READING
THESE
UNITED
STATES

READING THESE UNITED STATES

Federal Literacy in the Early Republic, 1776–1830

KERI HOLT

THE UNIVERSITY OF
GEORGIA PRESS
Athens

Paperback edition, 2023
© 2019 by the University of Georgia Press
Athens, Georgia 30602
www.ugapress.org
All rights reserved
Set in 10/13 Adobe Caslon Pro by
Graphic Composition, Inc., Bogart, Georgia

Most University of Georgia Press titles are
available from popular e-book vendors.

Printed digitally

Library of Congress Cataloging-in-Publication Data

Names: Holt, Keri, author.
Title: Reading these United States :
federal literacy in the early Republic, 1776–1830 / Keri Holt.
Description: Athens : The University of Georgia Press, 2019. |
Includes bibliographical references and index.
Identifiers: LCCN 2018028386 | ISBN 9780820354538 (hardback : alk. paper) |
ISBN 9780820354521 (ebook : alk. paper)
Subjects: LCSH: Books and reading—Political aspects—
United States—History—18th century. |
Books and reading—Political aspects—
United States—History—19th century. |
United States—Intellectual life—1783–1965. |
Federal government—United States—History—18th century. |
Federal government—United States—History—19th century. |
Political socialization—United States—History—18th century. |
Political socialization—United States—History—19th century.
Classification: LCC Z1003.2 .H65 2019 | DDC 028.90973/09033—dc23
LC record available at https://lccn.loc.gov/2018028386

Paperback ISBN 978-0-8203-6614-2

Para mis padres

CONTENTS

ACKNOWLEDGMENTS
ix

INTRODUCTION
Drawing Together by Drawing Apart
1

CHAPTER 1
The United States Are Thirteen:
Representing a Plural Union
17

CHAPTER 2
Reading Parts and Wholes:
The Federal Imagination of American Almanacs
55

CHAPTER 3
Reading Differences Differently:
Magazines, Satire, and Federal Literacy
99

CHAPTER 4
Concurrent Sentimentality:
The Federal Logic of Captivity
138

CHAPTER 5
Federalism Redux:
Reading the Literary West
174

EPILOGUE
The Failure of Federal Literacy
219

NOTES
243

BIBLIOGRAPHY
269

INDEX
291

ACKNOWLEDGMENTS

★ ★ ★ ★ ★ ★ ★ ★ ★ ★ ★ ★

As with all book projects, I owe buckets of thanks all over the place. This project began, long ago, as a dissertation, and I am deeply grateful for the support and guidance of Philip Gould, Jim Egan, Nancy Armstrong, and Deak Nabers, who helped shape the foundations of this book. Those early years of research and writing were also supported by many wonderful friends whose questions, conversations, and reasons to take a productive break or two kept me going. Many thanks to Patricia Akhimie, David Babcock, Daniel Block, Lisa Brocklebank, Manu Chander, Julie Davis, Matt Delmont, Heather Fielding, Avak Hasratian, Chris and Katie Holmes, Jonna Iacono, Stephen and Heidi Koelz, Chris Lee, Wendy Lee, Jake Leland, Linda Liu, Corey McEleney, John Melson, Lelia Menendez, Asha Nadkarni, Eric Ong, Laurel Rayburn, Stephen Satterfield, Bethany Shepherd, Mike Siegel, Zak Sitter, Mel Spencer, Ray Sultan, Rebecca Summerhays, Sarah Wald, Jacque Wernimont, and Gena Zuroski, as well as my buddies at the GCB: Brian and Debra Ballentine, Simon Feldman, Ed Goll, Stephen Grunschel, Sin Guanci, Jean Gullickson, Terry Linehan, Patrick Oaks, Mark Sonday, Don Ward, Kevin Wu, and Susan Yund. A special thanks to Allan Hazlett, whose excellent conversation and knack for extending the right words at the right time are always appreciated, as are his invitations to buffet. I also owe much to David Ben-Merre, whose support and love, which began at the start of this project, hold a special place in my heart.

On the ever-exciting scene of early American scholarship, I am grateful to many fantastic friends and colleagues who have provided me with valuable feedback as I hammered out this manuscript. I presented much of this work at conferences sponsored by the Society of Early Americanists, the Charles Brockden Brown Society, the Western Literature Association, and C19, and I owe much to the conversations that these organizations foster. Andy Doolen,

Michael Drexler, Duncan Faherty, Ned Watts, and Ed White all gave me particularly useful advice and opportunities for sharing ideas. A particular shout-out to my "Carwin" gang who, in addition to their insightful encouragement, keep me attuned to the delightful weirdness that can be found in early America, from sympathetic gymnastics to cross-species spies. Thanks to Tad Davies, Sîan Silyn Roberts, Brian Sweeney, and especially John Funchion, whose insightful comments on my drafts were crucial for shaping chapters 4 and 5. I owe all of you many flagons of ale.

Here in Utah, I offer my thanks to two other academic support groups. My department's monthly reading group, which usually includes Christine Cooper-Rompato, Brock Dethier, Pat Gantt, Keith Grant-Davie, Melody Graulich, David Hailey, and Rebecca Walton, read numerous drafts of these chapters and did much to strengthen and clarify my arguments. Thanks also to my variously acronym'd women's group of Sarah Case, Dory Cochran, Anne Diekema, Carrie Durward, Kerry Jordan, Karin Kettenring, and Whitney Matson, whose steady presence brings much-needed cheer to my life, particularly as I wrestled with final revisions. Their encouragement and friendship, which always comes with warm smiles and a much-appreciated meal, does much to refuel my goals every other week.

Thanks to the English department and College of Humanities and Social Sciences at Utah State University for travel funding and research leave that allowed me to complete this book. I am grateful to have many outstanding colleagues here who also have given me helpful guidance on this project, particularly Christine Cooper-Rompato, Paul Crumbley, Lawrence Culver, Evelyn Funda, Lisa Gabbert, Shane Graham, Keith Grant-Davie, Melody Graulich, Benjamin Gunsburg, Phebe Jensen, Joyce Kinkead, Brian McCuskey, Kris Miller, Ryan Moeller, Colleen O'Neill, Nathan Straight, Steve Shively, Jennifer Sinor, Jeff Smitten, and our department chair, Jeannie Thomas, along with many others who make our department a good place to work.

This project was also supported by a short-term fellowship from the American Antiquarian Society, which was crucial for conducting research on early American almanacs and federal imagery, and I am indebted to the wonderful suggestions of the excellent library staff. I am equally grateful to the librarians and staff at the Filson Historical Society and the archives at the Museum of the Cherokee Indian, as well as George Frizzel, head of Special Collections at the Hunter Library at Western Carolina University who assisted with my research on the *Cherokee Phoenix*. Thanks also to Paul Cohen who was so generous with his time and resources regarding Abel Buell's *New and Correct Map of the United States*.

Finally, thanks to my family who has always been there. As part of this family, I include my friends from St. Mary's College of Maryland who did much to cheer my spirits at the low points of this project and who, as the work went on and on, gave me much relief by not asking me how it was going. Thanks to Eric Baugher, Lauren Brandes and Kari Cohen, Mark Buenaflor and Laurel Keene, Eric Hermann and Kate Greene, Joey Hipolito and Sarah Pauly, Mike Johnson, Jeff Leasure and Adam Griffiths, Sarah Loff, Theresa Sotto and Mike Eaton, and, most of all, Elizabeth Botton, whose regular phone calls always give me a boost of energy and whose appreciation for the glories of archives and the Masons reminds me that there are always new things to discover in a library. Thanks also to my god-brother Scott Knackstedt and his shared enthusiasm for early America.

An extra special thanks to my very best friends, Joey Marquart and Jeni Jones, who will not have to hear me tell them that I'm "almost done" with my book anymore. I hope the two of you get to meet some day, when we will drink tea, eat Battenberg cakes, and discuss murder in Mrs. Wasaman's parlor.

To Mark Roark, thanks for your continual support and encouragement, despite all the messes that come with my writing. Your smile goes a long way on a tough day. Thanks also to Linda and Metro, whose love travels long distances, often with delicious fudge, jams, and other treats.

I hope this book makes my grandparents proud. Thanks to Maria and Salomon Espinoza and Bob and Luvenia Holt, whose hard work and commitment to education set an inspiring example for their grandchildren to follow. A special thanks to my Aunt Janice, who kept me well supplied with pens and flair as I wrote this. My brother and sisters also make for a pretty inspiring collective. Robby, Tricia, Becky—I love that we love spending time together, and the three of you continually give me new ways to think about the world as I hear about your experiences (hence my incessant questions, Beto). Thanks for always being there, and thanks also for the wonderful people you've brought to the family—Cameron, Dave, Claire, Wallace, and Harrison. Y'all keep the fun conversations going, and I'm excited for more in the years to come.

Most of all, thanks to my parents, Bob and Cece Holt, to whom I owe the most of all. From my very first days of word scavenging, you have encouraged me to think critically, to be creative, to try new things, to always be up for the next adventure, and to always be myself and take pride in the work that I do. Every day, I'm trying to follow the example you set for us, and your guidance and sense of fun have seen me through this whole long process. As I've said before, I can always look forward because I know the two of you are always behind me. This book is dedicated to you.

READING
THESE
UNITED
STATES

INTRODUCTION

★ ★ ★ ★ ★ ★ ★ ★ ★ ★ ★

Drawing Together by Drawing Apart

> Various orders, in one form, sublime.
> ——*Geography: An Amusement*

In the archives of the American Antiquarian Society is a box filled with eighteenth- and nineteenth-century geography games. These games, which were designed to make the study of geography "agreeable" and "pleasing" for young students, include an eleven-foot-long "ribbon map" that, when unrolled, charts the path of the Mississippi River; jigsaw puzzles that depict the nation in various parts and pieces; and several boxes of flashcards, among them a set titled *Geography: An Amusement*. Printed in 1805 and sold throughout New England and the mid-Atlantic states, *Geography: An Amusement* tells us a great deal about the way citizens imagined unity in the early republic. The set contains more than one hundred 3×6-inch cards identifying "the boundaries, situation, extent, divisions, chief towns, rivers, mountains, lakes, religion, and number of inhabitants of all countries, kingdoms, and republics, in the known habitable globe."[1] Of particular interest is the card—or, rather, cards—for the United States. A single card titled "United States" provides information for the nation as a whole, including its official boundaries, total population, major rivers, agricultural and industrial productions, and constituent states. In addition to this single card, the set also represents the United States with nineteen individual state cards that provide information about the boundaries, definitive landmarks, and major industries for each. The heading for "Government" on the single "United States" card explains this dual structure of representation, noting that the government of the United States "is vested in a President and Congress; and each State is a little Republic."

This description highlights the federal dimensions of early U.S. unity, which defined the nation in terms that were singular and plural at the same time. As a federal republic, the United States represented a single, unified nation that was also defined through the representation of its many parts—a model of unity exemplified by the national motto *E pluribus unum*. By representing the United States through both a single national card and the various state cards, these flashcards attempt to convey the federal structure of the nation's union. In doing so, however, they also highlight the representational challenges posed by this unusual and somewhat paradoxical model of nationhood.

Although the state cards provide a comprehensive portrait of the United States' constituent elements, a close look shows little ground for connecting them. Like the cards for all the other independent nations, each state stands alone as a clearly bounded space with its own definitive characteristics, and, taken together, the state cards represent an extremely varied range of people, landscapes, and industries. The card for New Hampshire, for instance, reports a population of 183,858, identifies the Merrimack and Piscataqua Rivers and the Blue Hills as its central topographic features, and lists poultry, Indian corn, and beef as its major "Productions." Meanwhile, the card for Virginia lists a much larger population of 886,149, identifies a separate set of definitive landmarks and waterways (the Potomac and Shenandoah Rivers and the Allegheny and Blue Ridge Mountains), and reports dominant industries that include cotton, flax, iron, and whiskey. The Virginia card also lists the names of three major colleges (William and Mary, Hampden Sydney, and Washington College), in contrast to New Hampshire, which lists none. Such differences regarding topography, population, industry, and infrastructure emerge across all the state cards, suggesting that the residents of these "united" states shared few common characteristics or experiences. Given this variety, the flashcards illuminate a problem that was central to the federal union—how was it possible to view the nation's constituent differences in unified terms? How could this plural nation comprising many "little republics" signify a single, united republic?

Interestingly, the flashcards also provide a potential answer to this question. Printed on the outside of the box are a few lines of verse that acknowledge the plural character of the United States while also suggesting how the nation's many parts can be linked together:

> 'Tis he alone whose comprehensive mind
> From situation, temper, soil, and clime
> Explored, a nation's various powers can bind
> And various orders, in one form, sublime.

Here, the poem attributes the unity of the nation to the efforts of a reader whose "comprehensive mind" can examine and reflect on its varied conditions and characteristics. Rather than emerging as an inherent characteristic of the nation, national unity is something produced by individuals who take the time to explore the nation's "various powers" and "various orders." By thus gaining a comprehensive knowledge of the different locations, communities, and interests that compose the United States, the nation's readers can "bind" the diverse nation into "one form, sublime."

Understanding national unity as a condition produced through a process of reading is hardly a new idea. From the beginning, U.S. citizens considered literacy and the establishment of a strong literary culture to be crucial for uniting the nation and establishing an independent national identity in the early republic. "Too much pains cannot be taken to teach our youth to read and write our American language with propriety and elegance.... It is the first accomplishment in a republic and often sets the whole machine of government in motion," wrote Benjamin Rush in 1786.[2] If literature and literacy played a central role in defining the early nation, however, it is important to consider what *kind* of unity these texts helped imagine. The *Geography: An Amusement* flashcards suggest that citizens learned to recognize the United States as a diverse, composite nation whose unity was produced by cultivating a comprehensive knowledge of its local differences. This model of union might seem to run counter to conventional arguments that define nationalism in relation to an imagined sense of similarity—political, cultural, and temporal. Imagining national unity in terms of variety makes sense, however, when we recall the federal dimensions of early U.S. nationalism.

In the decades following independence, the United States was regularly figured and imagined as a union of differences rather than similarities. Although the former colonies had all been part of the British Empire, these communities were, as Richard Beeman notes, "extraordinarily disconnected from one another, displaying among themselves and within themselves significant varieties of political behavior."[3] These colonial distinctions carried over to the states, creating a nation that was defined by different histories, economies, laws, and social norms, not to mention variations in climate, topography, and infrastructure. Unable to combine the states on the basis of shared beliefs or characteristics, the leaders of the early nation turned to federalism as a practical means for uniting what John Adams described as "such heterogeneous ingredients."[4] Members of the Continental Congress, most notably James Madison, John Dickinson, John Witherspoon, and Thomas Jefferson, carefully studied the different federal systems proposed by John Locke, Baron de Montesquieu, Hugo Grotius, and Samuel von Pufendorf, as well as the federal models of government used in Switzerland and the Netherlands, to inform their efforts to forge a diverse union. British attempts to consolidate the governments of their North American colonies also informed these efforts, most notably in the form of the

Albany Plan of Union proposed in 1754. On the basis of these considerations, political leaders pushed for the adoption of a federal governing structure for the new United States soon after declaring independence. "I humbly apprehend, that every argument from honor, interest, safety and necessity, conspire in pressing us to a 'confederacy,'" asserted John Witherspoon in a speech before the Second Continental Congress in 1776. "A well-planned confederacy among the states of America," he continued, would not only "hand down the blessings of peace and public order to many generations," it would also mark "a greater step from the former disunited and hostile situation of kingdoms and states . . . to a state of more perfect and lasting union."[5]

Although federalism offered a promising model for organizing a diverse nation, it also marked an unusual and counterintuitive model for national unity, particularly in the late eighteenth century. Even today, nations are typically defined in terms of some degree of political, cultural, or ethnic homogeneity, an idea that can be traced back to Plato and Aristotle, who argued that citizens needed to share common values, language, and history to maintain a stable and productive republic.[6] Enlightenment thinkers such as Francis Hutcheson, John Locke, and Adam Smith continued to theorize nationalism in terms of similarity, arguing that the citizens of successful nations were bound together by shared experiences and sentiments that were further solidified by a capacity for sympathy.[7] Within this homogeneous model of nationalism, differences—political, social, or economic—were largely perceived as destabilizing forces that threatened to undermine the unity of a nation as a whole.

This understanding of national unity—as a condition of shared political, social, or cultural beliefs and experiences—has continued to shape contemporary studies of nationalism, exemplified by the work of Ernest Renan and Ernest Gellner or, more recently, John Breuilly and Michael Hechter, among others.[8] This homogeneous model of nationhood, however, would not work in the newly independent United States. In the early republic, citizens were more likely to identify themselves in relation to their localities—as residents of New York or Virginia or Massachusetts—than in relation to their nationality, largely because there were so few similarities between their respective experiences. Forging a unified national identity in this environment required citizens to find a way to foreground, rather than downplay, this variety, which is how federalism comes into play. Within a federal nation, sovereignty is divided between multiple constituencies who are united by their agreement to share power in ways that equally benefit and protect one another. Because unity is produced by an agreement to share power, rather than an agreement to share interests, a federal system can operate as a unified community while simultaneously allowing for the expression and representation of differences. In fact, rather than threatening national unity and stability, within a federal nation, differences can actually support and strengthen national unity. James Madison famously describes this principle in Federalist No. 10: "Extend the sphere and you take in a greater variety of parties and interests; you make it less probable that a majority of the whole will have a common motive to invade the rights of other citizens; or if such a common motive exists, it will be more difficult for all who feel it to discover their own strength, and to act in unison with each other.... Hence it clearly appears that the same advantage ... is enjoyed by a large over a small republic."[9] Here, Madison identifies how the different interests and experiences represented within the federal nation serve as a check on division and instability. Because all the constituents are equally invested in the federal government, they will work hard to ensure that one constituency is not gaining more power over another. The more diverse the nation, the more vigilant each constituency will be in ensuring that power is distributed equally, thus reinforcing the stability of the union. On the basis of this logic, the strength of the federal union lies precisely in its ability to represent, preserve, and even promote variety, which boded well for a nation as diverse and expansive as the United States.

Early representations of the United States continually emphasized the nation's composite character. The national flag, for instance, was designed to represent the United States as a union of distinct and separate states joined together in a collaborative system, as indicated by Flag Act of 1777, "*Resolved*, That the flag of the United States be made of thirteen stripes, alternate red and white; that the union be thirteen stars, white in a blue field, representing a new Constellation." The design for the national seal similarly emphasized the singular pluralism of the federal union through its image of an eagle holding a shield of thirteen stripes positioned beneath a constellation of thirteen stars, so as to clearly convey "the several states all joined in one solid compact entire."[10] Other popular images of the United States likewise characterized the nation as a union made up of distinct yet interconnected parts, such as the image of the "federal edifice," which represented the nation as a building supported by many pillars or the image of a chain composed of interlocking links. Other popular images included a harp whose multiple strings were meant to represent a "harmonious" union or a quiver of thirteen arrows, which emphasized how the nation's varied constituencies could contribute to its security and strength.[11] The federal dimensions of union also found expression in public celebrations, where citizens gave toasts celebrating the characteristics and contributions of each state or participated in parades where people walked with props representing the dominant features or productions of their home states. Some of these celebrations even featured "federal cakes" that commemorated the composite character of the union by including thirteen layers or measuring thirteen feet in length.[12]

Print also provided an important medium for representing the nation in plural terms. Just as games such as *Geography: An Amusement* encouraged citizens to "bind" the nation together by cultivating a thorough knowledge of its many differences, popular forms of print such as almanacs, serial satires, magazines, and captivity narratives represented the nation in diverse and composite terms. More than simply representing the nation in parts, however, these texts also influenced the way citizens interpreted differences, providing strategies that enabled them to read the nation's differences in unifying terms. In this regard, early U.S. print helped imagine the federal nation in two distinct ways: first, by representing the nation as a union of diverse parts, and second, by fostering a *federal literacy*, whereby citizens learned to read the variety of the nation as a source of strength and stability rather than division and discord.

Over the past thirty years, literary scholars have devoted considerable attention to the ways that print helped citizens imagine the early nation. Within this scholarship, print has typically been characterized as a medium that enabled citizens to overcome their sense of difference and separation to imagine a national community rooted in a sense of shared feelings and experiences. Benedict Anderson's conception of the nation as an "imagined community" that emerges through the circulation of printed materials represents the best-known version of this argument, and subsequent studies have revised and expanded Anderson's ideas, exploring, for instance, how print helped draw citizens together by creating a shared language of republican eloquence and civility, promoting bonds of sentiment and sympathy, or facilitating the creation of a republican public sphere.[13] While important differences exist among these arguments, all remain committed to the idea that print helped define the nation by mediating differences and establishing a sense of imagined homogeneity. This model, however, relies on the assumption that nationalism can only be produced by imagining a sense of sameness among citizens, an assumption that fails to account for the federal dimensions of nationalism in the early republic.

By foregrounding the role that federalism played in early U.S. politics and culture, *Reading These United States* attempts to correct a fundamental misreading of early U.S. nationalism in studies of print culture. If national unity in the early United States was contingent on recognizing and representing the many differences that made up the nation, we need to reexamine early U.S. print culture in relation to these federal dynamics. To this end, I argue that instead of creating an imagined sense of similarity, early U.S. print culture encouraged citizens to recognize and read the nation as a plural union of differences. In short—and rather ironically—the literature of the early republic drew citizens together by drawing them apart.

More than simply recovering a lost political vision, *Reading These United States* engages in a broader reassessment of the politics of literacy and literary form. As citizens struggled to engage with a nation defined through the representation of its many parts, the early decades of the republic became a period of intense literary experimentation as writers, editors, and readers sought ways to represent diversity in unifying terms. Taking a formalist, reader-oriented approach, *Reading These United States* examines a range of popular print forms and genres to examine how their structure and aesthetics taught citizens to read differences cohesively in the early republic. In doing so, this study follows the work of Matt Brown, who argues that close attention to the formal dimensions of the "steady sellers" within a given culture can help us understand "the aesthetic effects of writing and reading practices within certain social formations."[14] Brown's attention to the formal features of primers, catechisms, and commonplace books and their relationship to the devotional religious culture of colonial New England serves as an illustrative model for my own efforts to situate popular genres of the early United States, such as almanacs, satires, magazines, and captivity narratives, within a culture of federal nationalism. In the case of almanacs, for instance, formal features such as its calendar pages, road tables, and astrology charts enabled citizens to imagine a cohesive plural union by providing them with literary experiences that enabled them to negotiate productive relationships between parts and wholes. Satires, magazines, and captivity narratives likewise provided U.S. readers with new opportunities for linking seemingly incompatible beliefs and experiences and experimenting with multivoiced formats that helped them assert and situate their local positions within a larger federal whole, while also illuminating the value of representing different views and interests within the nation.

In exploring the relationship between the formal features of literary texts and their cultural effects, it is particularly important to pay attention to specific reader responses. As Brown writes, although difficult, attending to specific practices of reading gives rise to a more productive "sociology of literacy" that allows us to explore the cultural and political implications of literature and print culture in greater depth.[15] In tracing the federal dimensions of early U.S. texts and images, I have tried to document specific reader responses whenever possible in order to illustrate the effects of this federal literacy in more concrete terms, most notably in the case of U.S. almanacs where readers often recorded their responses directly within these texts. Although charting and examining these particular reading experiences is important, the extensive archival work needed to fully address them—work that involves analyses of bookseller catalogs and records, library inventories and circulation histories, and letters, diaries, and family histories—is ultimately beyond the scope of this project. By foregrounding the formal dimensions of these federal reading experiences, however, this study invites further inquiry into the practice of federal literacy that draws on the critical methods of book history to examine the dissemination and reception of these federal literary texts.[16]

In addressing the federal diversity of early U.S. print and national culture, *Reading These United States* joins with other recent efforts to highlight the variety and volatility of the early republic. Work by Christopher Castiglia, Jason Frank, Benjamin Irvin, Edward Larkin, Trish Loughran, Eric Slauter, and Carroll Smith-Rosenberg has similarly challenged the traditional print culture thesis by examining the heterogeneous character of the early nation.[17] As Smith-Rosenberg describes it, the early United States is better understood and studied as an "eclectic" nation composed of "multiple, often inharmonious parts," and these scholars have argued for new models that can better address the diverse and locally oriented dimensions of early U.S. print culture, as well as the varied audiences and experiences associated with different forms of print.[18] In highlighting the heterogeneous dimensions of U.S. print culture, however, there remains a tendency to interpret this diversity as evidence of a *lack* of unity in the early republic, with print culture producing, as Loughran writes, a "nation [in] fragments called regions and sections, rather than as the great unionizer and unifier it is so often remembered as."[19]

While I agree that early U.S. print provides us with a portrait of a fragmented nation, this study interprets the effects of this fragmentation differently. Instead of reading the nation's local variety as a reason to challenge or question the existence of national unity and stability, I argue that this heterogeneity was a central condition for the United States' unity and stability. Within the early republic, reading and representing the nation in "fragments" did not inhibit or undermine the development of an imagined national community. To the contrary, the diverse characteristics and literary forms associated with early U.S. print culture provided citizens with the knowledge and interpretive practices that they needed to imagine unity in a federal republic. By foregrounding the federal structure and ideology of early U.S. nationalism, *Reading These United States* argues that the diverse and seemingly disconnected dimensions of early U.S. print culture emerge not as an obstacle to unity but as a necessary condition of it.

Drawing attention to the federal dimensions of print nationalism also offers a productive opportunity for unsettling assumptions about the concept of the nation itself. Over the past two decades, American studies scholarship has aggressively challenged the primacy of the "nation" as a category for analysis, replacing fixed and bounded definitions with approaches that emphasize how nations are constructed through complex interactions, interdependencies, and varying forms of exchange. This revised understanding of nationhood has produced a significant "transnational turn" as scholars examine how the United States has been shaped by various transatlantic, transpacific, and transhemispheric relationships. Although *Reading These United States* remains focused within the national boundaries of the United States, its emphasis on federalism nevertheless contributes to this critical revision of the nation by turning the critical insights of transnational studies inward to explore how the United States was shaped by complex networks of exchange, interaction, and interdependency *within* its own borders—a move that can similarly illuminate the flexible, transitory, and expedient dimensions of nationalism as an organizational concept. Alongside this transnational turn, this study also contributes to ongoing efforts to explore the spatial dynamics of early American literature and culture. The composite dimensions of the federal United States were, quite literally, mapped onto the physical space of the nation through the establishment of distinct and bounded states, and U.S. almanacs, magazines, and captivity narratives were deeply implicated in helping citizens situate those spaces in a unified national framework, a complicated process that involved continual practices of spatial reorientation and renegotiation. By exploring these dynamics, this study is closely aligned with the work of Martin Brückner, Hsuan Hsu, Anne Baker, Ralph Bauer, Hester Blum, and others who similarly seek to reimagine U.S. culture through the production "of multiple and often conflicting geographies."[20]

Other challenges to studies of U.S. nationalism have concerned the United States' relationship to empire. Since the early 1990s, American studies scholarship has challenged the exceptionalist paradigm that denied U.S. involvement in imperial practices and power relations. In addressing, as Amy Kaplan famously described it, "the absence of empire from the study of American culture," early American scholarship has emphasized how the United States operated as an imperial power from its earliest origins, focusing specifically on the ways that the United States marginalized and exploited its regional, African American, and Native American communities to serve the interests of a dominant and largely urban Anglo-American elite.[21] Edward Larkin and Julian Go have recently argued that federalism itself operated as an imperial discourse in the early United States. Through "innovative political forms such as the Articles of Confederation and the U.S. Constitution," writes Larkin, the federal structure of the United States enabled Americans to "imagine a new kind of empire" whose crucial difference lay in its approach for managing and valuing its diverse constituencies.[22] Within a traditional empire, diversity was important to represent and cultivate because it was profitable. Diversity was equally profitable in a federal nation, but federalism also attaches additional value to its constituent differences for contributing to the nation's intellectual strength and political stability, while also fostering a more equitable and participatory form of government. This ability to represent the rights and authority of its constituencies on equal terms was one of the primary reasons that federalism was figured as an "exceptional" form of empire in the early republic, laying the foundation for Jefferson's famous description of the United States as an "empire for liberty."

Just because federalism was represented as an exceptional form of empire in the early republic does not mean that it proved be to exceptional in practice. Although federalism was meant to represent and value its diverse residents equally, there were clear limits on the specific kinds of difference the federal nation would acknowledge and support. Work by Jodi Byrd, Laura Doyle, Mark Rifkin, and Ann Laura Stoler has drawn attention to the significant points of exclusion, oppression, and exploitation inherent in the ideology of early U.S. nationalism.[23] Even in a nation that was predicated on representing variety, defining the federal United States required, as Stoler writes, "locating the boundaries of what and who was 'inside' or 'out.'"[24] In examining the plural dynamics of U.S. federal nationalism, this study will explore how the United States granted value and equality to some kinds of differences (regional, political, religious, etc.), while limiting and obscuring others (race and gender). Literary texts played an instrumental role in defining and reinforcing these points of exclusion in the federal nation while at the same time providing opportunities to criticize and transform those exclusions as well.

Ironically, since federalism was, by definition, a discourse devoted to pluralism, those excluded from the federal nation often relied on the logic, language, and structures of federal nationalism to argue for their rights to be included within it. In exploring the plural dimensions of literary forms such as the almanac, magazines, satire, and captivity narratives, this study takes a close look at the way writers such as Benjamin Banneker, Judith Sargent Murray, Royall Tyler, James Hall, Elias Boudinot, and David Walker drew on these same forms and principles to argue for including African Americans, Native Americans, women, Muslims, Catholics, and other cultural and ethnic minorities within the nation on more equitable terms.[25] Within these works, we can begin to see how the federal literary culture of the early United States defined the nation in exclusive terms while simultaneously providing writers and readers with the tools for challenging and dismantling its exclusions. By teaching citizens to read differences differently, the federal literary culture of the early United States encouraged them to continually reimagine and revise the terms of the nation's pluralism—revisions that would ultimately push the federal nation to its breaking point with the beginning of the Civil War.

The plural yet cohesive model of federal nationalism that defined the initial decades of the United States would ultimately be short lived. The rapid expansion of the United States in the early nineteenth century raised questions about the limits of federal unity as the nation grew to encompass a greater range of geographic, social, economic, and cultural variety. Even though the federal structure of the nation was designed to accommodate differences, many feared that incorporating so much new territory—which included former French and Spanish colonial territories and numerous Native American nations—would destabilize the foundation of the original republic, producing, as John Quincy Adams described it, "a Union totally different from that for which the Constitution had been formed."[26] As the nation grew, the different characteristics and interests of these newly added states and territories increasingly became a source of conflict and division, particularly as arguments over slavery, Indian policy, intrastate commerce, and infrastructural development pitted local and national authorities against one another. Over time, imagining and representing the United States in terms of its diverse parts ceased to serve as a means of supporting and strengthening national union and, instead, gave rise to a divisive sectionalism as the states increasingly saw themselves in conflict with the federal government, eventually culminating in the secession of the southern states and the outbreak of the Civil War.

The destructive consequences of the war prompted a radical rethinking of federal structures and principles in the latter half of the nineteenth century. Anxious to avoid the sectional conflicts and political instabilities that arose from the federal politics of the antebellum era, citizens began to embrace more consolidated conceptions of union in the postbellum decades. Although the United States was still a federal republic, Reconstruction policies, combined with a gradual strengthening of the authority of Congress and the presidency, the rise of a national middle class, and rapid advances in transcontinental communication and transportation eroded the composite conception of national unity that dominated the national imagination in the early republic.[27] Instead of representing a union of differences, the United States was increasingly figured through a rhetoric of shared experiences and common views—a shift illustrated by the grammatical transformation of the "United States" from a plural to a singular noun over the course of the late nineteenth century.[28]

This singular understanding of the United States has had a lasting influence in popular and academic culture, to the point that, when we talk about the nation, we assume that it represents the singular form that has only been dominant since the late nineteenth century. *Reading These United States* returns to the plural understanding of union that shaped public conceptions of the nation in the early republic. Even though this period of federal literary nationalism is relatively short, recalling the plural dimensions and representations of the early United States has important consequences for how we understand the role of print and its relationship to nationalism in the early republic. It also provides some provocative points of comparison regarding the ways the United States continues to grapple with issues of pluralism and diversity in the present. By recalling the early nation's commitment to variety and its efforts and struggles to read and represent the nation's differences equitably, we can find models, both positive and negative, for the United States' ongoing efforts to imagine and govern a union that continues to be composed of many.

The chapters in this book examine how various forms of popular print—including maps, currency, nationalist iconography, almanacs, magazines, serial satires, and novels—encouraged citizens to imagine national unity, not by obscuring the nation's differences but by foregrounding them. In examining each genre, these chapters emphasize how the form of these texts influenced the ways that citizens read and interpreted differences. More than simply representing the nation as a union composed of many parts, these texts presented citizens with strategies for learning how to read differences equitably and cohesively—strategies that, I argue, constitute a federal literacy. By examining how these texts, in various ways, trained readers to view the nation as a union of differences, this book explores how citizens in the early republic were encouraged to view the nation in plural terms, reading the United States, in effect, as these United States.

The plural dimensions of the genres I examine in these chapters are not, of course, unique to the United States. Of the genres that I address in this study, only the captivity narrative has any claim to represent a distinctly "American" form of representation, which makes it much easier to attribute its plural tactics and reading practices to a federal literary nationalism, since this genre was so closely associated with an American cultural consciousness. In the case of almanacs, satire, and magazines, however, the specific formal features and literary tactics that I end up associating with the practice of federal literacy—such as the road tables or the astrology signs of the almanacs or the multivoiced dimensions of satire and magazines—can be found in any example of these genres throughout the world. If these plural dimensions are a definitive feature of these genres and not unique to the United States, how can I argue that they constitute a distinctive practice of federal literary nationalism, as opposed to simply participating in a broader aesthetic and political discourse of pluralism?

A number of scholars have recently argued that the eighteenth century did, in fact, see the emergence of a new aesthetics of "copiousness" as writers and artists sought to reflect the increasingly diverse conditions produced by the expansion of the British Empire and the new and active networks of transnational exchange that accompanied these imperial politics and enterprises.[29] The discourse of cosmopolitanism was central to this new aesthetics of pluralism and variety, which played a significant role in eighteenth-century print culture.[30] Federalism and federal literacy are likewise an important part of this cultural and aesthetic movement to foreground diversity and multiplicity in the eighteenth century. In acknowledging that there is a larger critical frame for theorizing the representation of differences in the eighteenth century, however, I would argue that federalism represents a very specific political and aesthetic practice within this pluralist discourse, a specificity that comes across in U.S. almanacs, satires, and magazines. As I explore the plural structures and tactics of these literary works, I will show how, in the case of U.S. almanacs, satires, and magazines, the content of these works carefully connects their plural dynamics to the political, social, and geographic space of the United States, a connection that makes it possible to link their pluralism specifically to a federal national consciousness rather than a broader imagination linked to cosmopolitanism or the concept of "copia." Although formal features such as astrology tables or the Anatomy Man can be found in almanacs throughout the world, in U.S. almanacs the presence of these figures alongside content that was deeply rooted in representations of U.S. regional geography, court schedules, and congressional representation provided a specific framework for reading them in distinctly federal terms. U.S. satires and magazines likewise made a specific effort to position their plural structure and tactics in relation to content that emphasized the federal structures and political discourse of the early nation. Although pluralism was everywhere in eighteenth-century writing and aesthetics, these chapters show how the pluralism of early U.S. literature took on a distinctly federal hue.

The first chapter begins by exploring the representational problems posed by the federal structure of the early republic. As a nation defined by the representation of its many parts, citizens struggled to find a way to represent the United States as a united nation while also respecting the differences and boundaries of its constituent states. The first half of this chapter examines the political philosophy of federalism, particularly its emphasis on preserving the representation of clear and specific local differences within a republic and the value of those differences in ensuring national union. Following this discussion of the political philosophy of federalism, the chapter turns to print culture, looking specifically at the visual strategies used to represent the United States as a union of different constituent parts. By looking at a range of images, including maps, state and national emblems, broadside illustrations, and early U.S. currency, this opening chapter explores how print was used as a central medium for promoting and supporting a federal conception of national unity, and its analysis of visual strategies for representing the federal nation sets the stage for the book's subsequent analysis of federal literary strategies.

The next chapter examines how early U.S. almanacs, one of the most popular and prevalent genres in the early republic, helped promote a federal vision of the nation. Despite the dominance and popularity of these texts in early American life, few scholars have studied their influence in the development of early nationalism, primarily because their local focus and limited circulation do not seem to contribute to a shared sense of national community. By looking at a range of almanacs from the New England, mid-Atlantic, and southern states, this chapter argues that almanacs did play a crucial role in tying the nation together by teaching citizens how to situate themselves as a unique part of a diverse, yet consolidated, whole. The geographic focus of the almanac, combined with its formulaic yet locally specific content, produced a model of reading that encouraged citizens to define themselves as part of a distinct local community, while also learning how to position that community as a part of a larger, interconnected, and collaborative union. The chapter concludes with a look at how those who were excluded from the nation—in this case, African Americans—also turned to the almanac as a literary form that allowed them to argue for an equal place within the plural federal union, focusing specifically on the almanacs published by Benjamin Banneker in the late 1790s.

The third chapter examines magazines and epic satires, focusing specifically on a set of serial satires published in several early U.S. magazines, including Jeremy Belknap's *The Foresters* (1787), John Trumbull's *M'Fingal* (1775), and *The Anarchiad* (1786–87), which was collectively written by Joel Barlow, Lemuel Hopkins, David Humphries, and John Trumbull, commonly known as the Connecticut Wits. Satiric poetry is another genre that, while among the most popular literary forms of the late eighteenth century, has been overlooked in contemporary studies of U.S. print culture. This chapter examines both the popularity and national influence of satire in the early United States, as well as their close connection to the nationalist dimensions of early U.S. magazines. Rooted in the conditions of disagreement, criticism, and competing perspectives, literary satires and magazines produced experiences of reading that generated productive understandings of difference and conflict, which, in turn, helped support a federal understanding of national unity. Although epic satires such as *The Foresters*, *M'Fingal*, and *The Anarchiad* sought to argue for the triumph of one particular political opinion, their formal aesthetics, combined with their placement in the multivoiced space of early magazines such as the *Columbian Magazine*, the *American Museum*, and the *Massachusetts Magazine*, encouraged readers to develop a healthy respect for and dependence on the representation of different views and experiences. By examining how these serial satires encouraged citizens to engage with different opinions in a humorous format and how the magazines that published them, in turn, invited citizens to participate in the debates brought forward within the satire, this chapter explores how the serial publication of satire supported a federal model of unity, while also providing citizens with a medium for enacting the federal principles of diverse representation. The chapter concludes by exploring how women turned to these same genres to argue for equality and representation within the federal nation, focusing specifically on the work of Judith Sargent Murray. As in the case of almanacs, the federal dynamics of U.S. magazines and satire made it possible to criticize and counteract the nation's significant points of exclusion.

Chapter 4 turns to a more canonical set of texts by examining how early U.S. captivity narratives encouraged citizens to read national differences productively. Although I discuss a number of works from this genre, the chapter primarily provides a case study of two specific works, Mary Rowlandson's *A Narrative of the Captivity and Restoration of Mrs. Mary Rowlandson* and Royall Tyler's *The Algerine Captive*. Although Rowlandson's narrative was originally published in 1682, her account was widely reprinted during the 1770s and the 1790s, making it one of the most popular texts in the early republic. In exploring this second wave of popularity, I argue that Rowlandson's *Narrative*, which engages with issues of dual allegiances and a split sense of self, provided citizens with a model for imagining the conflicted nature of federal citizenship, which required citizens to reconcile local and national forms of affiliation without compromising either identity. Specifically, I show how Rowlandson's narrative encourages readers to develop a new understanding of community founded on the establishment of concurrent sentiments, where unity can be imagined as a product of compatible yet ultimately separate feelings and experiences. The second half of the chapter turns to *The Algerine Captive* (1797), a fictional account of a man who is first held captive by his own U.S. culture before being taken captive in Algiers. By exploring the protagonist's varied efforts to read and interpret the many differences he encounters, my analysis shows how this captivity narrative encouraged readers to become more accepting of religious, political, and cultural differences and, moreover, to recognize the stabilizing and unifying consequences of this tolerance. In doing so, *The Algerine Captive* produces a more diverse yet ultimately cohesive model of national unity that opens the door for a more inclusive and expansive model of federal nationhood as the United States expanded in the early nineteenth century.

Chapter 5 moves into the early nineteenth century to explore how writers both revived and revised the practice of federal literacy in the context of westward expansion. Focusing specifically on the print culture of the Ohio and Mississippi river valley regions during the 1820s and 1830s, this chapter explores how western writers such as Timothy Flint, Daniel Drake, and James Hall sought to reinstate the federal reading practices of the early republic to make space for western regional differences, while also providing a mechanism for contending with the increasingly divisive relationships between the states and the central government. Within the West, federal literary nationalism took more institutionalized forms, becoming integrated into local educational and social structures to teach citizens how to read the nation's many differences—regional, cultural, political, ethnic—in more cohesive terms. Western writers also made an effort to include a wider range of differences in their representations of the federal nation, encouraging readers to accommodate French and Spanish cultural practices as equal and valued expressions of U.S. nationalism. For as much as the literary culture of the West worked to reaffirm and revitalize these federal practices, however, this revival proved unable to resolve the regional and racial divisions that came to dominate the United States as the nation moved toward Civil War, as evident by the crises over Indian removal and slavery.

The book concludes with an epilogue that explores the racial limits of federal nationalism by examining the anti-Removal writings published in the *Cherokee Phoenix* in the late 1820s and 1830s and David Walker's *Appeal to the Coloured Citizens of the World* (1829). Both of these works draw on the principles of federalism and the practice of federal literacy to criticize the racist policies of the United States and argue for their equality and authority. On the one hand, their reliance on these federal strategies illuminates the extent to which the plural structure and logic of the United States should have required U.S. citizens to recognize and represent racial differences within the nation on equal terms. On the other, the failure of their federal arguments also illustrates the extent to which U.S. citizens in the mid-nineteenth century refused to include racial differences as part of the federal nation. Although antebellum citizens still wanted to insist that the United States was a plural federal union—a commitment that was evident in the increasingly fervent assertions of states' rights and state authority at this time—this pluralism was restricted to the regional identities and affiliations of the nation's white citizens only. In the end, however, maintaining these racial restrictions within the federal nation would ultimately be enough to set its different states against one another. By promoting the pluralism of the states over the pluralism of the nation's residents, the restrictive federal dynamics of the United States would ultimately dissolve the union, and the *Cherokee Phoenix* and Walker's *Appeal* provide clear illustrations of both the promise and the breakdown of federal literacy in the years leading up to the Civil War.

CHAPTER I

The United States Are Thirteen
Representing a Plural Union

> The proposed Constitution, therefore, is, in strictness, neither a national nor a federal Constitution, but a composition of both.
> ——JAMES MADISON, Federalist No. 39

What is federalism? Before examining the challenges involved in representing and supporting a federal union, it is important to understand what defines a federal union in the first place. Federal definitions are fairly flexible, and the federal structure and significance of the United States has often been subject to change. The residents of the British American colonies experimented with limited forms of federal governance long before independence, and citizens continued to experiment with different models for defining and representing the federal union thereafter. Before considering how literary texts helped imagine the early federal nation, this chapter examines the political history of federalism in the early United States and the different forms the federal government took between the 1770s and the 1790s, while also exploring the strategies citizens used to make sense of this paradoxical model of unity in the popular and political realm.

Rather than delineating a specific form of government, federalism is better understood as a philosophy of governance founded on the belief that national sovereignty can be divided and shared among multiple constituent polities. In a federal system, authority is distributed among a single central government, which serves the collective interests of the union, and a set of various local governments, which serve the interests of their immediate communities. The structure of a federal nation can take many forms, depending on how power is allocated. No matter how it is organized, a federal system departs from traditional models of unity by defining the nation through the representation of its social, political, and geographic differences rather than its shared similarities.

The origins of federal governance can be traced to ancient Greece, where independent city-states joined in leagues or alliances called "foedera" to share responsibility for selected civic duties and common defense.[1] Federalism emerged as a modern political philosophy during the seventeenth century when changing views about the nature of sovereignty, natural rights, and individual authority transformed political conceptions of nationhood. Hugo Grotius, Samuel von Pufendorf, and Johannes Althusius were particularly influential in developing the principles of divided sovereignty that are central for federal governance. Rejecting the concept of absolute sovereignty that defined monarchical systems, these philosophers argued that citizens had the right to establish governments that were designed to serve their local needs and interests.[2] Pufendorf addressed the benefits of forming a "system of states" where the citizens of different communities could join together to contend with local issues without fully surrendering their sovereignty. "These Unions submit only some certain Parts of Sovereignty to mutual Direction . . . [while] the particular States reserve to themselves all those Branches of that supreme Authority," wrote Pufendorf, who argued that such "systems of states" would produce more responsive and locally attentive modes of governance.[3] These ideas were expanded into more formalized theories of federal governance during the eighteenth century in the work of John Locke, Jean-Jacques Rousseau, and Charles-Louis de Secondat, baron de Montesquieu, whose 1752 work, *The Spirit of Laws*, became one of the most influential federal treatises. As Montesquieu describes it, "This form of government is a convention by which several petty states agree to become members of a larger one, which they intend to establish. It is a kind of assemblage of societies that constitutes a new one, capable of increasing by means of further associations, till they arrive at such a degree of power as to be able to provide for the security of the whole body."[4]

Two important distinctions emerge in Montesquieu's definition, the first being his assertion that a federal government constitutes a "new" society. Although it is formed from multiple existing communities, a federal government is nevertheless distinct from its constituencies, representing power and interests that its constituent states cannot represent on their own. By characterizing a federal union as a new political entity, this definition differentiates federalism from other forms of composite union, such as an empire, where local authority is absorbed by a dominant government that retains its preexisting identity and is not necessarily accountable to its acquisitions. Furthermore, within a federal union, these constituent states enter this assemblage willingly and collaborate equally to establish a system of governance that ensures their mutual security and stability, in contrast to an imperial union, where colonies are brought into the assemblage by force or conquest and are made subject to a preexisting authority whose interests take precedence over their own. This equal participation and retention of local authority and autonomy marks the second significant feature of a federal union. In agreeing to form a federal "assemblage," the constituent states do not completely relinquish their sovereignty to the newly established government. Instead, the states retain their own "equal authority and credit," agreeing to abide by the laws passed by their confederated government, while simultaneously representing their distinct interests within that government on equal terms.[5]

In practice, of course, a federal union may fail to deliver on these principles of mutual consent and equal representation when governing its constituent communities, a failure that can lead a federal system to operate very similar to an empire. Julian Go and Edward Watts offer compelling assessments of the ways that the federal United States did not admit its new territories on equal terms but, instead, kept them as "subordinated dependencies"; in addition, Go, along with Onuf, Larkin, and Greene, has drawn convincing parallels between the federal structure and policies of the early United States and the imperial structure and policies of Great Britain.[6] Although a federal union may end up operating, in practice, like an empire, the emphasis placed on these principles of mutual consent and equal representation and collaboration among its varied constituencies nevertheless distinguished a federal political structure from the traditional models of empire in the late eighteenth century, and examining these distinctions can help us understand how federalism offered an alternative model for representing and interpreting variety in the early United States.

Early American political thinkers and writers were aware of the close relationship between empire and federal nationalism, and the terms were often closely associated with one another. A 1779 account describes the United States as an association of "several states in the union of the empire," and, as Peter Onuf has argued, residents of the United States habitually "imagined that their own de-centralized regime, a federal union of self-governing republics, was a worthy successor to Britain's empire in America."[7] Rather than simply mimicking the imperial structure of Great Britain, however, the federal structure of the United States was meant to revise and improve on Britain's imperial model by offering an alternative approach to the representation and management of its diverse constituencies. Much like an empire, the federal structure of the United States was designed to govern a heterogeneous group of people through a centralized structure, but this federalism assigned a different set of values and functions to its varied components. Within an empire, heterogeneity is valued and cultivated for its ability to maximize profits for the imperial government. The greater the variety within an empire, the more opportunities to translate its constituent resources into capital and profits.[8] Within a federal system, heterogeneity continues to have economic value. As Hamilton wrote, "commercial enterprise will have much greater scope, from the diversity in the productions of different States."[9] Variety, however, also took on new forms of significance in the federal United States, particularly regarding its ability to promote representative and participatory forms of governance. This variety was also valued as a means of promoting intellectual growth and protecting individual rights. As James Madison wrote, "In the extended republic of the United States, and among the great variety of interests, parties, and sects which it embraces, a coalition of a majority of the whole society could seldom take place on any other principles than those of justice and the general good."[10]

As mentioned in the introduction, these distinctions gave rise to an exceptionalist rhetoric that masked the imperial dimensions of U.S. federalism. For as much as federalism was meant to represent a new and improved approach to the representation of variety, the federal dynamics of the early United States also led to oppressive practices of imperial appropriation, marginalization, and abuse, and I will draw attention to these points of exclusion and contradiction in later chapters. For now, I simply want to emphasize the extent to which the ideology and rhetoric of U.S. federalism tried to define a different kind of plural nationalism in the late eighteenth century.

The ability to establish a government that was unified, yet also capable of representing and responding to the varied interests of its constituent states, is precisely what made federalism so appealing for residents of the new United States. As part of the British Empire, the American colonies were increasingly dissatisfied with their lack of representation and participation within the imperial government, and it was their desire to actively represent their local interests that led to rebellion. Although the colonists wanted a government that could represent their distinct localities after declaring independence, they soon realized that the extensive variety of the new nation made it difficult to establish points of unity, a difficulty compounded by the lack of reliable modes of transportation and communication. As one colonial governor described it, "the different manner in which they are settled, the different modes under which they live, the different forms of charters, grants, and frames of government they possess ... the different interests which they actuate, the religious interests by which they are actuated, the rivalship and jealousies which arise from hence ... [point to] the impracticability, if not the impossibility of reconciling and accommodating these incompatible ideas and claims."[11] More than simply hindering union, these differences also made conflict more likely. "In a period such as this, sir, when Thirteen Colonies unacquainted in great measure with each other are rushing together into one mass, it would be a miracle if such heterogeneous ingredients did not at first produce violent fermentations," wrote John Adams in a letter to a friend in 1775, highlighting widespread fears that the differences represented within the newly proposed union were more likely to produce feelings of conflict and division rather than affinity and affiliation.[12]

Because the variety of the former colonies could not be circumvented and representing this variety was a condition for declaring independence, federalism provided the most viable model for establishing a nation that was diverse and united. Those involved with orchestrating the new government were well educated in theories of federalism, and John Witherspoon, John Dickinson, Benjamin Franklin, John Adams, Thomas Jefferson, James Madison, Alexander Hamilton, and James Wilson drew extensively on the writings of Pufendorf, Grotius, Locke, and Montesquieu to design the federal nation, in addition to examining federal examples set by Switzerland, Germany, and the Netherlands.[13] The federal structure of the United States was also influenced by the nation's colonial history. As White and Yurish have argued, the establishment of the federal republic did not arise, exclusively, from a post-Revolutionary synthesis of Enlightenment ideologies and political philosophies, but, rather, must be viewed as a movement "with its early roots in the nature of the colonial enterprise."[14] At various moments, the British American colonies turned to federal structures and principles to improve British imperial governance. In 1643, for instance, the colonies of Plymouth, Massachusetts, and Connecticut joined in a confederation they termed the "United Colonies of New England." Under a written agreement, these "United Colonies" entered into "a firm and perpetual league of friendship and amity" to provide "offence and defense, mutual advice, and succor ... for their own mutual safety and welfare."[15] This association, which lasted forty years, was a stable and productive alliance that enabled the New England colonies to share resources and defend themselves from advances by Native American, Dutch, and French forces, and it was often cited by colonial and early national leaders as an example of the security and benefits derived from a confederated model of union.

The colonies also gained experience with federalism through their local governments. Each colony was governed by two institutions—a Crown-appointed governor and governing council and an assembly of locally elected delegates. Although the power of these elected assemblies was limited and subject to the authority of the royal appointees, these assemblies were active and effective in managing local affairs, and their success gave the colonists a sense of how sovereignty could be divided effectively between national and local forms of governance and, moreover, how this system of shared authority could better manage and respond to local interests and concerns. These colonial experiences laid a strong ideological foundation for federalism that citizens would build on after 1776.[16] Ultimately, it was Great Britain's failure to acknowledge the legitimacy and effectiveness of these local colonial governments that prompted their rebellion, a failure that the federal structure of the United States was designed to rectify.

This conflict between the colonists' desire for local autonomy and sovereignty and their status as colonial subjects is evident in the failure of the Albany Plan of Union in 1754. In contrast to the United Colonies of New England, which involved only a few colonies from the same region, the Albany Plan sought to join all thirteen British American colonies "under one government as far as might be necessary for defense and other general important purposes."[17] In the context of the British Empire, there was a precedent for granting sovereign status to its dominions through the case of Scotland, which joined with England in the Act of Union of 1707. The American colonists studied Scotland's example with great interest, believing it offered a model for their own efforts to be recognized as sovereign constituencies within Great Britain.[18] The primary goal of the proposed Albany alliance was security, enabling the colonies to combine their resources to defend themselves during the French and Indian War. Under the Albany Plan, colonial defense would be overseen by a "grand council" of elected delegates and a Crown-appointed "president general," and together, this alliance would have the authority to make treaties with Indian tribes, levy taxes, and allocate funds. By establishing this centralized system of authority, the Albany Plan represented a definitive attempt to organize the colonies in federal terms, and its supporters emphasized its unifying potential by providing residents with an opportunity to improve "our disunited state and . . . weakness arising from such a want of union."[19]

Though many colonists supported the Albany Plan in principle, the proposal failed to win approval from the colonial governments and the British Empire. In the eyes of Parliament, the unified government proposed by the Albany Plan gave the colonial governments too much power, and they preferred to deal with the colonies separately, rather than negotiating with them in a consolidated union. Meanwhile, many of the colonial assemblies objected to the Albany Plan because they feared it would compromise their local authority, believing that the proposed union, as long as it remained under the oversight of a Crown-appointed president, would become yet another form of imperial control. In this regard, the failure of the Albany Plan exemplified how the goals and advantages of a federal union could not be realized within an imperial structure of government.

While it failed to produce a successful union in the 1750s, the Albany Plan served as the primary model for drafting the Articles of Confederation after independence was declared in 1776. The Articles of Confederation closely followed the language of the Albany Plan, whereby the states agreed to "severally enter into a firm league of friendship with each other, for their common defense, the security of their liberties, and their mutual and general welfare."[20] Determining the specific form that this federal "league of friendship" would take, however, proved to be difficult. Under the Articles, delegates initially designed a federal system that privileged the authority of the states by establishing a nation that was defined by strong and visible state governments and a weak central authority. While this structure was effective for quickly uniting the former colonies and combining their resources to fight Great Britain, this model of federalism was unable to provide political and financial stability for the nation after the war. The inadequacies of the Articles were widely discussed throughout the 1780s, eventually leading to the Constitutional Convention where delegates sought "to devise such further provisions ... to render the constitution of the Federal Government adequate to the exigencies of the Union."[21]

The Constitutional Convention produced yet another model of federal governance that, in this case, established a much stronger central government whose powers were more clearly outlined and prioritized over the states. Although the states still retained some degree of autonomy and authority, under the new Constitution, their influence was more carefully constrained by the structure of the federal Congress, which was designed to mitigate the sectional conflicts and rivalries that dominated the federal nation under the Articles of Confederation. Delegates agreed that this new federal Congress needed to provide a forum for representing the nation's constituencies justly and equally, serving, as George Mason described, as a "grand repository" that "ought to know and sympathize with every part of the community."[22] Determining an effective form for producing this equal and comprehensive representation, however, proved to be difficult, and arguments over whether the states should be represented equally or proportionally in the federal Congress nearly brought the convention to a halt in July 1787. Although this conflict was eventually resolved by structuring Congress as a bicameral legislature that would use both systems of representation, this solution reveals the extent to which the federal government of the United States was always tied up with issues of form and competing interpretations of federal representation and equity.[23]

Debates over form and interpretation would continue to dominate the federal United States, beginning with the ratification process. During ratification two partisan positions emerged that were rooted in two distinct versions of federal interpretation, positions that would eventually lay the groundwork for the nation's two-party system. On one side were the Federalists, who believed that a federal government should focus on representing a consolidated union, exemplified by the presence of "an energetic and active national government" that exercised careful control over its constituent states to avoid promoting "weakness, disorder ... and calamities."[24] On the other side were the Anti-Federalists who, despite their name, were firmly committed to the principles of federalism, believing that "a confederacy ... is precisely the principle which has hitherto preserved our freedom."[25] The Anti-Federalists, however, believed that a federal government should primarily represent the authority of its constituencies, and, for this reason, they opposed the new Constitution because it granted too much power to a central government while minimizing the authority of the states. "This government is to possess absolute and uncontrollable powers ... [and] it appears from these articles that there is no need of any intervention of the State governments," wrote the Anti-Federalist writer "Brutus," who concluded that "the government, then, so far as it extends, is a complete one and not a confederation."[26]

Patrick Henry summarized these two competing interpretations of federalism in his speech to the Virginia Ratifying Convention delivered in June 1788, where he asked his audience to consider the implied significance of the Constitution's preamble. "The fate of this question and of America may depend on this. Have they said, We, the States? Have they made a proposal of a compact between states? If they had, this would be a confederation. It is otherwise most clearly a consolidated government."[27] By focusing on the significance of the collective term "we," Henry distinguishes between two different forms of national union. If "we" refers to the "people," then the Constitution represented a federal nation that was defined by a collective body of citizens and emphasized its status as a centralized union, rather than a composite one. By contrast, if "we" refers to the states, then the Constitution would privilege the plural dimensions of the federal union over its consolidated status. For Henry and the other Anti-Federalists, a constitution whose language clearly emphasized the power of the states represented a more legitimate form of federal government than the one proposed, whose language privileged the power of the central government. In either case, Henry's arguments reveal how the federal structure and significance of the United States was produced, quite literally, through careful practices of reading and writing.[28]

In the end, the Federalist language and interpretation of federal nationalism prevailed when the Constitution was ratified with its emphasis on a strong central government intact. The form and significance of the federal union, however, would continue to be subject to endless processes of rereading and rewriting in the early decades of the republic as citizens continued to argue over whether the United States represented a consolidated or a composite model of nationhood. These arguments were aided by the ambivalent language of the federal Constitution whose wording left the specific relationship between the central government and the states open to interpretation. James Madison addressed the flexible significance of the nation's federal character in the Federalist No. 39, where he describes the Constitution as a document that is "neither wholly *national* nor wholly *federal*." "Were it wholly national, the supreme and ultimate authority would reside in the *majority* of the people of the Union," he writes. "Were it wholly federal, on the other hand, the concurrence of each State in the Union would be essential to every alteration that would be binding on all.... The proposed Constitution, therefore ... is, in strictness, neither a national nor a federal Constitution, but a composition of both."[29] By defining the United States as a union that was both "national and federal" at the same time, the language of the Constitution made it possible for citizens to interpret the United States in multiple ways, representing either a consolidated or a state-centered system of governance, as needed. The rise of the two-party system was defined by these two competing models of federal interpretation, and as political conflicts quickly erupted over issues such as western expansion, the establishment of the Bank of the United States, the Whiskey Rebellion, and the Alien and Sedition Acts, citizens were continually asked to determine—and reconsider—what kind of federal union the United States was supposed to be. Because the meaning of the federal United States was so contingent on the ways citizens chose to represent and interpret it, practices of reading and writing became central to the development of a federal national consciousness in the early republic.

Singular and Plural: The Federal Union in the Public Sphere

The politics of federalism are evident in the everyday grammar of the early nation. The Articles of Confederation and the Constitution both declared "The United States of America" as the official name of the new nation, and from the beginning, there was considerable uncertainty as to whether this name should be treated as a singular or a plural noun. Documents from the early republic—formal and informal—show significant variations.[30] Sometimes "United States" is treated as a singular noun, taking singular verbs and articles, while in other cases "United States" is treated as a plural noun, with plural verbs and modifiers. This grammatical usage reflects the competing interpretations of federal nationalism that emerged in the early republic, where the singular usage of "United States" signified a consolidated model of union while the plural usage emphasized the nation's diverse constituencies. Use of the singular or plural forms of "United States" did not track neatly to Federalist and Anti-Federalist positions, however, and the usage of "United States" varied depending on what aspect of the federal union a speaker wanted to emphasize.[31] Noah Webster tried to strike a middle ground by defining the United States in both singular and plural terms in his *Grammatical Institute of the United States*, where he writes that "the United States of America are Thirteen."³² By defining the United States as a singular noun (through use of the article "the") that nevertheless takes a plural verb ("are"), Webster sought to emphasize the singular and plural dimensions of the federal union in everyday usage. While this joint singular and plural usage represents the federal character of the nation, however, the awkwardness of this phrasing reflects another difficulty of representing the federal union. How could citizens represent the nation's paradoxical singular and plural character in terms that were practical and effective, as opposed to confusing and contradictory?

The need for popular and effective forms for representing the federal nation was particularly important given the uncertain conditions of union at this time. As Lester Olson writes, the Articles of Confederation and Constitution "call[ed] into being a condition among its members that had not and did not, in fact, exist."³³ Even though the United States had been defined as a federal nation, citizens had to create the bonds that would tie the different states together. Jedidiah Morse, author of the nation's leading geography textbooks, describes this discrepancy between the nation's federal definition and the conditions of its unity. "The American Republic is composed of almost all nations, languages, characters, and religions which Europe can furnish; the greater part, however, are descended from English; and all may, perhaps, be distinguishingly denominated *Federal Americans*," he reports in his 1796 edition of *Geography Made Easy*.³⁴ Although "Federal Americans" provides an appropriate way to "distinguish and denominate" the citizens of the United States, Morse is quick to acknowledge that this term unites the citizens in name only, reporting that these "Federal Americans, collected together from various countries, of different habits, formed under different governments and of different languages, customs, manners and religions, have not yet assimilated to that degree as to form a national character."³⁵ Morse goes on to predict that these Federal Americans will soon establish a "vigorous, powerful, and respectable" nation, but he takes care to insist that this identity does not yet exist in the United States and, moreover, that producing it will take a great deal of work.

It is also worth noting the limitations placed on this not-yet-realized federal American identity. Although Morse emphasizes that "Federal Americans" are defined by their regional, cultural, linguistic, political, and religious variety, he is careful to insist that this variety is acceptable only insofar as it can be traced to the differences "which Europe can furnish." Europe represented a large range of variety regarding languages, cultural practices, religious beliefs, and so on, but Morse is very clear that the federal heterogeneity of the United States is not open ended. The variety that defines Federal Americans is restricted to those of

European cultural and political origins, and it does not include residents with connections to Africa, Asia, or any indigenous communities.

U.S. citizens were actively involved in developing the heterogeneous federal nationalism that Morse tries to call into being in his geography texts. Throughout the late eighteenth century, residents experimented with different media, organizational strategies, and aesthetic forms to represent the nation's diverse characteristics in unified terms. In developing these public representations, however, citizens had to contend with the contradictory and disruptive consequences of representing diversity as a sign of union. Highlighting the varied dimensions of the United States was a relatively easy task. More difficult was finding ways to ensure that those differences would convey a sense of unity and stability to viewers. Federal nationalism thus required citizens to think very carefully about issues of form. What kinds of designs and organizational structures could portray the nation's differences as a sign of its unity, rather than an indicator of its absence? And what forms could simultaneously celebrate the nation's differences while also delineating those who were excluded from it?

Geography was widely perceived as an effective discourse for defining and supporting this federal nationalism. By representing the nation's physical space and including detailed descriptions of its diversity, maps, atlases, gazetteers, and geography textbooks could provide citizens with a comprehensive knowledge of the different parts of the nation in a format that represented these differences within clear national boundaries. More than simply educating citizens about the diverse content of the federal nation, geography texts were also believed to foster feelings of sympathy and unity among a widely dispersed population. As Noah Webster wrote, the study of national geography will "call home the minds of youth and fix them upon the interests of their own country" and "assist [them] in forming attachments to it, as well as in enlarging the understanding."[36] Geography was considered so important for unifying the new nation that it became a required part of the primary and secondary educational curriculum, and geography texts were among the most popular works of print sold in the United States during the 1780s and 1790s, transforming, as Brückner writes, "the representation of personal, regional and political difference into material figures of national consent."[37]

While geographic texts provided an effective means for imagining a united federal nation, they also drew attention to its divisions and points of exclusion. Although geography books sought to foster a united and sympathetic understanding of the nation's differences by representing "the history, policy, commerce, productions, particular advantages, and interests of the several states," at times these representations could have antagonistic effects.[38] Morse's textbooks, for instance, often included critical comments that highlighted regional rivalries and conflicts. His descriptions of the southern states, for instance, often emphasize their "indolent" and "dissipated" characteristics and criticize the practice of slavery, while the northern states are described in more positive terms as "frugal" and "industrious" and praised for their commitment to "liberty."[39] These comparisons highlight regional tensions within the United States, and Morse's criticism of the southern states characterizes these differences as a source of conflict rather than a sign of union. Morse's descriptions indicate divisions among the northern states as he criticizes some states for their local particularities. Morse singles out Rhode Island, for instance, whose residents "exhibit a melancholy proof of those evils which ever follow a relaxation of moral principles," and he criticizes the people of Connecticut whose "litigious spirit" leaves them "remarkably fond of having all their disputes, even those of the most trivial kind, settled according to law."[40] Rather than fostering a unified understanding of the nation, these judgmental descriptions present readers with a picture of the federal nation that is not quite as harmonious as it was imagined to be.

The organizational structure of Morse's textbooks emphasizes how writers had to walk a fine line in presenting the nation's differences in unifying or divisive terms. "The American republic, of which we have given a general account, consists of three grand divisions, denominated the Northern, or more properly Eastern, Middle and Southern States," writes Morse, who arranges his descriptions of the states according to these three regional categories. Although this organizational structure was meant to emphasize the similarities between the states in each region, grouping the states into these "grand divisions" also suggests that these regional collections of states were fundamentally different and separate from one another. Morse acknowledged the problematic effects of this organizational structure and terminology in later editions of his geography books, where he apologetically explains, "Though these divisions are merely nominal and may be liable to some objections . . . yet the convenience of using the appellations northern, middle, and southern, in writing and conversation is considered as sufficient reason for adopting this classification."[41] Here, the difficulty of representing the differences of the nation in unifying terms is readily apparent. Though Morse tries to downplay the implications of his use of the term "division" by calling it "nominal," he also recognizes its problematic consequences. The fact that the term "division" is the most "convenient" for representing the different characteristics of the nation illuminates the extent to which the federal structure of the nation required citizens to become comfortable with paradoxical or contradictory forms of representation. As Morse's geography texts make abundantly clear, learning how to recognize the plural United States as a singular nation involved learning how to read its "grand divisions" as a paradoxical sign of union.

Embedded within Morse's geography texts are additional signs marking differences that were not intended to be read or interpreted as part of the union. These points of exclusion are most evident in his state-by-state depictions of the U.S. population. The demographic information in Morse's geography books shows that each of the states categorized their "Inhabitants" differently.[42] Many of the states divided their populations into racial categories by identifying the number of "black" and "white" residents (Connecticut, Georgia, Maryland, New Jersey, New York, North and South Carolina, Rhode Island, Virginia), although some states did not mark racial divisions at all (Delaware, Massachusetts, New Hampshire, Pennsylvania). A few states made further refinements under the category of "black" residents by listing the number who were free and the number who were enslaved (New Jersey, Virginia), while others made distinctions under the category of "white" residents to identify those who were eligible to serve in a militia (Connecticut, Massachusetts, Pennsylvania, Virginia). Only two states recorded information about "women" residents (Connecticut and New Jersey), and only one state, Connecticut, included Native Americans as part of their "Inhabitants," listing them under a category titled "Total Blacks: Indians and Negroes." New York referred to Native Americans only to record their diminishing presence in the state, noting that "the few Indians who remain are, in general, friendly." Otherwise, Native Americans were not represented as "Inhabitants" at all, with New Hampshire specifically stating that "there are no Indians in the state" and Georgia asserting that all of its population data was "exclusive of Indians." A few states used religion as a population category, most notably Massachusetts, New Jersey, and Pennsylvania, which broke their populations down into specific denominations (Episcopalians, Baptists, Quakers, etc.) with data for each category.

This population data suggests that these categories carried different levels of significance in each state. In some cases, these categories simply marked important points of distinction. States that identified the number of white men capable of serving in the militia, for instance, likely had a particular need for military engagement and protection, which made this a significant category for representation, and the efforts of Massachusetts, New Jersey, and Pennsylvania to represent their religious demographics suggest that these communities played an important political, social, or economic role in these particular states but not in others. In the case of race and gender, however, these categories marked different points of value and exclusion. Black residents were typically granted fewer rights and privileges in nearly all the states, and enslaved black residents counted as only $3/5$ of a person for purposes of congressional representation, which is why this racial category appeared so often in this population data. The near absence of Native Americans in these population charts likewise reveals the extent to which these communities had little value or recognition within the United States, a position shared by women, whose absence reflects the prevailing laws of coverture where women were presumed to be represented by their husbands or fathers.[43] While this population data clearly represents the United States as a nation with diverse residents, these categories also reveal a nation that did not grant equal rights or value to those diverse residents, specifically those who were women, African American, or Native American. Instead, the differences that *were* granted equal value concerned the states' distinctive policies for managing their respective populations. Morse's population charts show that each of the states represented and valued their residents differently, and he presents these variations as equally valid expressions of local governance and identity. Within the federal United States, the different policies and practices of the states were represented in equal terms. The different people living within those states, however, were not.

This privileging of the diversity of the states over the diversity of their populations was problematic for a nation founded on the equitable representation of its constituent variety, and Morse addresses this discrepancy when he addresses the practice of slavery in the United States. "While we exhibit the fair side of the character of Federal Americans, we would not be thought blind to their faults," stated Morse, who acknowledged that slavery violated the nation's principles of federal equity by placing states' rights over the rights of individuals, noting that "a European writer has justly observed that 'if there be an object truly ridiculous in nature, it is an American patriot, signing resolutions of independence with one hand and with the other, brandishing a whip over his affrighted slaves.'" For Morse, the practice of slavery, which denies any rights or autonomy to black residents, is incompatible with the values of independence and equal representation that the federal government was supposed to exemplify, which leads him to assert that "under the Federal government, from the measures already adopted, we have reason to believe that all slaves in the United States will in time be emancipated." He acknowledges that this process will be "attended with difficulties," but he argues that the logic of federalism must ultimately be extended to include and represent African American residents equally.[44] By making these arguments, Morse's textbooks celebrate the diversity of the federal nation, while also identifying and seeking to remedy important and visible points of federal exclusion.

Maps were another important medium for representing the federal union, and these texts also reveal tensions over how to represent and manage its singular and plural dimensions. The issue of representing state boundaries was a matter of particular concern for early U.S. cartographers. Many mapmakers chose to de-emphasize state boundaries on national maps, marking them in faint or partial forms or, more often, leaving them out entirely. The national maps included in Morse's geography textbooks, for instance, did not include state boundaries and identified the states simply by printing their names over their respective territory. This border-free design provided a more unified image of the United States by representing the nation as a single landmass, whose identity was defined solely by its national borders, rather than the boundaries of its constituent states.[45] Other cartographers, however, felt that this style failed to accurately represent the federal character of the nation.[46] By depicting state boundaries, these maps pushed viewers to recognize the plural and constituent dimensions of the federal nation, providing citizens with the information they needed to recognize and engage with the union's many parts.[47]

Other maps reflected the paradoxical nature of federal union through their decorative elements. Abel Buell's *New and Correct Map of the United States of North America*, which was printed in New Haven, Connecticut, in 1784, provides a particular case in point (fig. 1). Buell's *New and Correct Map* was the first national map to be printed and published in the United States by a U.S. citizen, and it was also the first map to be copyrighted in the United States, thanks to early copyright laws passed by the state of Connecticut. A well-established New Haven engraver and printer, Buell was responsible for the entire project, from drafting and design to printing and distribution, and he hoped, as he noted in his copyright proposal, that this map would earn him the position as "Geographer for the State of Connecticutt." The map depicts the full extent of the United States following the 1783 Treaty of Paris, including its new western and northern territories. To compose the map, Buell drew on preexisting works, most notably John Mitchell's 1755 *Map of the British and French Dominions in North America*, which had been used in negotiating the Paris treaty, as well as more recent, locally oriented maps such as Thomas Hutchins's *The Western Parts of Virginia, Pennsylvania, Maryland and North Carolina* and Jonathan Carver's *A New Map of North America from the Latest Discoveries*, both published in 1778.[48]

While Buell's depiction of the United States' physical geography was very similar to these earlier maps, he included additional decorative elements to emphasize the United States' new national status. The cartouche clearly identifies the map as a unified national document with its title, *New and Correct Map of the United States of North America*. To further support the map's national focus, the cartouche also features an American flag at the top of the design, which, by 1784, was widely recognized as a symbol of national strength and unity. The lower right-hand corner of the cartouche rounds out this nationalist focus with an image of the figure of Liberty seated above a plaque inscribed with the words "Independence, July 4, 1776," thus establishing the date of independence as the unifying foundation for the nation depicted on the map.

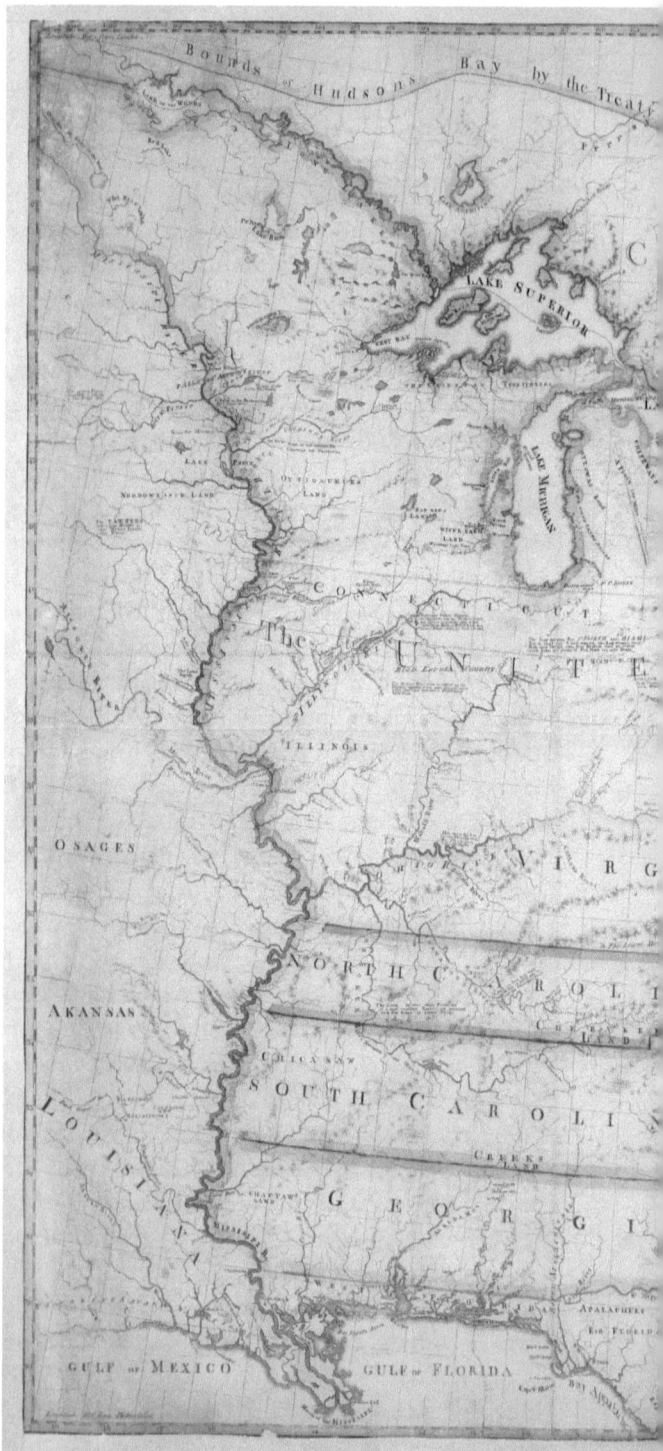

FIG. 1. Abel Buell's *New and Correct Map of the United States Layd down from the Latest Observations and Best Authorities Agreeable to the Peace of 1783*. New Haven, Connecticut, 1784. © The British Library Board. Cartographic Items Maps * 71490.(150.)

In the midst of these emblems of national unity, however, the cartouche also emphasizes the influence of local interests. Having proposed this map to obtain a position as Connecticut's official geographer, Buell's efforts to celebrate U.S. nationalism share space with his efforts to promote the interests of this particular state. After asserting that this map provides a "correct" representation of the new nation, Buell notes that it is also "humbly inscribed to his Excellency the Governor and Company of the State of Connecticut," a move that repositions this national map for use by a specific state. Buell further emphasizes Connecticut's claim to the map by including an image of the state seal—three grape vines positioned on an oval background—at the top of the cartouche, directly below the image of the national flag. After the Revolution, many states developed their own official seals, flags, and mottos as a way of asserting their distinct identities and sovereignty within the federal union.[49] The general assembly of Connecticut, which had used the image of the grapevines as its colonial seal since the seventeenth century, declared this image to be its official state seal in 1784, the same year that Buell's map was published. In presenting viewers with one of the first images of the nationally independent United States, Buell's *New and Correct Map* also presented one of the first official representations of Connecticut statehood. With Connecticut's seal positioned below the U.S. flag, the state's identity is clearly subordinate to the nation's. Nevertheless, these two images are nearly equal in size on the cartouche, suggesting their equal importance. Though subtle, an uneasy tension emerges here between Buell's desire to represent the national union and, at the same time, privilege one particular part of it, a tension that speaks to the larger difficulty of representing a federal nation where citizens were asked to define their national affinity through the expression of their local interests and authority.

Buell's depiction of U.S. geography continues to show this tension between the map's national and state-oriented focus. Unlike Morse's maps, Buell's carefully identifies the boundaries for each state. On one hand, this clear demarcation emphasizes the map's national focus by representing the United States as it had been "layed down" by official authorities. This nationalist interpretation of these state boundaries, however, becomes complicated when considering Buell's representation of the United States' western borders. When Buell's map was printed, the United States had not officially organized the western territory acquired under the Treaty of Paris. Many of the states with existing western borders, such as Georgia, the Carolinas, and Virginia, had made preliminary claims to this territory on the basis of their colonial charters, and, in the absence of any official legislation, Buell's map reflects these early state claims, extending the western boundaries of Georgia, Virginia, and the Carolinas as far west as the Mississippi River. Buell's map also presents an extended western boundary for the state of Connecticut, which stretches to the Mississippi River and as far north as the Great Lakes. Although Connecticut argued that this claim was supported by their colonial charter, this extended western boundary was considered to be more controversial and disruptive, particularly since it hopscotched over the state of Pennsylvania to claim land that was not contiguous to its existing territory. Under this proposed boundary, Connecticut emerges as one of the largest states in the nation, a projection that would have accorded the state much greater authority in the federal union. Buell's representation of these projected state boundaries thus reveals his interest in promoting and privileging the interests of Connecticut on this "national" map, conveying a much more conflicted portrait of the union than its nationalist imagery suggests. As Patrick Spero has argued, the early United States was beset by numerous border conflicts as the states struggled to assert their power and identity in the new republic.[50] Rather than simply presenting a "correct" image of the various states that make up the nation, Buell's map reflects these conflicted relationships, where states such as Connecticut were vying with their neighbors for greater visibility, influence, and power within the union.

The dual focus of Buell's *New and Correct Map*, which is split between its representation of national and state interests, is an inevitable consequence of the United States' federal structure. In a nation composed of distinct and sovereign states, expressions of federal nationalism must inevitably contend with local affiliations and interests. In some cases, the representation of these local and national interests could coalesce and complement one another, as represented by the U.S. flag, but in other cases, these joint affiliations could counteract and conflict with one another, as evident in Morse's and Buell's geographic representations of federal nation. To this end, remarks Waldstreicher, the practice of federal nationalism created opportunities "for both divisive activity and real consensus," such that "one day's happy identification of region and nation could be the next day's intractable political dilemma."[51]

Maps such as Buell's also illustrate the practices of exclusion at stake in mapping the federal nation. While Buell's maps clearly reflect the complementary and conflicting relationships between the unified nation and its constituencies, this map also defines this federal nation in terms that are restricted to Anglo-American claims. Missing from this map are any representations of Native American nations or their own claims to this land. In 1782–83, when Buell was composing this map, the Pequot and Mohegan nations were actually in the process of petitioning the Connecticut Assembly to clarify the status and boundaries of their territorial possessions by asking for an official survey of their claims.[52] The absence of any boundaries marking Mohegan or Pequot land on Buell's map exemplifies how these claims held little value or recognition for state or national audiences. Nearly all maps of the early United States convey these principles of exclusion regarding Native Americans. As Brückner writes, "the act of mapping . . . is inherently oppressive" for those communities outside of those cultural norms.[53] In the early United States, the process of mapping its boundaries, settlements, and topography necessarily diminished and, in most cases, completely erased the presence of Native Americans and their claims to the lands that made up the new nation, not to mention their different strategies and approaches for representing and imagining space.[54]

We Are One . . . but How?
Designing Images of Union

Since geography proved to be a difficult medium for controlling the potential divisions posed by the federal structure of the nation, citizens turned to other forms of visual expression to represent the nation's variety productively. As James Wilson argued in a speech delivered at the Grand Federal Procession in Philadelphia, it was not enough for citizens to simply recognize all the different states that made up the union; they also needed to develop a sense of how "each gains from all, and all gain from each."[55]

Finding popular images that could represent the federal union in these mutually supportive and interdependent terms, however, was challenging. During the Revolution, the most famous image of the federal union was the rattlesnake, whose bisected body represented each of the states alongside the statement "Join or Die." After the Revolution, however, the image of a rattlesnake did not seem to be an appropriate national emblem. As Olson observes, "The image of the snake designating the United States lost its widespread popularity after national independence had ended the oppressive circumstances that had made serpentine values seem so necessary for survival."[56]

The design of the national flag represented one of the first and most successful attempts to represent the federal union. Different versions of the stars and stripes design had been used during the Revolution, but Congress approved an official design on June 14, 1777, which stated "that the flag of the United States be thirteen stripes, alternate red and white; that the union be thirteen stars, white in a blue field, representing a new Constellation."[57] Several factors contributed to the success of this design. First, the thirteen stars and stripes effectively represented the states as distinct yet equal entities. Second, these components all worked together to produce a larger effect, with the stripes combining to make up the complete cloth of the flag, while the stars represented the complete and unified shape of a circle.[58] Another advantage of the flag's federal symbolism was its flexible and inclusive dimensions. By representing the nation's plurality through the images of stars and stripes, which had no specific local connotations, this imagery avoided the appearance of privileging one constituency over another, while also providing an open-ended symbolism that could be interpreted in multiple ways. Although these images portrayed the United States as a plural union, they did not stipulate the specific kinds of variety that the nation represented. By leaving the plurality of the federal nation open ended, the flag allowed U.S. residents to tailor their interpretations of the nation's variety to meet their individual needs and expectations.

On the same day that independence was declared, the Continental Congress appointed a committee composed of Benjamin Franklin, John Adams, and Thomas Jefferson to "bring in a device for the seal of the United States of America." Their first proposal focused on allegorical images, with Franklin proposing an image of Moses parting the Red Sea, and Jefferson one of the Israelites emerging from captivity, while Adams turned to classical mythology, proposing an image of Hercules choosing between a path of Virtue and a path of Vice.[59] Unable to come to a joint decision, the committee consulted with Pierre Eugène du Simitière, a Philadelphia artist with experience designing heraldry who suggested a design that emphasized the federal structure of the new nation. Simitière's design featured a shield emblazoned with symbols representing "the Countries from which these States have been peopled," which was, in turn, surrounded by a circle of plaques bearing the initials of each of the constituent states. The figures of Lady Liberty and an American soldier were positioned on either side of this central image; at the top was an image of the protective "Eye of Providence," and, at the bottom, a banner bearing the motto *E pluribus unum*, which emphasized the composite union that the seal was designed to represent (fig. 2).[60]

Franklin, Adams, and Jefferson presented Simitière's design to Congress on August 20, 1776, but the motion for approval was tabled, and Congress did not revisit the issue until 1780 when they appointed a new committee to redesign the seal. By this time, the United States had formally adopted the national flag, and, hoping to capitalize on the success of this image, the committee of 1780 enlisted Francis Hopkinson, the flag's original designer, to compose the national seal. Hopkinson's proposal depicted a shield with thirteen alternating red and white stripes positioned beneath a constellation of thirteen stars. Much like Simitière's design, this shield was flanked by two figures, in this case, a goddess of peace holding an olive branch and a Native American warrior, although Hopkinson soon replaced the Native American warrior with a soldier in classical Roman dress in a second design drafted soon after. A banner with a new motto, *Bello Vel Pace Paratus* ("prepared in war or peace"), was featured at the bottom

FIG. 2. Design for the Seal of the United States: The First Design. Pierre Eugène du Simitière, 1776. Library of Congress, Prints and Photographs Division, LC-USZ62-45728.

(fig. 3). Despite its similarity to the flag, this design was again rejected by Congress, and the matter of a national seal was left unresolved until 1782, when the United States needed it to ratify its peace treaty with Great Britain at the end of the Revolutionary War.

A third committee proposed a design that was very similar to Hopkinson's 1780 proposal, once again featuring a shield emblazoned with thirteen alternating red and white stripes, although in this image the constellation of stars had been replaced with the image of an eagle. The entire image was flanked by two different figures, an American soldier and a woman representing the "Genius of America" (fig. 4). Concerned that this proposed design was too busy, Congress referred the image to Charles Thomson, the secretary of the Congress, for further revision. Thomson's design featured a simpler and more consolidated image that retained a shield of alternating stripes centered on the body of an eagle that clutched both an olive branch and a set of thirteen arrows (fig. 5). Above the eagle's head was a constellation of thirteen stars, as well as a banner that reinstated the motto originally featured on the first design, *E pluribus unum*. In his final report to Congress, Thomson emphasized the seal's ability to convey the

FIG. 3. Second Design for the Great Seal Obverse
by Francis Hopkinson, 1780. The National Archives, no. 595252.
Papers of the Continental Congress, 1774–89.

federal dimensions of the national union. "The pieces ... represent the several states all joined in one solid compact entire, supporting a Chief [eagle], which unites the whole and represents Congress. The Motto alludes to this union ... [which is] kept closely united by the Chief, and the Chief depends on the union and the strength resulting from it for its support, to denote the Confederacy of the United States of America & the preservation of their union through Congress."[61] By emphasizing this seal's ability to represent the nation's plural dimensions "joined in one solid compact entire," Thomson's proposal illustrates how the nation's composite elements depend on one another for support. Thomson continued this emphasis on the back of the seal, which featured the image of a thirteen-step pyramid with "1776" written in roman numerals at the base, an image borrowed from Continental currency to signify how the thirteen states made up a nation founded on its assertion of independence. Pleased with Thom-

FIG. 4. Design for the Recto of the Great Seal of the United States by William Barton, 1782. The National Archives, no. 595258. Papers of the Continental Congress, 1774–89.

son's proposal, Congress finally approved this design on June 20, 1782, and the seal was cast several months later.

The length of time it took to design and approve the federal seal illustrates how hard it was to find effective ways to represent this plural model of union. The congressional record provides very little information as to why Congress objected to the earlier proposals or why Thomson's version ultimately met with approval, but comparing the successive designs provides some possible insights. All the designs contain multiple elements, but while the earlier proposals portray these components as separate entities, Thomson's design represents all its elements as part of a single image, where all the components are connected to the body of the eagle, with the federal motto *E pluribus unum* highlighting the overall effect of the seal's imagery. The unified representation of these different components would have provided a more stable and assertive representation of the United States' federal union. Moreover, Thomson's design also represents one of the most equitable representations of the nation's many differences. Each of

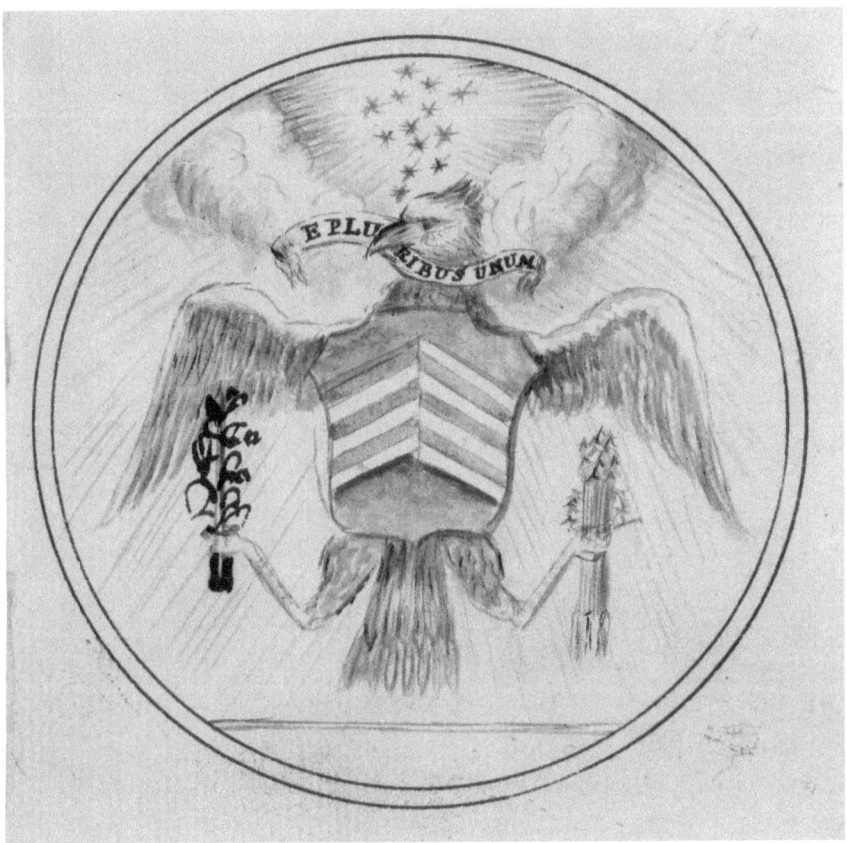

FIG. 5. Design for the Verso of the Great Seal of the United States by Charles Thomson, 1782. The National Archives, no. 595257. Papers of the Continental Congress, 1774–89.

the federal images—the stripes, the arrows, and the stars—represents the states in distinct but equal terms, in contrast to Simitière's attempt to represent the federal nation through plaques bearing the initials of the states, a form of representation that many delegates may have found objectionable by emphasizing the different names of the states, as opposed to the more harmonious equitability implied by Thomson's nameless images.

Citizens experimented with other visual forms to represent the federal nation throughout the 1770s and 1780s. The most successful designs, like Thomson's design for the great seal, represented the diverse components of the nation while simultaneously conveying the productive and mutually supportive effects of their union. Two popular examples include a candelabra with thirteen lit candles

FIG. 6. Benjamin Franklin, *One Sixth of a Dollar*, Philadelphia, 1776. Library of Congress, Prints and Photographs Division, LC-USZ6-861.

and a harp with thirteen strings. In these images, the candles and the strings have a greater effect when joined together than they would have had alone, and their respective effects—in the case of the candelabra, light, and in the case of the harp, harmonious music—further portray diversity as a positive attribute. Other images likewise emphasized the productive effects of a federal union, as well as its improved security and strength, such as the image of bees at a hive or arrows gathered in a quiver. While the influence of one single bee or arrow was small and negligible, the united efforts of many could have strong and productive effects. Like the images of the national flag and seal, these images also represented variety in open-ended terms, allowing citizens to define the specific variations recognized by the nation in their own terms, rather than establishing proscribed designations.

Benjamin Franklin's image of interlinked chains was another popular design for asserting the strength and stability of the federal union. This image depicts thirteen interlinked rings that form a circular chain (fig. 6). In this image, the states are represented as independent, self-sufficient entities that, when joined together, produce a chain whose strength and unity is contingent on the presence of each individual link. In the middle of the ring is a short statement, "We are One," which forcefully asserts the central paradox of the federal union—a plural term that represents a single union. Rather than trying to explain or shift attention away from this seeming contradiction, Franklin's design confidently asserts this paradox as a foundational fact of the union, relying on the support of the visual image that surrounds this statement—that of the linked chain—to support the credibility and coherence of the words "We are One."

Franklin's image originally appeared as part of his design for Continental currency, and it was first printed as part of the $\frac{1}{6}$ dollar note issued in 1776 and was later used on the first one-cent coin for the United States, known as the "fugio cent." Most of the images used to represent the new federal nation also originally appeared on early national currency, including the images of the harp, candelabra, bees, and arrows, and their presence on currency further illuminates their unifying influence. Paper money had been used in the colonies since the early seventeenth century, though it was closely monitored by Great Britain. Following independence, the individual states immediately began issuing their own currencies as a sign of their independent sovereignty, and these currencies featured images that evoked their distinctive local character. On the eve of independence, Connecticut issued its own local currency with an emblem of grapevines that would shortly become the official state seal, and New Jersey's currency depicted the state coat of arms, which featured three plows to represent the state's agricultural production (fig. 7).

Many of these state currencies also tried to signify their connection to the larger national union by featuring federal images such as the harp, a candelabra, or a quiver or arrows. The Continental Congress also issued its own "national" currency that was designed to hold value in all the states, and this Continental currency also featured federal images, although the resonance of these images was slightly different. If the federal images featured on state currencies helped link the states to the national union, the presence of these federal images on the Continental currency reminded citizens that this national currency still represented its constituent parts. In other words, while the federal images on the state currencies reminded citizens to see themselves as part of a whole, the federal images on the Continental currency reminded citizens to recognize that the whole was composed of parts (see fig. 8).[62]

These federal images migrated to other popular formats, appearing on the mastheads of U.S. newspapers and magazines, on state flags and seals, in political cartoons, and on broadside illustrations. Amos Doolittle printed a number of popular broadsides that represented the United States using a picture of President Washington surrounded by images of the state seals arranged in interlinked

FIG. 7. Connecticut currency for nine pence with emblem of grapevines, 1780, and New Jersey currency for twelve shillings 1783. Courtesy American Antiquarian Society.

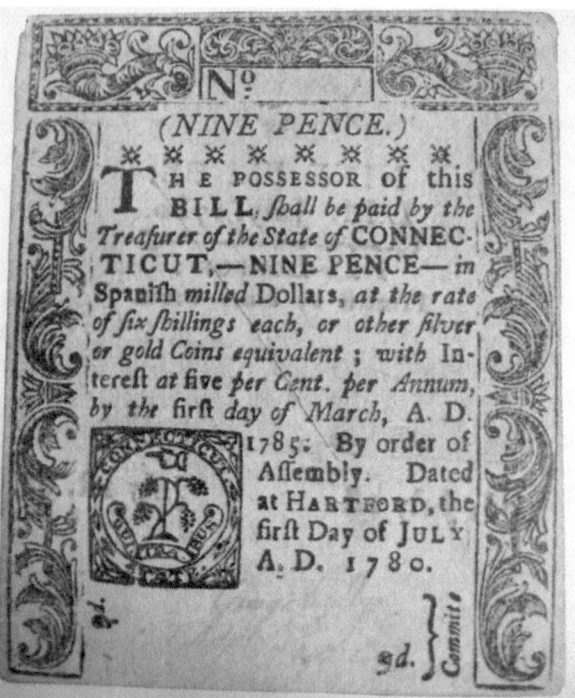

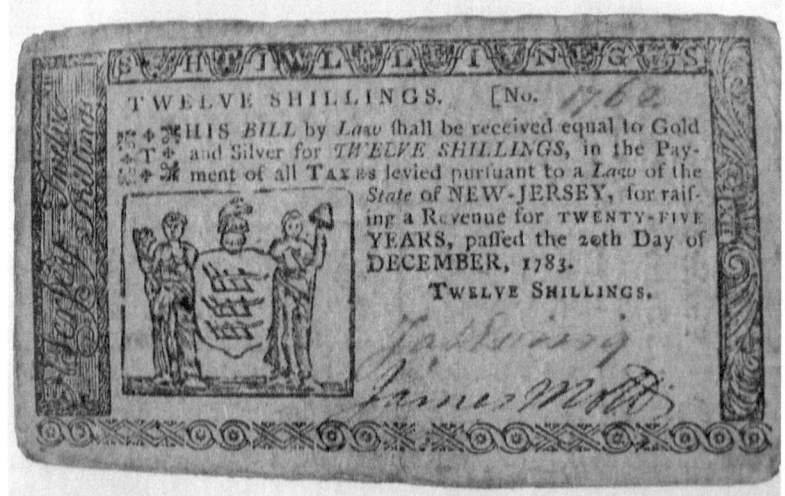

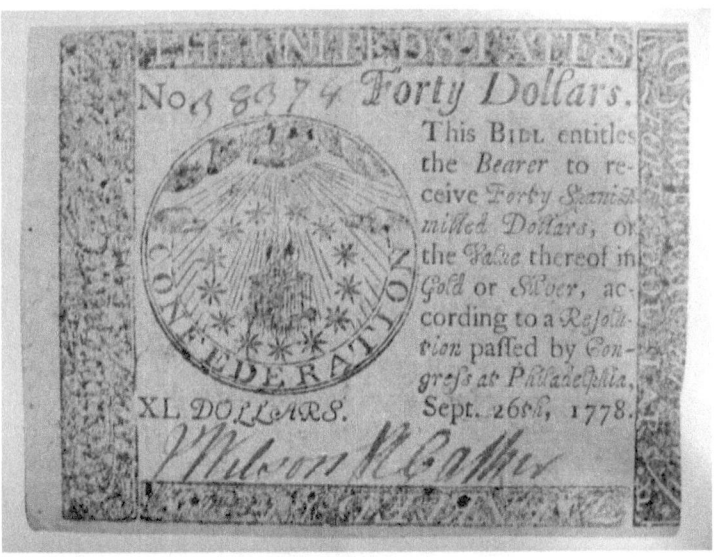

FIG. 8. Continental currency featuring federal images of the ring of stars and the harp. Courtesy American Antiquarian Society.

FIG. 9. Amos Doolittle, "A Display of the United States of America."
New Haven, Conn.: A. Doolittle, 1794. Library of Congress,
Prints and Photographs Division, LC-DIG-pga-03662.

chains (fig. 9). This image was so popular that he followed it with another broadside featuring President Adams surrounded by images of the states following Adams's election in 1797.[63] These federal images also appeared on domestic goods, including hand-stitched samplers, buttons, plates, bowls, pitchers, and even textiles and carpets. Martha Washington had a set of china made with Franklin's design of interlinked chains, eventually leading to the mass-market production

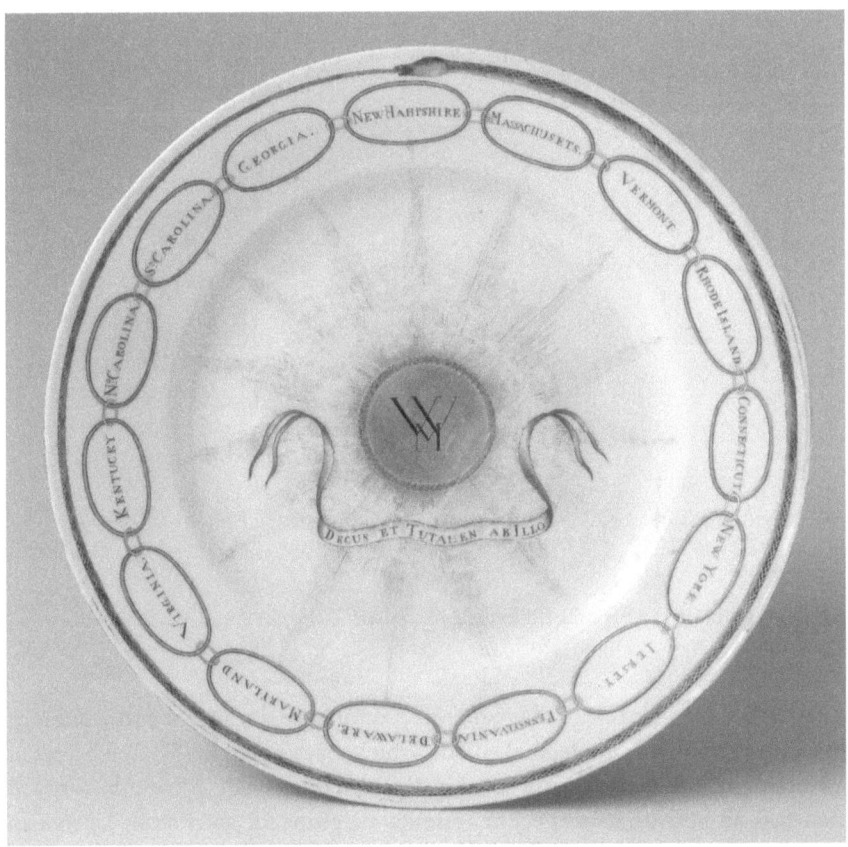

FIG. 10. Plate from a service for George Washington, designed by Andreas Everardus van Braam Houckgeest, 1796. Philadelphia Museum of Art: Gift of the McNeil Americana Collection, 2006. 2006-3-7.

of this pattern, which became known as the "Martha Washington service" (see fig. 10).[64] The prevalence of these federal images in popular culture testifies to the power of these images in generating public support for federal nationalism, while also promoting public acceptance of this paradoxical model of union. The relatively open-ended significance of these symbols of federal pluralism, which were often featured on items intended for domestic use, also made it possible for those excluded from official federal citizenship—such as women and slaves—to imagine themselves as part of the plural nation, while also fostering anger and resistance as their lack of official recognition and representation within this "equitable" plural union became increasingly apparent.

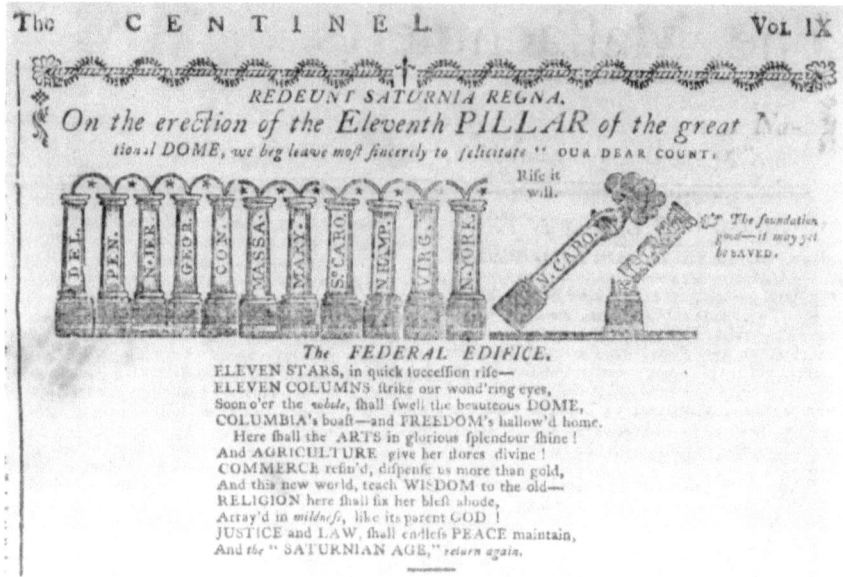

FIG. 11. The Federal Edifice, *Massachusetts Centinel*, August 2, 1788.

Another popular image that came to prominence during the ratification of the Constitution was the federal edifice, which represented the United States as a building whose roof was supported by thirteen pillars. Eric Slauter has argued that this architectural imagery represents a significant shift from European images of government, which typically represented the state through human-oriented metaphors for the "body politic."⁶⁵ Much like Franklin's image of the interlinked chain, the image of the federal edifice emphasized not only permanence but also the composite strength of the federal union, since the support of each pillar contributed to the strength of the entire structure. In addition, this image also emphasized the stability created by a federal union, since the addition of each pillar created a more stable structure. This growing strength and the stability of the federal union was illustrated by a series of cartoons published in the *Massachusetts Centinel* that featured the addition of a new pillar each time a state ratified the Constitution that would "facilitate 'OUR DEAR COUNTRY.' Rise it will. The foundation is good."⁶⁶ Images of the federal edifice became even more widespread following the ratification of the Constitution in 1788, and the image was often depicted as a frontispiece in periodicals such as the *Columbian Magazine* and the *Massachusetts Centinel* and appeared in pamphlets, newspapers, and popular engravings (fig. 11).

Visual representations of the federal union were also prominent during the public celebrations that followed ratification. Between 1787 and 1788, each of the states held public celebrations that were known as the "Grand Federal Processions."[67] The federal processions of Boston, Philadelphia, and New York were well documented, and local newspapers provided detailed descriptions of the ways that citizens chose to represent the federal union. Francis Hopkinson provided one of the most thorough accounts of the Grand Federal Procession held in Philadelphia on July 4, 1788, which was published as a popular pamphlet and reprinted in the *Columbian Magazine*. Hopkinson's account describes the presentation of "the new roof or grand federal edifice on a carriage," which was "a dome supported by thirteen Corinthian columns, raised on pedestals proper to that order; the frieze decorated with thirteen stars.... On the pedestals of the columns were inscribed in ornamented cyphers, the initials of the thirteen American states."[68] For as much as this elaborate celebration of the nation's federal structure was meant to publicize its plural stability, the precarious position of this particular federal edifice, balanced on top of a carriage, introduces an interesting irony by suggesting that this plural union may not be as stable or as fixed as its citizens would like it to be—an irony that political satirists and writers whose positions in the federal nation were marginalized would later exploit in their own literary works, as I will explore in later chapters.

Citizens also celebrated the federal structure of the nation through parades that included groups of citizens "each bearing a flag with the name of the state he represented in gold letters and walking arm in arm, emblematical of the union."[69] The processions also featured representatives "of the mechanical and learned professions," each bearing a banner identifying their respective trade, with the goal of providing a comprehensive portrait of the many skills and industries that made up the economic foundations of the state. In addition to showcasing their variety, which included farmers, merchants, manufacturers, and repair and service industries, the processions also illustrated the interdependent relationships between the different professions, which was suggested by the inclusion of carpenters, housepainters, brickmakers, bricklayers, stonecutters, blacksmiths, sailmakers, ship joiners, clock- and watchmakers, carvers and guilders, potters, wheelwrights, weavers, bakers, butchers, tallow chandlers, printers, and others.[70] By representing such a diverse range of professions, these processions emphasized how the nation's diversity could lead to economic security and stability. To reinforce this unifying potential, many of these professional groups carried emblems representing the federal union, including the familiar images of thirteen-branched candelabra, a harp, sheaves of wheat, and various configurations of thirteen stars and stripes. Others carried flags with federal mottoes, such as "By unity we support society" and "United in one." In all instances, reports of the processions emphasize how these expressions of the nation's "beautiful variety"—however limited—produced feelings of unity and peace. "All was order, all was harmony and joy," reports Hopkinson, who quickly translates the effects of the procession into nationalist terms by declaring that the procession "has been the happy means of uniting all our citizens in the government." Anticipating the argument that the federal feelings and unity produced by these processions would be short lived, Hopkinson emphasized their lasting effects, noting that the procession "has made such an impression on the minds of our young people that 'federal' and 'union' have now become a part of the household words of every family in the city."[71] As Hopkinson describes it, the experience of witnessing this diverse celebration has made it possible for citizens to imagine the federal nation as a possible and practical reality in their daily lives, and he hopes that his written account of it will have the same effect on those who read about it.[72]

Though these unified federal feelings are presented as a natural and immediate response to these processions, it is important to recognize that these celebrations were carefully organized to produce this effect. A great deal of time and attention was devoted to planning these events—from the images represented, to the timing of the toasts and speeches, to the order in which each group would march through the streets in order to promote feelings of unity.[73] Hopkinson continually remarks on the ordered structure of the processions, as well as the equally ordered and unified reaction of the crowd. "I return from this digression to relate one more fact, that out of seventeen thousand people who appeared on the green . . . [there was] not a single quarrel or even dispute heard of during the day."[74] Whether or not this statement is true, Hopkinson's repeated emphasis on the orderly effects of the celebration is important, particularly regarding his sense of surprise as he reports these results. Rhetorically, Hopkinson's tone of awe and amazement suggests that the peace and harmony of this celebration, while welcome, are also unexpected, a reaction that further indicates the extent to which federalism required citizens to interpret variety differently. In contrast to the expected response—that the diverse displays of the federal processions would produce discord and conflict—Hopkinson emphasizes how the structure of the celebration, combined with the mottoes, images, and sentiments expressed over the course of the day, enabled citizens to interpret these many differences in "flourishing and secure" terms.[75]

Hopkinson's concluding remarks identify a few other factors that influenced the harmony of the processions. The final page of his report calls for establishing a commemorative monument on the green inscribed with the following message: "In honour of American beer and cyder, it is hereby recorded . . . that

17,000 people assembled on this green on the 4th of July 1788 to celebrate the establishment of the Constitution of the United States and that they separated at an early hour without intoxication or a single quarrel—They drank nothing but beer and cyder. Learn, readers, to praise those invaluable Federal liquors and to consider them as the companions of those virtues that can alone render our country free and respectable. Learn likewise to despise SPIRITOUS LIQUORS as Anti-federal and to consider them as the companions of all those vices that are calculated to dishonor and enslave our country."[76] This inscription, which is printed inside a decorative frame to illustrate how it would appear on the monument, attributes the national effects of this celebration not just to its events but to the beverages its attendees were drinking. Beer and cider are celebrated as "federal beverages" because of the cohesive effect they have on the assembled citizens, in contrast to the feelings of antagonism and conflict that result from drinking "Anti-federal" alcohol. By drinking beer and cider, citizens experience peaceful and tolerant feelings of goodwill, making it possible for a large and diverse group of seventeen thousand people to share the same space and express their nationalist sentiments without "quarreling." Through these final observations about the "federal" effects of drinking beer and cider, Hopkinson's account emphasizes how the future of the federal nation depends not just on the way that differences are represented in the federal nation but also on the way that citizens perceive and interpret them. If drinking beer and cider had a favorable influence on the way citizens responded to the variety of the new nation, Hopkinson's final remarks suggest, indirectly, that there must be other, equally influential ways to shape the way citizens respond to the different constituencies of the United States, which brings us, at last, to literature.

As suggested by Hopkinson's own desire to recapture and reconstitute the unifying effects of the federal procession by publishing a written account of it, literature provided an influential medium for representing the plural and singular dimensions of the federal union while, at the same time, training citizens to read the federal nation as both a plural and also singular union. For as much as literature provided a means of promoting plural nationalism more widely, however, it also placed further restrictions on the racial, ethnic, and economic dimensions of this federal nationalism, since literacy was largely restricted to educated white residents with some degree of financial stability. Unlike the open-ended visual representations of federal union, which invited all kinds of residents—black, white, female, illiterate, poor, and so on—to imagine themselves as part of the nation's plural union, literary representations of federal union placed more restrictions on the kinds of diversity that the plural nation would represent. Over time, however, the inclusive and flexible dimensions of the early federal imagery of the United States would eventually find expression in U.S. literature as those excluded from the federal nation likewise turned to print culture to argue for their equal representation in the United States.

Federal Literacy:
Reading These United States

Visual representations of the United States, whether in the form of geography, iconography, or popular celebrations, played a crucial role in helping citizens embrace the federal union by providing credible models for envisioning its paradoxical character. Images such as the federal edifice, Franklin's conjoined rings, and the stars and stripes offered clear representations of how a nation composed of different parts could constitute a strong and stable union. These visual strategies, however, had their limitations. While emblematic images could illustrate federal cohesion, they could not provide citizens with the skills needed to contend with the nation's differences in everyday practice. Literature, by contrast, could. In addition to illustrating the structure of the federal nation, early U.S. literary texts provided citizens with forms that taught them to read political, social, economic, and geographic differences in equitable terms.

From the late 1790s through the mid-1800s, hundreds of newspaper articles, essays, pamphlets, speeches, and letters related to the drafting and ratification of the Constitution were reprinted and recirculated, with some works—such as the speeches and proceedings of the various state ratifying conventions—appearing in new and specialized editions. In addition to reprints of these primary documents, essays and editorials that interpreted these documents were also widely printed. "The range of sources invoked to establish the original understanding of the federal constitution was staggering," writes Saul Cornell, "[and] virtually all of the available texts produced during ratification had the potential to be reinterpreted and reread in the struggle to ascertain the meaning of the Constitution."[77] Over the course of the late eighteenth century, citizens came to understand the federal union precisely through this continual process of reading and interpreting "federal" texts, an interpretive process that quickly extended beyond strictly political documents to include popular and imaginative literary forms, and these popular texts and genres became a powerful means of promoting federal nationalism and enacting federal principles.[78]

Many writers supported the federal union by mimicking popular visual strategies and metaphors. Stories and poems published after the ratification of the Constitution frequently drew on the image of the federal edifice, among them Francis Hopkinson's allegorical narrative titled "The New Roof" and a poem titled "The Raising: A Song for Federal Mechanics," which was distributed at the Grand Federal Procession in Philadelphia and widely reprinted in early U.S. periodicals.[79] These works expanded on this metaphor to emphasize features of the federal union that were not as evident in a visual representation. In "The New Roof," for instance, the narrator points out how the combined support of the rafters makes it difficult to view any of them separately, describing "thirteen rafters so strongly braced together [that] the individual and separate strength of each rafter would be lost in the compounded and united strength of the whole."[80] Likewise, "The Raising" highlights not just the support provided by the states but also their comprehensive expanse.

> Up! Up with the rafters—each frame is a state
> How nobly they rise! Their span, too, how great!
> From the north to the south, o'er the whole they extend
> And rest on the walls, while the walls they defend.[81]

Literary texts also introduced other popular metaphors for representing the federal union, such as the image of a family. In 1789 the *American Museum* published a story titled "The Farmer and His Thirteen Sons, an Allegory," which tells the story of how thirteen sons, each "of a sanguine, vigorous, and enterprising turn," find ways to combine their skills to ensure "the[ir] joint security."[82] Another popular metaphor was that of a business partnership, exemplified by "The Story of the Thirteen Partners," which described "thirteen persons [who] once entered into a company" under the agreement that "each member ... should make advances out of his own pocket for the good of the whole."[83] In both cases, writers emphasized the various strengths and skills of each family member or business partner to show how these differences could contribute to the success of the whole. In "The Farmer and His Thirteen Sons," the brothers discover they each have different ideas and experiences to draw on for raising wheat, and they agree to divide up the farm and tend to their sections "in proportion to the age, ability, and industry of each brother," a decision that ensures "their future establishment and prosperity."[84]

These metaphors also highlighted strategies for maintaining this plural unity by dramatizing moments of conflict between the different members. In "The Story of the Thirteen Partners," their joint business arrangement runs into problems due to the "unequal contributions of the different members," and, for a time, their meetings are diverted from effective planning to engage in arguments about the "bad bargains some of the members had made." The members of the business eventually work out their differences and regain success but doing so requires a great deal of conversation and compromise as each member represents and evaluates their respective "claims and charges."[85] In contrast to visual images such as the federal edifice, these familial and entrepreneurial metaphors suggest that supporting a federal union required more than simply establishing a federal structure. In order to succeed, a federal union required citizens to engage in debate and pursue compromise.

Though these figurative representations of the federal union could be very effective, there were only so many metaphors that could reasonably account for the federal structure of the United States. The limits of these federal metaphors become evident when considering some of the less successful federal images used to represent the nation, as in the case of a 1787 poem titled "The Continental Medley" published in the *Columbian Magazine*. In this work, the federal United States is likened to a pie composed of "a curious collection of substances strange." Each of the states provides an ingredient for the pie, which include "The Yankey's their onion and fish," "the Yorker's superfine flour," "the pork of the largest the Jersey's had sent," a dash of Maryland's "powdered tobacco, delightful to smell," and even a helping of "sawdust" from "poor little Georgia," while North Carolina "joins in" with pitch and South Carolina "tinge[s] it with shadings from Indigo blue." Although the end result is described in unified terms, as "a nice little parcel" and "a treat complete," the contents of the pie create an image that is far from practical or appealing.[86] Rather than providing a persuasive image of federal unity, this metaphor seems overly constructed and unconvincing, undermining the legitimacy and credibility of the federal union that it is supposed to affirm.

Literary texts would ultimately deploy more complex and creative strategies to represent the federal nation, and the remaining chapters will examine these strategies in detail, looking specifically at almanacs, magazines, satires, and captivity narratives. More than simply helping citizens make sense of the paradoxical structure of the federal union, these genres enabled citizens to contribute to the unity and stability of the federal United States by teaching them how to read differences equitably and to position their interpretations in relation to other possible frameworks and perspectives. Showing how these literary genres fostered a federal nationalism through the practice of federal literacy provides a new framework for considering how early American literature helped make the federal United States not only visible but also viable and meaningful. Furthermore, these literary texts also provided those excluded from the plural nation with opportunities to criticize and counteract its critical points of exclusion.

CHAPTER 2

Reading Parts and Wholes

The Federal Imagination of American Almanacs

> No one who would penetrate to the core of early American literature ... may by any means turn away, in lofty literary scorn, from the almanac——most despised, most prolific, most indispensable of books, which every man uses and no man praises.
>
> ——MOSES COIT TYLER, *History of American Literature*

Almanacs are the foundation of American print culture. Second only to the Bible in production and circulation, almanacs dominated the American print market from the seventeenth through the early nineteenth centuries. The first American almanac was printed in Cambridge, Massachusetts, in 1639, predating the *Bay Psalm Book* by nearly a year. Almost every major town in the British American colonies published its own almanac, and four or five different almanacs circulated concurrently in cities such as Philadelphia, New York, and Boston. Audiences for these almanacs came from diverse social, economic, and educational backgrounds, and printers drew attention to their wide appeal, boasting of the almanac's ability to serve readers of "every Rank and Character," including "the Clergyman, the Lawyer, the Physician, the Merchant, the Husbandman, the Soldier, the Sailor, and every occupation of human life."[1] Because of their broad audiences, almanacs were consistently profitable. The standard print run for most almanacs was 2,000–3,000, with some editions selling more than 50,000 copies annually, an unusual success story at a time when printers struggled to find viable markets for newspapers, periodicals, and full-length books.[2]

Given their prevalence and popularity, almanacs were enormously influential in shaping the way people understood the world and determining how they should act within it. This influence was particularly felt as the colonies transformed into an independent nation. As one of the most commonly used forms of print, almanacs played an instrumental role in helping readers define and

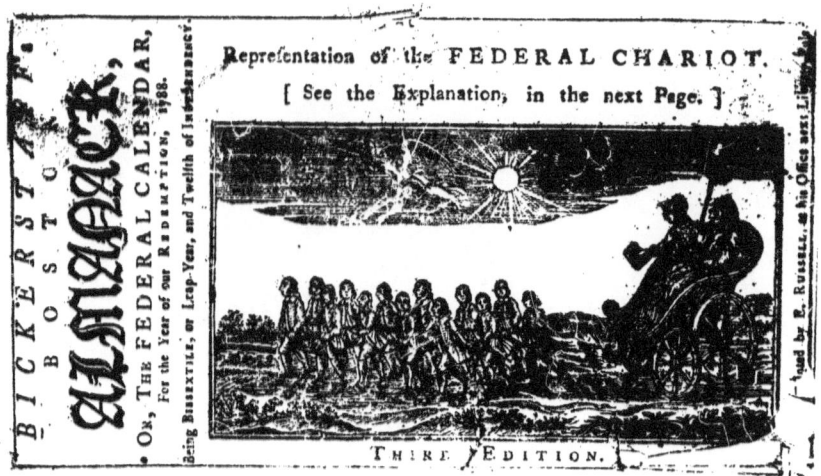

FIG. 12. "Presentation of the Federal Chariot," *Bickerstaff's Boston Almanack, or, The Federal Calendar for the Year of Our Redemption 1788.* Boston: E. Russell, 1787. *Early American Imprints*, Series I, No. 45040.

embrace the newly independent United States, particularly regarding its federal structure. Almanacs included articles that taught readers how the federal nation was organized, how power would be distributed within it, and how the different states would contribute to the union. Some almanacs reprinted complete copies of the Articles of Confederation and the Constitution, as well as proceedings from the Continental Congress. Others featured articles explaining the various branches of government and provided lists of the names, term lengths, and duties of currently elected senators and representatives, as well as information about the history, geography, and dominant industries of the different states.[3]

Many almanacs also provided images to help readers visualize the federal character of the union. *Bickerstaff's Boston Almanack* opened its 1788 edition with a front-page illustration of "The Federal Chariot" (fig. 12). The attendant "Explanation" of the image states that it "depicts the truly patriotick Washington and Franklin, triumphantly seated in the Federal Chariot, drawn by 13 Freemen, figurative of the happy Union now forming by these states." The image of the Federal Chariot is also illuminated by the rays of a sun that, according to the accompanying "Explanation," "shines resplendently on the American Federal Union, denoting that every ray of light has now burst forth and beautifully illumes the whole United Continent of America."[4]

The 1789 edition of *Bickerstaff's Boston Almanack* opens with a picture of two angels unveiling a set of thirteen columns beneath a heading that states "Rising Glory of America," and the 1785 edition of *The Continental Almanac* of Phila-

FIG. 13. Image of federal pillars and stars, *The Continental Almanac, for the Year of Our Lord 1785*. Philadelphia: Anthony Sharp, 1784. *Early American Imprints*, Series I, No. 18759.

delphia likewise uses the image of an arch supported by thirteen pillars and decorated with thirteen stars, which later became the official heading for its title page between 1780 and 1785 (see fig. 13).[5] The frontispiece for *The Columbian Almanac or North-American Calendar for 1791* also features multiple emblems of federal unity, including a constellation of thirteen stars, a sun emitting numerous rays of light, and an eagle holding a shield with thirteen stripes, which are all juxtaposed against a banner bearing the federal motto *E pluribus unum*.[6] Through images such as these and articles describing the federal government and its constituent states, these early national almanacs operated as a kind of federal "primer" whose content was designed to teach readers how to visualize and support the composite model of nationhood that bound them together.[7]

Not all almanacs, however, taught readers to recognize and embrace the federal union in such direct terms. While the almanacs described above were actively invested in promoting the federal union, such explicit federal content was not common. Most almanacs of the early United States avoided printing anything related to national or local politics, focusing instead on information related to weather, travel, farming, and domestic advice to appeal to the broadest possible range of readers. Almanacs featuring federal imagery, federal documents, and other information related to the federal character of the United States were the exception, rather than the rule. Of the nearly 1,700 almanacs published in the early United States between 1776 and 1800, fewer than 20 percent comment on national politics, policies, or proceedings related to the establishment of the federal nation in any extensive detail. Only about twelve almanacs printed copies of the Articles of Confederation and ten printed copies of the Constitution, while approximately seven contained outlines or listings of the federal government and its elected officials. The almanacs featuring this federal information were also published in a limited area, concentrated almost exclusively in Boston and Philadelphia, with a few others in Virginia and South Carolina.[8]

Although most almanacs did not address the federal structure or government of the United States directly, I argue that almanacs did encourage and support a federal model of union. Recognizing the federal function of this genre, however, requires looking beyond their specific content to explore their form. By exploring the formal and conventional features of almanacs, particularly their representations of space, time, and community interests, this chapter explores how almanacs provided citizens with a means of defining and asserting their distinct local characteristics, while also situating themselves within a larger network of interconnected communities. By training readers to position themselves as a distinctive part of a diverse yet unified whole, almanacs provided citizens with the interpretive tools needed to imagine unity in federal terms.

This ability to foster a sense of federal "positionality" was not a post-Revolutionary phenomenon. As White and Yurish have argued, the roots of U.S. federalism can be traced to the culture and politics of the colonial era.[9] Long before the establishment of a formal federal government in the United States, colonial almanacs were training readers to imagine federal unity through the diverse and composite terms set forth by this genre. The federal nationalism that defined the United States after the Revolution owes a great deal of its acceptance and stability to the models of literacy promoted by American almanacs during the colonial era.

Oddly enough, despite their dominating presence and influence, almanacs have long been neglected in studies of early American print nationalism. The critical turn toward the politics of print within the last thirty years has produced generative reevaluations of other genres such as newspapers, broadsides, and magazines, as well as public reports of celebrations and oratory.[10] Almanacs, however, have remained something of an elephant in the room. Although their prevalence and importance are often noted, their political and cultural influence has remained largely unexplored. Moses Coit Tyler's criticism of the "despised" status of "that most indispensable of books" noted at the beginning of this chapter represents an early example of this attitude, which continues in the present. Contemporary critics such as David Waldstreicher, Lily Santoro, and Thomas Horrocks have all commented on the "unexplored," "marginal," and "lamented" status of the almanac, which is a common critical response.[11] To some extent, this neglect is due to the practical challenges of studying this genre, which includes more than 1,700 different works housed in numerous public and private collections. The rise of full-text, searchable digital databases has mitigated some of these difficulties by improving their accessibility, but the sheer size and scope of the archive continues to make comprehensive studies difficult.

Ideological factors also account for this critical neglect. As texts designed for local use, almanacs tend to reflect the interests of small, regionally specific communities. These texts not did circulate nationally, and, rather than promoting a sense of common feelings and experiences, almanacs seem to reinforce their readers' sense of local distinction and separation from other communities. As a result, almanacs have long been overlooked because these texts seem to contradict or, at the very least, lie outside the long-standing models of U.S. print nationalism that characterize print as a means for transcending the local differences and distinctions that almanacs specifically seek to emphasize.

Reorienting the study of print nationalism according to a *federal* model of unity, however, transforms the way we interpret these locally oriented texts. As Matthew Brown observes, "Almanacs themselves collected a heterogeneous set of voices, images, and knowledges," and the local specificity and regional diversity of early American almanacs look different when we examine them in relation to a composite understanding of national unity.[12] Instead of representing regional disconnection and fragmentation, the diversity and local focus of early American almanacs emerge as a means of enacting a federal model of unity. Reading early American almanacs effectively trained residents to interpret the nation's plurality in unified terms, producing a federal literacy that would be further developed by other literary genres in the early United States.

To illustrate how early American almanacs promoted this federal literacy, this chapter is divided into three parts. The first section examines the local specificity and variety of colonial and national almanacs. By comparing almanacs published in different locations, this section shows how almanacs encouraged readers to define themselves, first and foremost, as members of distinct and bounded local communities. Rather than producing myopic and isolated perspectives, however, these locally oriented almanacs contained formal features that enabled their readers to position their local communities within a larger united network. The second section examines some of these specific formal features in detail, which include road and distance charts, directional markers, time measurements, legal schedules, and the layout of calendar pages to show how almanacs taught citizens to read the disparate communities of the nation in united terms. In this section, I will also examine some of the marginal notes and diaries that were often interleaved within personal copies of almanacs. By providing information about the daily use and reading experiences of these texts, these notes and diaries provide further insights into the federal dynamics of these texts. The chapter concludes by examining how the plural dimensions of U.S. almanacs also provided a useful format for those excluded from the federal nation to argue for an equal place within it, exemplified by the almanacs of Benjamin Banneker.

Reading the Many:
The Diversity of American Almanacs

Before examining almanacs as a genre, I would like to begin with some definitions. Derived from the Spanish Arabic term "al manakh," which means "the count," an almanac is an annotated calendar designed to mark the passage of time and provide information about annual events and local conditions for a specific area. The first almanacs had their origins in ancient Babylon and Egypt where they were used to chart the stars and keep track of religious feasts. These calendars became more detailed with Greek advancements in astronomy, and the form continued to develop throughout Europe from the twelfth century onward. European almanacs featured monthly pages listing astronomical data, such as the dates of eclipses, moon phases, and times for sunrise and sunset, as well as astrological predictions, weather forecasts, and dates for religious and secular holidays. The genre remained popular in Europe throughout the sixteenth through the eighteenth centuries, and almanacs rose to particular prominence in England where the genre expanded to include a much wider range of information, including practical household and professional advice, moral and political essays, humorous anecdotes, short biographies, poetry, and puzzles—the form we commonly recognize today.[13]

Given their popularity in England, almanacs transferred readily across the Atlantic to the British American colonies, where they became even more prevalent than their English predecessors.[14] In 1760, for instance, more than twenty different almanacs were published in the American colonies, compared to only twelve in England. The popularity of almanacs grew even faster in the aftermath of U.S. independence, such that by 1790 the United States was home to nearly eighty different almanacs, compared to twenty in England. The content of these

American almanacs was similar to their English counterparts, providing information about astronomy, astrology, and weather, as well as essays and household advice. A notable difference, however, emerged in their regional specificity and variety. In England almanacs were relatively uniform texts whose content was directed toward national rather than local audiences. English almanacs were all calculated from the meridian of London, which meant that all English almanacs contained roughly the same information regarding tides, sunrises and sunsets, and other astronomical and weather information. Furthermore, for more than two hundred years, English almanacs were compiled and printed by the Royal Stationer's Company, which held a royally sanctioned monopoly on the production of almanacs through the mid-eighteenth century. As a result, English almanacs maintained a high level of consistency with regard to form and content across different editions.[15] While some almanacs were directed toward specialized audiences such as women, farmers, or gentlemen, these audiences were always addressed in national rather than local terms.[16] The relatively small size of England, which encompassed approximately fifty thousand square miles of similar terrain and climate, combined with its largely homogeneous population, made this centralized format and content effective. An almanac calculated for the meridian of London could provide reliable information for readers living throughout the country, and the existence of an expansive road system ensured that these English almanacs could circulate easily through the whole country.

In contrast, the size and diversity of the British American colonies and, later, the United States required a more varied range of almanacs. Encompassing more than 360,000 square miles of territory that included different climates and terrain, as well as varying economies, political structures, and populations, the colonies and, later, states were too diverse and widely separated to be served by an almanac that was calculated or distributed from a single location. As a result, American almanacs were much more locally oriented than their English counterparts, providing content and organizational structures that were designed to respond to the needs and interests of their local readers. As Spero notes, early American almanacs should be viewed as "the local products they were, influenced by local exigencies that gave new form and shape to this genre depending on location."[17]

Some of the clearest variations in American almanacs emerge between northern and southern publications due to differences in climate and topography. Southern almanacs often included year-round gardening calendars that explained which kinds of fruit, vegetables, and flowers should be planted each month. The *South-Carolina and Georgia Almanack* of 1776, for example, instructs readers to plant strawberries in February and kidney beans in March. These year-round gardening calendars, however, had no place in northern almanacs such as *The New England Farmer's Almanack* or *The United States Almanack*, which instead featured articles about caring for northern crops such as Indian corn, storing fruits and vegetables, and tending to livestock in winter conditions.[18]

Differences in content were not solely dictated by geography and climate. Readers living in different locations also had different political, social, and literary preferences. Marion Stowell observes that "southern almanacs typically contained more literature," and "the content of Southern almanacs was generally (though not always) less pious than the Northern in theme and diction."[19] A quick comparison of *The Virginia Almanack* (compiled by William Rind between 1767 and 1773) and *The New-Jersey Almanac* (compiled by William Ball between 1743 and 1770) supports this claim. Within its standard run of forty-eight pages, *The Virginia Almanack* typically devotes more than half of its content to literary works, including various forms of verse (commemorative odes, comic satires, pithy rhymes) and short, humorous anecdotes. In contrast, *The New-Jersey Almanack* devotes the majority of its pages to practical data such as tables of interest rates, duties and taxes, and schedules for local legal courts, Quaker meetings, and county fairs. Such regional variations, however, were not absolute. Benjamin Franklin's *Poor Richard* almanacs and John and William Dunlap's *Father Abraham* series (both published in Philadelphia) tended to avoid the didactic tone of other northern almanacs and often featured humorous literature and trivia similar to *The Virginia Almanack*. Likewise, for all its humorous overtones, *The Virginia Almanack* also published moral essays on topics such as "Maxims on the Conduct of Life" and "Advice to Ladies." Despite these exceptions, the content of most northern and southern almanacs was different enough to suggest that the early American colonies and states contained distinctive reading communities that were defined by regionally specific interests.

A set of almanacs compiled by John Tobler exemplify the extent to which American almanacs were shaped by local concerns. Tobler, a Swiss emigrant who settled in South Carolina in the 1730s, compiled successful almanacs for two different locations—*The Pennsylvania Town and Country-man's Almanack*, which was printed in Wilmington, Delaware, from 1754 to 1777, and *The South-Carolina and Georgia Almanack*, which was printed in Charleston, South Carolina, and Savannah, Georgia, between 1764 and 1792.[20] Compiling an almanac was a time-intensive process, and, given the costs and the labor involved, we might expect to find many similarities between Tobler's almanacs. A comparative analysis, however, reveals substantial differences between Tobler's northern and southern almanacs that illuminate their intensive local focus and the regional variations of the early nation.

Tobler's *Pennsylvania* almanacs have a complicated layout that displays different kinds of information (temporal, historical, and literary) on a single page

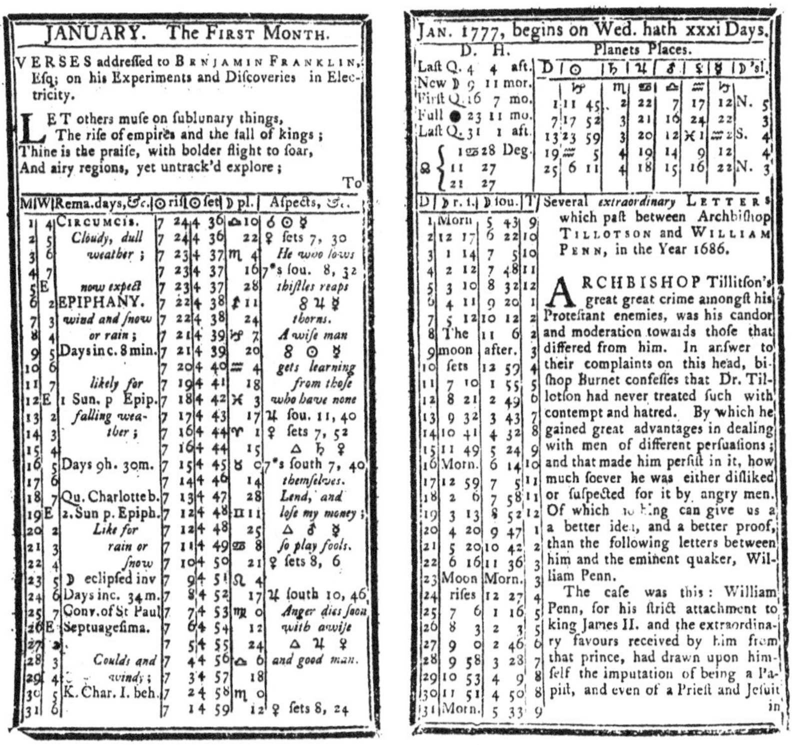
JANUARY. The First Month.

VERSES addressed to Benjamin Franklin, Esq; on his Experiments and Discoveries in Electricity.

LET others muse on sublunary things,
The rise of empires and the fall of kings;
Thine is the praise, with bolder flight to soar,
And airy regions, yet untrack'd explore;

JAN. 1777, begins on Wed. hath xxxi Days.

Several extraordinary LETTERS which past between Archbishop TILLOTSON and WILLIAM PENN, in the Year 1686.

ARCHBISHOP Tillitson's great great crime amongst his Protestant enemies, was his candor and moderation towards those that differed from him. In answer to their complaints on this head, bishop Burnet confesses that Dr. Tillotson had never treated such with contempt and hatred. By which he gained great advantages in dealing with men of different persuasions; and that made him persist in it, how much soever he was either disliked or suspected for it by angry men. Of which no thing can give us a better idea, and a better proof, than the following letters between him and the eminent quaker, William Penn.

The case was this: William Penn, for his strict attachment to king James II. and the extraordinary favours received by him from that prince, had drawn upon himself the imputation of being a Papist, and even of a Priest and Jesuit in

FIG. 14. Sample calendar pages printed in John Tobler's *Pennsylvania Town and Country-Man's Almanack for the Year of Our Lord, 1777*. Wilmington, Del.: James Adams, 1776. *Early American Imprints*, Series I, No. 15116.

(fig. 14).[21] The monthly calendar extends across two leaves, where the left-hand side presents astronomical data about the phases of the moon, times for sunrises and sunsets, other astrological positions, and weather predictions. Interspersed with this information are short aphorisms, such as "He who sows trifles reaps thorns" and "Anger dies soon with a wise and good man," as well as selections of verse. This example from 1777, for instance, features lines from a poem in praise of Benjamin Franklin. The right-hand side of the calendar page presents additional information about the movement of the stars and the weather, along with literary articles devoted to moral instruction, history, biography, and domestic advice. The right-hand side of the January 1777 page features letters exchanged between the Archbishop Tillotson and William Penn on the subject of tolerance, which continue for successive months, followed by other articles featuring domestic advice, including a recipe for "Making Common Salt" and "Remedies for a Bruise."²² After the calendar pages, the *Pennsylvania* almanacs always conclude with lists of taxes and interest rates, schedules for court sessions in Pennsylvania, New York, and Maryland, the dates for Quaker meetings and annual fairs, and a table of roads and distances between regional towns and cities.²³

In contrast to the varied page layout of the *Pennsylvania* almanacs, Tobler's *South-Carolina and Georgia* almanacs have a different organizational structure. Unlike the *Pennsylvania* almanacs, the *South-Carolina* almanacs maintain a clear separation between its calendrical data and its literary content. The calendar pages for these almanacs are shorter, focusing strictly on astronomical information, weather predictions, annual holidays, and gardening advice for each month, rather than featuring any formal articles, aphorisms, or poetry. The content for each calendar page was also condensed to a single page, as opposed to the two-page calendar structure of Tobler's *Pennsylvania* almanacs (fig. 15).²⁴ Literary content is not entirely absent from the *South-Carolina and Georgia* almanacs, however. These almanacs typically included an extensive selection of essays, poetry, anecdotes, and domestic advice. The 1777 edition, for example, includes a copy of the Declaration of Independence, as well as a poem celebrating the defeat of the British at Sullivan's Island, another poem on "The Impossibility of Pleasing Everybody," and a full section devoted to recipes, remedies, and other household advice.²⁵ This written content always appears *after* the calendar pages in a separate section. They are not integrated within the monthly pages as in Tobler's *Pennsylvania* almanacs.²⁶

Significant differences also emerge when comparing the literary content of these two almanacs. While both feature home remedies and medical advice, such articles play a more prominent role in the *South-Carolina and Georgia* almanacs than in the *Pennsylvania* almanacs. The *Pennsylvania* almanacs typically printed two or three brief remedies per issue, with most focusing on relatively minor ailments such as ulcers, bruises, or headaches. The *South-Carolina and Georgia* almanacs, on the other hand, typically devote at least three full pages to articles published under the heading "Valuable Receipts and Directions."²⁷ These articles, in turn, cover a much wider range of conditions and treatments, including chronic and severe illnesses (scurvy, asthma, rheumatism, and the "bloody flux"), minor aches and pains (sore throats, swollen ankles, upset stomach, toothaches, etc.), and common accidents (cuts, rattlesnake bites, and bee stings). The *South-Carolina and Georgia* almanacs also provide more detailed household advice, including articles on how to pickle meats and vegetables, how to remove stains from various fabrics, how to get rid of vermin such as fleas, bedbugs, and rats, and how to make items such as soap, dye, or gunshot. The regional focus of this almanac is particularly evident when these articles

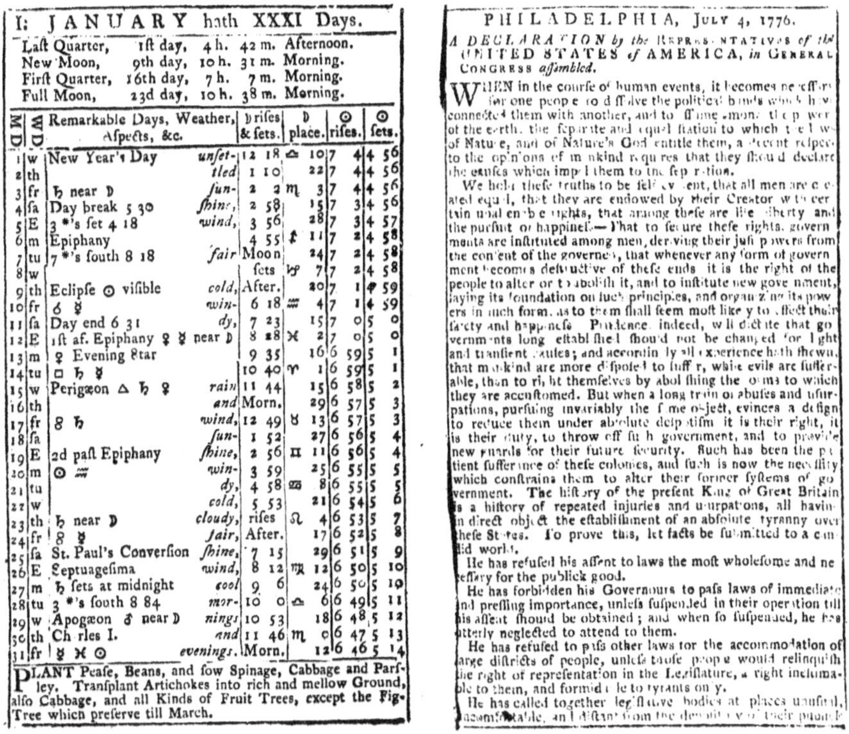

FIG. 15. Sample calendar page and copy of the Declaration of Independence printed in John Tobler's *South-Carolina and Georgia Almanack, for the Year of Our Lord, 1777*. Charleston: Robert Wells & Son, 1776. Early American Imprints, Series I, No. 15117.

mention that their domestic advice was acquired from slaves, as in the description of "The Cure for the Bite of a Rattlesnake, as discovered by Sampson, a Negro, for which discovery the province of South Carolina purchased his freedom and allowed him an annuity" or "the Negro Caesar's cure for Poison, for discovering which the Assembly of South Carolina purchased his freedom and gave him an annuity of 100 pounds."[28]

The *South-Carolina and Georgia* almanacs also have a more overt political focus than the *Pennsylvania* almanacs. During the 1770s the *South-Carolina and Georgia* almanacs printed numerous articles about national independence and revolution. The 1775 edition features a pointed essay on "Liberty," as well as extensive excerpts from "The Votes and Proceedings of the American Continental Congress," and the 1776 edition contains a copy of a congressional declaration on "The Causes and Necessity of Taking Up Arms," as well as an essay on "The Beginnings of the Swiss Confederacy," which is presented as a possible model for the newly united colonies. By contrast, even though it was published near Philadelphia at the height of independence debates in the early 1770s, the *Pennsylvania* almanacs contain few direct references to political topics. References to the Continental Congress, the Declaration of Independence, or any other events related to independence or the Revolution do not appear at all in Tobler's *Pennsylvania* editions, and the closest this almanac comes to commenting on the Revolution occurs in a 1776 article titled "Substitutes for Tea," which offers indirect support for colonial resistance to the tea tax.[29]

The differences between these two almanacs indicate both the variety and separation of early American reading audiences. As a compiler, Tobler was clearly aware that the content and organization of an almanac was not regionally transferable. Information and formatting that was useful and profitable in South Carolina was not necessarily useful or profitable in Pennsylvania. The political articles featured in the *South-Carolina and Georgia* almanacs suggest that readers from this region were interested in and largely supportive of national independence, while the lack of political content in the *Pennsylvania* almanacs indicates that such articles would not have had a receptive audience in this region.[30] Other differences in content, such as the detailed domestic and medical advice in the *South-Carolina and Georgia* almanacs, suggest that southern readers were more interested in using almanacs for practical domestic purposes, while readers of the *Pennsylvania* almanacs used them as a means of moral and historical instruction.[31]

The organization and layout of these editions also suggest that regional audiences preferred different kinds of reading experiences. The clear separation between the calendrical data and literary content in the *South-Carolina and Georgia* almanacs suggests that these southern readers preferred a more compartmentalized, subject-specific experience, where they could engage with the text by selecting from its separated sections (calendar, household advice, political articles, etc.). In contrast, the more integrated layout of *The Pennsylvania Town and Country-Man's Almanack* suggests that these mid-Atlantic readers preferred a more multifaceted, comparative reading experience, where they could engage with a range of topics and information at one time.

Tobler's almanacs, then, not only demonstrate the extent to which early American print culture was shaped by local considerations. They also show how American readers encountered and engaged with print in different ways—an observation that challenges the argument that print enabled readers to overcome their sense of local particularity in the early nation. As Trish Loughran has noted, "too few literary accounts of print culture in the early national period emphasize its provincial and plural nature."[32] As texts that were carefully tailored to address the interests and needs of regionally specific audiences, Tobler's two almanacs illustrate quite clearly the "provincial and plural" characteristics of early American print culture and early American readers. Rather than providing a means of experiencing information in homogeneous forms, early American almanacs defined and reinforced a clear sense of regional boundaries and distinctions.

Other studies show variations between almanacs in much closer proximity. In his study of the mid-Atlantic almanacs of the 1770s and 1780s, Joseph S. Tiedemann notes that there were at least thirty-two different almanacs published in this region during this period. Although the almanacs for this region shared similar conditions regarding astronomy, weather, crops, and roads, there were still substantial variations in these texts, particularly regarding their religious and astrological content.[33] Spero likewise shows how "local production forged two different forms of the almanac" by comparing editions published in Boston and Philadelphia between 1720 and 1790. Philadelphia almanacs, for example, tended to be longer than Boston almanacs, running between 30 and 40 pages and containing more "entertaining miscellany" such as "prescriptive literature, maxims, excerpts from histories, jokes, and stories of faraway lands, along with recipes, medicinal cures, and various astronomical information." In contrast, Boston almanacs averaged 16–24 pages and feature more practical or utilitarian data. The result, concludes Spero, is that Boston and Philadelphia almanacs ultimately represent "two vastly different forms of the same genre."[34]

Just because almanacs reaffirm the distinct and diverse local dimensions of early American culture does not mean that these texts challenged the development of a unified nationalism. Scholars have often been quick to read the "provincial and plural nature" of American almanacs as evidence of the tenuousness of colonial and national unity, revealing, as Spero writes, "how fragmented the Atlantic world of print could be."[35] Recognizing the dominant localized character of early American print, however, does not necessarily negate or undermine its unifying functions. Even though almanacs were produced for distinct local audiences with particular and bounded interests and tastes, early American almanacs did not promote myopic perspectives that prevented national sentiments or affiliation. For as much as almanacs represented and served local interests, their organizational structure and spatial representations provided readers with a means of situating their local communities in the midst of a larger interconnected union.

One among Many:
Reading the Federal Almanac

How, then, did almanacs produce strategies for reading local differences cohesively? As discussed at the beginning of this chapter, a few almanacs promoted a composite model of unity through their content, including articles, documents, and images that endorsed the federal structure of the nation directly. Almanacs also enabled citizens to recognize and embrace the federal nation through their form, particularly regarding the ways they represented space and time. These formal features ultimately had a wider impact on the national imagination of U.S. citizens than the specific federal content found in the early national almanacs of New England because these formal features were not only more standardized and widespread. They also provided citizens with strategies for interpreting variety in unified terms.

As a genre, almanacs are deeply invested in the representation of time and space. Although almanacs rarely contained maps or spatial illustrations, the geographic and temporal information contained within them—including weather predictions, hours of daylight, schedules for planting and harvests, tax information, tide tables, road tables, and essays, poems, and anecdotes—provided readers with a clear picture of the interests, features, and conditions of their specific locations and how those conditions varied by time and place. More than simply representing distinct local spaces, the formal features of almanacs encouraged readers to position their local communities as part of a larger, collaborative whole. The manner in which almanacs identified their points of calculation, their representations of time, the visual layout of their pages, and their road tables, court schedules, and astrological symbols all contributed to this "situational" understanding of space, and by continually reminding readers that their experiences and interpretations were one among many, almanacs taught citizens how to read their localities in relation to other communities, producing an interpretive framework that helped readers understand and embrace the federal union.[36]

In examining these formal features, my analysis relies on the perspective of the "implied reader" to explore the cultural and national effects of the almanac's conventional features. Whenever possible, I will supplement my formal analysis with the perspectives and experiences of specific readers, drawing on the marginal notes and diaries found in personal copies of early American almanacs. As texts designed for daily use and timekeeping, almanacs, more than any other early American text, provide a great deal of evidence about their daily use and reader responses to them, which, as Brown observes, "make for a thickened, interactive genre best understood through its readers."[37] As Molly McCarthy writes, the marginal notes contained within almanacs illuminate the "interactive" dimensions of these texts as readers "left crosses and dashes alongside the calendar to signal important dates or scribbled notes about matters both trivial and momentous."[38] In addition, readers often used almanacs as personal diaries and account books where they recorded daily events, financial information, and notes about travel, weather, health, and other memoranda. To accommodate this information, customers could pay to have additional pages interleaved within their almanacs to keep personal diaries. Almanac makers and booksellers regularly advertised this service, and archival collections are filled with examples of these interleaved almanac diaries. George Washington and Thomas Jefferson kept almanac diaries, with Washington labeling each of his interleaved diary pages "Where and How My Time Is Spent."[39] These marginal notes and diary entries are usually very brief and cursory, and they do not contain much reflective detail or sentiment. Most almanac diaries record notes about the weather, identifying that a day is "clear," "cloudy," "windy," and so on, or they refer to daily activities, such as "I was at home," "Dined at Johnson's," "Planted corn," and so on.[40] Though brief, these entries provide valuable insights into the ways readers used these texts to structure their experiences, which, in turn, can help illuminate how these texts helped create a distinctly federal understanding of national identity and culture.

One of the most prominent "situational" features of American almanacs can be found on the title page, which identifies the meridian used to calculate its contents. Typically, this directional statement provides the precise meridian coordinates for the almanacs, followed by a short description of other locations where the almanac's information could be used. A few representative examples are included below (emphasis mine):

1767: Poor Richard Improved: Being an Almanack and Ephemeris ... for the year of our Lord 1767 ... Fitted to the latitude of forty degrees, and a meridian of near five hours west from London; but **may, without sensible error, serve all the northern colonies.**

1770: The Virginia Almanack for the year of our Lord 1770: ... The whole calculated and referred to the horizon of 38 degrees north latitude; and a meridian of 5 hours west from London. **Fitting Virginia, Maryland, North-Carolina, &c.**

1775: The South-Carolina Almanack, or Lady's and Gentleman's diary, for the year of our Lord Christ 1775 ... **Calculated for the lat. of 32 deg. and 45 min. north; but, without any sensible error, may serve from Maryland to East-Florida.**

1780: Thomas's Massachusetts, New-Hampshire, and Connecticut Almanack for the year of our Lord Christ 1780: ... **Calculated for the**

> meridian of Boston, lat. 42. 25. n. but will serve without any essential variation for either of the four New England states.
>
> 1781: The Maryland, Delaware, Pennsylvania, Virginia, and North-Carolina almanack, and ephemeris, for the year of our Lord, 1781; . . . Calculated for the meridian of Baltimore-Town, lat. 39 deg. 30 min. north, and long. 4 hours and 59 min. west, from the observatory at Greenwich; but may, without sensible error, serve all the adjacent states.
>
> 1783: The United States Almanack, for the year of our Lord Christ, 1783; being the third after bissextile or leap year. Calculated for the meridian of Hartford, in the state of Connecticut, lat. 41 deg. 56 min. north long. 72 deg. 50 min. west and will serve for any of the adjacent states without any essential difference.
>
> 1786: Bickerstaff's New-England Almanac, for the year of our Lord, 1786 . . . Calculated for the meridian of Norwich, but will serve without any essential variation for the states of Connecticut, Rhode-Island, New-Hampshire, Massachusetts, and Vermont.

By stating the precise meridian of calculation, these statements identify the specific local focus for each almanac. After asserting this local focus, though, these statements direct their readers' attention outward, asking them to situate their specific location in relation to other neighboring colonies or states. By stating that the information calculated for one location can be easily "adapted" for use in another ("without any sensible error," "without any essential variation," or "without essential difference"), these statements suggest that readers in one distinct community could have compatible relationships and engage in cooperative forms of exchange with other nearby communities. Although differences between these localities must inevitably exist, these statements suggest that such differences are not substantial enough to cause conflict or fundamental misunderstandings. Learning, for instance, that an almanac "calculated for the meridian of Hartford, in the state of Connecticut, lat. 41 deg. 56 min. north long. 72 deg. 50 min. west" can also "serve for any of the adjacent states without any essential difference" defines a clear and bounded Hartford community while also implying that the residents of Hartford have—or can potentially have—a friendly, interactive relationship with its neighboring communities. From their very first page, then, almanacs provide information that encourages local readers to situate themselves within a larger network of cooperative communities.

Almanacs also produce this sense of situatedness through the road tables included in most editions. Usually located on the final pages, these road tables list potential routes from one major city to another, identifying the towns and other possible stopping points between them. Each location is usually followed by two columns of numbers (see fig. 16). The first column lists the mileage between the intermediate points, and the second lists the total miles from the starting point. In this regard, these road tables use the same formatting of contemporary digital maps, which typically provide the total distance for a trip alongside a point-by-point breakdown that lists the mileage for each component of a given route. By adding or subtracting distances in each column, readers can use the information in the tables to calculate shorter or more specific routes, depending on their needs. This structure provides an excellent model for imagining a plural model of national union. The routes depicted on these tables can be represented in two ways, either in terms of their total distance, where a route is represented as a single continuous space (i.e., Philadelphia to Pittsburgh equals 320 miles), or in terms of their component distances, where a single route is represented by many smaller communities (i.e., Philadelphia to Pittsburgh represents 40 communities whose respective distances add up to 320 miles). Through these road tables, the space of the nation is imagined, quite literally, by adding up its many constituencies, a compelling image of a federal whole composed of its many parts.

Of particular importance are the imaginative dimensions of these road tables. Although these tables represent real physical locations and were meant to provide information for actual travel, their factual significance is less important than the way they encourage readers to imagine national space. Whether or not citizens ended up traveling these routes, the information on these tables encourages them to view the nation's many constituencies as connected to one another with ample opportunities for communication and exchange. People using these road tables, for instance, could identify possible markets for buying and selling goods to one another. They could also project opportunities for maintaining regular correspondence or arranging visits or imagine opportunities for sharing personal or political information. A farmer in New York could imagine how his wheat could reach markets in Boston, and a homemaker in Connecticut could trace how her letters will reach her parents who live in Maryland. These kinds of interactions may never occur, but the road tables nevertheless encouraged readers to imagine these possible connections between many different points.

The road tables also encouraged readers to map the nation in ways that privileged local spaces and reflected their own local needs. Most road tables tried to provide a fairly comprehensive view of the nation. Some charted distances from the nation's most northern boundaries in Maine to its southern boundaries in Georgia, while others provided a more contracted focus that stopped at Boston or Philadelphia in the North and Virginia in the South. No matter their limits, these road tables made an effort to represent the nation in terms that extended beyond an almanac's immediate vicinity. This comprehensive national focus,

ROADS WESTWARD.

FRom Philadel.		To-	Scott's	9	75
to Schuylkill	2	tals 2	Bayley's	5	80
Black-horſe	4	6	Hughs's	4	84
Prince of Wales	4	10	Sample's	4	88
Buck	1	11	Sweetarra	3	91
Sorrel-horſe	1	12	Taylor's	3	94
Plough	1	13	Harris's Ferry	8	102
Unicorn	3	16	Hendrick's	3	105
Blue-ball	4	20	Chalmer's	11	116
Admiral Warren	3	23	Carliſle	3	119
White-horſe	3	26	Shippenſburg	21	140
Downing's	7	33	B. Chambers's	11	151
The Ship	2	35	Fort Loudon	13	164
Waggon	6	41	Fort Littleton	18	182
Miller's	6	47	Juniata	19	201
Douglaſs's	3	50	Bedford	14	215
The Hat	4	54	Foot of Alleg.	15	230
D. of Cumber.	3	57	Stoney-creek	15	245
Red-Lion	3	60	E. ſide Lau. H	12	257
Coneſtogo creek	4	64	Fort Ligonier	9	266
Lancaſter C. H	2	66	Pittſburg	54	320

Diſtance of Places from *Louisburgh* to *Pittsburgh*.

From Louiſburg		To	Ontario	60	800
to Quebec	360	360	Niagara Falls	160	960
Three Rivers	80	440	The Store-h.	20	980
Montreal	90	530	Lake Erie	10	990
La Galette	120	650	Fort Preſquiſle	90	1080
Fort Frontenac	90	742	Fort Beauf R.	15	1095
Oſwego acroſs the East End of Lake			Pittſburg	120	1215

A TABLE of COINS.

COINS.	Wt. dw	gr	L. M. l.	s.	d.	Pennſylva. l.	s.	d.	Sterling. l.	s.	d.
A GUINEA	5	9	1	8	0	1	14	0	1	1	0
Half Guinea	2	16	0	14	0	0	17	0	0	10	6
Moidore	6	22	1	16	0	2	3	6	1	7	0
4 Piſtole Piece	17	8	4	8	0	5	8	0	3	6	0
2 Piſtole Piece	8	16	2	4	0	2	14	0	1	13	0
1 Piſtole	4	8	1	2	0	1	7	0	0	16	6
Double Johannes	18	10	4	16	0	12	0	0	3	12	0
Single Johannes	9	5	2	8	0	6	0	0	1	16	0
Half Johannes	4	14	1	4	0	3	0	0	0	18	0
Quarter Johannes	2	7	0	12	0	1	10	0	0	9	0
Crown Silver	19	8	0	6	8	0	7	6	0	5	0
Dollar	17	12	0	6	0	0	7	6	0	4	6
Half Dollar	8	18	0	3	0	0	3	9	0	2	3
Quarter Dollar	4	9	0	1	6	0	1	10½	0	1	1½

R O A D S.

Road to Boſton.

FROM Providence to Pawtucket	4	
Attleborough	5	is 9
Wrentham	9	18
Walpole	8	26
Dedham	6	32
Roxbury	3	35
Boſton	9	44

Road from Boſton to Portſmouth.

FROM Boſton to Medford	5	
Malden	2	is 7
Lynn	4	11
Danvers	6	17
Salem	2	19
Beverly	1	20
Wenham	6	26
Ipſwich	6	32
Rowley	3	35
Newbury	7	42
Saliſbury	5	47
Saybrook	2	49
Hampton	4	53
North-Hampton	3	56
Greenland	4	60
Portſmouth	5	65

Road from Portſmouth to Caſco-Bay and Machias.

FROM Portſmouth to Old York	9	
Wells	13	is 22
Kennebunk	9	31
Saco	8	39
Scarborough	10	49
Falmouth	7	56
Falmouth-Town	5	61
New-Caſco	7	68
Nor. Yarmouth	6	74
Brunſwick	18	92
Heardnell's Fer.	13	105
Wiſcaſſet	12	117
Newcaſtle	10	127
Waldoborough	12	139
Thomaſtown	11	150
Camden	13	163
Belfaſt	18	181
Penobſcot	11	192
Blue-Hill	13	205
Union River	14	219
Kilkenny	6	225
New-Briſtol	8	233
Goldſborough	8	241
No. IV.	14	255
Pleaſant River	12	267
Chandler River	9	276
Machias	8	284

Road to Philadelphia.

FROM Providence to Pawtuxet	5	
Greenwich	10	is 15
North-Kingſ-town	8	23
Tower-Hill	8	31
South-Kingſ-town	4	35
Charleſtown	10	45
Weſterly	6	51
Stonington	12	63
Groton Ferry	8	71
New-London	1	72
Rope Ferry	5	77
Lyme	8	85
Saybrook Ferry	3	88
Killingſworth	13	101
Guilford	9	110
Branford	10	120
New-Haven	9	129
Milford	6	135
Stratford	8	143
Fairfield	7	150
Norwalk	12	162
Stanford	10	172
Rye	10	182
Marineck	7	189
Eaſt-Cheſter	7	196
Kingſbridge	6	202

R O A D S.

From Richmond to Charleſton (*S. C.*)

To Oſborne's 15 miles, Peterſburg 10, Hall's 21, Hick's Ford 24, Halifax 28, Enfield 12, Tar river 26, Poſniquot bridge 26, Quotankney creek 11, Eaton's 10, Neuſe ferry 21, Dixon's 31, N. E. branch of Cape Fear 40, Wilmington 10, N. W. branch of Cape Fear 2, Town creek 8, Lockwood's Folly 16, Beal's 24, Eaſt end of Long Bay 13, Weſt end of do. 15, Wackamaw ferry 23, Black River do. 3, George Town 5, Cooke's ferry Santee 12, Hugh's 10, White's 18, Mulatto Town 5, Button's 10, Charleſton 4.

From Richmond to Portſmouth (N. H.)

To Norvel's 12, Hanover court-houſe 10, Lynch's 13, Bowling Green 12, Todd's 10, Fredericksburg 12, Garret's 13, Dumfries 9, Colcheſter 9, Alexandria 16, Bladenſburg 14, Roſe's 14, Spuriers 7, Baltimore 13, Philip's 13, Buſh 12, Suſquehanna ferry 6, Charleſtown 9, Head of Elk 12, Chriſteen 10, Wilmington 9, Cheſter 12, Philadelphia 15, Frankford 5, Briſtol 15, Trenton 10, Princeton 13, Brunſwick 17, Woodbridge 10, Elizabeth Town 10, Newark 6, New York 9, Kingſbridge 15, Eaſt Cheſter 6, New Rochel 4, Rye 5, Horſeneck 6, Sanford 7, Norwalk 10, Fairfield 12, Stratford 8; Milford 4, New Haven 10, Wallingford 13, Durham 7, M. Town 5, Weathersfield 11, Hartford 3, Windſor 8 Enfield 8, Springfield 10, Kingſton 15, Weſtern 9, Brookfield 6, Spence 8, Leiceſter 6, Worceſter 6, Shrewſbury 5, Marlborough 10, Sunbury 11. Watertown 19, Boſton 10, Marblehead 9, Salem 8, Ipſwich 14, Newbury 12, Hampton 7, Portſmouth 15.

From Richmond to the Sweet Springs.

To Allen's 10, Peers 10, Payne's 25, the Bird 11, Allegrees 14, Charlotteſville 10, Wood's 10, Blue Ridge 18, Teas 3, Staunton 10, Acres 8, Kinkead's 14, Hamilton's 6, Cow Paſture 8, Warm Springs 19, Morris's 14, Brown's 19, Reeſes 3, Red Spring 14, Sweet Spring 1.

FIG. 16. Road tables from *Father Abraham's Pocket Almanack for the Year 1777* (Philadelphia: John Dunlap, 1777); *The New-England Alamanack . . . for the Year of Our Lord 1783* (Providence: John Carter, 1782); and *The Virginia Almanack, for the Year of Our Lord, 1790* (Richmond: John Dixon, 1789). *Early American Imprints*, Series I., Nos. 15063, 17795, 45425.

however, was always oriented in relation to the needs of each respective locality. In the examples provided in figure 16, each set of road tables is oriented from the major towns in each area. The tables in *Father Abraham's Pocket Almanac*, which was published in Philadelphia, all extend from the major towns in Pennsylvania (Philadelphia, Reading, and Louisburg). The road tables in the *New-England Almanack* are likewise oriented from Boston, Portsmouth, and Providence, and the road tables in the *Virginia Almanac* have an even narrower focus, orienting all of its routes from the city of Richmond. In doing so, these tables encourage citizens to read the nation in terms that represent the specific needs and interests of each locality. A reader of the *New England Almanac* will imagine the nation in terms that represent and facilitate the local needs, interests, and connections of the people of Boston, just as a reader of the *Virginia Almanac* will imagine the nation in terms that privilege southern needs and interests. Within these road tables, imagining the nation as a whole goes hand in hand with representing and asserting the interests of a locality, yet another way these road tables promote a federal understanding of national unity and space.

The marginal notes and personal diaries recorded in individual copies of almanacs provide a more concrete illustration of the ways readers used these texts to situate their own experiences within the nation. Readers often recorded brief notes about their travels in their interleaved almanac diaries, writing down places they visited and how long it took to get there, placing check marks next to the names of places they visited, and noting the distance traveled. In some cases, these trips were taken for matters of business, as in the case of Nathaniel Lovejoy, a trader from Andover, Massachusetts, who traveled throughout his state and recorded the various places he visited for his transactions within his almanacs.[41] John Moore, a New York customs agent who also conducted a successful mercantile business, likewise recorded his frequent travels throughout Connecticut and parts of New York in almanacs that were designed to serve the mid-Atlantic region.[42] In other cases, readers recorded trips taken to visit friends and family, as in the almanac diaries kept by John Pierce, a farmer from Lancaster, Massachusetts, who carefully recorded the dates and locations of these social visits in his 1791 edition of Osgood Carlson's *An Astronomical Diary or an Almanack* calculated for Boston.[43] Moore likewise supplemented his records of business transactions with even more detailed accounts of his own dinner parties and guests, as well as the club meetings he attended in his local community.[44] George Washington's almanac diaries also provide an extensive overview of his social engagements as he reports the various people he set out to "visit" or "dine with" each week.[45] Although these notations are brief, they indicate the ways readers used these almanacs to locate themselves within the larger spaces of the nation and, more importantly, how almanacs allowed them to chart their points of connection and interaction with the nation's different spaces. Through these annotations and diary entries, the United States emerges as a space that is composed of diverse but interconnected personal and economic networks.

A federal consciousness also emerges in the way almanacs represent time. A number of critics have explored how almanacs contributed to a sense of national time in the early republic by looking at the historical "chronologies" featured in many almanacs throughout the colonial and early national periods.[46] Prior to 1776, these chronologies represented significant events in continental British history, such as the dates of major military battles, the passage of important parliamentary legislation, and the birthdays and coronation anniversaries for the British monarchy. As the colonies moved toward independence, however, almanac makers revised these time lines, replacing events in British history with events specific to the American colonies, such as the dates of major Revolutionary battles such as Lexington and Concord, laws and decrees passed by the Continental Congress, and birthdays and anniversaries associated with figures such as George Washington and other Revolutionary leaders. Through these revisions, almanacs presented readers with an American rather than British view of the past, which, as Spero argues, helped "reorient history ... toward a new nation."[47]

A closer look at these historical chronologies shows that, in addition to representing a shared national history defined by the Revolutionary War and the new federal government, these chronologies also encouraged readers to recognize the presence and history of the individual states within the nation. Nearly all of these chronologies begin with Columbus's discovery of South America and continue with the settlement of North America and the establishment of the British American colonies. Accounts of this colonial history varied. Some almanacs only list the date for the colony that would become their home state, as in the case of the Philadelphia-based *Poor Will's Almanack*, whose 1788 chronology lists only the founding of the Pennsylvania colony. Other almanacs provide a more comprehensive account of British colonial history, as in the case of South Carolina's *Palladium of Knowledge or the Carolina and Georgia Almanac* for 1788, which lists dates for the establishment of each of the original thirteen colonies. Whether an almanac chose to list solely their local colonial history or the colonial history of the nation as a whole, these chronologies nevertheless make a point of emphasizing that the history of the United States needs to be understood in relation to the history of its parts.

If anything, almanacs actually seem to work against development of a shared sense of national time because their locally oriented content was more likely to remind readers of the extent to which residents of the colonies and, later, the states did *not* share the same experiences of time. The specific temporal information included in almanacs, such as information about the hours of daylight, the times of tides, or the lengths of growing seasons, would have made readers aware of how their experiences of time were shaped by their specific locations. Other place-specific information, such as the orientation of road tables, recipes, remedies, and gardening and farming practices further emphasized the extent to which people living in these specific locations used time in different ways. Given the ways that almanacs made readers aware of how their experiences of time were shaped by specific locations, it seems more likely that their temporal information might cause them to question any sense of shared national time, rather than helping them produce it. The personal diaries kept within these almanacs emphasize the highly personalized dimensions of their use, which, in many ways, seem to preclude a sense of national consciousness as readers used these texts to mark events that would have had little significance beyond their immediate experience, such as the births and deaths of family members.[48] The almanac diaries of Robert Wormeley Carter exemplify this individualist focus as he uses his almanacs to comment on his gambling practices and how they affected his personal relationships with his family members, information that had little bearing on his sense of a shared commitment to the experiences of his fellow citizens.[49]

And yet, by representing these different temporal experiences within a single text, American almanacs still provided readers with a means of locating their unique, local temporalities within a unifying frame of reference. Returning once again to the information printed on the title page, almanacs always included a statement about the year in which they were published. Prior to 1776, most almanacs described this year in reference to Christian time (e.g., "For the year of our Lord Christ," "For the year of our Lord," or "For the year of the Christian era") or, in some cases, the reigning monarch (e.g., "in the reign of George III"). Under these annual headings, the distinct temporal experiences of each local community were united under a shared sense of identity, either as Christians or as British subjects. Although their local conditions might differ from one another in a given year, the leading description of the year links all readers as people sharing in a common Christian and British history and identity.

Following the Declaration of Independence, U.S. almanacs continued to use these yearly headings as a point of communal identification, but instead of referencing the king's reign, the yearly headings now took two forms, referring to either "the year of our Lord" or the "year of Independence" (see figs. 12 and 13).[50] Just as they had in the British colonial almanacs, references to "the year of our Lord" continued to connect almanac readers through a shared Christian identity. References to the "year of Independence," however, had a different unifying effect. By marking time in relation to an ongoing time line of national independence, these headings united citizens under a shared national history that also included and represented their local experiences. Within this time frame, the only condition for national unity was a shared engagement with national independence, which could be experienced in many different ways, depending on location. Conceiving of national time in relation to the condition of independence allowed readers to position their localities within a larger history of national independence without asking readers to assume that their experiences of that independence must necessarily be the same. By reminding readers to position the locally specific information in the almanac in relation to this time line of national independence, almanacs taught readers to view national history as something that was simultaneously diverse and locally oriented—an experience that reinforced a federal understanding of plural union.

The records kept in personal almanac diaries likewise show how almanacs enabled citizens to situate themselves in relation to national events. During the American Revolution, readers often made personal notes marking significant battles or developments and their experiences and observations involving the war effort. John Stanton, a store manager and captain in the militia for Worcester, Massachusetts, records how Henry Knox led his troops through Worcester as they transported a British cannon captured at Fort Ticonderoga in his diary interleaved in Nathanael Low's *Astronomical Diary or Almanack* for 1776.[51] Belcher Noyes adds additional entries to his almanac's chronologies and calendars that note the specific events leading up to the outbreak of the war in Boston, as well as a more extended account of his family's efforts to escape Boston following the British siege in late 1775.[52] Samuel Man and William Powell likewise expand their almanac chronologies by noting the specific movements of troops under the leadership of Generals Arnold, Gates, Burgoyne, Howe, and Washington, paying particular attention to those that were close to their homes in Wrentham, Massachusetts (Man), and Boston (Powell).[53] Through these notes, we can see how almanacs enabled readers to connect and situate themselves locally in relation to the events of the war, while also illustrating their awareness of its broader national significance. Furthermore, their efforts to supplement the existing records of these national events within their almanacs show just how important it was for U.S. readers to be able to imagine the nation's emerging history in locally specific terms.[54]

Local court schedules also contributed to this federal understanding of time and place. As with the road tables, most almanacs included a schedule identifying the days and times that various courts were in session. These lists did not just focus on an almanac's specific area or state but also included court schedules for surrounding states. For instance, *Father Abraham's Almanack*, published in

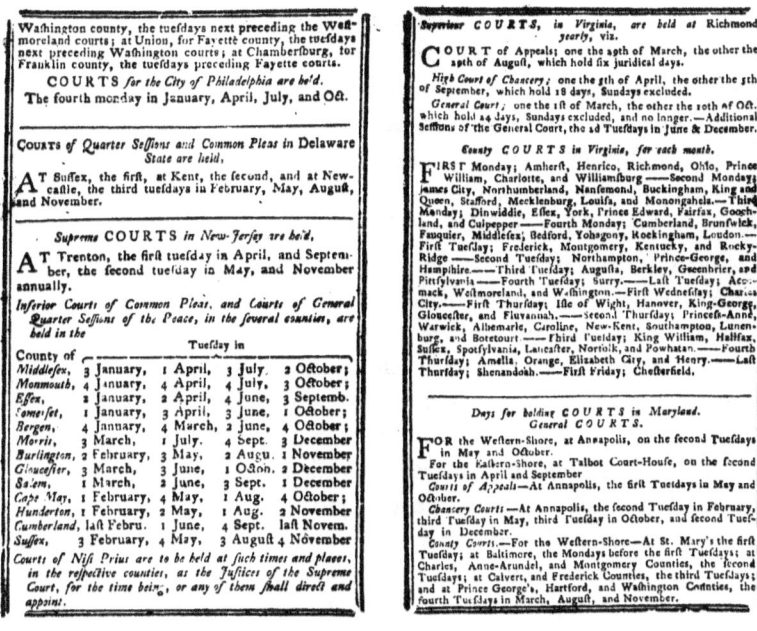

FIG. 17. Court schedules, *Poor Will's Almanack, for the Year of Our Lord 1788*. Philadelphia: Joseph Crukshank, 1787. *Early American Imprints*, Series I, No. 20853.

Boston, includes court schedules for the city of Boston, as well as for Connecticut, Rhode Island, and several other major towns in Massachusetts. *Poor Will's Almanack*, published in Philadelphia, contains listings for courts in Pennsylvania, as well as Virginia, Maryland, and New Jersey, and the New York–based *Hutchin's Improved* features schedules for New York, Connecticut, and New Jersey (see fig. 17). In reading these schedules, it becomes abundantly clear that these states have different judicial structures and forms of organization. For the state of Pennsylvania, one can find schedules for a single "Supreme Court," as well as a set of "Nisi Prius courts," "Courts of Quarter Sessions and Common Pleas," and various "City Courts." Virginia, by contrast, relies on a larger system of "Superior Courts" that include a court of appeals, a high court of chancery, and a general court, as well as a system of "County Courts." Maryland also relies on a large system of "General Courts" that include chancery courts and multiple courts of appeals, as well as a more diverse body of local courts including "County Courts," "Orphan Courts," and "Mayor's Courts."[55] This lack of uniformity among the court systems of the different states—which also extends to the schedules themselves as different courts sit for different lengths of time in each state—highlights the diversity of local governance in the early nation. Citizens reading over the court schedules would immediately recognize that these states were governed on a widely variable local scale.

At the same time, these court schedules also point to relationships of underlying compatibility and connection. Including several sets of court schedules in a single almanac suggests that citizens needed this extended information, either because they worked across different jurisdictions (as attorneys, printers, or law enforcement, for instance) or because legal disputes often took place or were settled across the court systems of different states.[56] Furthermore, even though each state shows minor differences regarding the structure and legal focus of their respective court systems, the fact that people worked across different jurisdictions suggests that these variations did not hinder regular interaction between residents of the different states. Citizens were clearly able to work within the legal systems of the neighboring states, provided they had the necessary information about the different kinds of courts, jurisdictions, and schedules for each location. The almanac diaries of Samuel Bridge illuminate these interconnections as Bridge makes notes about the opening dates for the various courts in the region surrounding Worcester, Massachusetts. As a town constable and court crier, Bridge needed to conduct business in these various systems, and the almanac enabled him to plot out his plans and travels for doing so in his own local but varied community.[57] The publication of these multiple court schedules, like the road tables, thus reminded readers to view the nation as a composition of different and distinct local governments, while also suggesting that citizens could easily work with one another across these local boundaries in orderly and productive ways.[58]

A final word on the marginal notes and diary entries interleaved within personal copies of American almanacs. As mentioned earlier, when examined on an individual basis, these personal notes and records seem to emphasize the highly individualized and locally specific interpretive frameworks of early American readers. The commentary and observations recorded in these notes focus on issues that are relevant to each user—such as the weather, daily chores, harvest records, births, deaths, and illnesses—but do not necessarily convey a sense of collective community or national consciousness. These highly individualized uses, however, nevertheless reflect the federal dimensions of these almanacs as they show how readers took information that was designed for a larger, regional American community and sought to situate themselves—in locally specific and distinctive terms—within that larger space. The marginal notes and diary entries recorded in early American almanacs show readers in the process of integrating their local experiences within a text that was designed to represent a larger whole, a process that not only allowed readers to experience a sense of national connection and unity but also encouraged them to recognize that their collective experience, as Americans, must always be rooted in a strong sense of local distinction, particularity, and preferences.

Design and Visual Language: The Layout of the Almanac Page

The layout or visual design of the almanac was equally influential in training readers to read variety cohesively. There is more to reading a text than just attending to its linguistic or literary features, and, in the case of almanacs, we need to pay close attention to its visual and spatial dimensions.[59] In considering these visual dynamics of the almanac, however, I am not just referring to their use of pictures and illustrations. Almanacs typically contained very few visual images. Sketches, cartoons, and engravings were expensive and difficult to reproduce, making them impractical for a text that was meant to be affordable and annually replaceable. Even though almanacs contained few illustrations, the layout and content of their pages represent a significant part of their visual dynamics. As George Landow writes, "Print employs a greater diversity of visual information than people usually take into account," including the "spacing between words, paragraphing, changes of type style and size, formatting to indicate passages quoted from other works, [and] assigning specific locations on the page."[60] Almanacs, which are organized in distinct sections and rely heavily on tables, charts, and astrological and astronomical symbols, present readers with a complex visual layout that influenced the way that citizens experienced and interpreted variety in the early republic.

At the level of the page, almanacs present a very diverse visual experience. As reference texts, almanacs have a highly compartmentalized structure, where information is carefully set apart in sections that include calendar pages, as well as sections featuring farming and gardening advice, government information, essays, poems, recipes, remedies, anecdotes, and tax, interest, and exchange rates, to name some of the most common sectional spaces. The sample page from the New Jersey–based *United States Almanac* for 1789 illuminates this compartmentalized structure, where the almanac is clearly broken in separate sections that provide financial information, moral advice, a recipe, and a home remedy (see fig. 18). The specific sections within an almanac, of course, varied widely. Some almanacs limited their organizational structure to calendar information and reference data that was easily reproducible, such as road tables, tax and interest rates, court schedules, and lists of people holding political office, exemplified by the Connecticut-based *Stafford's Almanack*. Other almanacs provided more col-

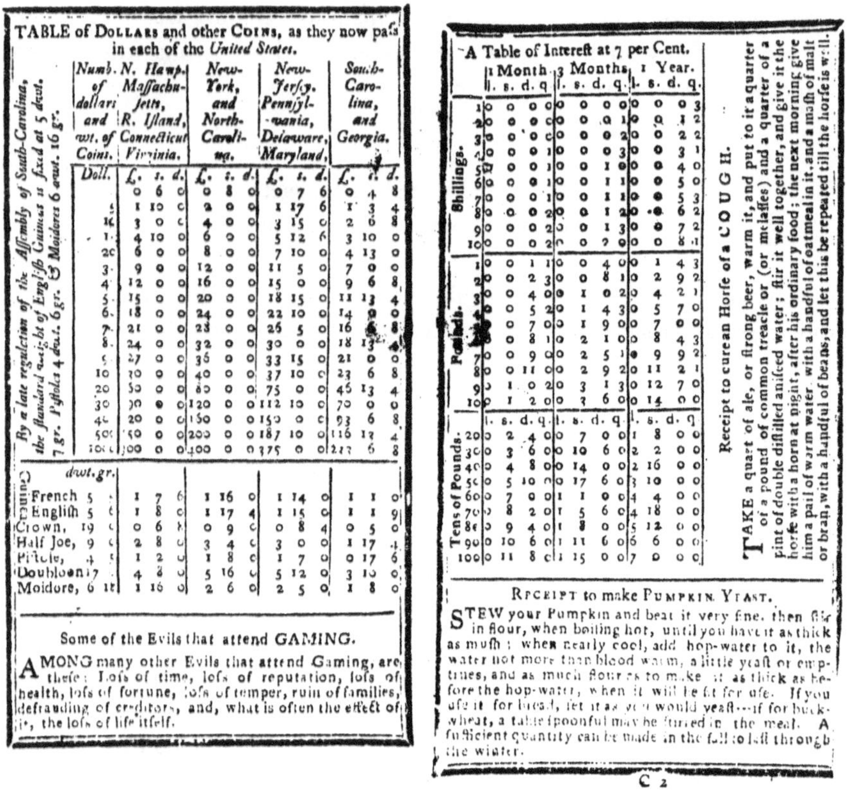

TABLE of DOLLARS and other COINS, as they now pass in each of the *United States*.

By a late regulation of the Assembly of South-Carolina, the standard weight of English Guineas is fixed at 5 dwt. 7 gr. Pistoles 4 dwt. 6 gr. & Moidores 6 dwt. 16 gr.

Numb. of dollars and wt. of Coins.	*N. Hamp. Massachusetts, R. Island, Connecticut Virginia.*			*New-York, and North-Carolina.*			*New-Jersey. Pennsylvania, Delaware, Maryland,*			*South-Carolina, and Georgia.*		
Doll.	£.	s.	d.	£.	s.	d.	£.	s.	d.	£.	s.	d.
	0	6	0	0	8	0	0	7	6	0	4	8
5	1	10	0	2	0	0	1	17	6	1	3	4
10	3	0	0	4	0	0	3	15	0	2	6	8
1.	4	10	0	6	0	0	5	12	6	3	10	0
20	6	0	0	8	0	0	7	10	0	4	13	0
3	9	0	0	12	0	0	11	5	0	7	0	0
4	12	0	0	16	0	0	15	0	0	9	6	8
5	15	0	0	20	0	0	18	15	0	11	13	4
6	18	0	0	24	0	0	22	10	0	14	0	0
7	21	0	0	28	0	0	26	5	0	16	[illegible]	8
8	24	0	0	32	0	0	30	0	0	18	13	4
9	27	0	0	36	0	0	33	15	0	21	0	0
10	30	0	0	40	0	0	37	10	0	23	6	8
20	60	0	0	80	0	0	75	0	0	46	13	4
30	90	0	0	120	0	0	112	10	0	70	0	0
40	20	0	0	160	0	0	150	0	0	93	6	8
50	50	0	0	200	0	0	187	10	0	116	13	4
100	00	0	0	400	0	0	375	0	0	233	6	8
dwt. gr.												
Guineas French 5 [illegible]	1	7	6	1	16	0	1	14	0	1	1	0
Guineas English 5 6	1	8	0	1	17	4	1	15	0	1	1	9
Crown, 19 [illegible]	0	6	8	0	9	0	0	8	4	0	5	0
Half Joe, 9 [illegible]	2	8	0	3	4	0	3	0	0	1	17	4
Pistole, 4 5	1	2	0	1	8	0	1	7	0	0	17	6
Doubloon 17	4	8	0	5	16	0	5	12	0	3	10	0
Moidore, 6 18	1	16	0	2	6	0	2	5	0	1	8	0

Some of the Evils that attend GAMING.

AMONG many other Evils that attend Gaming, are these: Loss of time, loss of reputation, loss of health, loss of fortune, loss of temper, ruin of families, defrauding of creditors, and, what is often the effect of it, the loss of life itself.

A Table of Interest at 7 per Cent.

		1 Month				3 Months				1 Year			
		l.	s.	d.	q.	l.	s.	d.	q.	l.	s.	d.	q.
Shillings.	1	0	0	0	0	0	0	0	0	0	0	0	3
	2	0	0	0	0	0	0	0	1	0	0	1	2
	3	0	0	0	0	0	0	0	2	0	0	2	2
	4	0	0	0	1	0	0	0	3	0	0	3	1
	5	0	0	0	1	0	0	1	0	0	0	4	0
	6	0	0	0	1	0	0	1	1	0	0	5	0
	7	0	0	0	1	0	0	1	1	0	0	5	3
	8	0	0	0	2	0	0	1	2	0	0	6	2
	9	0	0	0	2	0	0	1	3	0	0	7	2
	10	0	0	0	2	0	0	2	0	0	0	8	1
Pounds.	1	0	0	1	1	0	0	4	0	0	1	4	3
	2	0	0	2	3	0	0	8	1	0	2	9	2
	3	0	0	4	0	0	1	0	2	0	4	2	1
	4	0	0	5	2	0	1	4	3	0	5	7	0
	5	0	0	7	0	0	1	9	0	0	7	0	0
	6	0	0	8	1	0	2	1	0	0	8	4	3
	7	0	0	9	0	0	2	5	1	0	9	9	2
	8	0	0	11	0	0	2	9	2	0	11	2	1
	9	0	1	0	2	0	3	1	3	0	12	7	0
	10	0	1	2	0	0	3	6	0	0	14	0	0
		l.	s.	d.	q.	l.	s.	d.	q.	l.	s.	d.	q.
Tens of Pounds.	20	0	2	4	0	0	7	0	0	1	8	0	0
	30	0	3	6	0	0	10	6	0	2	2	0	0
	40	0	4	8	0	0	14	0	0	2	16	0	0
	50	0	5	10	0	0	17	6	0	3	10	0	0
	60	0	7	0	0	1	1	0	0	4	4	0	0
	70	0	8	2	0	1	5	6	0	4	18	0	0
	80	0	9	4	0	1	8	0	0	5	12	0	0
	90	0	10	6	0	1	11	6	0	6	6	0	0
	100	0	11	8	0	1	15	0	0	7	0	0	0

Receipt to cure an Horse of a COUGH.

TAKE a quart of ale, or strong beer, warm it, and put to it a quarter of a pound of common treacle or (or melasses) and a quarter of a pint of double distilled aniseed water; stir it well together, and give it the horse with a horn at night, after his ordinary food; the next morning give him a pail of warm water, with a handful of oatmeal in it, and a mash of malt or bran, with a handful of beans, and let this be repeated till the horse is well.

RECEIPT to make PUMPKIN YEAST.

STEW your Pumpkin and beat it very fine, then stir in flour, when boiling hot, until you have it as thick as mush; when nearly cool, add hop-water to it, the water not more than blood warm, a little yeast or emptines, and as much flour as to make it as thick as before the hop-water, when it will be fit for use. If you use it for bread, set it as you would yeast---if for buckwheat, a table spoonful may be stirred in the meal. A sufficient quantity can be made in the fall to last through the winter.

C 2

FIG. 18. Compartmentalized page structure, *United States Almanac, for the Year of Our Lord 1789*. Elizabethtown, N.J.: Shepard Kollock, 1788. *Early American Imprints*, Series I, No. 21182.

loquial forms of information that were presented in sections devoted to domestic activities, such as cooking, gardening, and mending, or social advice involving marriage, courtship, and raising children. Many almanacs also had sections devoted to educational topics, featuring articles about history, mathematics, the natural sciences, and government, and still others had sections devoted exclusively to entertainment, including humorous anecdotes, jokes, and songs. The Tobler almanacs discussed earlier in this chapter exemplify how the layout and sectional organization of almanacs varied from place to place.

While the specific layout and sectional organization of almanacs varied, this compartmentalized format also provided readers with a visual structure that was designed for multiple uses. Broken up into different sections, the pages of an almanac were not meant to be read linearly. Instead, their design encouraged readers to select the specific type of information they wanted at a given moment, depending on their individual needs. Brown describes this as an "indexical" reading process that is highly informed by the choices and circumstances of individual readers.[61] Readers interested in obtaining information related to farming, for instance, would refer to the calendar pages listing sunrise, sunsets, and weather predictions or the sections devoted to gardening and agricultural advice. Readers interested in business would refer to charts listing taxes and interest rates, or travel information available on the road tables. Meanwhile, readers interested in household management would focus more on recipes, home remedies, or essays on education. Whatever their readers' immediate interests, the compartmentalized visual structure of the almanac creates a range of different reading paths depending on where, when, and who might be using the text at a given moment.[62]

Literary scholarship offers a range of theoretical frameworks for contending with texts that offer these kinds of plural structures and multiple interpretive pathways. In the case of novels, Bakhtin's concept of heteroglossia is used to account for the diverse perspectives, voices, and intensions that define this narrative form. Works of satire and irony are also interpreted through frameworks that foreground multiple modes of representation and interpretation as readers must negotiate competing forms of literal and figurative significance that can vary depending on their own location and knowledge. Literary works representing the experiences and perspectives of marginalized communities also exhibit multivoiced and pluralist frameworks, often examined in terms of hybridity, performance, or, in the case of Deleuze and Guattari, the process of "becoming minor," as they contend with and resist the dominant power dynamics that shape their experiences.[63] While these critical approaches provide helpful starting points for contending with almanacs, they cannot fully account for the plural structures and multiple reading experiences represented by these texts, particularly because almanacs are intended for uses that are not, exclusively, literary. As McCarthy points out, almanacs were, to some degree, meant to be read as literary texts through the essays, poems, sermons, anecdotes, and stories that were often included within their contents, but almanacs also had many other nonliterary purposes, serving as a timepiece, a calculator, a diary, a calendar, a map, a weather guide, a recipe book, a medical handbook, and more.[64] Likening the multiple uses and practical applications of early American almanacs to the modern-day smartphone, McCarthy argues that we should turn to critical studies involving technological literacy to explore the plural dynamics of almanacs more effectively. In this regard, we might think of examining almanacs as "multimodal" texts—a term coined by contemporary media theorists to describe texts whose organizational and design features foster multiple uses within a single work.[65] As Charles Kostelnick notes, one of the distinctive features of multimodal texts is their ability to foster an awareness of different reading pathways. In contrast to traditional narrative texts where all readers are asked to follow the same path of organization for a given set of content, multimodal texts require readers to select their own reading paths from a number of possible and equally valid options. Kostelnick uses the modern metaphor of a freeway to describe this kind of reading experience, where "drivers on the freeway follow the same general rules, even though they have different destinations and drive in different lanes at different speeds," an image that helps illustrate how readers can participate in a shared network while also exercising their individual interests and authority.[66]

While this concept of multimodality provides a useful model for accounting for the plural structure and uses of early American almanacs, we might also situate its multiple pathways of representation and reading more firmly in the aesthetics of the eighteenth century. As Daniel DeWispelare has recently argued, political changes in the eighteenth century, which included the expansion of the British Empire in the Americas, the American Revolution and establishment of the United States, and the development of new transnational and transatlantic networks of exchange, "generated aesthetic ideas that praised mixture as a maker of forms," a shift that resulted in a new representational framework that privileged and celebrated "copiousness."[67] This aesthetics of "copia" provided useful strategies for representing the increasingly heterogeneous views of population, nationhood, and experience that defined British and American national identity, and while DeWispelare and others primarily explore these dynamics of copia in relation to British imperial culture and linguistics, I argue that these aesthetics can also be used to examine the pluralism of early American almanacs, particularly with regard to the close relationship between the principle of copia and a heterogeneous sense of politics and nationhood.

Combining this awareness of the eighteenth-century aesthetic emphasis on copiousness with attention to the practical dimensions of multimodality can lead us to a productive framework for contending with the multiple forms, functions, and reading experiences associated with early American almanacs. American almanacs foregrounded and celebrated their multiple content and uses in terms that drew attention to their plurality while also making it possible for readers to reinforce their distinctive identities and interests based on their specific motives and needs. At the same time, as they flipped through the compartmentalized structure of the almanac, readers came to recognize the existence and possibility of other equally valid uses and interests. Because these different uses and interests are all built into a single text, the pages of the almanac make readers aware of these differences in a productive and cohesive format. More importantly, even though almanacs introduce readers to many different uses, interests, and reading paths, they do not create experiences of chaos or incoherence for readers. Instead, the diverse reading experiences contained within their compartmentalized layouts create a generative and exceptionally useful text that can better serve the interests of a given community precisely because of their ability to represent multiple uses and perspectives at the same time. The visual layout of the almanac thus trains readers to view themselves as distinctive members of a community that is always made up of a larger array of interests and practices. Similar, then, to the road tables, court schedules, and other temporal markers, the visual layout of almanacs fostered a sense of "situatedness" in early U.S. readers, which supported a federal conception of unity. In selecting information from the crowded visual pages of an almanac, readers were continually reminded that, moreover, their own local views and experiences were one among many, and that these different uses, experiences, and motives could be bound together, productively, within a single text and a single nation.

Another important visual aspect of the almanac concerns the layout of the calendar pages themselves. All almanacs had these calendar pages, which were organized to provide information for each month. Each month, in turn, was broken down into information about each day of the month, and each day of the month, in turn, was broken down into information about the weather and the movements of the sun, moon, and stars for each twenty-four-hour period. All of this information was provided in a detailed chart, composed of anywhere from six to ten columns, that was filled with numbers and symbols to represent the varied information available for each day. Although there were some variations in the way this information was presented to readers, the layout of this day-to-day data was standardized enough that most almanacs did not provide any information about how to read or interpret the material provided on the calendar pages. The editors and compilers of the almanacs simply assumed that readers knew how to read and interpret this information, an assumption that poses a challenge for contemporary readers who might find themselves flummoxed by the complicated arrangements of numbers, columns, and symbols presented on the calendar pages without any points of reference (see fig. 19, right-hand side, as well as figs. 14 and 15).

A few almanacs did provide reference guides to explain the layout and the data provided on the calendar pages, such as this example from *The Universal Calendar and North American's Almanack for 1788* (Boston) (see fig. 19, left-hand side). This "Explanation of the Calendar Pages" briefly describes the significance of each column for each day. The first two columns identify the numeric date and the day of the week, also rendered as a number where 1 = Sunday, 2 = Monday, and so on. The next column provides information about the weather and also identifies feast days and holidays. The fourth column gives times for the rising and setting of the sun, and the fifth column provides "clock equations" in the

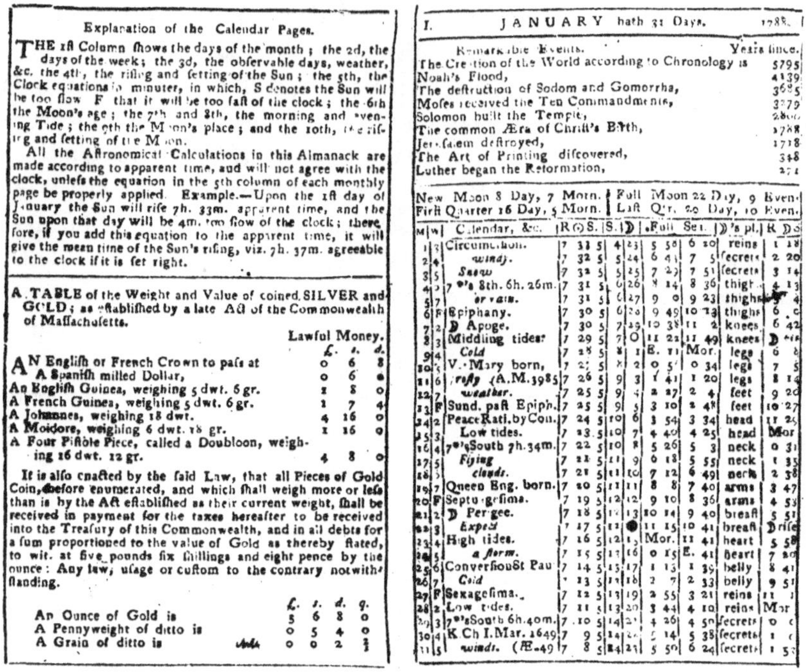

FIG. 19. "Explanation of the Calendar Pages," *The Universal Calendar and North-American's Almanack for the Year of the Creation . . . 1788*. Boston: Edes & Son, 1787. *Early American Imprints*, Series I, No. 20725.

form of minutes, which were needed to calculate the sunrise and sunset times into accurate times on a clock. The next five columns all contain information related to the moon, including the phase of the moon (column six), the times for morning and evening tides (columns seven and eight), the moon's location in relation to its astrological significance (column nine), and the times for rising and setting (column nine). Not all calendar pages were as extensive as *The Universal Calendar*. The Tobler almanacs, for example, only included seven columns of information, and other almanacs had as few as four. No matter their specific divisions, these charts broke each day down into specific components of information. Taken on their own, each column represents a unique and singular temporal marker that signifies a specific aspect of the day. Although each component is significant on its own, understanding the day as a complete unit of time involves considering all of these temporal components, added together. Reading the calendar page thus becomes an experience of understanding how these varied parts can make up something that readers will also recognize as a whole. Each column of information is important on its own, but readers can only get a complete picture of the day and, by extension, the month and the entire year, by reading all of these component parts together. By enacting the experience of composing a union out of parts, these calendar pages provide an excellent framework for teaching citizens how to read and interpret the federal union.

As a final example of the federal dynamics of early American almanacs, I want to conclude with a look at the astrological dimensions of the genre. Astrology was always a definitive feature of the almanac, and, from their earliest beginnings, almanacs provided information that linked the movements of the moon and stars to human events, emotions, and relationships. Almanacs presented this information through a regularized system of signs and symbols representing specific constellations and astronomical events, and these symbols were displayed on the calendar pages to provide readers with specific astrological information for each day. Because the movement of the stars was believed to correlate with particular areas of the body, almanacs also included a "key" for interpreting the influence of these symbols through a figure known as the "Zodiac Man," the "Man of Signs," or, more commonly during the eighteenth century, the "Anatomy Man." This figure, which was represented by an image of a man with arrows pointing to specific body parts, identified how each astrological symbol corresponded to various physical conditions and experiences. When readers encountered astrological symbols on the calendar pages, they could refer back to the Anatomy Man to determine how the astronomical conditions for a particular day would affect them on a physical level (see fig. 20).[68]

The figure of the Anatomy Man was one of the most standardized features of American almanacs, a significant fact in a genre that otherwise varied so widely with regard to its content. All American almanacs included this figure somewhere in their pages, and the formatting of the Anatomy Man pages was relatively consistent, as evident by the two examples I have included from *The Wilmington Almanack* for 1782 (Delaware) and *Poor Richard Improved Almanack* for 1791 (Philadelphia). The persistence of these astrological elements in early American almanacs has often puzzled historians because astrology was declining in credibility and influence during the colonial and early national periods. As Bernard Capp observes, although almanacs continued to provide readers with astrological information and symbolic references, by the eighteenth century this system no longer served the same representational function as a source of legitimate information about the natural or social world.[69] Why, then, did American almanacs continue to provide this information for a public that was increasingly disinclined to use or value them?

To some extent, this astrological content remained in the almanacs because many people continued to view astrology as a useful system of knowledge in the late eighteenth century. As Peter Eisenstadt has argued, although there was an

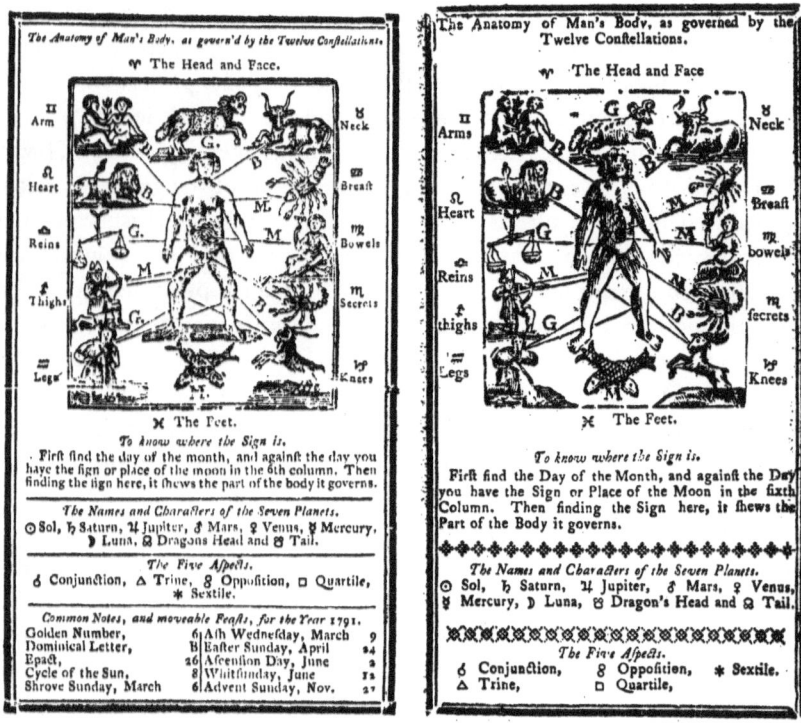

FIG. 20. Conventional images of the "Anatomy Man" or "Man of Signs," *Wilmington Almanack or Ephemeris for the Year of Our Lord 1782* (Wilmington, Del.: James Adams, 1781); *Poor Richard Improved: Being an Almanack and Ephemeris . . . for the Year of Our Lord 1791* (Philadelphia: Hall & Sellers, 1790). *Early American Imprints*, Series I, Nos. 17157, 22872.

increasing degree of "disenchantment" with astrological belief and interpretation in the age of the Enlightenment, astrology remained an important frame of reference for many readers, particularly those living in rural areas who typically lacked a formal education. Just because astrology was on the decline among the educated upper classes did not mean there was not still a popular market among other communities of readers, especially since astrology did not require traditional forms of literacy. It is also possible that this material persisted because people enjoyed reading it for entertainment or nostalgic purposes, similar to the role that horoscopes play in contemporary newspapers today, where zodiac-based predictions are printed alongside comic strips and advice columns.

I would argue, however, that astrological symbols and images continued to play a central role in early American almanacs because their structure provided a framework for understanding unity in composite terms. Although the representation of astrological signs is not overtly political, the process of reading the astrological data presented within the almanac requires readers to become adept at identifying and placing locally specific conditions in relation to a larger system. As far as the placement of this information on the calendar pages is concerned, I have already addressed how this astrological information serves as a component part of a reader's understanding of an entire day. If readers chose not to accept astrological beliefs, they could easily skip over this information and remove it from their conception of the day as a whole. What the astrology imagery does force citizens to do, however, is imagine a body composed of distinctly different yet equally important and contributing parts.

The image of the Anatomy Man itself promotes a literary strategy of reading parts in relation to an interconnected whole. Even though the image of the Anatomy Man is meant to depict an astrological view of the universe, this body and reference to the governing system of "twelve constellations" provides a useful metaphor for describing the structure of the federal republic. Indeed, as Slauter has pointed out, the unity of the new United States was often represented through such bodily imagery, with the different parts and functions of the body providing a useful visual metaphor for the federal "body politic." The astrological reference to the guiding influence of the constellations likewise aligns with popular rhetoric for describing the federal union, which was also likened to a system of stars or a governing constellation of states.[70] When considered in context of American independence, astrology provided a convenient metaphorical language for imagining unity in the new federal nation.

Of course, all almanacs—not just American almanacs—used these astrological signs and conventions, which begs the question: can we really read these features as producing a federal literacy that was specifically linked to the development of U.S. nationalism? If such astrological signs and symbols were used in almanacs printed throughout the world, under a range of different political systems—monarchal, parliamentary, and imperial—what makes it possible to argue that almanacs helped foster a federal literacy?

Ultimately, I believe that we can read the astrological content of early American almanacs in federal terms because of their persistence and popularity in the United States at this particular time. As mentioned, astrological signs and references continued to be a significant presence in early American almanacs when such references were in decline elsewhere. The prevalence of this form in the colonies and early United States throughout the late eighteenth century suggests that this imagery and symbolism had a particular use and importance for early national readers. T. J. Tomlin has recently tried to explain the persistence of astrological representation in early American popular culture during the late colonial and early national eras, arguing that astrology provided readers with a "useful narrative and epistemological framework" for explaining and understanding other forms of discourse, most notably Christian theology. By examining the central emphases of astrology, such as the representation of an ordered universe and the suggestion of moral punishment and reward, Tomlin argues that "almanacs and their astrological formulations complemented and even promoted orthodox Christianity," a unique reading that interprets astrology as a rhetorical system for supporting a different system of religious values and beliefs, in contrast to the "pagan" or "occult" practices that astrology was originally intended to represent.[71] By juxtaposing these astrological tables and imagery alongside the other content of U.S. almanacs, which was firmly rooted in portraying a diverse and locally oriented national space, associating these formal features with a federal imagination also seems more credible. Within a British almanac, where the Anatomy Man was *not* surrounded by content that oriented readers in relation to a diverse but unified space, this figure would not have had a federal resonance. In a U.S. almanac, where the rest of the content was, in fact, designed to cultivate this plural spatial and cultural imagination, the astrological features could take on this nationalist significance.

Building on Tomlin's argument that astrology serves as a critical framework for "complementing and promoting" other forms of knowledge, I maintain that astrology also provided a useful epistemological framework for imagining the federal nation by encouraging residents to read the world through a relationship of parts to wholes. The same case can be made for other conventional elements of the almanac that I have identified here as fostering a federal literacy. Although road tables, court schedules, and directional and temporal markers were also common features in European almanacs, these conventions took on a different resonance in the colonies and early nation as a result of the diverse and locally oriented focus of the American texts. American almanacs differed from their European counterparts because of their regional focus and diversity. In contrast to the nationally oriented focus of their English predecessors, the content and organization of American almanacs consistently made readers aware of the local dimensions of their reading experiences. Through these local frameworks, the road tables and court schedules produced a different kind of spatial sensibility for American readers, who were continually asked to situate their local experiences in relation to a larger community. Instead of training readers to recognize the space of the nation in uniform terms, organized around a shared geographic and political center such as London, American almanacs encouraged readers to develop a sense of national or communal space that was centered on the particular experiences and preferences of one community, yet nevertheless oriented in relation to surrounding communities. This ability to foster a dual awareness of one's position as a member of both a local and a larger colonial and, eventually, national community enabled readers to recognize and accept the paradoxical nature of federal unity at a time when the meaning and understanding of such a union was beginning to take hold.

The almanac's success in promoting this plural model of unity is perhaps most apparent in the way that those excluded from the federal union turned to this literary form to argue for their right to be represented as a legitimate and equal part of the nation's diversity. At the end of the eighteenth century, Benjamin Banneker, a free African American writer, surveyor, farmer, and scientist, published a series of almanacs that argued for African American equality. In making these arguments, Banneker drew specifically on the plural structure and reading practices of the almanac to critique the racial limitations of U.S. federal nationalism and situate African Americans within that federal nationalism. Through the pages of his almanacs, Banneker endorsed and celebrated the plural dynamics of the federal union while simultaneously arguing for the rights of African American people to be included within it.

"We Are All of the Same Family": The Almanacs of Benjamin Banneker

Born just outside Baltimore in 1731, Banneker was a free, self-educated black man who was widely respected as a skilled farmer, scientist, engineer, surveyor, and writer in the early republic. Between 1792 and 1797, Banneker published a series of almanacs that circulated widely in Maryland, Pennsylvania, Delaware, and Virginia. By carefully framing and marketing his almanacs as the work of "a sable descendent of Africa," Banneker used this literary genre to assert the equal rights and citizenship of African Americans at a time when the United States was beginning to sharply limit their rights and roles in the federal nation.

Although he lived his entire life as a free man, Banneker was acutely aware of the precarious and limited dimensions of his freedom. As the grandson of a free white woman and a former slave, Banneker's mixed-race heritage complicated his family's free status because Maryland law prohibited interracial marriage. The Bannekers lived in relatively isolated terms for many years to avoid attracting attention, although, over time, the family improved their status by purchasing property, which provided a clear legal record of their freedom.[72] As a result of this stability, Benjamin attended school for a few years where his teachers quickly recognized his exceptional abilities, although the needs of the family farm ended his formal schooling in the early 1740s. Banneker continued to educate himself by borrowing books and keeping extensive farm records that allowed him to make scientific inquiries involving botany, crop rotation, and irrigation.[73] Banneker also devised useful improvements for tools and equipment, and in 1753 he designed and built a wooden clock that earned him a widespread reputation as a local prodigy who was often consulted for advice on matters related to farming, mathematics, and engineering.[74]

Banneker's accomplishments coincided with a broader shift in the status of African Americans in eastern Maryland and the country at large in the late eighteenth century. Even though Maryland remained a slaveholding society, the region surrounding Baltimore and the Eastern Shore became more open and welcoming for African Americans due to the influence of a growing Quaker population.[75] In 1762 the Maryland Yearly Meeting of Friends declared buying or selling slaves to be a disownable offense, and the antislavery writings of John Woolman and Anthony Benezet circulated widely throughout the region, promoting not just abolition but equal rights and treatment for African Americans. The outbreak of the American Revolution likewise seemed to offer African Americans a chance to acquire greater rights and opportunities, and many black Americans readily embraced the Revolutionary rhetoric of liberty, equality, and just representation, believing that the United States would, as Charles Cerami writes, "bring freedom for the slaves and a new status for all blacks."[76] Banneker strongly supported the Revolution on these grounds, and he was deeply impressed by the "true and invaluable doctrine" stated in the Declaration of Independence "'that all men are created equal; that they are endowed by their Creator with certain unalienable rights,'" believing, as he would later write to Thomas Jefferson, that the new nation would live up to its founding principles by extending equal rights and citizenship to African Americans.[77]

These expectations, however, were followed by immediate disappointments as the United States passed laws that sharply restricted the rights of African Americans after the war. Despite the promises posed by the nation's founding rhetoric of pluralism and equality, race became a more visible and exclusionary determinant in defining U.S. rights and citizenship during the 1780s and 1790s, and these limitations were particularly evident in the state of Maryland.[78] Under colonial law, Maryland had actually granted free black men the same rights as free white men, including the right to vote, own property, and file a lawsuit. As Maryland's population of free blacks expanded after the Revolution, the state's white residents, fearful of losing their dominant authority, imposed new limitations on them. In 1783 the Maryland legislature passed a law that rescinded the rights of free black residents to vote, hold office, testify against white people, or "enjoy any other rights of a freeman, other than to hold property and to obtain redress in law"; other states passed similar laws throughout the 1780s and 1790s.[79] Delaware restricted voting rights for African Americans in 1792 and Massachusetts in 1795, while Connecticut prohibited free blacks from settling in the state in 1784, followed by New Jersey in 1786.[80] Publications promoting African American inferiority also began circulating widely, most notably Thomas Jefferson's *Notes on the State of Virginia* (1785), which argued that "the blacks, whether originally a distinct race, or made distinct by time and circumstances, are inferior to the whites in the endowments both of body and mind."[81] Such arguments provided a convenient logic for restricting the rights of African Americans in the new republic, giving rise to a definition of citizenship that was increasingly determined by race.

It was in the context of these changes that Banneker first began to think about publishing an almanac. Although he had never been a political activist, the contradictions between the federal rhetoric of the early United States and the racial restrictions imposed on African Americans spurred Banneker to take a public stance. For Banneker, an almanac offered an ideal means for showcasing the intellectual strengths of African Americans since calculating an almanac took considerable scientific, mathematical, and literary expertise. The value and equality of such an almanac could easily be determined by comparing his work with others, allowing him to present his arguments for racial equality to a large audience in clear and accessible terms. Banneker began drafting his first manuscript in 1790, with the goal of producing an almanac calculated for 1791.

Banneker's work on the 1791 almanac was interrupted, however, when Andrew Ellicott invited him to join his team surveying the new national capital, known as the "Federal Territory," an experience that further strengthened his desire to challenge the principles of exclusion embedded in the federal nation.[82] Banneker was a close friend of the Ellicotts, a prominent Quaker family who ran a successful milling operation on the Patapsco River and were strong advocates for African American rights and abolition. Andrew Ellicott's decision to hire Banneker for the survey of the national capital was both a practical and a political move. Ellicott was well acquainted with Banneker's skills as a surveyor and had great confidence in his mathematical abilities. He was also keenly aware of the political significance of having Banneker help survey the capital for a nation that celebrated diversity but did not recognize his equality. Washington and his advisers wanted the new capital district to serve as a symbolic space that embodied the plural principles of the federal government, and the subsequent design by Charles L'Enfant was meant to serve as an "allegory of the Constitution" where the different constituencies of the nation could be represented within a unified whole. The press responded favorably to L'Enfant's design, which structured the city as a network of diagonal avenues that created numerous parks and squares, praising the city for its emphasis on diversity and harmony. "A variety of elegant prospects are produced," noted a widely reprinted "Description of the City of Washington," which extolled the city's many public squares that "may be appropriated to the different States composing the Union."[83]

By hiring Banneker for the survey of this "Federal Territory," Ellicott wanted to illuminate a critical oversight in this federal plurality by highlighting the presence and contributions of the nation's African American residents. Although he did not voice this argument directly, Ellicott's insistence on placing Banneker on the survey team at equal pay shows his interest in criticizing the nation's unequal treatment of African Americans and asserting a more inclusive model of community that justly mirrored the symbolic pluralism of the city's design.[84] The political implications of Ellicott's decision were noted by the *Georgetown Weekly Ledger*, which reported that the survey team for the Federal Territory included "an Ethiopian whose abilities as a surveyor and astronomer clearly prove that Mr. Jefferson's conclusion that this race of men were void of mental endowments was without foundation."[85]

Banneker served with distinction on the federal survey, where he operated the astronomical clock whose data was used to refine and correct the survey measurements. Despite challenges posed by weather and difficult terrain, his calculations were detailed and accurate, and his work earned the admiration of his colleagues. As Ellicott's daughter later reported, "Banneker's deportment throughout the whole of this engagement, secured their respect, and there is good authority for believing that his endowments led the commissioners to overlook the color of his skin to converse with them freely and enjoy the clearness and originality of his remarks on various subjects."[86] As they surveyed a city that was supposed to celebrate the nation's diversity, however, Banneker and his colleagues were continually confronted with the limitations of that federal vision as Banneker—whose work was so crucial for the survey—was not represented equally within the United States.

After completing his work on the survey in April 1791, Banneker returned to his almanac with a bolder critical agenda. Determined to use his almanac to promote racial equality and citizenship for African Americans, Banneker sought the support of antislavery societies in publishing it, and he ended up working closely with James Pemberton, president of the Pennsylvania Abolition Society, who helped Banneker secure printers in Philadelphia, Baltimore, and Alexandria who were eager to highlight Banneker's race and equality in promoting the almanac while also expanding its circulation.

Calculated for 1792, *Benjamin Banneker's Pennsylvania, Delaware, Maryland and Virginia Almanack and Ephemeris* presents its arguments for racial equality by asserting both its difference and similarity to other U.S. almanacs. All editions for the 1792 almanac open by identifying Banneker's race, stating that the almanac had been "calculated by a sable descendent of Africa." This statement of racial difference is followed by an immediate assertion of the almanac's equality, which "evinces, to demonstration, that mental powers and endowments are not the exclusive excellence of white people, but that the rays of science may alike illuminate the Minds of men of every clime (however they may differ in the colour of their skin)." The almanac also included a letter from James McHenry, a prominent Maryland statesman who, again, asserts Banneker's racial difference by reporting that "his father was an African and his mother the offspring of African parents," followed by another statement of equality. "I consider this Negro as fresh proof that the powers of the mind are disconnected with the colour of the skin," writes McHenry, who goes on to argue that Banneker's almanac should serve as incontestable "proof" that "the system that would assign to these degraded blacks an origin different from the whites . . . must be relinquished."[87] Through these opening materials, Banneker's almanac creates a critical framework recognizing African Americans as distinct but equal citizens whose rights should not be limited in the United States.

Although these opening pages highlight Banneker's race as a distinguishing feature of the almanac, the rest of its content is virtually indistinguishable from any other U.S. almanac. Banneker's almanac follows all the standard structures and conventions. His calendar pages feature the usual information about sunrises, sunsets, astronomical readings, and weather predictions, and his literary content features the typical variety of essays and anecdotes, including a short description of the solar system, philosophical reflections on "the Swiftness of Time," and "The Balance of Happiness," several poems, a humorous excerpt from the *London Magazine* on "The Origin of the Grey Mare's Being the Better Horse," and remedies for illness and injuries. The almanac concludes with the expected list of court schedules, road tables, and charts of interest and exchange rates. If anything, Banneker's almanac places slightly more emphasis on the federal structure of the United States than other almanacs. At the end of each calendar page, for instance, he provides the date when each state was founded, reminding readers of the composite dimensions of the union, and, at the end of the almanac, he also lists all the branches of the government and the names of the senators and representatives for every state. Banneker's decision to include this information shows his interest in emphasizing the plural dimensions of the federal nation, an emphasis that supports his claims for racial equality and inclusion.

The conventional dimensions of Banneker's almanac were strategic. By following the traditional form and content of other U.S. almanacs, Banneker could clearly assert the equality of his work since it could be easily compared to almanacs compiled by white authors. After clearly identifying himself as a black writer on the first page, the subsequent equality of the almanac's content prevented his readers from interpreting his racial difference as a sign of inferiority. Instead, the juxtaposition of Banneker's racial difference with the indistinguishable dimensions of the almanac's content made it easier for U.S. readers to imagine African Americans as equal members of the national community. The fact that the almanac itself was a literary form that encouraged readers to recognize the nation as a plural union of differences further reinforced Banneker's arguments for racial equality and inclusion. Since U.S. almanacs already represented the United States as a union of differences, the almanac's form suggested that extending this plurality to include African American residents should not seem disruptive or threatening.

Only one article in Banneker's almanac addresses race in specific terms, a short essay excerpted from the *Columbian Magazine* that argues for the abolition of slavery. This article is attributed to David Rittenhouse, a noted scientist and fellow compiler of almanacs who, as noted on the title page, had personally verified the calculations in Banneker's almanac. Within his article, Rittenhouse condemns the practice of slavery as a violation of the United States' national principles, arguing that this "inhuman traffic" is particularly reprehensible "in a country, too, where the natural rights of men are perfectly understood and where the civil rights of the citizens are better defined and secured than in any other."[88] By calling out this contradiction between the United States' commitment to equality and pluralism and the nation's refusal to extend those rights to African Americans, Rittenhouse articulates the same argument that the form and content of Banneker's almanac were meant to convey. In contrast to Banneker, who must rely on his readers' interpretations of the almanac to convey this argument, Rittenhouse can state this argument explicitly, and in this regard, Rittenhouse's article highlights the different subject positions of these writers, as well as the different literary strategies they could use to express their arguments for racial equality. By including Rittenhouse's claims as part of his almanac, Banneker also strengthens his almanac's arguments for equality by showing how these views were shared by other citizens in the nation. Rather than representing a single voice for African American equality, Banneker's almanac provides a plural assertion of that equality, once again reinforcing the federal dynamics of his argument.

Although Banneker's almanac presents a compelling argument for African American equality and inclusion on its own, he took steps to magnify its impact by sending a handwritten copy to Thomas Jefferson, along with a letter explaining his reasons for doing so. Banneker's letter is a rhetorical tour de force that, unlike the implied dimensions of his almanac's critique, aggressively confronts Jefferson with the contradiction between the United States' principles of equality and pluralism and its practices of racial oppression.[89] Instead of relying exclusively on his almanac to present this argument, Banneker begins by asking Jefferson to examine his own writing in the Declaration of Independence, where he defined the United States as a nation that recognized "'that all men are created equal; that they are endowed by their Creator with certain unalienable rights.'"[90] Banneker goes on to denounce the United States for failing to live up to these founding principles, expressing his anger and frustration that a nation "impressed with proper ideas of the great violation of liberty and the free possession of those blessings" should "at the same time counteract" these principles by "detaining by fraud and violence so numerous a part of my brethren under groaning captivity and cruel oppression" (8). For Banneker, the hypocrisy of the United States—"that you should at the same time be found guilty of that most criminal act, which you professedly detested in others, with respect to yourselves" (8)—is just as damaging to the nation as the institution of slavery itself. In making this argument, Banneker characterizes the racist practices of the United States as a violation not just of the rights of African Americans but of the nation's own values and identity, and he pushes his audience to recognize African American equality as a means of restoring their own commitment to the federal union. "Sir, I have long been convinced, that if your love for yourselves and for those inestimable laws, which preserved to you the rights of human nature, was founded on sincerity, you could not be solicitous that every individual, of whatever rank or distinction, might with you equally enjoy the blessings thereof" (5).

By identifying the critical contrast between the nation's foundational values and its current views and policies toward African Americans, Banneker's letter to Jefferson illuminates the racial limits of federal nationalism. Although the United States was founded on the principles of just and equal representation—principles that should produce a racially heterogeneous national union—Banneker criticizes the ways that the United States only extends those rights and protections to its white residents. In place of this racially restricted practice of federal nationalism, Banneker pushes Jefferson to embrace a more diverse conception of federal pluralism where racial differences are represented as a legitimate part of the nation's federal dynamics. "I am of the African race and in that color which is natural to them of the deepest dye," he informs Jefferson, and, as a black man, Banneker asserts his right to "tast[e] of the fruition of those blessings which proceed from that free and unequaled liberty with which you are favored" (6). As far as Banneker is concerned, the United States can and should include racial difference as part of its federal identity, producing a nation that affirms "however variable we may be in society or religion, however diversified in situation or color, we are all of the same family" (5).

It is only at the very end of his letter that Banneker finally references his almanac, offering it to Jefferson as "a present ... I humbly request you will favorably receive" (9–10). Noting his almanac's "correctness and accuracy," Banneker intends for his work to provide concrete evidence of African American equality, which is why he emphasizes that he has sent Jefferson a copy written "in my own hand writing" (9).[91] In the end, though, Banneker's letter to Jefferson suggests that the burden of proof for asserting African American equality should not rest solely with the nation's black residents. Instead, the federal principles of the United States should make all citizens responsible for ensuring the equal representation of African American residents. For Banneker, including black Americans as equal members of the federal nation should be a national fact rather than a matter of debate.

The long-term effects of Banneker's arguments are difficult to determine. Jefferson sent him a brief reply where he stated his willingness to consider Banneker's arguments, without providing a definitive response to them. "No body wishes more than I do to see such proofs as you exhibit, that nature has given to our black brethren talents equal to those of the colors of other men," he writes. "I can add with truth that no body wishes more ardently to see a good system commenced for raising the condition, both of their body and mind, to what it ought to be" (11). Jefferson sidesteps, however, the issue of addressing racial equality at the national level, not contesting Banneker's claims but neatly avoiding them. He concludes his letter by promising to forward Banneker's almanac to the Academy of Sciences at Paris, effectively shifting his arguments about racial equality outside of the United States and reframing his work as a matter for intellectual and scientific inquiry, rather than placing it in the political sphere.[92]

By publicizing this exchange, however, Banneker ensured that his arguments received considerable public attention. He published both letters in a pamphlet that became an immediate best seller, going through two editions in 1792, and these letters were also reprinted and quoted in other magazines and almanacs throughout the 1790s, including the *Universal Asylum and Columbian Magazine*, the *Providence Gazette and Country Journal*, and *Poor Richard Revived: Being the Farmer's Diary; or, Barber & Southwick's Albany Almanac*. Responses to Banneker's almanac and exchange with Jefferson were mixed. In the North, antislavery societies and abolitionists embraced Banneker's arguments, praising both the letters and his almanac for publicly affirming that African Americans "are equally capable of improvements with yourselves."[93] Readers in the southern states reacted less favorably, rejecting Banneker's claims of equality and, in the case of the letters, condemning Jefferson's willingness to "fraterniz[e] with negroes, writing them complimentary epistles ... [and] congratulating them on the evidences of their genius."[94] These varied opinions demonstrate the widespread impact of Banneker's work, which, for a time, prompted a significant national discussion about racial equality in the United States.

Banneker's influence on the racial politics of the nation, however, was short lived. Following the publicity surrounding his first almanac, Banneker continued to pursue his arguments for racial equality in his second almanac published in 1793, although there were significant regional variations in its content. The Philadelphia edition of Banneker's 1793 almanac was dedicated, explicitly, to the subjects of racial equality and abolition. Nearly all the articles in the Philadelphia almanac address issues of race in some way, either by criticizing slavery, arguing for equal rights and education, or promoting peaceful and egalitarian approaches for resolving community conflicts, and these topics would have found a receptive audience among the numerous Quaker and abolitionist communities in Pennsylvania.[95] The content of Banneker's Baltimore edition, however, was much more muted in its treatment of race. Although the Baltimore almanac opens by reprinting Banneker's exchange with Jefferson, the rest of the almanac offers no additional commentary on matters related to race or slavery, focusing instead on moral tales and household advice before concluding with the conventional road tables, court schedules, and interest rates.[96] This difference in content suggests that Banneker's Maryland audience was no longer as receptive to arguments about racial equality as it had been the year before, a condition that was likely influenced by growing concerns about the rising number of free blacks settling in eastern Maryland.

By the time Banneker published his 1794 almanac, there were no references or arguments related to racial equality or slavery in his work at all, and he would continue to avoid these topics in his remaining almanacs. Several factors can explain this shift in focus. Banneker's work faced greater competition as more almanacs entered the market in the mid-1790s, which may have made him less inclined to engage in controversial topics. The passage of a national Fugitive Slave Law in 1793 may also have heightened his concerns about publishing arguments for African American rights and equality because such positions could be interpreted in criminal terms. News of the ongoing Haitian revolution, which was orchestrated by self-liberated slaves, stoked further fears and suspicions about the status and significance of African Americans in the United States. All of these issues would have made it very difficult for Banneker, as a black man, to continue to advocate for racial equality as publicly as he had once done, and his silence on this topic in these later editions says much about the nation's increasingly restrictive and oppressive view of racial differences by the end of the eighteenth century. Banneker published his final almanac in 1797 and retired to his farm where he lived until his death in 1806. The day of his funeral, his home caught fire, destroying a great deal of his written records and manuscripts, which has made it difficult for scholars to examine the full extent of his political and scientific engagements over the course of his life. His almanacs, however, stand out as a powerful record of his efforts to challenge the racial limits and exclusions of U.S. federalism, while also illuminating the powerful role that almanacs played in managing and promoting the terms of the nation's pluralism.

CHAPTER 3

Reading Differences Differently
Magazines, Satire, and Federal Literacy

> For my part, I entertain a high idea of the utility of periodical publications: insomuch that I could heartily desire copies of the Museum and Magazines as well as common Gazettes might be spread through every city, town, and village in America. I consider such easy vehicles of knowledge more happily calculated than any other to preserve the liberty, stimulate the industry, and meliorate the morals of an enlightened and free people.
>
> ——GEORGE WASHINGTON, "Letter to the Printer of *The American Museum*"

If almanacs laid the foundation for federal literacy, magazines were the medium for imagining its future. Washington's "high idea of the utility of periodical publications" illuminates their national importance in the post-Revolutionary republic. Characterized as "easy vehicles of knowledge," magazines were primary agents in the ideology of diffusion that defined the politics of print nationalism in the early United States.[1] By thus circulating information "through every city, town, and village in America," magazines were seen as a crucial means for fostering nationalist sentiments and drawing citizens together as they participated in a widespread literary exchange.

More than simply distributing information, magazines were also valued for the variety of information they dispersed. As evident from their name, which refers to a storehouse or repository of goods, magazines were always meant to provide readers with a diverse collection of topics and materials, but U.S. editors took this miscellaneous form to new heights in an effort to appeal to the expansive interests and locations of their national audiences. Compared to their British counterparts, U.S. magazines covered a much wider range of topics and styles, providing readers with "a universe or smorgasbord of discursive modes and texts."[2] Supporters of early U.S. magazines praised them for the "variety of [their] exertions," which "opened a way to every kind of inquiry and communication."³ "The intelligence and discussion contained in them are very various and extensive ... which, in a certain degree, hath enlarged the public understanding," remarked a 1790 editorial published in the *New York Magazine*, while the *Massachusetts Magazine* likened its varied contents to "a rich treasure, constantly accumulating, supplied with new veins [that are] continually opening."⁴ "A Magazine," asserts another, "ought literally to be a *shop* where stuffs of all conceivable or vendible kinds ... should be offered for sale, wrought into all textures, dyed of all colors, and cut into all shapes."⁵

The variety of these magazines made them particularly suited for supporting federal nationalism. A magazine was actually the source of the United States' federal motto, *E pluribus unum*, which originally appeared on the title page of the *Gentleman's Magazine*, a popular British periodical that was widely read in the British American colonies. John Adams, Benjamin Franklin, Thomas Jefferson, and Pierre Eugène du Simitière selected this phrase as the motto for the national motto from the magazine's heading, believing that its unifying sentiment provided an excellent model for representing the new federal union.⁶ By introducing citizens to a variety of topics, writing styles, and opinions and presenting that variety in a form that was unified and productive, magazines helped citizens become more comfortable with a nation that was likewise composed of many different people, places, and perspectives. "Radically inclusive yet rigorously organized, polyphonous yet unified," notes Jared Gardner, magazines provided a useful "metaphor for national unity."⁷ The fact that editors frequently used terms such as "museum," "repository," "bouquet," and "cabinet" to describe the content of their magazines further illustrates their federal focus by evoking objects that were composed of different materials, with practical, profitable, and secure results.

In addition to their miscellaneous form, early U.S. magazines supported federal nationalism through the literary works they published. Magazines led the way in publishing the first literary essays, short fiction, novels, and poetry written by U.S. authors. Of the many different works featured in these publications, satire was one of the most popular and prominent genres.⁸ The eighteenth century was the golden age of literary satire, and U.S. writers readily embraced satire as a powerful mode of political and social critique. During the late 1780s and early 1790s, most U.S. magazines published at least one, if not several, satiric essays, poems, or stories per issue. The *American Museum* even had a special literary section devoted specifically to "Satire and Humor" in its 1788 publications.⁹ Three of the most popular literary works of the post-Revolutionary era were works of satire, and all three were published serially in U.S. magazines, namely, Jeremy Belknap's *The Foresters*, which appeared in the *Columbian Magazine* between June 1787 and April 1788, *The Anarchiad*, which was collectively written by John

Trumbull, Joel Barlow, Lemuel Hopkins, and David Humphreys and published in the *New-Haven Gazette and Connecticut Magazine* between October 1786 and September 1787, and John Trumbull's *M'Fingal*, which was published in multiple U.S. magazines between 1787 and 1788, including the *American Museum*, the *Massachusetts Centinel*, and the *New-Haven Gazette*.

Just as the structure of the magazine helped citizens recognize and embrace the federal structure of the nation, the formal dimensions of satire had a similar effect. Satire is inherently a dialogic form, where significance is produced through the expression of many different voices, styles, and alternating perspectives.[10] Rather than relying on a single, definitive voice, satire forces readers to engage with multiple and often competing viewpoints and levels of meaning as the literal significance of the text often differs from its figurative implications. The experience of reading satire asks people to recognize that a text representing multiple and conflicting ideas and positions can still form a cohesive and coherent work, and by providing citizens with a means of experiencing this unusual relationship, satire was another literary form that supported the United States' own plural union.

The Foresters, *The Anarchiad*, and *M'Fingal* illustrate the ways that magazines and satire contributed to the development of a federal literacy. Critics have examined the federal dimensions of these literary forms before, focusing specifically on their engagement with the ideology of the Federalist Party. The authors of *The Foresters*, *The Anarchiad*, and *M'Fingal* were all committed Federalists, and these works, which were all published or reprinted during the Constitutional Convention, have typically been read as partisan arguments promoting a strong, centralized government.[11] The editors and contributors for most of the leading early U.S. magazines were also affiliated with the Federalist Party, most notably Noah Webster, Matthew Carey, and Josiah Meigs, and the content of these magazines often reflected Federalist views by promoting a strong central government and supporting the establishment of a consolidated banking system and a strong military.[12] Gardner has recently explored the Federalist dimensions of early U.S. magazines in a different light by focusing not just on the political views of their editors but on the politics of the editorial function itself. By "discriminat[ing], arrang[ing], and organiz[ing] the material so that it will be more usefully and agreeably consumed," magazine editors served as a "centralized authority" that brought order and stability to a potentially chaotic literary form, a role that, for Gardner, closely aligns the magazine with the model of governance embraced by the Federalist Party.[13]

While early U.S. magazines and works of satire are clearly invested in Federalist politics and ideology, I am less interested in exploring the partisan motives and affiliations of their authors and editors than in examining the role that these literary forms ascribe to their readers. While authors and editors played a crucial role in shaping the way citizens encountered the material presented in magazines and satire, these literary forms also required readers to take responsibility for producing order from their diverse contents. To this end, this chapter examines the federal politics of the magazine and the works of satire published within them, focusing specifically on the demands and expectations these texts placed on their readers.

An editorial essay printed in both the *New York Magazine* and the *Massachusetts Magazine* focuses specifically on the effects that magazines were meant to have on their readers. The experience of reading a magazine was likened to that of a man who, "after the fatigues of the day are over, may thus sit down in his elbow chair and, together with his wife and family, be introduced, as it were, into a spacious coffee-house." Within this imagined space of encounter, the magazine becomes a unifying medium where "men of all ranks and of all nations, however widely disjointed from each other, may be said to be brought together here to converse at their ease, without ceremony or restraint."[14] This description makes a point of noting how magazines can produce unity even when its contents are "widely disjointed from each other." Significantly, the experience of reading a magazine is not intended to establish points of similarity. The goal, rather, is simply to bring diverse points together for sincere consideration "without ceremony or restraint"; by producing this reading experience, magazines helped foster a federal conception of unity where differences could be represented and acknowledged without producing instability or conflict.

A significant difference emerges here between the experience of encountering the miscellaneous content in the magazine and encountering the different materials of an almanac. Almanacs also presented readers with a wide range of material, most of which was encountered selectively as readers chose the information they needed for different uses. As a result, almanacs tended to privilege the immediate interests and experiences of their readers, and they fostered a federal conception of unity by enabling residents to situate their distinct interests and circumstances in relation to a larger network of equally diverse communities. In contrast, the miscellaneous content of a magazine was meant to be read comprehensively by audiences who had the leisure time to reflect on the magazine's varied contents. To this end, magazines encouraged readers to recognize not so much their unique circumstances but the diversity of the nation as a whole. If almanacs helped readers recognize themselves as *one* among many, magazines took the next step of helping readers to see how a nation of *many* could be recognized as one.

Satire similarly encourages readers to see how the representation of many different views and perspectives can still lead readers to a single, unified conclusion. The satiric form of *The Foresters*, *The Anarchiad*, and *M'Fingal*, which were prominently featured in the leading post-Revolutionary magazines, depict people and places beset by disorder and chaos. At the level of form, they present this chaos using a diverse array of rhetorical arguments and perspectives. Despite this expansive and seemingly disordered structure, satires use these varied forms and voices to convey a unified and coherent argument, provided, of course, that their readers are attentive enough to interpret the formal features of the satire correctly. By making readers aware of their own role in producing the significance of the text, these popular satires not only helped readers recognize how differences could produce a stable and productive union. They also showed how this unity depends on the way that citizens choose to interpret those differences. As the federal structure of the United States was debated and put into place through the Constitution, magazines and literary satires helped citizens develop a sophisticated and effective federal literacy by training them how to read and interpret differences in ways that would support, rather than destabilize, a composite model of union.

The Genius of Foederate America: The *Columbian Magazine* and *The Foresters*

Founded in Philadelphia in 1786, the *Columbian Magazine* was the first post-Revolutionary U.S. magazine to earn a national reputation and gain lasting success. The *Columbian Magazine* was published continuously between October 1786 and December 1792, making it the longest-running U.S. magazine until it was eclipsed by the *Massachusetts Magazine* in 1796. It also had the largest circulation of any eighteenth-century American periodical, including nearly 1,500 subscribers over the course of its run.[15]

The *Columbian Magazine* began as joint venture by five Philadelphia printers, editors, and businessmen: Matthew Carey, William Spotswood, Charles Cist, James Trenchard, and Thomas Seddon. Carey soon left the partnership to start his own magazine, the *American Museum*, in 1787, and control of the *Columbian Magazine* devolved to William Spotswood and, for a brief time, James Trenchard, who, in conjunction with Francis Hopkinson and Alexander James Dallas, also served as the magazine's editors. While its management was somewhat tumultuous, the magazine retained a consistent focus, which was to foster the "native industry and the useful arts" of the United States.[16] Like all periodicals of the time, the *Columbian Magazine* reprinted work from European publications, but its editors made a concerted effort to publish work by U.S. authors, promising to provide its readers with "as great a variety of original essays, instructive and entertaining, as the extent of the work will admit."[17]

Variety was a hallmark of the *Columbian Magazine*, which published essays on politics, agricultural and business ventures, education, and moral philosophy, as well as letters, biographical sketches, works of history, local and national legislation, and literary reviews. The *Columbian Magazine* also covered events taking place throughout the nation, and each issue included a section titled "American Intelligence" or "Domestic Intelligence" that featured short articles about political, social, scientific, and infrastructural developments in the various states. The *Columbian Magazine* also published engravings and descriptions of notable sites and attractions throughout the nation, including the state houses of Pennsylvania, Maryland, and New York, Virginia's Natural Bridge and Passaic Falls in New Jersey, and sketches of local curiosities, such as an unusual set of fossils found along the Ohio River. In this regard, the *Columbian Magazine* not only served the varied interests of its readers, it also helped them gain a wider knowledge of the nation as a whole.

The *Columbian Magazine* also far outpaced the other magazines of this period by publishing the work of U.S. writers. Within its literary section titled "The Columbian Parnassiad," the magazine featured the work of poets such as Lemuel Hopkins, Joel Barlow, and David Humphreys, as well as the fiction, poetry, and essays of Francis Hopkinson, who also served as editor between 1787 and 1788. The *Columbian Magazine* also published women writers such as Sarah Graeme Fergusson and Ann Young Smith, and it featured some of the first serial novels as well, including *Amelia, or The Faithless Briton* (1787) and *The History of Miranda and Cleander: An American Tale* (1790–91).[18]

The run of the *Columbian Magazine* also coincided with the drafting, ratification, and implementation of the new federal Constitution, and the magazine was deeply invested in covering the process of composing and debating the nation's federal structure and principles. Articles and letters published in the magazine gave voice to many of the central issues involving the revised federal structure of the United States, particularly regarding the respective powers of the states and the central government, and the need for a national bank and centralized military.[19] An early frontispiece for the magazine exemplifies the magazine's interest in representing the federal structure and identity of the nation by depicting "The Genius of Foederate America" as a woman surrounded by images of federal unity, including a harp, the federal edifice, and the national seal with its collection of stars, striped shield, and quiver of arrows.[20]

As testament to its commitment to the revised federal nation, the *Columbian Magazine* printed a complete copy of the Constitution in its September 1787 issue, along with a letter from George Washington, who presented the document to readers for "the consideration of the United States." Washington encouraged readers to consider the central challenge that the delegates faced in drafting the document, noting that "it is at all times difficult to draw with precision the line between those rights which must be surrendered and those which must be reserved," and he asked citizens to keep this difficulty in mind as they evaluated the Constitution in the hopes that they would interpret it as an acceptable means of balancing the interest of "our Union" with the "situation, extent, habits, and particular interests" of the states.[21]

The *Columbian Magazine* embraced Washington's push to think critically about the complicated relationship between the states and the central government in the new federal system. The magazine published extensive coverage of the state ratifying conventions, highlighting the varying interpretations of local and national sovereignty that emerged in these debates. Although the editors of the *Columbian Magazine* had Federalist leanings, the magazine tried to represent both Federalist and Anti-Federalist arguments, a strategy that caused problems when Benjamin Rush, a prominent Federalist, took issue with the magazine's efforts to represent Anti-Federalist arguments at the Pennsylvania ratifying convention. Accusing the magazine of bias, Rush argued that the *Columbian Magazine* had deliberately "misrepresent[ed] the proceedings and speeches" to privilege the Anti-Federalist positions, which led many prominent Federalists to cancel their subscriptions, causing considerable financial hardship for the magazine.[22] The speed and severity of the Federalists' response to the *Columbian Magazine*'s content says a great deal about the power U.S. magazines had over public opinion and their influence on the ratification debates. For many citizens in the early 1780s, the future of the federal nation seemed very much to lie in the pages of U.S. magazines.

In addition to its coverage of the ratifying conventions, the *Columbian Magazine* engaged with the politics of the newly proposed Constitution through its literary publications. Between June 1787 and April 1788, neatly coinciding with the drafting of the Constitution and the major ratifying conventions, the *Columbian Magazine* published a work of comic historical fiction titled *The Foresters*. Crafted as a satirical allegory, *The Foresters* retells the nation's colonial history by depicting John Bull's bumbling and misguided attempts to settle an expansive Forest, which becomes inhabited by a motley collection of Foresters who represent each of the colonies. The narrative was written by Jeremy Belknap, a minister and frequent contributor to the *Columbian Magazine* who was already a well-known writer of history thanks to the publication of the first volume of his *History of New Hampshire* in 1784. Belknap was widely praised for his meticulous research methods, which relied on a detailed analysis of primary documents, as opposed to privileging oral and religious traditions, earning him a reputation as one of the new nation's leading historians. The humorous, allegorical rendering of history in *The Foresters* marked a significant departure from Belknap's usual style, which accounts, in part, for his decision to publish the work anonymously. "I must not be known as the author," he wrote in a letter to a friend, "for I shall take great liberty and tell some sad truths in pretty coarse language."[23]

Coarse and fictionalized though it may be, Belknap's comic depiction of U.S. colonial history presents a creative critical engagement with the issues posed by the new federal Constitution. At first glance, *The Foresters* might seem to be more interested in maligning Great Britain than tackling federal politics. By poking fun at the foolish behavior of John Bull and his disastrous policies, this narrative can easily be read as a harsh critique of British colonial politics, but there is more at stake here than just an anti-British hatchet job. At the beginning of the work, the narrator invites readers to compare this story with the United States' present conditions. "We need not be surprised if we find a family likeness prevailing among the persons whose history we are about to recite, most of whom were formerly residents in Mr. Bull's house."[24] Through its satiric representation of colonial history, *The Foresters* invites readers to think critically about the parallels between the United States' colonial experiences and their present status as an independent nation. In describing the colonial Forest, *The Foresters* depicts a society that is defined by variety and local autonomy, but also subject, at times, to a controlling central government. Sometimes, the variety and local autonomies within the Forest are beneficial and the central government is harmful, while at other times, the reverse is true. By prompting readers to consider the benefits of maintaining a diverse and locally controlled community, as well as the risks involved in supporting those principles, *The Foresters* served as a useful allegory for considering the structure of the new federal nation.

Previous studies of *The Foresters* have argued that the narrative presents a Federalist argument by warning citizens about the dangers of local sovereignty and emphasizing the need for a stronger, centralized government.[25] While some aspects of the text do seem to argue for consolidated national authority, at other times the narrative seems to criticize consolidated forms of government as exploitive and impractical. Ultimately, *The Foresters* does not align neatly with either a Federalist or Anti-Federalist position. Instead of trying to advance a particular partisan agenda, *The Foresters* is more interested in the role that citizens need to play to support a stable federal union. In the end, *The Foresters* argues that the federal United States will be better served by attending to the interpretive habits and strategies of its citizens, rather than arguing over the specific structure of its government. In making this claim, this satire emphasizes the importance of federal literacy in the early United States, as well as the federal importance of the nation's literary forms.

The nine installments of *The Foresters* cover the colonial history of the United States from the founding of Virginia through the passage of the Stamp Act.[26]

The narrative begins with promising prospects as all of the Foresters leave England to pursue a future where they will have the liberty to live "in their own way."[27] The Foresters are named for the dominant products or characteristics of their settlements: Walter Pipeweed (Virginia), John Codline (Massachusetts), Humphrey Ploughshare (Connecticut), Roger Carrier (Rhode Island), Peter Bull-Frog (New York), Robert Lumber (New Hampshire), Julius Caesar (New Jersey), William Broadbrim (Pennsylvania), Frederick Marygold (Maryland), Peter Pitch (North Carolina), Charles Indigo (South Carolina), George Trusty (Georgia), and Casimir (Delaware). These names and their attendant significations were provided for readers in a formal table in the narrative's eighth installment.[28]

In describing the Foresters' settlements, the satire moves back and forth between representing the productive dimensions of their diversity and the problems that local variety and sovereignty can cause. Walter Pipeweed (Virginia) establishes the first settlement where he cultivates "a certain plant of narcotic quality" that is unique to the soil and climate of his chosen location.[29] Pleased by his ability to earn a successful living "in his own way," Pipeweed invites his friends to leave England and establish their own settlements according to their respective inclinations. He specifically emphasizes the "charms of liberty" in the Forest, where each will be free to manage his own livelihood and adopt "whatever posture was most easy to him." The result is a collection of new settlements that represent a range of different industries and characteristics, depending on their location. John Codline (Massachusetts) "had taken a great fancy to fishing and thought he could wholly or chiefly subsist by it," while Humphry Ploughshare (Connecticut) "had a mind to farm."[30] Peter Pitch's settlement (North Carolina) got its name "from collecting the resinous juice of the numerous pines which grew thereabouts," and Charles Indigo (South Carolina) capitalizes on his settlement's "wet and miry" conditions to cultivate indigo and rice. Other settlements are defined not so much by their products but by the philosophies of their founding leaders. William Broadbrim (Pennsylvania) chooses a "level piece of ground" where "persons of all nations and characters [may] come and take shelter."[31] Roger Carrier (Rhode Island) likewise establishes a settlement known for its variety and tolerance, where "it was a rule in his family not to refuse any who should come."[32]

When the Foresters are left to manage their settlements as they see fit, they all do very well. Each capitalizes on the strengths of their local conditions to produce goods that are best suited for their specific settlement, and, rather than producing competition, their different productions create cooperative relationships that benefit the security and stability of the whole. Robert Lumber (New Hampshire), whose settlement specializes in the production of wood, builds a sawmill to supply his neighbors with building materials, and in return they provide him with "powder, shot, and flint and sen[d] hands to help him" to fight the wild animals that plague his settlement.[33] On another occasion, recognizing that they do not have the resources to protect themselves from attack by the Indians on their own, they agree to "form an association for the mutual safety" where each contributes "some from one principle, and some from another."[34] On the basis of these relationships, the Foresters operate as "distant members of a family," where each settlement is clearly defined and separate, yet they are all also bound together by feelings of cooperation, affiliation, and interdependence.[35]

The Foresters' cooperative use of these varied skills and products mirrors Anti-Federalist arguments about the need to represent and protect state interests under the federal government. "All the states have local advantages, and in a considerable degree separate interests. They are, therefore, in a situation to supply each other's wants," argued Agrippa, the pseudonymous author of a series of Anti-Federalist editorials published in the *Massachusetts Gazette* from November 1787 to January 1788.[36] By celebrating these different productions, the Anti-Federalists argued that the states could foster productive and unifying relationships without the control of a central government. "A diversity of produce, wants, and interests produces commerce; and commerce . . . produces friendship," asserted Agrippa, a position that is clearly supported by the unified conditions of the varied Foresters.[37]

The Foresters continues to express its support for local governance and variety in its description of Roger Carrier's settlement. Within this settlement, Carrier "made it a rule in his family not to refuse any who should come, whether lame or blind, short or tall, whether one had two eyes or one, whether they squinted or stammered or limped." His settlement is also defined by "another rule that everyone should bear with the infirmities of his neighbours and help one another as they were able." The first rule ensures that Carrier's settlement is very diverse, containing people with different strengths, weaknesses, interests, and abilities. The second ensures that these diverse residents find ways to collaborate and cooperate with one another, resulting in new forms of productivity. The narrator describes the productive effects of these rules with the following anecdote: "I remember once as I was passing through Roger's plantation I saw one man carrying another on his shoulders, which at first, I thought, a very odd sight; upon coming up to them I perceived that the lower one was blind and the upper one was lame, so as they had but one pair of eyes and one pair of legs between them. The lame man availed himself of the blind man's legs, and he of the other man's eyes, and both went along very well together."[38] Although its results may look "odd," the variety of Carrier's settlement transforms traditional weaknesses into strengths. By representing and supplementing the weaknesses or deficiencies of their neighbors, all of the residents benefit, and these interdependent relationships, in turn, bind the residents closer together.

While the first half of the poem celebrates the local management and successes of these various settlements, *The Foresters* takes a turn when John Bull decides to exercise greater control over them. One of his first interventions occurs in George Trusty's settlement (Georgia), where Bull decides to dictate its productions. Because he needs wine and silk, he informs the settlers that "their business was to cultivate vines and mulberry trees and to manufacture wine and silk," without consulting anyone with knowledge or experience in the area. Bull also issues "strict orders" regarding their day-to-day operations, which include working six days a week, requiring all laborers to transfer their possessions through a male lineage, and "expressly forbidd[ing]" the consumption of grog, all of which depart from previous practices.[39]

Because of these controlling efforts, the settlement begins to fail miserably. The land and climate of Georgia are unsuitable for growing mulberry trees and grapes, and Bull's "strict" laws fail to attract an adequate labor force. Only when Bull loosens his control and grants the settlers the authority to choose their own crops and manage their own labor does the settlement finally begin to deliver "adequate returns." Left to their own devices, the settlers immediately begin "cultivating rice and indigo ... instead of silk and wine," with much greater success, an example that leads readers to conclude that local governance rooted in the concerns and conditions of its immediate community is more suited to ensuring stability and productivity than a distant and absolute voice of authority.[40] The narrator criticizes other instances where Bull's dominant and distant authority disrupts the Foresters' settlements, and he compares Bull's behavior to forcing the settlers to "try on a new coat, which was so strait that it split in several places, and never could be altered so as to fit him, but he was obliged to wear it."[41] Through this metaphor, *The Foresters* once again argues that these settlements are best managed when local residents have the authority to choose the laws and policies that fit them best.

The Foresters' emphasis on the value of local governance and the dangers imposed by a dominant and distant authority would have had immediate relevance to the debates surrounding the Constitutional Convention. Although it was widely agreed that the revised government needed a stronger centralized authority, delegates and citizens remained concerned about preserving the local authority and autonomy of the states. "Whatever power may be necessary for the national government, a certain portion must necessarily be left in the states," argued George Mason, who, along with many delegates, insisted that "the state legislatures ought to have some means of defending themselves against encroachments of the national government."[42] The support for local governance and suspicion of centralized authority expressed within *The Foresters* echoes these concerns, once again aligning this narrative with the arguments of the Anti-Federalist Party, which was similarly suspicious of central authority and a strong supporter of states' rights. "To promote the happiness of the people it is necessary that there should be local laws; and it is necessary that those laws should be made by the representatives of those who are immediately subject to the want of them," argued Agrippa in a 1787 editorial, which appeared one month after *The Foresters*' critique of John Bull's mismanagement of these fictional settlements.[43]

The Foresters continues to promote the importance of variety and local governance in its discussion of relations between the colonists themselves. The third installment addresses "the cause of a quarrel" between John Codline (Massachusetts) and Roger Carrier (Rhode Island). The argument arises when Codline insists that the residents of his settlement all follow his example: "He bade them welcome and was their very good friend, *as long as they continued to be of his mind* for he . . . loved to have his own way in everything." When Roger Carrier refuses to conform by introducing some new "innovations" into the settlement, which include changing the way he pronounces "certain letters and syllables" and refusing to bear arms, Codline demands that he "reform his principles and practice" and return to the settlement's norms.[44]

This allegorical rendering of the establishment of Rhode Island allows *The Foresters* to address the relationship between liberty and variety and the proper exercise of authority in a diverse community. Carrier argues that establishing a settlement on the principle of liberty will inevitably lead to variations. In defense of his "innovations," Roger Carrier asks Codline, "Didst thou not come hitherunto for the sake of enjoying thy liberty and did I not come to enjoy mine?" Persuaded by this logic, Codline agrees that such variations are acceptable, with one exception, that "no man ought to have the liberty to do wrong"—a distinction he uses to banish Carrier from the settlement. Here the conversation takes a different turn to address not just the value of differences but the source of governing authority. After Codline deems his unconventional behavior to be "wrong," Carrier asks, "Who is to be judge . . . [of] what is right or what is wrong? Ought not I to judge for myself? Or thinkest thou it is thy place to judge for me?" In answer, Codline argues that the authority to determine right and wrong derives from the settlement's written laws, whose authority is best understood and interpreted by Codline himself. "Who is to be the judge (said John), why *the book* is to be the judge, and I have proved by the book over and over again that you are wrong and therefore you are wrong." Carrier challenges Codline's interpretive authority, however, arguing that his own interpretation of the "book" has the potential to be just as valid. "But friend John (said Roger) who is to judge whether thou hast proved my opinions or conduct to be wrong."

Thou or I?"[45] As Carrier points out, the significance of this book is not absolute or inherent. Each interpretation will be influenced by the views and interests of the person reading it, and Carrier's questions encourage citizens to recognize how authority is produced, not by a single definitive document but by the way people read and interpret written rules of law.

Carrier's arguments are clearly an allegory for Roger Williams's attack on the governing authority of the Bible and his push for religious tolerance in the Massachusetts colony, but this scene can also be read as an allegory for the debates surrounding the new Constitution, which were similarly invested in determining the authority of a single governing text. The Constitutional Convention and ratifying debates were preoccupied with questions about the many ways this document could be interpreted and the consequences of those interpretations. Many argued that the language of the Constitution defined the powers of the new central government too broadly, allowing Congress the freedom to establish laws that were "*paramount* to the laws of the different States . . . [since] it will be theirs to explain the powers that have been granted to them."[46] The wording of the "necessary and proper" clause was a particular source of concern, because many feared that its open-ended and flexible language would enable the central government to eliminate the powers of the states. The addition of this clause—which took place in August 1787, the same month that the Carrier episode was published in the *Columbian Magazine*—was extremely controversial, leading several delegates, including Elbridge Gerry, Edmund Randolph, and George Mason, to refuse to sign the Constitution because they felt its language gave Congress too much undefined power. "Under their own construction of the general clause at the end of the enumerated powers, the Congress may . . . extend their power as far as they shall think proper so that the state legislatures have no security for the powers now presumed to remain to them or the people for their rights," wrote Mason in his "Objections to the Proposed Constitution," a statement that conveys the widespread concern that granting Congress the power to determine the scope of their own authority would lead them to exercise unlimited control.[47]

For as much as *The Foresters* seems to prioritize variety and local authority, the narrative also asks readers to consider the dangers of variation and local control in its depiction of William Broadbrim's settlement (Pennsylvania). Much like Roger Carrier, Broadbrim establishes his settlement on the principles of openness and tolerance, issuing "a standing invitation to persons of all nations and characters to come and take shelter under his roof."[48] As a result, his settlement becomes the most diverse of any in the Forest, where it was "sometimes compared to the Ark of Noah because there was scarcely any kind of human being, of whatever shape, size, complexion, disposition, language or religion but what might be found there." As with Carrier, this variety is initially a source of great success for the settlement, where "nothing was wanting to make them as happy as family as any in the world." As the settlement grows, however, this variety becomes a problem as competition and conflict emerge. "While the family was small," the narrator reports, the community was disposed "to live in peace," but "when the encreased number of the family had penetrated farther into the forest . . . ambition, jealousy, avarice, and party spirit had frequent outbreakings among them," requiring Broadbrim to exercise more control over his residents to keep the settlement safe and productive.[49]

Similar problems arise in Roger Carrier's settlement. Although variety initially made this settlement very productive, maintaining order and stability in this diverse settlement requires a lot of work. The narrator describes these challenges through an image of the settlement's fences. "As I passed along," he reports, "the fences were in some places made of very crooked, knotty rails, but the crooks and knots were made to say into each other so cleverly that the fences were as tight as they had been made of stuff sawed ever so even, a circumstance which convinced me that very crooked things might be put together to advantage if proper pains were taken about it." This image of a strong, united fence composed of crooked, nonuniform parts echoes the diverse composition of Carrier's settlement. In praising the union of these varied components, however, the narrator notes that creating and maintaining this unity requires careful skill and attention. Such a union does not form easily or naturally—"proper pains" must be taken to produce and maintain it. Furthermore, without careful maintenance, this form of union will eventually deteriorate, which the narrator discovers on a later visit. "I have since heard that the old crooks and knots have got out of order and that they have not the art of making new ones say into one another so well as formerly," a comment that, once again, highlights the difficulty of preserving a union composed of such varied materials.[50] In order to maintain a stable community made up of differences, citizens need to develop a specific plan or "art" for holding the various pieces together and maintaining it over time.

By drawing attention to the problems caused by a diverse union and the need for visible and centralized forms of authority, *The Foresters* now seems to voice the views of the Federalists, who argued that the federal United States required a strong central government to bring order to "the prejudices, the passions, and the interests of every member of which it is composed."[51] In contrast to its earlier suspicion of centralized authority and support for local sovereignty, in these later scenes *The Foresters* suggests that the differences of the Forest, while necessary and valuable, still require some form of centralized management to maintain a stable and productive union. Despite the clear Federalist dimensions of these arguments, *The Foresters* does not completely abandon its previous Anti-

Federalist concerns. As the narrative proceeds, *The Foresters* continues to extol the values of diversity and local governance, while also identifying the problems that can arise from these conditions, and by presenting both sides, the narrative does not definitively endorse one side over the other. Instead, the narrative encourages citizens to think critically about the merits and the limits of both positions. Just as Washington invited readers to reflect on the difficulty of "draw[ing] with precision the line between those rights which must be surrendered and those which must be reserved" as they read the Constitution, *The Foresters* provides citizens with a literary opportunity to reflect on these issues. Rather than providing readers with a clear sense of where this line should be drawn, however, *The Foresters* provides them with interpretive literary exercises to help them determine whether the new Constitution had drawn that line effectively.

Ultimately, *The Foresters* locates the stability of a federal government not in its governing documents but in the interpretive powers of its citizens. Whatever form the federal government will take, *The Foresters* insists that its citizens will be responsible for determining the proper exercise of local and national power, which is why the narrative consistently privileges the interpretive actions of its own readers. Returning, once again, to the example of Roger Carrier, the questions he poses about the authority of Codline's "book" illustrate the extent to which governing authority ultimately derives from those who read and interpret the law. If producing a just and stable republic lies in the interpretive powers of its citizens, then a federal nation needs to produce readers who know when and how to strike a balance between local and national interests. William Broadbrim stabilizes his own diverse settlement when he shifts his authority to the interpretive judgment of his residents. In an effort to improve the security of the settlement, Broadbrim issues a law that gives each citizen "a certain sum to provide for *the necessaries of life*," leaving them to decide how they want to interpret its terms.[52] Given the diversity of his settlement, Broadbrim recognizes that one specific law cannot adequately serve the varied circumstances of everyone. By using language that allows his residents the opportunity to put "their own constructions on the words," Broadbrim makes it possible for his residents to interpret and enact the law as they see fit, a move that necessarily requires striking a balance between their personal preferences and communal safety.

The Foresters attempts to produce this reader through its own varied content, which continually invites readers to evaluate the virtues and limitations of both a local and centralized use of authority. *The Foresters* also helps produce this reader through its form, which likewise emphasizes the role that readers play producing authoritative significance. As a satiric allegory, *The Foresters* does not present its arguments about the value of variety, the importance of local authority, and the need for centralized control directly. Arriving at these arguments requires the audience to read against the literal significance of the text and recognize the other, alternative interpretations represented by this language, a process that involves the active participation and interpretive involvement of readers. In this regard, the form of the satiric allegory forces readers to reflect not just on the work's significance but on their own role in creating that significance—a realization that trains citizens to recognize their own responsibility for shaping the stability and unity of the federal government. To this end, *The Foresters* reimagines the United States as a plural nation that can be fairly governed, not just by a federal document but also by the federal literacy of its citizens. Other literary works of the early republic would similarly draw on this form of satiric allegory to promote this federal literacy, foregrounding the important role that readers play in the federal nation in more aggressive terms.

Hearing the Voice of Union: The Satiric Structure of *The Anarchiad*

Part poem, part prose narrative, *The Anarchiad* is another popular satire that was also published as the Constitution was being drafted and ratified. Like *The Foresters*, *The Anarchiad* highlights the critical role that citizens play in determining the form and function of the federal government. Unlike *The Foresters*, however, *The Anarchiad* presents a more anxious view of the federal nation's varied dimensions, while also highlighting the political power of literature to unite differences in more overt terms. According to *The Anarchiad*, literature and literacy provide the best means of protecting and supporting the federal union, more so than the institutions of the federal government.

The Anarchiad was written by John Trumbull, Joel Barlow, Lemuel Hopkins, and David Humphreys, who would subsequently become known as the Connecticut Wits. Composed as an epic satire, *The Anarchiad* was published in twelve installments in the *New-Haven Gazette and Connecticut Magazine* between October 1786 and September 1787, appearing two weeks after the delegates to the Annapolis Convention made a formal announcement to revise the Articles of Confederation and concluding shortly after the newly drafted Constitution was released to the public.[53] Much like *The Foresters*, *The Anarchiad* was the literary centerpiece of another newly established national periodical, the *New-Haven Gazette and Connecticut Magazine*, which was founded the same year as the *Columbian Magazine* in February 1786. Although smaller and less financially stable than the *Columbian Magazine*, the *New-Haven Gazette* was widely read and respected throughout New England, where it was known for its comprehensive coverage of state news, its Federalist-leaning editorials, and its publication of "original" American poetry.[54]

Framed as an ancient document recently discovered "in the western territories," *The Anarchiad* tells the story of a mythic federal nation under siege by the god Anarch, who seeks to instill "confusion, chaos, chance, and darkness" and cause the "federal union [to] sink in endless shade."[55] The books of the poem identify specific sources of this disorder, which include the use of paper currency (book 3), the destabilizing influence of mobs and faction (books 4 and 6), and the self-interestedness of state leaders (book 7). By highlighting these causes, *The Anarchiad* serves as an allegory for the chaotic and fragmented conditions of the post-Revolutionary United States, which was similarly unsettled by a growing national debt, a widespread currency crisis, rampant land speculation, and violent local uprisings such as Shay's Rebellion. The poem's authors were particularly concerned with what they perceived as a nation "rush[ing] headlong on its ruin."[56] By joining forces to write *The Anarchiad*, Humphreys, Trumbull, Barlow, and Hopkins sought to convince their readers of the need to establish a stronger federal government, making the work an early and influential expression of Federalist Party politics.[57]

The Anarchiad offers a sophisticated assessment of the ways that chaos and disorder are rooted in the structure of a federal system. In book 10, the poem warns readers of

> The giddy rage of democratic States,
> Whose pop'lar breath, high-blown in restless tide,
> No laws can temper, and no reason guide;
> . . . .
> They see no object, and perceive no cause;
> But feel, by turns, in one disastrous hour,
> Th' extremes of license, and th' extremes of power. (461)

In these lines, *The Anarchiad* points to the chaotic potential inherent in a federal system. By granting its constituent states a degree of independence and autonomy, a federal union is susceptible to destabilizing expressions of individual interests. "Giddy" with their own freedom, these "democratic states" have the power to act on their immediate interests without considering how they may affect the nation. By granting states their own degree of sovereignty, a federal government will always be subject to disruption, depending on the extent to which the states choose to exert their "pop'lar breath."

Building on this potential, the poem goes on to imagine the destructive consequences of this federal structure, where the nation's varied interests, if left unchecked, threaten to transform the federal union into a monstrous body politic.

> In this weak realm, can countless kingdoms start,
> Strong with new force, in each divided part—
> While empire's head, dissected into four,
> Gains life by severance of diminish'd power?
> So, when the philosophic hand divides
> The full-grown polypus, in genial tides,
> Each severed part, infused with latent life,
> Acquires new vigor from the friendly knife;
> O'er peopled sands the puny insects creep,
> Till the next wave absorbs them in the deep. (461–62)

This image of a federal body run amok presents readers with a nightmarish national future, where the separate parts of a once-united "polypus" are "dissected" and dispersed, each "severed part" taking on a life of its own until the power and integrity of the original body is thoroughly "diminish'd." Without a strong force to hold this "weak realm" together, the federal nation will be divided and its constituent parts reduced to "puny insects" whose influence is lost in the ensuing chaos. In forecasting this destructive future, *The Anarchiad* echoes widespread concerns about the Articles of Confederation, a document that was likewise considered too weak to control the "vigor" of the nation's constituent parts. By painting the future of this "weak realm" in such frightening terms, the poem evokes the rhetoric of the emerging Federalist Party, which argued for a stronger central government to control the nation's potentially divisive parts. Book 10, in fact, was published on May 24, 1787, the day before the opening of the Constitutional Convention, a publication date that was carefully timed to bolster public support for establishing a more consolidated central government—a position that was clearly heard by the delegates, considering that the bulk of the conversation on the first day of the convention was devoted to "the prospect of anarchy from the laxity of [this] government."[58]

There is more at stake in this poem, however, than a straightforward Federalist agenda. Although *The Anarchiad* clearly argues for a stronger centralized government, it also identifies several nongovernmental factors for bringing order to a federal system, suggesting that citizens can find other ways to control and unify the nation aside from simply writing a new constitution. In book 6 Anarch gives a speech that describes the conditions needed to ensure his chaotic rule, noting that

> The lamp of science must be quench'd in night,
> Till none, or next to none, can read or write;
> The press, anon, in brazen chains must groan,
> First watch'd and guarded by our saints alone;

> The numerous schools that live along the shore,
> Must fall, successive, and must rise no more;
> The wits be hang'd; the Congress forc'd to flee
> To western wilds, or headlong to the sea. (445)

Here, the satiric form of the poem requires us to read Anarch's words against their literal meaning. As Anarch argues in favor of suspending scientific knowledge, silencing the press, hindering literature, literacy, and education, and banishing Congress to preserve his conflicted and disordered realm, readers of this poem are meant to pursue the opposite actions in order to ensure national unity and stability. According to the poem's satiric logic, the best way for a federal nation to counteract its own chaotic potential is to produce a nation filled with well-educated readers and writers who have multiple opportunities to educate themselves and participate in the free exchange of ideas. Arriving at this argument, however, requires citizens to read against the grain of the poem's literal significance and embrace the opposing view. This satiric portrait of Anarch's restrictive and silencing governing principles thus argues that a stable federal union can be produced and maintained when citizens have access to a wide range of information and can read, write, and represent themselves in equally varied formats and forums.

Ironically, *The Anarchiad* also suggests that, by permitting this expansive literacy and promoting an open public sphere, a stable federal republic must inevitably retain a certain degree of chaos. Encouraging widespread education and literacy and sustaining a free press and an open, active public sphere will necessarily give rise to "dang'rous foes ... in learning's dress / Arm'd with the pen and ambush'd in the press" (444). The poem continually characterizes the nation's writers and readers in disordered terms as "unnumber'd whirlwinds" hurtling "through the void," who cannot be controlled by "distance, time, or place." This satiric representation of the chaotic effects of writing and literacy, however, allows *The Anarchiad* to show how this literary spirit spurs citizens to productive action. At the beginning of the poem, the narrator of *The Anarchiad* describes how the "potent voice" of literature "shall burst the deathful chain / and raise him active in thy toils again" (432), and the poem continually represents writing as a means of prompting action and change, characterizing it as "the flame that draws / Chiefs, mobs, conventions, to support thy cause" (431). For this reason, Anarch expresses his fear of those who can "read and write," since their efforts can transform chaos into a productive and unifying force. By highlighting the unifying political power of educated readers and writers, *The Anarchiad* argues not simply for the establishment of a stronger central government but, more specifically, for the national importance of literary forms.

The satiric form of *The Anarchiad* provides a particularly compelling example of the way a literary text can foster a plural sense of unity that is produced by the active engagement of readers. Satire, with its ability to imitate and undermine traditional forms of authority, lends itself readily to political engagement, and Trumbull, Hopkins, Barlow, and Humphreys specifically chose the satiric form of the mock epic because of its close association with national critique. *The Anarchiad* was modeled on two specific mock epics, Alexander Pope's *The Dunciad*, which criticizes the declining state of England's literary and intellectual culture, and another collectively authored work titled *The Rolliad*, which criticized the administration of the British prime minister, William Pitt the Younger. In the case of *The Anarchiad*, however, the satiric form of the text accomplishes more than simply criticizing the politics of the Constitutional Convention. In this work, the satiric form of the mock epic supports a federal model of nationalism by showing readers how different and even opposing views can be represented with productive and stabilizing results. If the content of *The Anarchiad* argues that the local differences within the federal nation need to be carefully controlled, the form of the epic satire provides a framework for controlling these differences.

Recognizing the federal implications of this literary satire requires paying close attention to the kind of reading experience that satire produces. As numerous critics have observed, satire produces a multivoiced reading experience, where readers must encounter the constant "juxtaposition of conflicting frames of reference [and] systems of beliefs."[59] Throughout *The Anarchiad*, for example, the character of Anarch continually voices his plans to produce chaos and disorder in the nation. His arguments, however, become a crucial means for expressing and supporting the opposite argument, as in the example cited earlier where Anarch's ideas for fostering chaos provide readers with information they need to counteract it. While representing one specific argument while simultaneously conveying the opposite argument might seem antithetical, when expressed in the form of a satire, these competing arguments do not necessarily produce a confusing or disordered text. Instead, these opposing perspectives all contribute to the same argument. This unified argument, however, depends on the critical participation of the reader. While all literary works rely on the interpretive power of their readers, satire makes readers particularly aware of the role they play in producing the significance of a text. Since the views and statements in a satire are not meant to be read literally, readers must take greater responsibility for determining the central argument of a satiric text. Because the multivoiced structure of a satire does not convey a clear voice of authority on its own, the reader holds the primary authority for determining a satire's central, authoritative significance. Since the significance of a work of satire depends on the way that readers exercise their critical judgment, this form continually reminds readers of their responsibility.

The Anarchiad draws attention to the authoritative power of its readers at the end of book 10, where it addresses the poem's definitive significance. Although the narrator maintains that the "voice of Union" speaks to readers throughout the poem, it is ultimately up to the reader to figure out how to locate and interpret this voice in a text that is otherwise defined by its disordered and divisive subject matter.

> Through ruined realms the voice of Union calls
> Loud as the trump of heaven through darkness roars . . .
> On you she calls! Attend the warning cry:
> "YE LIVE UNITED, OR DIVIDED DIE!" (462)

Here, the narrator insists that "the voice of Union" calls out loudly to its readers through the lines of the poem. To hear this voice, however, readers must engage with all the ideas, images, and experiences in the poem that seem to run counter to the concept of unity. Attending to the "voice of Union" requires critically evaluating the countless images of discord and disunion—the "ruined realms," the "wild riots," the "maddening mobs," the "faithless factions," the "bickering fires," the "dark'ning shadows," and the "reign of anarchy"—where this voice is allegedly conveyed. Inviting readers to arrive at a shared call for union by navigating varied representations of the opposite argument, the satiric form of *The Anarchiad* requires citizens to participate in this production of union by actively engaging with its varied content.

By training readers to see how engaging with opposing views and perspectives can produce a cohesive, coherent, and convincing conclusion, the literary form of the satire taught citizens how to contend with the conflicts and divisions that would inevitably arise in a federal union. The antagonistic debates over the federal Constitution made it clear that this plural model of nationhood, no matter what form it took, would always be defined by "a diversity of opinions on great national questions" and an "ardor for new and opposite forms," as Madison noted in his records of the Constitutional Convention.[60] By electing delegates who had the ability to carefully consider and reflect on the expression of these different views, however, Madison and others argued that this heterogeneous body could still arrive at an "unexpected unanimity." Producing such unity, however, required developing concrete strategies for contending with conflict. In the case of the federal Congress, delegates worked to implement strategies of equitable representation and debate that would help them "reconcil[e] their discordant opinions, assuag[e] their mutual jealousies, and adjus[t] their respective interests."⁶¹ Training readers to engage with different views could similarly foster unity and consensus, which is one way that satire helped citizens recognize that the chaotic and divided dimensions of the union could still be interpreted in cohesive terms. If the United States required active writers, a free press, and a literate body of citizens to stave off anarchy, the satiric form of *The Anarchiad* went a long way toward fostering both a federal literature and a nation of federal readers.

M'Fingalick Federalism: Turning the World Upside Down

M'Fingal, a satiric poem by John Trumbull, who was also involved in writing *The Anarchiad*, was one of the most popular literary works of the early republic. The poem was originally written as a piece of Revolutionary propaganda that satirized the pompous speeches of Squire M'Fingal, a Tory loyalist, who argued ineffectively against his patriot opponents during a colonial town meeting.⁶² The first edition, which consisted of two cantos, appeared in Philadelphia in 1775; by lampooning loyalist arguments and casting M'Fingal, the Tory spokesman, as a foolish and bombastic elitist, *M'Fingal* did much to bolster support for national independence and promote the Revolutionary cause.

After the American Revolution, Trumbull returned to the poem and completely revised and expanded it, and this new second edition was published in 1782, shortly before the end of the war. In terms of form, Trumbull made substantial changes to the poem's literary structure by expanding its classical and historical allusions, tightening its rhythm and rhyme scheme, and constructing it more deliberately as a Hudibrastic mock epic. This second edition also revised the content of the original two cantos. Instead of simply criticizing the loyalist position, the 1782 work revised the town meeting to show the destabilizing effects of faction and partisanship by depicting both the Tories and the patriots as equally ridiculous and problematic. The 1782 edition also included two new cantos where M'Fingal delivers some significant speeches, one at a liberty pole in the public square and the other at a private meeting where he addresses the future of the new nation. With these changes, Trumbull transformed *M'Fingal* from a work of Revolutionary propaganda into a narrative that was more carefully aligned with the issues of federal unity and nationalism that citizens had to contend with after the Revolution, particularly regarding the representation of variety and strategies for managing the nation's complicated and conflicted diversity.⁶³

The 1782 edition of *M'Fingal* was even more popular than the first. The work went through seven editions between 1782 and 1792, and John Adams, Thomas

Jefferson, and George Washington all had copies of the 1782 edition in their personal libraries.[64] Noah Webster chose *M'Fingal* to represent U.S. literature in his 1785 textbook, *A Grammatical Institute of the English Language*, where he reprinted selections from the first two cantos as an example of "the modern manner of writing."[65] The poem enjoyed a particular resurgence in 1787 and 1788 when, much like *The Foresters* and *The Anarchiad*, *M'Fingal* became closely associated with the debates surrounding the Constitutional Convention. A new edition of the poem was published in Philadelphia in 1787, and selections from *M'Fingal* were frequently quoted in the press during the convention and the ratification debates.[66] In April 1787 Matthew Carey published the full text of *M'Fingal* in the *American Museum*, where it was reprinted alongside a series of letters offering "A View of the Federal Government of America, Its Defects, and a Proposed Remedy."[67] Between 1786 and 1788 selections of the poem were also reprinted in the *Massachusetts Centinel* and the *New-Haven Gazette*, which were primarily known for their coverage of the constitutional debates, as well as political satire.[68]

The first two cantos of *M'Fingal* address the familiar issues of variety and disorder in the context of a plural union. The action takes place in a town meeting where "voters of all colors" gather to "weave ... the public weal," a setting that easily serves as an allegory for the proposed federal Congress, which was likewise meant to provide a forum for representing and debating an array of positions, with the goal of arriving at a reasonable consensus.[69] Unfortunately, the town meeting in *M'Fingal* cannot play this unifying role because its delegates are too divided and distracted to represent their positions in ways that make coherent sense. Instead of fostering productive discussions, this meeting is "torn by feuds of faction" (20) that are dominated by two positions. On one side are the Tory loyalists, who argue for a strong centralized government under "good King George" (53), and on the other side are the Whig patriots, who want to reject this "proud oppressor" (80) and establish a government founded on the people. In the context of the 1780s, these loyalist and Whig positions correspond roughly to the political views of the Federalist and Anti-Federalist parties that were beginning to emerge in the post-Revolutionary nation, but these partisan distinctions actually end up being beside the point. Instead of pitting these two sides against one another, *M'Fingal* makes little effort to distinguish between them and, instead, casts both the Tories and the patriots as equally incoherent and destabilizing forces. As the meeting proceeds, both sides emerge as ridiculous and insubstantial, defined more by their desire to fight with one another than their desire to represent and enact a clear agenda. Rather than singling out one side as more reasonable or persuasive than another, the poem maintains that both positions represent "truth and falsehood, wrong and right," and the narrator groups both of them together as a unified force of disorder, describing how these "Whigs, Tories, orators, and bawlers / With ev'ry tongue in either faction / Prepar'd like minute men for action" (22). By the end of the morning session, the town meeting is compared to the Tower of Babel as the town meeting transforms from a promising representative space to an incomprehensible "gabble,"

> [Where] ev'ry creature talk'd at once,
> Or like the variegated gabble
> That craz'd the carpenters of Babel.
> Each party soon forgot the quarrel,
> And let the other go on parole;
> Eager to know what fearful matter
> Had conjur'd up such gen'ral clatter. (85)

With this image, *M'Fingal* provides a negative portrait of the consequences of federal representation. Even worse, the disordered and nonsensical results of this forum cause the delegates to lose interest in the legislative process altogether. Unable to follow their own "crazed clatter," the members of each party forget why they had chosen to assemble, transforming the town meeting into an institution that is both insignificant and nonproductive. Without any means of controlling their loud and shifting arguments, the meeting dissolves into "a gen'ral rout in chorus" as participants "could scarce be heard . . . ami'd th' increasing roar" (32).

By focusing on the disorder and mayhem that can arise from a plural body politic, *M'Fingal* is closely aligned with *The Anarchiad*, which likewise emphasized the chaotic effects of representing diversity. In contrast to *The Anarchiad's* fantastical and otherworldly imagery, however, *M'Fingal* hits readers a little closer to home by using the setting of the town meeting, which invites immediate parallels to the Continental Congress, which, at the time of *M'Fingal's* 1782 publication, was similarly caught up in divisive debates about how to represent the nation's varied interests under the Articles of Confederation that would continue throughout the 1780s. Reprinted in a new edition in 1787, *M'Fingal's* representation of the disordered town meeting continued to echo the concerns of the Constitutional Convention that a federal Congress would be "too numerous to act with any care or decision . . . composed of such heterogeneous and discordant principles, as would constantly be contending with each other."[70] Although Congress was supposed to mediate these conflicts by representing the varied interests of the states "on equal footing," *M'Fingal* offers a very cynical view of the unity and stability of such a body.[71] In fact, the town meeting in *M'Fingal* became so closely associated with this conflicted and ineffectual mode of politics that citizens coined the term "M'Fingalick" to describe the divisive and increasingly partisan conditions that defined U.S. government throughout the late eighteenth century.[72]

Ultimately, *M'Fingal* argues that the solution to these ineffective, oppositional politics was located outside the political sphere altogether. Rather than posing a legislative solution to the nation's variety and disorder by establishing a more forceful moderator or restricting the voices of the delegates, the narrator of the poem turns to his own readers to bring order to this chaos, calling on them to critically evaluate these varied voices and draw significance from this disordered scene:

> my critic-brothers
> May help me out, as well as others;
> And 'tis design'd, tho' here it lurk
> To serve as preface to this work. (33)

Although the town meeting has failed to produce a coherent or productive debate, the narrator argues that his "critic brothers" can transform this chaotic scene into a meaningful experience by evaluating the "error[s] ... of the prater" and composing a new "preface" for the town meeting that can better express the ideas that "lurk" within the chaos (33). By assessing the convoluted views expressed in the town meeting, these readers can write a new text that represents those differences coherently, and he implores his audience to take on this critical interpretive role. He praises readers who "ma[ke] objection / That what they scribbled must be fiction" and states his wish that, at every meeting, "The Muse was by, with table-book" to "[stand] clerk and [keep] the cue" to catch "some blunder [that] might ensue" (33). To this end, the poem suggests that Congress can be made more productive and less susceptible to division by training citizens outside of the political sphere to read and critically assess these debates and present their independent observations to others. By investing so much power in the authority of its readers, *M'Fingal* joins with *The Foresters* and *The Anarchiad* in arguing that the stability and unity of the federal nation does not lie solely in the structure of its government. Like the other works explored in this chapter, *M'Fingal* argues that the United States needs careful, objective readers and a free press to represent the nation's varied views in a useful format. The literary sphere, rather than the political sphere, emerges as the best forum to ensure the success of the federal union.

In the second half of the poem, *M'Fingal* introduces a new dimension to this federal literacy by arguing that citizens also need to be willing to change their minds and question their own assumptions as they engage with the differences represented in a federal nation. This new condition of federal literacy emerges in canto 3 when the Whigs and Tories move outside to continue their arguments in the public square. Unlike cantos 1 and 2, which did little to distinguish the Whigs and Tories from one another, canto 3 represents their differences very clearly. Loudly proclaiming their commitment to freedom, public interest, and representative government, the Whigs raise a flag "inscribed with . . . liberty and thirteen stripes," actions that would have prompted immediate sympathy and support from U.S. readers (88). In contrast, the Tories, under the leadership of M'Fingal, denounce the Whigs for their democratic politics, criticizing these "dirtbred patriots" for overturning the traditional social order by electing leaders "from every workshop thro' the street," a move that transforms "the commonwealth [into] a common harlot / The property of every varlet" (99, 92, 96). For M'Fingal, by elevating the "leather apron'd" working class and diminishing the authority of the elite, the Whigs threaten the stability and integrity of the nation by instituting a government that functions "by the rule of topsy-turvys" (94).

> You've push'd and turn'd the whole world up-
> Side down and got yourselves a-top:
> While all the great ones of your state
> Are crush'd beneath the pop'lar weight. (94)

With these comments, the poem's satiric force is on clear display. As M'Fingal condemns the Whigs for turning the world upside down with their democratic principles, readers are meant to turn M'Fingal's own words upside down and view the Whigs' position with admiration and M'Fingal's Tory views with derision. In contrast, then, to cantos 1 and 2, canto 3 begins by establishing a clear binary opposition to these two positions, where the Whigs emerge as the patriotic heroes and the Tories as the anti-American villains, such that, by the end of M'Fingal's speech, readers expect that the Whigs will continue to show their commitment to liberty, justice, and equality while the Tories will remain "their en'mies" whose "errors [are] clearly spied" (107, 108).

As canto 3 continues, however, Trumbull doubles down on these topsy-turvy dynamics by refusing to provide readers with this expected oppositional narrative. Immediately following M'Fingal's speech, the Whigs respond with aggressive force, attacking M'Fingal "with handirons, tongs and shovels . . . clubs and billets, staves and stones" until he is "stretch'd on the ground" (102, 106). At this point, having "got their en'mies in their pow'r," they hoist him up the liberty pole where "they swung him like a keg of ale" (107). Described as a "conq'ring crew" composed of "rav'ning lions" (101, 115), these images immediately distance the Whigs from their admirable patriotic values, requiring readers to shift their position as the Whigs now seem to embody the savage and tyrannical displays of power that they were supposed to oppose. The poem completes this critical reversal when the Whigs bring M'Fingal down from the pole and brutally tar and feather him. By transforming M'Fingal into a creature who can no longer "prove his claim to human nature" (113), the Whigs not only emerge as violent oppressors; they also recast M'Fingal as an object of sympathy. The irony of this transformation is clearly expressed as the Whigs "paraded round our feather'd 'Squire . . . And hail'd great Liberty in chorus" (114). For as much as U.S. readers may have initially admired the Whigs and their commitment to liberty, equality, and justice, the topsy-turvy occurrences of canto 3 make it difficult for readers to continue to endorse the Whigs' actions wholeheartedly. Their rapid transition from democratic principles to mob violence illuminates the fine line between productive federal pluralism and destructive mayhem, a distinction that looks ahead to the challenges posed to the nation by populist uprisings such as Shay's Rebellion and the Whiskey Rebellion in the coming years.

By requiring readers to reverse their original perceptions of the Whigs and the Tories in this scene at the liberty pole, *M'Fingal* introduces a new dimension to the practice of federal literacy. Instead of simply training readers to recognize the value of different views and opinions—which is the federal literacy promoted by *The Foresters* and *The Anarchiad*—*M'Fingal* requires its readers to question their initial assumptions and continually reevaluate the way they interpret the nation's varied constituencies. Instead of consistently supporting the same set of points and relationships throughout, the satiric form of *M'Fingal* requires readers to constantly alter and revise their former perspectives in response to the changing circumstances of the poem. As the significance of the Whigs and Tories continually changes, readers must separate themselves from their prior assumptions about what constitutes a "right" or a "wrong" position and embrace a more flexible and open-minded practice of interpretation. In doing so, *M'Fingal* models a more active and engaging practice of federal literacy where citizens learn to read the nation not just as a collection of static differences but as a union defined by diverse and ever-changing perspectives and experiences.

In considering the future of the nation, the poem's greatest fear is not partisan divisions or mob violence, but citizens who are not willing or able to change their opinions in response to changing conditions. The poem continues trying to produce readers with these qualities in the last canto, where M'Fingal, having extricated himself from the liberty pole, delivers a final speech concerning his vision of the American future. Rather than predicting a future of disorder and destruction for the new nation, as he did at the start of canto 3, M'Fingal concludes by prophesying the successful rise of the United States:

> Her glory, wealth, and fame [will] ascend
> Her commerce rise, her realms extend . . .
> Her cities, towers, and columns rise
> And dazzling temples meet the skies. (165)

Although readers were previously meant to read M'Fingal's statements satirically, in this canto he is represented as a sincere voice who speaks of the rise of the future nation in terms that one might expect from the Whigs. The end of the poem thus provides readers with a final reversal, as the Tory character of M'Fingal becomes the most definitive and authoritative source for expressing U.S. national sentiments and ideals. In recognizing the value and legitimacy of M'Fingal's concluding remarks, readers must acknowledge the extent to which their own interpretive habits have changed as M'Fingal foretells the nation's productive future.

A final word on the medium where *M'Fingal* most often appeared—the magazine. As discussed at the beginning of this chapter, magazines were an ideal form for practicing and promoting a federal literacy because they taught readers how to encounter and interpret different topics, styles, and forms in a unified framework. Much like the text of *M'Fingal*, magazines were also an ideal form for unsettling readers' assumptions and teaching them how to change their positions and reinterpret the world from altered perspectives. Gardner describes early U.S. magazines as a "deeply collaborative and interactive" space where readers were expected to engage actively with their miscellaneous content.[73] Editors regularly invited readers to send in letters expressing their responses to particular articles and information, and magazines were widely perceived as texts that produced active critical conversations. As one early U.S. editor wrote, in magazines, "knowledge, instead of being bound up in Books and kept in Libraries and Retirements, is thus obtruded upon the Public; [where] it is canvassed in every Assembly and exposed upon every Table."[74]

While all magazines invited readers to enter into dialogues with their varied content, this collaborative and dynamic relationship is particularly evident in the *American Museum*, where *M'Fingal* was reprinted in 1787. Published in Philadelphia by Matthew Carey between 1787 and 1792, the *American Museum* exemplified its title by attempting to "collect" and "preserve" a representative range of the literary, historical, political, legal, agricultural, industrial, and domestic interests of the United States.[75] More than simply covering a wide range of different topics, the *American Museum* represented an extremely wide array of opinions. In each of its issues, the magazine featured at least one section that covered a single topic from numerous perspectives. The May 1788 issue, for instance, featured a set of "Papers Reflecting the Late Private Transactions with the Oneida Indians," which addressed an attempt to renegotiate a land lease with the Oneida nation that had been previously denied by the governor of New York.[76] Rather than providing a single, authoritative summary or assessment of this event, the *American Museum* includes a series of petitions, speeches, and legal proclamations that present the differing views of the various parties involved. In an official 1788

"Proclamation" delivered to the state of New York, Governor Clinton outlines his rationale for denying the legality of the lease, while two other documents feature petitions from local New York businessmen that state their arguments for seeking the lease. The *American Museum* also included a speech given by the Oneida Indians to the New York legislature where the Oneida voice their distrust of any formal land agreements with the governments based on their prior negative experiences. By presenting this issue in relation to multiple perspectives, the magazine refuses to present its readers with a definitive opinion, encouraging them, instead, to read and evaluate the documents as they see fit and recognize the extent to which political decisions require the consideration of multiple sides.

Other articles in the *American Museum* likewise encouraged citizens to interpret the United States from a variety of views and experiences. The January 1787 issue includes a series of "Documents Respecting the Battles of Lexington and Concord" that represents this definitive moment through a diverse set of depositions taken from military leaders, volunteer soldiers, local merchants, idle spectators, and even a woman who was confined to her home by an illness.[77] Other articles feature varying opinions on the best methods to counter the destructive effects of the Hessian fly, where readers were instructed to refrain from settling on a specific remedy until they had a chance to consider the "several communications" respecting this subject.[78] By continually representing its featured topics in relation to these varying views and positions, the *American Museum* carefully trains its readers to interpret its contents—and, by extension, the nation—by considering multiple views and sources of information.

The different perspectives represented in the *American Museum* also enabled readers to become more comfortable with changing their initial interpretations or assumptions. Articles published in the *American Museum* were often followed by letters and essays in subsequent issues that were meant to alter the views expressed in the original publication. A notable example can be found in the March, April, and May issues of 1787, where the *American Museum* published several responses to the "Account of Jemimah Wilkinson," which was originally published in the February 1787 issue. The first article offers a condemnatory account of "the religious imposture" of Jemimah Wilkinson, who "professes she is Jesus Christ, come again in the flesh a second time."[79] A second essay, published in March, presents a different interpretation of the same events where the author counters the arguments made in the first article, paragraph by paragraph, arguing that the author has repeatedly drawn "wrong conclusions" and relied too heavily on "hearsay" instead of legitimate facts. In light of this critique, the author invites his own readers to reconsider the charge of "religious imposture" and instead view the previous essay as a work of "slander" and "calumny."[80] The *American Museum* then published a third response, which was split into two parts in the April and May issues. In this essay, the author acknowledges the prior critique by agreeing that the first essayist, in some places, relied too heavily on hearsay to support his points. Rather than dismissing his argument entirely, however, the third essayist introduces new eyewitness evidence about Wilkinson's behavior to offer a more convincing set of "charges" against her.[81] By including these successive responses and reinterpretations, the *American Museum* invites readers to change their minds about the case as they read and evaluate the different arguments and evidence presented.

The *American Museum* repeatedly provided readers with these opportunities to engage in these serial exchanges and revise and reinterpret their original perceptions of its content. In one particularly notable case, the magazine linked its emphasis on these shifting interpretive practices directly to the structure and stability of the federal government. In 1789, following the final ratification of the Constitution, the *American Museum* reprinted a series of documents related to the Albany Plan of Union, which was the colonists' failed attempt to form a federal alliance in 1754.[82] True to form, the magazine provided a diverse range of perspectives on the subject, including an essay on "Reasons for the Proposed Plan of Union among the American Colonies," "Reasons against Partial Unions," and, finally, a complete copy of the proposed "Plan of Union" itself. By inviting readers to interpret the Albany Plan from a variety of perspectives, the *American Museum* encourages citizens to engage with the nation's federal principles using the same critical practices of reading and reinterpretation. More importantly, these articles also force readers to recognize the ways that public perceptions of federal nationalism had changed over time. When the Albany Plan was originally proposed in 1754, its ideas of plural union were unfamiliar; ultimately they were interpreted as unviable, which is why the plan failed to earn approval. In 1789, however, the Albany Plan looked very different to U.S. citizens whose leaders had incorporated many of its ideas and much of its language into the newly ratified Constitution. While the American colonists of 1754 did not read the Albany Plan as a practical or productive model of union, these same documents laid the foundation for a stable federal union in 1789, reminding readers of the extent to which the structure and stability of the federal nation were contingent on citizens who were willing to change their critical interpretations and reconsider perspectives they had previously rejected.

By providing citizens with opportunities to experiment with different perspectives and develop productive methods for interpreting that variety, magazines and satires illuminate how the stability and success of the federal nation depended on the way that citizens were taught to read and interpret differences in the popular and public sphere. Representing the nation's constituent differences in the formal environment of Congress was not enough to produce a stable or successful federal union. The United States needed alternative forms to represent and manage the nation's differences, and magazines and satires went a long way toward helping citizens negotiate the unusual and often contradictory dimensions of their newly established federal nation. Even more importantly, by training citizens to continually unsettle and alter their opinions and interpretations, these literary forms provided citizens with the skills they needed to redefine this plural union in the future, particularly with regard to imagining federal citizenship in more expansive terms.

"Is the Needle and Kitchen Sufficient?" The Federal Literacy of Judith Sargent Murray

One of the specific ways that magazines promoted an altered interpretation of the nation's federal dynamics concerned their attention to women. Magazines, with their varied content, offered a logical point of entry for women to participate in the nation's plural culture, and editors made a concerted effort to attract women readers and writers following the ratification of the Constitution. "The fair sex merits our highest attention. If their taste has not hitherto been consulted or the delicacy of their fancy gratified, we flatter ourselves that the succeeding numbers will make compensation for their former negligence," asserted the *Massachusetts Magazine* in 1793.[83] Magazines such as the *American Magazine* (New York City), the *Columbian Magazine* (Philadelphia), the *National Magazine* (Richmond), the *Gentleman and Lady's Town and Country Magazine* (Boston), the *Lady's Magazine and Repository of Entertaining Knowledge* (Philadelphia), the *Lady's and Gentleman's Pocket Magazine of Literary and Polite Amusement* (New York), and the *New York Magazine* (New York) actively solicited submissions from "the elegant polish of the Female Pencil."[84] More than any other medium, magazines offered women the best opportunities for publication in the early republic, providing them with access to a public sphere from which they were, otherwise, largely excluded.

As the leading public forum for female voices, magazines became a prominent site for reimagining women's roles in the new nation. As Susan Branson writes, early U.S. magazines "helped to develop an American public discourse on gender roles and gender relations in the early republic," and in the midst of these varying views and debates, a particular voice stands out, that of Judith Sargent Murray, one of the most prolific and popular magazine writers of the early United States who drew specifically on the principles of federal pluralism to argue that women should be included and represented as equal and active participants within the nation's public sphere.[85] Between 1790 and 1794, Murray was a regular contributor to the *Massachusetts Magazine*, where she wrote two popular series known as "The Repository" and "The Gleaner," as well as other essays and editorials. Although she published all her work anonymously, her authorship was widely known and celebrated. John Adams, Jeremy Belknap, Fisher Ames, Jedidiah Morse, and other leading authors and statesmen publicly admired her work, and George Washington praised her as "the first literary Lady as was ever seen in any country."[86] Murray's popularity eventually led her to compile her "Gleaner" articles and other previously unpublished works into a three-volume collection that she published by subscription in 1798, an accomplishment that set a new standard for women's social and political involvement in the public sphere.[87]

Murray's magazine work addressed numerous topics, from national policies of diplomatic neutrality to the role that religious belief should play in republican culture. Her primary focus, however, concerned the rights and roles of women in the United States, particularly regarding their access to equal education. In making these arguments, Murray drew heavily on the logic of federal nationalism to argue for women's status as different, but equal, citizens in the United States. She also used satire to criticize widespread assumptions about women's inferiority and promote a more diversified understanding of the ways that men and women could contribute to the nation. Although she stopped short of arguing that women should participate in the federal government directly, Murray's work identifies print culture and the domestic sphere as places where women can represent themselves as active, engaged, and equal citizens within a diverse federal nation.

Understanding Murray's engagement with federal literary nationalism requires recognizing the tentative position women held in the republic following the ratification of the federal Constitution. Although women are not mentioned at all in the text of the Constitution, the framers intended for women to be recognized as citizens.[88] Their rights and interests were not represented directly, however. Under the prevailing laws of coverture, women were assumed to be represented through the voices and actions of their husbands.[89] According to this logic, women were considered to be adequately represented in the Constitution by their husbands or male family members. The rhetoric of pluralism and just representation that surrounded the new federal Constitution, however, raised serious questions about the logic of coverture in the early republic.[90] Abigail Adams's famous request for her husband to "remember the ladies" in drafting the nation's laws exemplifies this expectation that women needed to be represented more visibly and actively within the new federal nation, and Judith Sargent Murray likewise pushed her readers to imagine alternative roles for women to play in the nation's public political sphere.

Murray's engagement with the politics of federal literary nationalism is evident in her most famous essay on women's rights, "On Equality of the Sexes," which she began writing in 1779 but did not publish until 1790 when it appeared in the *Massachusetts Magazine*. In this essay, Murray presents a masterful argument for educating women according to the same standards as men, writing that "If we are allowed an equality of acquirement [and] let serious studies equally employ our minds ... we will bid our souls arise to equal strength."[91] Despite her claims for gender equality, Murray insists that men and women will not necessarily exhibit their intellectual skills and interests in the same way or at the same level. At the heart of Murray's essay is a larger argument about the variety of intellectual abilities that exist within a community and how best to represent and interpret that variety—a critical focus that reveals the federal dimensions of her arguments.

Murray begins her essay with a poem that identifies variety as a fundamental fact of existence, writing, "That minds are not alike, full well I know / This truth each day's experience will show" (3). She follows this assertion by describing these intellectual variations, noting that "to heights surprising some great spirits soar," while others "wish not to improve / Who never can the path of knowledge love" (3). Such differences, she argues, must always be recognized and represented as inevitable and indisputable. She objects, however, to the way these differences are usually interpreted, where intellectual inferiority is attributed exclusively to women and intellectual strength to men:

> As if a woman's form must needs enrol
> A weak, a servile, an inferiour soul
> And that the guise of man must still proclaim
> Greatness of mind and him to be the same. (4)

Rather than denying the existence of intellectual differences, Murray wants her readers to change the way they *interpret* this variety and acknowledge that women can be represented among those who show "heights surprising" and not relegated exclusively to those who are "stupidly dull" (4).

Although she does not refer to federalism directly, Murray's emphasis on recognizing these intellectual differences and finding ways to represent this variety equitably echoes the representational values of a federal system. She clearly states that the world will always be defined by a range of intellectual abilities. What she wants is a more just and equitable way of representing and interpreting this intellectual variety, which, in turn, will lead to a more productive use of the nation's varied resources. She talks at length about how denying women's intellectual abilities and excluding them from education detracts from the harmony and productivity of the nation. "At length arrived at womanhood, the uncultivated fair one feels a void which the employments allotted her are by no means capable of filling. What can she do? . . . Fashion, scandal, and sometimes what is still more reprehensible are called in to her relief" (6). Without any recognition of their intellectual skills or potential, women engage in activities that undermine the values and stability of their community. In contrast, granting women an equal education so their intellectual skills can be justly recognized eventually leads to more productive and unifying behaviors. "A mind, thus filled, would have little room for the trifles with which our sex are, with too much justice, accused of amusing themselves," asserts Murray. "Fashions, in their variety, would then give place to conjectures which might perhaps conduce to the improvement of the literary world; and there would be no leisure for slander or detraction" (7). Educating women equally will not only allow women to contribute to their communities with more substance (particularly, as she notes here, through their literary productions); it will also eliminate actions and sentiments that lead to conflict and division, such as gossip and slander.

Murray carefully limits the scope of her arguments. Although she wants women to be included as part of the nation's intellectual variety, particularly within its advanced levels of knowledge and accomplishment, she does not encourage women to exercise those abilities outside of the domestic or, at most, the literary sphere. "Will it be urged that those acquirements would supercede our domestic duties?" she asks, confronting widespread fears that equal education would lead women to seek more active roles in business or politics. Murray assures her readers that educating women will simply strengthen and improve their current roles, rather than radically alter them. At the same time, she also argues that education will transform the domestic sphere into a place where women can exercise political agency and authority. "Nay while we are pursuing the needle or the superintendency of the family, I repeat, that our minds are at full liberty for reflection," writes Murray. "If we were industrious we might easily find time to arrange [our ideas] upon paper or, should avocations press too hard for such an indulgence, the hours allotted for conversation would at least become more refined than rational" (7). By asserting that the domestic sphere can accommodate a more diverse range of thoughts and actions, Murray redefines its political scope. Rather than engaging in activities that only benefit their own homes and families, educated women can use the domestic sphere to participate in political and social discussions that will benefit the nation. Such arguments laid a foundation for the concept of republican motherhood, where women's political roles were defined by their ability to raise active and responsible citizens within stable and civically informed households.[92] While indirect, Murray's arguments for the political significance of the domestic sphere nevertheless redefine the home as a place where women can participate in the political culture of the nation.

Murray also identifies print culture as another space where women can engage with political issues and represent themselves as active and equal citizens. She mentions several times that equal education will also enable women to "conduce to the improvement of the literary world" (7), and she intended her own essay to stand as evidence of women's abilities to contribute to the nation's political discussions in print. To this end, she paid close attention to the formal dimensions of her writing, which brings us to her use of satire, a literary form that enhanced her efforts to position her voice within a plural national framework. Although Murray's use of satire is not as overt or aggressive as the other works examined in this chapter, she uses the same tactics of representing the views of her opponents to offer alternative interpretations of their positions, an approach that encourages readers to view the world in more diverse and productive terms. In "On the Equality of the Sexes," Murray satirizes arguments that represent a singular, homogeneous view of women to show readers that there are other, more effective ways to interpret women's interests and abilities. At various points, Murray presents some of the prevailing views of the "lordly sex" regarding women, including their claims that "your domestic enjoyments are sufficient" (7), that "our judgment is not so strong" (5), and that "ornamenting our exterior ought to be our principle object of attention" (9). In referencing these statements, Murray does not endorse their literal significance. Instead, she satirizes these views to convey their opposite claims, arguing that women's domestic duties are insufficient, that women's judgment is, indeed, strong, that women's interests extend beyond their physical appearances, and that men are not, in fact, a "lordly sex" at all. Just as *The Foresters*, *The Anarchiad*, and *M'Fingal* used satire to show how the world can be made up of multiple views and, moreover, how representing and engaging with those different views can lead readers to develop stronger, shared conclusions, Murray's satiric representation of traditional gender norms achieves the same ends.

Perhaps the best example of Murray's engagement with federal literacy emerges in her closing supplement to "On the Equality of the Sexes," where she reinterprets the biblical story of Adam and Eve. She presents this critical rereading as a response to a letter she received that asserted the superiority of men over women, and she opens by satirically asking her male correspondent to "assist" her in understanding why "the superiority of your sex hath ... been time out of mind esteemed a truth incontrovertible." She then proceeds to discredit this truth by comparing different practices of reading. First, she describes her own process of interpretation, which relies on "selecting some arguments from nature, reason, and experience" (11). She also notes that she specifically avoided consulting any "sacred testimonials" because she felt that religious texts had no credible bearing on the subject. "I held them to be merely metaphorical, and thus regarding them, I could not persuade myself that there was any propriety in bringing them to decide in this *very important debate*" (11). She next describes her correspondent's interpretive methods, which rely exclusively on the Bible to supply the "supposed proofs" of women's inferiority (11). By juxtaposing these two different reading practices, Murray's satiric tactics are on full display. Although she describes her own process of interpretation as "weak and presuming" (11), she clearly intends her audience to recognize that her methods of analysis are superior to those of her male correspondent. Her reliance on reason and experience and rejection of religious authority would have stood out as preferable practices for U.S. readers, allowing Murray to counter her correspondent's claims of male superiority while also showing that women were capable of using these rational intellectual skills.

More than simply demonstrating her exceptional intellectual capabilities, Murray emphasizes how she arrives at her arguments for gender equality by considering these different processes of reading. Although she disagrees with her correspondent's views of women, she is willing to consider how he arrived at his interpretation. "However, as you, sir, confine yourself entirely to the sacred oracles" (11), she agrees to examine his biblical interpretation, and this effort to represent and consider her opponent's view exemplifies the practice of federal literacy. For Murray, the best way to promote a more inclusive and equitable view of gender in the United States is to engage in multiple forms of interpretation and reading. She begins by acknowledging her correspondent's interpretation, where Eve is blamed for the downfall of humankind due to her "sensual appetite" and marked as inferior because she "was first in the transgression" (12). Murray then challenges this interpretation by showing how the same story can support the opposite conclusion. In the case of Eve, Murray points out how her actions were "governed . . . by a desire of adorning her own mind," in contrast to Adam, whose actions had nothing to do with "the accumulation of knowledge" but, rather, were motivated by "a bare pusillanimous attachment to a woman" (13), an interpretation that suggests that women are superior figures due to their reason, independence, and intelligence, in contrast to men who are driven by their emotional and physical attachments. Rather than presenting her interpretation as definitive "proof" of female superiority, however, Murray encourages her readers to recognize the potential validity of both readings and embrace a figurative, rather than fixed, perception of both genders. Although it might seem that Adam "is manifested as a figure of strength . . . we must not regard him as anything more than a figure" (14), Murray wants her readers to recognize that men and women can both be interpreted according to the qualities of strength and weakness represented in the Bible. When Murray writes, "His soul is formed in no sort superior but every way equal to the mind of her who is emblem of weakness" (14), she puts forward not a single, definitive reading of gender but an interpretation of it in diverse and multiple terms. Only by being open to alternative interpretations will the citizens of the United States be able to represent their differences equitably and productively.

Murray continued to present her arguments using multiple voices and perspectives, and these plural literary tactics culminated in her *Gleaner* essays, which were published as a regular column in the *Massachusetts Magazine* between 1792 and 1794. Murray published thirty-two essays in the *Gleaner* series, which she later expanded to one hundred essays in her three-volume collection that she published under the same title in 1798. Unlike her previous work, Murray adopted a male persona for narrating these essays, casting herself as a "Gleaner" whose authorial role determined the plural structure of her work. Instead of providing a single, authoritative voice, the Gleaner presents himself as a disinterested collector whose goal was to gather and present information from a wide variety of sources. As he announced in the first essay, "With diligence, then, I shall ransack the fields, the meadows, and the groves ... deeming myself privileged to crop with impunity a hint from one, an idea from another, and to aim improvement upon a sentence from a third." From the beginning, then, Murray structured the *Gleaner* essays as a miscellaneous survey of the nation, providing citizens with a means of encountering the different people, places, and concerns of the United States, with the goal of assembling these varied components into an "ample harvest" that all citizens could enjoy and appreciate.[93]

Diversity is the definitive feature of the *Gleaner* essays. Presented as an endless exchange of letters between the Gleaner and his fictional friends, family, and readers, this format allows Murray to provide a fairly representative portrait of the nation's variety that covers the perspectives of all kinds of citizens—men and women, rich and poor, urban and rural, educated and uneducated, young and old—as well as an equally diverse range of topics that include the development of political parties, policies for managing debt, female education, conventions of courtship and marriage, the current status of the theater, national responses to the French Revolution, the secrecy of the Masons, and many more. In the end, the specific content of the *Gleaner* essays is less important than the expansive processes of reading and exchange that these essays foreground. Nina Baym comments on how the *Gleaner* essays continually emphasize these varied networks of engagement, noting that "often a single essay will contain several layers of different narration, presenting voices within voices, enclosing letters within letters, mediating one discourse by another discourse, until the question of who is writing or speaking becomes untraceably labyrinthine."[94] Though it might seem that this style would be prone to disorder and chaos, the Gleaner argues that the experience of encountering these numerous exchanges enables readers to develop a productive understanding of the nation. "I have treasured even the *whispers* of conversation; my ear is constantly on duty ... and I am careful to hoard every remark," reports the Gleaner, who carefully assembles and presents this "multifarious burden" to his readers for "public observation."[95] By allowing his readers to access these various exchanges, the Gleaner's essays help them recognize that "their component parts ... are united, as it were, by a sympathetic thread."[96]

Murray directly associates these plural dimensions of the *Gleaner* essays with the federal structure of the United States. The Gleaner devoted an entire essay to the subject of federal nationalism, where he praises the United States for its commitment to representing the nation's many differences.[97] "Variety constitutes one of the principle beauties in the arrangement of [its] nature," asserts the Gleaner, and although he acknowledges that, at times, this diversity might lead to "faction ... and discord," he ultimately insists that representing the United States as a "heterogeneous collection" is the best way to produce a just, equitable, and successful form of government.[98] As he describes it, "federalism was the basis on which we were successfully building the superstructure of everything useful," and he encourages his readers to find new ways to contribute to "the complex and admirable intertexture of those united and separate governments which constitute our federalism." For the Gleaner, any efforts to "trace the varieties of nature" is "a fruitful avocation," and although he does not mention his own essays directly, readers would have seen an immediate connection between the plural dimensions of his writing and the political status of the United States. By representing the United States as "a people ... made up of all those varieties of constitution, intellect, passions, and corporeal strength which are commonly found in a community," the *Gleaner* essays, much like the federal government, are intended to bring "the requisite dignity, energy, execution, and obedience to the social order."[99]

What happens, then, to Murray's arguments about gender equality in the context of these diverse essays? Murray's decision to present these essays through a male persona might seem to diminish the authority of women within the federal nation, particularly as the Gleaner continually privileges his supervisory roles and responsibilities as a husband, father, businessman, and writer. Rather than taking the Gleaner's authority at face value, however, Murray uses the plural content of these essays to question and reevaluate his critical standing. By continually juxtaposing the Gleaner's views and statements with the equally strong and varied views of his numerous correspondents (which include both men and women), Murray encourages her readers to interpret the Gleaner not as a single, definitive voice but as one voice that needs to be evaluated, equally, alongside many others—a framework that, in turn, encourages citizens to focus more on the content of what these speakers are saying rather than on their gender. As many critics have noted, the *Gleaner* essays ultimately portray both men and women in very diverse terms. Some are capable of speaking with great authority, eloquence, and wisdom, while others are silly, uninformed, insincere, and deceptive. Sometimes these variations even emerge in the same character, as in the extensive "Margaretta" letters where the Gleaner describes his family's involvement with the education and marriage of their adopted daughter. Within these letters, at times, the Gleaner serves as the guiding voice of reason, but, at other moments, he makes foolish assumptions and errors in judgment that are corrected by the observations and insights of his wife and daughter and vice versa. By encouraging citizens to interpret gender in terms of these variations, the *Gleaner* essays refuse to attach any definitive moral or intellectual significance to men or to women, leaving readers free to interpret them on their own individual and equally complicated merits. Just as she did in "On the Equality of the Sexes," Murray uses the *Gleaner* essays to argue not that men and women are absolutely equal but that the process of interpreting men and women should be equal. Like so many of her fellow magazine writers and satirists, Murray, first and foremost, uses print to promote a plural understanding and interpretation of the nation. The crucial difference, however, is that, unlike most of her contemporaries, Murray includes women as an active, vital, and unquestionable part of the nation's federal diversity.

CHAPTER 4

Concurrent Sentimentality

The Federal Logic of Captivity

> I can remember the time, when I used to sleep quietly without workings in my thoughts whole nights together, but now it is otherwise with me.
>
> ——MARY ROWLANDSON, *A True History of the Captivity and Restoration of Mrs. Mary Rowlandson*

Captivity narratives tell stories of revision. As captive subjects are taken from their homes and transported into unfamiliar spaces, they change the way they look at the world, reorienting their former views of self and home to account for the different customs and experiences they encounter. Mary Rowlandson describes this process of revision at the end of her 1682 captivity narrative when she famously recounts her inability to sleep. Returned to her family in Boston, Rowlandson stands once again in the English Puritan community that she considers home, yet she recognizes that she no longer sees or experiences it in the same way. As she describes it, Rowlandson feels "otherwise" as she looks at her home, and she describes how she understands and experiences her community differently from her neighbors. "When all are fast about me, and no eye open but his who ever waketh, my thoughts are upon things past."[1]

In this concluding moment, Rowlandson revises her former view of home—where she felt and acted the same way as her neighbors—and replaces it with a new one that includes perspectives and experiences that her neighbors do not share. Lying awake with her thoughts running "upon things past," Rowlandson now orients her sense of self and community in relation to a much wider range of activities and beliefs than she did before her captivity. And yet, even though she admittedly feels "otherwise," her divergent position does not cause her to feel excluded or alienated from her English Puritan home. Despite her altered perspective, Rowlandson confidently reclaims her place as a faithful member of her home community, where, together with her neighbors, they are sustained by "the love and the goodness of God" (50).

Rowlandson's concluding position as a part of, yet also apart from her home introduces readers to a more heterogeneous understanding of community founded on what I would like to call "concurrent sentiments." Concurrence is a useful concept for thinking about differences within a unified system since concurring elements are defined by a joint relationship of distinction and similarity. Concurrent events take place in different locations but occur at the same time. Concurrent lines are distinct yet run in parallel directions. In legal contexts, concurrent opinions refer to a shared judgment reached by different arguments. Concurrence likewise explains Rowlandson's dual experience of inclusion and separation at the end of her narrative. Surrounded by her family and friends, Rowlandson returns to the same national, cultural, and religious community where her narrative began and where she still shares the same core practices and beliefs.[2] Her understanding of those beliefs and practices, however, has been reshaped by experiences that differ from her fellow colonists. Her identity as a faithful English Puritan is now defined by a much wider range of knowledge and perspectives than she previously thought possible.

Early American captivity narratives provide numerous examples of individuals who redefine their sense of self and community to accommodate the experiences and perspectives they encounter during their captivity, allowing them to develop a concurrent sense of national belonging. *A True Narrative of the Sufferings of Mary Kinnan* (1795) describes how Mary Kinnan develops a new interpretive framework during her captivity with the Shawnee and Delaware people. As her experiences "led to the exertion of faculties, which till then were not possessed, or at least lay dormant," Kinnan engages in a new range of activities and beliefs that she now finds acceptable, such that "I have supported *in reality*, what, *in idea*, had appeared impossible."[3] In *A Genuine and Correct Account of the Captivity, Sufferings, and Deliverance of Mrs. Jemima Howe* (1792), Howe similarly reports her ability to accommodate multiple perspectives in framing her own identity and behavior, noting how she learns "to behave in such a manner as at once to secure my own virtue and the good esteem of the [Abenaki] family in which I resided."[4] Other captivity narratives describe how captives develop a more diverse understanding of not just their own cultural identities but also those of their captives. "The difference in mankind ever struck me more sensibly than while a prisoner," remarks Ebenezer Fletcher, a Revolutionary solider taken captive by the British during the Revolutionary War. Although he initially expected his British captors to be a homogeneous group uniformly opposed to his own views, Fletcher reports that, over time, he comes to view the British in more varied terms, where "some would do everything in their power to make me comfortable and cheerful, while others abused me with the vilest of language."[5] Rather than interpreting the world in singular terms, Fletcher learns that his interests are better served by learning to recognize and engage with variety, a perspective that lends itself to a federal sensibility. Other captivity narratives similarly encouraged readers to recognize the value of understanding alternative perspectives and recognizing the political and cultural variety within a community, such as *The Adventures of Col. Daniel Boon* (1784) and the *Narrative of the Remarkable Occurrences in the Life of John Blatchford of Cape-Ann* (1788).

Captivity narratives reimagine the concept of community by making room for these subjects who learn to think and feel "otherwise" during their experiences away from home. By dramatizing cross-cultural encounters, captivity narratives inevitably tell stories of change and transformation. While captivity narratives inevitably produce "transcultural," "hybrid," or "dialogic" perspectives, however, few tell stories of complete conversion or assimilation.[6] Even though captive subjects observe and, in some cases, learn to tolerate and adopt some of the beliefs and practices of their captors, most retain a strong connection to their home communities and readily resume their former habits and identities when they return. If returned captives do not lose their communal identities or connections to home, they nevertheless return with an altered understanding of their community. Distinguished from their countrymen by their experiences in captivity, captive subjects must expand and diversify their understanding of "home" to include members who have been defined by different histories and frames of reference, producing a new sense of belonging founded on concurrent, rather than coincident, sentiments.

This ability to imagine a community composed of different, yet ultimately compatible, experiences aligns the genre of the captivity narrative with the discourse of federalism—a model of unity founded on the concept of concurrence. Rather than governing through a single body or uniform set of principles or interests, federalism imagines national unity in terms of what John Rawls calls an "overlapping consensus," where different experiences and perspectives are represented to produce a collaborative, though ultimately heterogeneous, union.[7] This diversified model of unity emerged from changes in the concept of sovereignty in the late seventeenth and eighteenth centuries as citizens began to imagine power in more multiple and dispersed terms. By relocating power in "the people" rather than a monarch or other absolute authority, the rise of liberal democracy produced more diverse and locally oriented models of representation where, as Alison LaCroix describes it, authority "could be shifted wholesale to reside ... in different location[s] within a political community."[8]

This chapter examines how captivity narratives contributed to this multiple and concurrent understanding of sovereignty in the British American colonies and early United States by enabling readers to imagine communities defined by different yet compatible experiences and expressions. Captivity narratives have long been read as central texts in the development of U.S. nationalism and literary culture. Often described as the first "American" literary genre, these narratives helped readers think through issues of liberty and resistance before and after the Revolution, providing useful allegories for imagining national identity, autonomy, and individual rights in the early republic.[9] Critics have also argued that captivity narratives laid the groundwork for modern conceptions of citizenship by imagining new models of subjectivity and sentimental affiliation, while also shaping the literary development of the novel.[10] Shifting away from these thematic and subject-oriented readings, however, I want to examine how captivity narratives influenced U.S. nationalism by experimenting with heterogeneous forms of unity. As captive subjects revise their view of home to account for a wider range of experiences and feelings, their narratives made it possible for readers to see how expressions of difference can produce stable forms of affiliation. Significantly, captivity narratives do not just produce an expanded awareness of differences. Captive subjects learn how to interpret differences in compatible terms, providing yet another model of how early U.S. literature helped citizens embrace and enact a federal nationalism.

To illustrate, I turn to two of the most popular captivity narratives of the early republic, *The Narrative of Mrs. Mary Rowlandson*, which describes Rowlandson's captivity with the Wampanoag Indians during King Philip's War, and Royall Tyler's picaresque novel of Barbary captivity, *The Algerine Captive*. Although Rowlandson's account was originally published in 1682, it was reprinted in the 1770s and again in 1790s, making it one of the most widely read texts in the early national era. Critics have often explained this renewed interest in relation to themes of liberty and resistance, arguing that "the frame of [her] captivity narrative—beginning and ending in freedom—endorsed the colonists' desire to regain liberties that were theirs by right."[11] Such thematic readings, however, do not fully account for the complex revisions of community that emerge in her narrative, nor do they explain its continued popularity in the 1790s when such revolutionary parallels were less relevant. Critical assessments of *The Algerine Captive* have similarly focused on the novel's engagement with liberty, particularly regarding its depiction of slavery, which provides a framework for recognizing individual rights and "the blessings of freedom" in the new nation.[12]

Rather than focusing on liberty, I argue that we might better understand the popularity and influence of these texts by situating them in relation to changing conceptions of sovereignty in the late eighteenth century. Americans were heavily invested in two separate, though related, arguments about the form of national sovereignty during the 1770s and 1790s, and Rowlandson's and Tyler's works provided readers with a means of addressing these issues. During the 1770s, the British American colonists were increasingly resistant to the singular and absolute model of sovereignty set forward by the British Crown through the passage of the Stamp Act, the Townsend Act, and various Intolerable Acts. Although most colonists still saw themselves as loyal British subjects sharing in "the common rights of Englishmen" under the Magna Carta, they also believed that their circumstances were distinct enough to require their own parliamentary representation. Inherent in their arguments was a plural conception of British sovereignty where power could be shared between the imperial government and its various colonies, and it was during this time that the British American colonists began referring to the colonies as a sovereign "part" of an imperial whole.[13] As Benjamin Franklin explained in his testimony to Parliament in 1766, rather than representing a "purely British" interest, the imperial government needed to be expanded to represent "conjointly a British and an American interest," a description that makes room for different, though ultimately linked, forms of sovereignty within the realm.[14] "Let us have an American Parliament, as well as provincial assemblies, and be gently tied together with the pleasant chords of a sovereign policy," argued "A Loyal Patriot" in a pamphlet published in response to the Stamp Act in 1768.[15] This image of sovereignty as a set of "pleasant chords" linking the distinct yet allied interests of the colonies and the British Empire provides an apt illustration of the model of concurrent governance that was taking shape in the colonies in the late 1760s and 1770s, a model that would be further endorsed by the plural dynamics of Rowlandson's account of captivity, which began to be reprinted around the same time.

These arguments for a plural yet collaborative model of sovereignty would come to the forefront of American politics again in the 1790s, although in this case, citizens were more concerned with how to make this model of plural sovereignty succeed rather than arguing for its existence. By this time, the United States had been clearly defined as a nation of concurrent sovereignties through the federal Constitution, but citizens continued to argue over how best to interpret and enact this plural model of authority as local uprisings such as the Whiskey Rebellion and the establishment of the Bank of the United States raised questions about the balance of power between the states and the central government. Meanwhile, international conflicts, such as the seizure of U.S. citizens by Barbary pirates and British press gangs, caused many to worry that the plural dimensions of the union only weakened its authority on the world stage, where "the union of the thirteen states is much too weak even to combat the machinations of any petty prince, however contemptible, who shall chuse to insult the American flag."[16] By the mid-1790s, the federal unity forged under the Constitution seemed precarious enough that George Washington even expressed his uncertainty about its future, concluding his "Farewell Address" with the unsettling question, "Is there a doubt whether a common government can embrace so large a sphere? Let experience solve it."[17]

As citizens debated the viability of the federal union, captivity narratives supported this plural model of nationalism by teaching citizens how to interpret differences in concurrent terms. While *The Narrative of Mrs. Mary Rowlandson* represents a tentative early step toward imagining communities composed of different experiences, practices, and perspectives, *The Algerine Captive* offers a much more assertive defense of the value and stability of diverse models of unity. Although they are different in form and focus, both narratives illustrate the potential of imagining a nation founded on concurrent experiences, where citizens who learn to think and feel "otherwise" can still make up cohesive and productive communities.

Of course, for as much as captivity narratives helped promote a more diverse understanding of national citizenship, these narratives also reinforced specific points of exclusion in the federal nation, particularly regarding race. While white captives benefit from their plural and concurrent perspectives, captivity narratives typically draw clear racial boundaries between those who can be included in the "civilized" nation and those who cannot. Rowlandson's and Tyler's captivity narratives, however, stand out as notable exceptions. Although these narratives are ultimately unwilling to recognize racial "others" as equals, they nevertheless encourage their readers to view racial and ethnic differences in more tolerant and understanding terms, laying a foundation for imagining more collaborative and peaceful relationships between white and nonwhite communities in the future.

While most captivity narratives affirm the racial limits of federal nationalism, they tend to offer more radical and inclusive possibilities for women. Most captivity narratives feature women who take thoughtful, authoritative, and independent action outside of the traditional domestic sphere, providing a framework that made it possible to imagine alternative roles for women in the federal nation. Once again, these narratives typically stop short of imagining women as equal citizens with the right to act directly in the political sphere. Nevertheless, captivity narratives do make it possible to imagine women as more active and influential participants in the nation, opening the door for a more inclusive federal future.

Imagining a Federal Puritan

Originally published in 1682 under the title *The Sovereignty and the Goodness of God*, Rowlandson's narrative was a colonial best seller. The book went through three editions in its first year, and the second and third editions sold more than one thousand copies each—an unprecedented number for this time. As Neal Salisbury notes, it is estimated that more than 1 percent of the New England colonial population purchased the book, which meant that the text itself had an even wider circulation among those who borrowed the text or heard it read aloud, encompassing an audience that included "large numbers of ordinary colonists as well as ministers and other members of the region's elite."[18] Directed toward a Puritan audience, these early editions emphasize the religious and spiritual dimensions of Rowlandson's experience, and her story of captivity and redemption was meant to testify to the power of God. Lest this spiritual message be overshadowed by the "extreme hazards" and "strange and amazing" details described in the text, these editions all began with a prefatory essay (likely written by Increase Mather) that sets forth a clear framework for interpreting the narrative as "an instance of the faith and patience of the Saints" and "the Sovereignty of God . . . who is indeed the supreme Lord of the world."[19]

The Sovereignty and Goodness of God was an enormously influential text in seventeenth-century New England. In addition to challenging and reconfiguring aspects of Puritan faith, Rowlandson's narrative offered new ways for thinking about individual subjectivity, Native American culture, and women's roles in colonial America. The text took on a very different political and cultural resonance, however, in the late eighteenth century when it experienced a second wave of popularity. Six new editions appeared in Massachusetts between 1770 and 1773, with another boom in publication occurring in the 1790s. Retitled *The Narrative of the Captivity and Restoration of Mary Rowlandson*, these later editions repackaged Rowlandson's story as a narrative of individual liberty and independence. Not only did these later editions eliminate the original focus on "God" in the title, they also cut Mather's religious "Preface to the Reader," replacing it, in some cases, with illustrations that depict Rowlandson as an aggressive and independent defender of her home. In one example, she blocks the doorway of a log cabin, aiming a rifle at a group of tomahawk-wielding Indians. In another, she stands alone in front of a fort, holding a rifle and wearing a soldier's tricorn hat, her breasts partially displayed above a tight bodice. Such images bear little resemblance to the "modest" and "pious" Puritan woman that Mather describes in his original introduction or to Rowlandson's description of the attack on her home.[20] Instead, these changes highlight the altered significance of Rowlandson's narrative for late eighteenth-century readers who viewed her text as a means of reflecting on liberty and resistance in the context of their own interests in revolution, individual rights, and national independence.[21]

Such readings, however, do not fully account for the renewed interest in Rowlandson's text in the 1770s and 1790s. While the narrative's emphasis on liberty would certainly have resonated with readers on the cusp of revolution, her revised conception of community, combined with her innovative rereadings of the Bible, would have been equally instructive and relevant for early national readers. The first wave of reprintings appeared in and around Boston, which was also the site of some of the most vocal arguments for colonial governance. Throughout the early 1770s, residents of Boston led the way in demanding the representation of "American" interests through the publication of pamphlets and editorials and more violent acts such as the Boston Tea Party. Arguments about the legitimacy of local sovereignty took a particularly radical turn in 1773 following a series of debates between the royal governor of Massachusetts, Thomas Hutchinson, and the local Massachusetts assembly, known as the General Court. Anxious to quell the growing demands for greater colonial autonomy, Hutchinson delivered a speech that drew heavily on English constitutional law to assert the absolute power of the Crown, arguing that "it was the sense of the Kingdom that [the colonies] were to remain subject to the supreme Authority of Parliament."[22]

To counter Hutchinson, members of the colonial assembly embarked on extensive rereadings of English constitutional and colonial documents, turning to the Magna Carta, the Massachusetts colonial charter, and the 1707 Act of Union to present an alternative interpretation of English law that supported local sovereignty and governance. "Although from the nature of government, there must be one supreme authority over the whole, yet this constitution will admit of subordinate powers with Legislative and Executive authority, greater or less, according to local and other circumstances," concluded the Massachusetts Council, making room for a more dispersed and diverse expression of political authority within the realm. "Thus we see a variety of corporations formed within the kingdom, with powers to make and execute such by-laws as are for their immediate use and benefit, the members of such corporations still remaining subject to the general laws of the kingdom."[23]

Of central importance here is the principle of compatibility, where the distinct interests and circumstances of a local community can be represented while "still remaining" a part of a national whole. As LaCroix notes, "The debates of 1773 signified an important transition in Anglo-Americans' thinking about sovereignty ... an illustration of a key conceptual breakthrough that helped bring about the development of federalism."[24] Although the colonists acknowledged that their local assemblies might look and act differently from the English Parliament so they could serve the "use and benefit" of their constituents, the Massachusetts General Court argued that these assemblies would nevertheless remain compatible with the central principles and laws of the British government. As the Massachusetts Council argued, "These modes of expression, convey the same meaning, and serve to show an intention, that the laws of the colonies should be as much as possible, conformable in the spirit of them, to the principles and fundamental laws of the English constitution."[25] This argument, that a nation can be composed of different yet "conformable" modes of political expression corresponds to the revised model of community that emerges in Mary Rowlandson's captivity narrative. Rowlandson's account dramatizes a shift between two different understandings of home—one founded on a sense of shared beliefs and practices, and another that makes room for expressing those beliefs and practices differently—and this transformation would have provided an instructive model for early American readers who were similarly trying to imagine a more expansive conception of power and nationalism. Just as Rowlandson learns to reinterpret her English Christian identity in ways that respond to local circumstances while still remaining compatible with her central beliefs, British American colonists and, later, U.S. citizens were also looking for ways to express their national identity and allegiance in locally specific yet inclusive ways. By illustrating this shift from a homogeneous model of community to one founded on feelings of concurrence, Rowlandson's narrative helped readers imagine more diverse forms of political and social belonging, which, in turn, laid the groundwork for a federal conception of unity.

The transformation of Rowlandson's sense of community begins early in her captivity. Her initial view of home, which is founded on a sense of religious and cultural uniformity, emerges in her description of the Indian attack, where she describes the "Christians lying in their blood, some here and some there, like a company of sheep torn by wolves. All of them stript naked by a company of hellhounds, roaring, singing, ranting, and insulting" (13). Here, Rowlandson clearly depicts her colonial community in uniform terms, united by their religious beliefs and their status as victims and defined in opposition to an equally homogeneous community of Indians, whose "savageness and brutishness" contrasts sharply with the character of the English Christians. She also views her community in relation to a comprehensive national identity at the beginning of the text. For Rowlandson, "Englishness" is such a cohesive and all-encompassing identity that it extends to anything the colonists have owned, constructed, or used, as evident in her homesick exclamations over evidence of colonial cows and footpaths: "I saw a place where *English* Cattle had been: that was a comfort to me, such as it was, quickly after that we came to an *English* path, which so took with me, that I thought I could there have freely lyen down and died" (23). Rowlandson's initial use of the Bible further reflects her belief that the English Puritans are bound together by shared knowledge and common experiences. Early in her captivity, when she feels particularly disconnected from her home, surrounded by "wilderness and woods and a company of barbarous heathen," the process of reading and even just "turning the leaves" of the Bible draws her back to her English Christian community through her contact with this common text, an experience that assures her that "though we were scattered from one end of the earth to the other, yet the Lord would gather us together" (19).

And yet, as much as she draws comfort from her homogeneous understanding of community, her experiences in captivity soon force her to develop a more expansive definition of it. This transformation begins early on, when she comes face to face with the "glittering weapons" of the Indians during their attack. "I had often before this said, that if the Indians should come, I should choose rather to be killed by them than taken alive," remarks Rowlandson, "but when it came to my trial, my mind changed; their glittering weapons so daunted my spirit that I chose rather to go along with those (as I may say) ravenous bears than that moment to end my days" (14). Confronted with physical harm, Rowlandson departs from what she once considered a steadfast belief—that she would choose death rather than be taken captive—and acts in a way that separates her from her community. Instead of expressing her faith through martyrdom (like many of her neighbors do), she makes a choice that had previously been unthinkable. Significantly, Rowlandson does not characterize this decision as a faltering or betrayal of her beliefs and identity but, rather, as an alternative expression of her Puritan faith, one that allows her to "see more of [God's] power, yea so much that I could never have thought of had I not experienced it" (16).

From this point forward, Rowlandson becomes a different kind of Puritan. Though she continues to see and portray herself as a faithful member of her English Christian community, she interprets and expresses this identity in new ways. When some of her fellow captives begin to make plans to "run away," for instance, Rowlandson once again departs from her community by refusing to join them: "they being to go one way, and I another" (19). In this case, she turns to the Bible to align her divergent decision with the faith of her fellow Christians, citing from the book of Psalms, "Wait on the Lord, be of good courage and he will strengthen thine heart, wait I say, on the Lord" (20). Ironically, Rowlandson's use of the Bible—to which she originally turned as a source of common belief and experience—repeatedly enables her to develop a more diverse understanding of Christianity that accepts a broader range of actions and beliefs. Throughout the narrative Rowlandson adopts a number of new behaviors that run counter to her former habits, such as working on the Sabbath, begging for food, and sleeping on the ground "like a Swine" (33). Though she readily acknowledges that these actions differ from her former Christian actions when "my family was about me, and relations and neighbors with us, [and] we could pray and sing and then refresh our bodies with the good creatures of God and then have a comfortable bed to ly down on," she turns to "comfortable Scripture" to characterize her new experiences as equal evidence of her faith and salvation. "Now we might say as Job, Naked I came out of my mother's womb and naked shall I return," she writes, using Job's example to interpret her altered appearance, habits, and circumstances as evidence of faith, rather than "brutishness" (24). At other moments, she cites the experiences of the prodigal son or accounts of suffering from the book of Psalms to justify "the change[s] that had come upon us" (24), again relying on scriptural interpretations to include her unconventional behavior as part of an acceptable Christian framework.

The most notable transformation of Rowlandson's expression of English Christianity concerns her eating habits. She frequently comments on how she learns to eat and even enjoy foods she would never have consumed at home, including ground nuts, tree bark, bear meat, and the feet, intestines, and internal organs of horses. "What (sayes he) can you eat Horse liver?" an Indian asks when she requests a piece, indicating the extent to which her new tastes run counter to those expected of a Puritan woman: "I told him I would try, if he would give a piece," she reports (23). Rowlandson clearly recognizes that these food choices would not be acceptable in her English Puritan community. She often "thinks how formerly my stomach would turn against this or that and *I* could starve and die before I could eat such things" (21), and, in addition to eating different foods, she also starts eating them in a different manner. Not only does she eat foods that she would normally "turn against," she consumes much of it in a manner that further departs from her traditional habits. Fearful of losing her piece of horse liver, for instance, Rowlandson eats it partially raw with "the blood about my mouth" (23). Another time, Rowlandson takes a piece of horseflesh from an English child who "could not bite it, it was so tough and sinewy, but lay sucking, gnawing, chewing, and slobbering it in the Mouth and Hand," an act that runs counter to both her former tastes and maternal sentiments. Nevertheless, "I took it of the Child," she reports, "and eat it myself and savoury it was to my taste" (36). In all these instances, she again turns to the Bible to interpret her unconventional actions as compatible expressions of her faith. Her enjoyment of the bloody liver testifies to the teachings of Proverbs, which states, "to the hungry soul every bitter thing is sweet" (23). Similarly, she renders her theft and consumption of the child's piece of horsemeat acceptable by aligning it with the experiences of Job. "That I may say as Job, Chap. 6. 7. *The things that my Soul refused to touch are as my sorrowful meat*" (36). By interpreting these experiences in relation to scripture, Rowlandson makes it possible to read her unorthodox behavior in compatible terms, noting that "the Lord made that pleasant and refreshing which another time would have been an abomination" (36).

More than simply reinterpreting her "savage" actions as evidence of her Christian faith, Rowlandson goes even further by characterizing this behavior as a means of improving her faith. "See I pray you how mine eyes have been enlightened because I tasted a little of this honey," she writes after eating "a piece of the ruff or ridding of the small guts [that] I broiled on the coals" (36). Her description here, which references the book of Samuel, illustrates the principle of concurrence. The "honey" she consumes in captivity is very different from "honey" as she would have interpreted it at home. Despite this difference, her consumption of this native "honey" still affirms and enhances her faith, suggesting to Rowlandson and her readers that there are different ways of representing, interpreting, and expressing Christian identity and beliefs.

This recognition—that multiple views and experiences can still lead back to a shared set of beliefs—represents one of the most important insights of Rowlandson's text. In the end, Rowlandson's ability to view her captive experiences as concurrent with the core beliefs and practices of her colonial community not only ensures her survival, it suggests to readers that communities can accommodate a diverse range of perspectives and interpretations without fundamental disruption. And while she remains somewhat unsettled by this altered sense of home (as evident in her inability to sleep), Rowlandson acknowledges that she can no longer view the world according to a single or uniform frame of reference, an insight she justifies with reference to the book of Psalms: "For my thoughts are not your thoughts, neither are your ways my ways, saith the Lord" (30). Acknowledging that there are different yet equally valid ways of interpreting and expressing a Christian identity, Rowlandson not only comes to view her own community in more diverse terms; she also comes to see variety as a central component of any enlightened community.

Rowlandson's revised understanding of community, which makes room for citizens who feel "otherwise," would certainly have been instructive in the 1770s as the British American colonists (soon-to-be rebel nationalists) tried to forge a more diverse and expansive model of British identity, which, in turn, would lay the groundwork for their subsequent federal American identity. Rowlandson's ability to imagine and recognize the validity of her revised Christian identity was equally instructive when her narrative once again became popular in the 1790s, although the specific nature of its instructive value and reasons for its popularity were different. In the 1790s Rowlandson's captivity narrative was important, not so much because it provided citizens with a plural model of identity but because of its ability to define federal citizenship in flexible and mutable ways.

Although the Constitution was successfully ratified in 1789, citizens and political leaders alike were unsure what it meant to represent, to govern, or to even define federal citizenship and federal legislation in the new nation. Christian Fritz has recently argued that the 1790s presented a "crisis of sovereignty" in the new federal republic as citizens struggled to identify themselves as both sovereigns and subjects and determine the appropriate balance of power between the states and the central government. "The constitution divided governmental power between national and state governments, a division creating a puzzle in identifying the sovereign of the federal Constitution," remarks Fritz, and, because "the federal Constitution reflected no consensus on how the people could express their sovereignty," citizens had to continually revise and reinterpret the signs and actions that defined their federal identity.[26]

Two major issues brought concerns about the meaning of federal nationalism and sovereignty to the fore in the 1790s: the establishment of the Bank of the United States and the Whiskey Rebellion. Both events prompted debates about the significance of the federal union and the degree of authority that should be granted to the central government and to the states. Proponents of the national bank argued that the United States needed to establish a centralized system to manage the national debt and support the economic growth of the nation. Such a bank, wrote Hamilton, was "essential to the being of the national government."[27] Opponents of the bank argued that the Constitution did not give Congress the power to establish such an institution, making it a violation of the federal compact. In 1791 Hamilton responded by arguing that the power to establish the bank was "implied" by the Constitution, an argument that further opened up the question of federal validity as the significance of federal legislation was now subject to a much wider range of interpretation. For some, the powers of the federal government were restricted to those mentioned explicitly in the document. For others, the powers of the federal government were open to any that were not explicitly restricted by the document. Within this environment, the definition of legitimate federal action or power could be in considerable flux.

The Whiskey Rebellion likewise introduced complicated problems of federal interpretation. When residents in rural Pennsylvania took up arms to resist the U.S. government's attempt to collect a national whiskey tax in the early 1790s, and Washington responded by sending in federal troops, divisive debates broke out over which side exemplified a just federal response. For some, the actions of the federal government were a tyrannical abuse of power that diminished the authority of the people whose interests they were supposed to represent and protect. "The government is *responsible* to its sovereign the people for the faithful exercise of its entrusted powers, and *any part of the people* have the right to express their opinions on the government," stated the president of the New York Democratic Society, one of the local groups that supported the rebellion and argued for greater local activism and representation by the federal government.[28] For others, the forceful government response to the Whiskey Rebellion represented an appropriate and legitimate use of federal power, characterizing the rebels and their supporting Democratic-Republican societies as extraconstitutional forces that threatened to "shake the government to its foundation."[29]

Whatever side they chose to take on these issues, citizens and political leaders all relied on the logic and rhetoric of federalism to defend their arguments, and these divided views regarding legitimate "federal" actions eventually led to the emergence of formal political parties that roughly broke down according to the ways they chose to interpret the Constitution—as a document privileging the power of the central government (Federalists) or the power of the states (Republicans). Both sides believed they were remaining true to the nation's federal ideals, even though they had radically different ways of interpreting the nation's federal identity and power, and over the course of the 1790s, they would continually engage in the process of interpreting and reinterpreting the federal language of the Constitution, of the documents surrounding the drafting and ratification of the Constitution, and the language of current legislation to find ways to support their respective models of the federal union. These endless processes of interpretation never produced a definitive federal "reading" of the nation. Instead, they continued to represent the nation in plural and, in this case, seemingly contested terms.

In the midst of these intense debates about the meaning of federal union and federal sovereignty, a text such as Rowlandson's captivity narrative would have been very reassuring for U.S. readers. Rowlandson's narrative shows that texts can be interpreted differently while still producing a unified national and cultural identity. It also reassures readers that the same single document can endorse a wide range of different actions and behaviors, even ones that might seem to be radically opposed to one's original perceptions of self or home. In the end, Rowlandson's narrative did not offer readers in the 1790s any specific solutions to the questions of sovereignty or federal identity in the early United States, nor did it provide a way to resolve the intensifying partisan politics that shaped the federal nation. What it does offer, however, is a framework for recognizing how these competing interpretations and opposing behaviors can still be seen as part of a unified nation.

In imagining the nation in terms of these plural, but concurrent, perspectives and behaviors, Rowlandson's captivity narrative does pose some radical alternatives regarding the roles that women can play in a national community. As discussed in the previous chapter, the plural dynamics of the early United States raised serious debates about whether women should be included as equal citizens within the federal nation, and Rowlandson's narrative seems to suggest that women can certainly take on more active, equal, and independent roles in the public sphere without fundamentally disrupting their own identities or communities. At the start of her captivity narrative, Rowlandson exemplifies the quiet, deferential, domestic qualities expected of Anglo-American women. Her actions revolve entirely around her role as a mother as she tends to her injured child;

she says very little and continually defers to the authority of her captors, even when she would rather not. "There was no resisting, but go I must," she writes of her first weeks in captivity, where she primarily "sat upon my knees with my babe in my lap . . . with a very heavy heart" (17). Over time, however, Rowlandson takes on a much more active and independent role in her new community, adapting her domestic skills to participate in the local economy where she exercises her individual agency and authority with great success. She describes her new activities as follows: "During my abode in this place, Philip spake to me to make a shirt for his boy, which I did, for which he gave me a shilling; I offered the money to my master, but he bade me keep it and with it I bought a piece of horse flesh. Afterwards he asked me to make a cap for his boy, for which he invited me to dinner. I went and he gave me a pancake. . . . There was a Squaw who spake to me to make a shirt for her sannup, for which she gave me a piece of bear. Another asked me to knit a pair of stockins for which she gave me a quart of pease. I boyled my pease and bear together and invited my master and mistress to dinner" (25). Here, Rowlandson is no longer a passive, deferential woman who is defined solely by her familial relationships. Instead, she actively participates in the local economy, where she successfully transacts business as an individual and manages her own exchanges and expenditures. These activities eventually enable Rowlandson to act as the head of her own household, as evident when she invites her master and mistress to dinner. Although such behavior would have been unheard of in her home community, Rowlandson embraces and thrives in these new roles, which not only improve her circumstances but also enhance her Christianity. As she becomes more self-sufficient, she writes, "I had time and liberty again to look into my Bible, which was my guide by day" (32), assuring her readers that her new forms of behavior have not radically altered her identity. Although she is acting differently, she is still a faithful Puritan woman who is committed to her domestic and religious tasks.

During her captivity, Rowlandson also begins to speak for herself in more direct and aggressive terms. At another point in her narrative, she describes a moment when "Philip's maid came in with the child in her arms and asked me to give her a piece of my apron to make a flap for it. *I* told her *I* would not; then my mistress bad me give it, but still *I* said no. The maid told me if I would not give her a piece, she would tear a piece off it: I told her I would tear her coat then" (31). In contrast to her quiet, deferential behavior at the start of her narrative, in this scene Rowlandson clearly and forcefully speaks for herself, even when she is confronted with opposition. Once again, this public display of independence, assertiveness, and resistance would not have been accepted or permitted in her home community. In this instance, though, Rowlandson expresses no feelings of regret or shame for her actions. She simply reports her behavior as a straightforward fact, affirming her sense of its legitimacy. If anything, her continual emphasis on the word "I" in this exchange emphasizes the pride she feels in asserting her own voice and authority, as well as the confidence she feels in expressing her position.

Although Rowlandson's efforts to exercise her own independent agency would have seemed unorthodox for readers in both the colonial period and the early United States, her narrative portrays her actions in wholly positive terms. Her ability to earn her own living, manage her own resources, speak for herself, and handle confrontation all have productive benefits for Rowlandson that reinforce rather than diminish her sense of self and home, granting her "time and liberty" to pursue other interests and allowing her to live "cheerfully, with the thoughts of going homeward" (34). On returning home, her interest in writing a formal account of her experiences indicates that she fully intends to continue exercising her own voice and authority in her English community. Her experiences in captivity have enabled her to imagine different but acceptable alternatives for defining her role as a female citizen, and these alternatives would have been inspiring for women in the early United States who were likewise looking to redefine their roles in the new nation. As Lisa Logan observes, "Rowlandson's text becomes a model for the issues American women struggle with when, as subjects, they enter the arena of representation."[30] By demonstrating her ability to engage in the public sphere without compromising her own identity or her traditional domestic roles, Rowlandson's narrative made it possible for early U.S. readers to imagine how women could similarly participate in the federal nation in positive and productive terms.

Other captivity narratives from this period likewise made room for women who felt, spoke, and acted differently. *A Genuine and Correct Account of the Captivity, Sufferings, and Deliverance of Mrs. Jemima Howe* (1792) and *A True Narrative of the Sufferings of Mary Kinnan* (1795) both provide accounts of female independence and assertiveness, with Howe engaging in political negotiations that allow her to procure "the means and manner of my own redemption" and Kinnan working closely with her brother "to concert some means of escape."[31] Fictional accounts of captivity reimagined women's roles in even bolder terms. Ann Eliza Bleeker's 1793 captivity novel, *The History of Maria Kittle*, foregrounds and privileges female agency by showing how Kittle and her female companions make better decisions than their male compatriots and contend with matters of political and national concern alongside their domestic duties.[32] Another fictional best seller, Abraham Panther's *A Surprising Account of the Discovery of a Young Woman Discovered in a Rocky Cave* (1787), makes even bolder claims for female agency and authority by depicting a woman who frees herself from captivity by brutally murdering and dismembering her captor. Although her actions are meant to be shocking, the protagonist is rewarded and admired for her actions, rather than punished. After securing her freedom, the Lady claims her captor's property and establishes a successful and civilized home. As she describes it, "I now found myself alone in possession of this cave in which there are several apartments," and she proceeds to live a "contented" existence, planting and cultivating a small crop of Indian corn. Despite her unconventional behavior, the hunters who find her describe her as an "agreeable, sensible lady" who is capable of caring for herself and maintaining a comfortable home without any male assistance, a radical argument for female independence and equality in the early republic.[33]

If captivity narratives push readers to imagine more active and assertive roles for women in the nation, they typically offer a more exclusionary and restrictive view of race. Returning to Rowlandson's narrative, even though she becomes more tolerant of the culture and customs of her native captors, she always draws a definitive line between those who are "English" and those who are "Indian" and refuses to entertain the idea that members of one community could become accepted members of the other. She emphasizes this clear cultural boundary when she is ransomed toward the end of her narrative, writing, "I was not so much hem'd in with the merciless and cruel *Heathen*, but now as much with the pitiful, tenderhearted, and compassionate *Christians*" (47).

Although she wants to maintain a clear distinction between the Indians and the English, Rowlandson's narrative nevertheless suggests that the lines between these communities are easily blurred. At the start of her narrative, she represents the Indians in uniform and oppositional terms, describing all of them as "barbarous," "savage," and "inhuman" (19). She continues to view many of them in these terms throughout her account, but, over time, she also describes Indians who treat her with "comfort" and "kindness," such as the Indian who "asked me if I would have a Bible" or the family who "gave me some groundnuts and bade me come again . . . yet they were strangers to me" (27), a description that echoes the language of Jesus in the New Testament.[34] These experiences allow Rowlandson to align these Indians with her own Christian values, diminishing her sense of difference and separation from them. She also develops a more equitable understanding of Indian cultural practices when she describes the "proud gossip" who refuses to eat when Rowlandson invites her to dinner "because I served them both in one dish" (25). Rather than dismissing this as "savage" behavior, Rowlandson's phrasing acknowledges that the Indians have their own well-established standards of politeness and civility, which, while different from her own, nevertheless represent a cultural similarity.

Rowlandson is clearly troubled by her changing perspective. As her perception of the Indians becomes more tolerant and equitable, she works hard to reassert the boundaries she wants to maintain, as is evident at the end of her narrative when she provides a list of the "remarkable passages of Providence which I took special notice of in my afflicted time" (43). Within this list, Rowlandson describes her surprise and confusion at the number of instances when her Indian captors seem to succeed and prosper while her English compatriots suffer setbacks and losses. "Strangely did the Lord provide for them" (45), she remarks, expressing her surprise at the "wonderful power of God, in providing for such a vast number of our Enemies in the Wilderness" while allowing "the destruction of many still amongst the English" (44). Rowlandson's unsettled feelings about "the strange providence of God in turning things about" such that "the *Indians were at the highest* [when] the *English at the lowest*" (45) indicate her desire to retain a strong hierarchical distinction between the English and the Indians, as well as her sense that this distinction might be false. On the one hand, she wants desperately to believe that the English are intellectually and morally superior to the Indians. On the other, her experiences suggest that she might need to revise this distinction as she discovers that the Indians seem much better able to handle the challenges posed by the landscape and conditions of the American wilderness than the English. Although she continues to portray the English and Indians as culturally distinct from one another, her experiences suggest that she might need to change the way she interprets these cultural differences and recognize that the cultural beliefs and practices of the Indians may have more legitimacy and value than she wants to believe.

In the end, Rowlandson reaffirms the cultural superiority of the English by interpreting their struggles as a test from God who "strengthened [the Indians] to be a scourge to his People" (44) in order to affirm their Christian faith. This interpretation, however, rings a bit hollow given the Indians' ability to manage and protect their communities more successfully than the English, and her assessment would have been particularly unconvincing to the more secular U.S. readers of the late eighteenth century. Although Rowlandson steadfastly tries to maintain a hierarchical distinction between the English and her Indian captors, her narrative cannot support that distinction as definitively as she would like, giving readers room to reinterpret the Indians and their cultural differences in more acceptable and even admirable terms. After reading Rowlandson's narrative, citizens in the early United States might be inclined to feel and act differently toward Native Americans. They may read the Indians as different, but they do not necessarily need to interpret the Indians solely as inhuman or inferior enemies.

By opening the door for these alternative interpretations, Rowlandson's account stands apart from most Indian captivity narratives of this time. As Frank Shuffelton writes, most captivity narratives provide "a means to insist on the inadequacy and distance of the ethnic Other," and popular captivity narratives of the late eighteenth century typically represent Native Americans as distinct from and inferior to Anglo-Americans.[35] Indigenous people are consistently portrayed as "savages," "heathens," "creatures," and "monsters" who are defined by violence, cruelty, and intellectual simplicity, as evident in top-selling accounts such as *God's Mercy Surmounting Man's Cruelty, Exemplified in the Captivity and Redemption of Elizabeth Hansen* (1728, reprinted in 1780), *The Redeemed Captive Returning to Zion: A Faithful History of Remarkable Occurrences in the Captivity and Deliverance of Mr. John Williams* (1707, reprinted throughout the 1770s and 1780s), *A Genuine and Correct Account of the Captivity, Sufferings, and Deliverance of Mrs. Jemima Howe* (1792), *A True Narrative of the Sufferings of Mary Kinnan* (1795), and the *Affecting History of the Dreadful Distresses of Fredric Manheim's Family* (1793). Some captivity narratives even include supplemental materials to ensure that their protagonists' ability to adapt to their captors' cultures would not be misinterpreted as an endorsement of native practices. *The Wonderful Escape of Dr. Knight and John Slover from Captivity* (1783) concludes with a letter from Hugh Henry Brackenridge that encourages readers to resist any urge to interpret the Indians depicted in the narrative favorably. Instead of "profaning ourselves by calling them brothers," writes Brackenridge, he encourages his readers to view them as "degenerate" and "incapable of all civilization." "They have the shapes of men and may be of the human species," he writes, "but certainly in their present state they approach nearer the character of devils."[36]

Toward the end of the eighteenth century, a few captivity narratives began to break with these racist dynamics and represent Native Americans in more compatible and inclusive terms. *The Adventures of Col. Daniel Boon [sic]* (1784) shows how Boone's experiences in captivity, much like Rowlandson's, lead him to abandon his former view of the natives as "savages," and he eventually portrays them in a more favorable and equitable light, to the point where he considers them to be members of the same family. "I spent my time there as comfortably as I might expect, was adopted, according to their custom, into a family where I became a son and had a great share in the affections of my new parents, brothers, sisters, and friends," writes Boone.[37] Boone's description promotes a radically different perception of Native Americans founded on mutual trust, respect, and affiliation, making it possible to imagine interactive and allied relationships between native and Anglo-American communities in the future. Jonathan Dickinson's *God's Protecting Providence* likewise promotes a more collaborative and equitable intercultural view. Originally published in 1699, Dickinson's account of his captivity in southern Florida was also reprinted numerous times in the 1790s, providing a detailed account of the customs, language, politics, and religious beliefs of the Jaega, Jobe, and Ais people. Dickinson's "proto-ethnographic" descriptions grant these indigenous communities greater authority and legitimacy than most captivity narratives of this period, and, although he continues to view the natives as culturally distinct from his own, his account also portrays them as skilled, intelligent, and compassionate people with sophisticated communities worthy of respect.[38] Dickinson also emphasizes how the natives and Anglo-Americans benefit from learning to work together and view one another on equal terms, as when the women agree to share responsibility for nursing one another's children, noting that this exchange "was a means of [the Indian woman] and our child reaping a benefit."[39] As Lisa M. Logan argues, by redefining Anglo and Native Americans in relationships of "cross-cultural collaboration," captivity narratives such as Dickinson's and Boone's make it possible for U.S. readers to recognize Indians as allies rather than enemies, setting a new interpretive framework for considering the nation's future engagements with native people.[40]

Fictional captivity narratives imagined these collaborative intercultural relationships in even more radical terms by representing Native American communities not just as equitable allies but as superior models for the United States to follow. *A Surprising Account of the Captivity and Escape of Philip M'Donald and Alexander M'Leod* (1786) tells the story of two Americans, M'Donald and M'Leod, who are caught in an indigenous community defined by peace, order, health, and productivity where the inhabitants are "prohibited by religion from war," "murder and infidelity are equally unknown among them," and their lands supply food with "great plenty." These observations easily convince M'Donald and M'Leod that this native community is superior to their own, and they admit that "we could have spent our lives among these people contentedly and never should have thought of seeking another home."[41] In *New Travels to the Westward* (1788), Alonso Decalves and his companions likewise find themselves temporarily trapped in an indigenous community defined by political, cultural, and moral order that could provide "a pattern to many civilized nations." War and armed conflicts are unknown, and the community's resources are abundant and evenly distributed, producing a nation that is "well-peopled and calculated for persons of ingenuity to live in." By the end of the narrative, one of his companions feels so welcome and happy that he chooses to remain within this native community, "adopt[ing] all their manners and customs," instead of returning home.[42] In both cases, characters who originally identified as American choose to fully adopt the beliefs and customs of these native communities or, at the very least, incorporate most of these customs and beliefs into their own culture when they return home, a radical reimagination of the relationship between indigenous communities and the United States. Rather than simply encouraging readers to interpret indigenous differences in compatible terms, these fictional narratives go a step farther by arguing that U.S. citizens would benefit by modeling their own nation after these native communities.

Captivity narratives ultimately offer readers a wide range of options for reimagining the roles and relationships of Native Americans and women in the United States. While some captivity narratives push for more radical forms of tolerance and inclusion than others, all of them share a commitment to imagining national identities and communities in more plural and expansive terms. Even when captivity narratives seem to reinforce points of racial and gender exclusion, their efforts to imagine and represent alternative and concurrent forms of experience open the door for readers to imagine a wider range of experiences and perspectives that can be included in a national community. In all cases, fiction definitely stands out for imagining these experiences of concurrence and pluralism in particularly revolutionary and transformative terms, which brings us to *The Algerine Captive*, Royall Tyler's 1797 novel of Barbary captivity that was one of the most popular fictional captivity narratives of the early national period. Like all captivity narratives, *The Algerine Captive* provides readers with a model for interpreting communities in ways that privilege heterogeneity and promote concurrent feelings of unity. Within this novel, however, Tyler pushes this federal tolerance and concurrence to its limits by asking readers to incorporate a much wider range of religious, cultural, and ethnic differences than had ever been considered for the nation, inviting readers to imagine a much more expansive and productive federal future for the ever-expanding United States.

"Exhibiting Our Own Manners": The Promise and Problems of Federal Representation

Published in 1797, *The Algerine Captive* was written by Royall Tyler, a writer deeply committed to establishing a strong national literary culture in the United States. Tyler gained early fame as the author of *The Contrast*, the first play to be written by an American citizen and performed professionally in the United States. *The Contrast* famously argued for the importance of representing U.S. manners, morals, and politics in the nation's literature, and Tyler continued to pursue this argument in *The Algerine Captive*, a novel that is heavily invested in promoting the federal dimensions of the United States. At the end of the novel, after traveling through the United States in search of work, followed by seven years of captivity in Algiers, the protagonist—Updike Underhill—returns home and reflects on what he has learned from his adventures. "I now mean ... to contribute cheerfully to the support of our excellent government, which I have learnt to adore in schools of despotism," he reports, "and thus secure to myself the enviable character of an useful physician, a good father, and a worthy FEDERAL citizen."[43] Here, Underhill specifically states that his experiences at home and abroad have taught him to value federal unity and citizenship. Furthermore, he argues that the experience of reading about his adventures will have a similar effect on his audience. "My ardent wish is that my fellow citizens may profit by my misfortunes," he continues, "[and] if they peruse these pages with attention they will perceive the necessity of uniting our federal strength to enforce a due respect among other nations" (225).

Underhill's emphasis on the term "federal" here is significant. As he describes it, those who "peruse these pages with attention" will learn to embrace a distinctive type of citizenship and union, becoming not just citizens but "worthy FEDERAL citizens" who belong to a nation defined by its "federal strength" (226). This qualifying emphasis would have had a strong resonance for readers in the late 1790s when the Whiskey Rebellion, the controversial establishment of the Bank of the United States, and George Washington's retirement raised serious questions about the meaning and viability of the federal union. By characterizing this novel as a tool for producing federal citizens and supporting federal unity, *The Algerine Captive* takes a clear political stance, one that endorses a heterogeneous model of national unity at a time when the future of such a union was a matter of serious debate.

Despite the politically charged nature of this term in the 1790s, scholars have rarely commented on Underhill's emphatic references to federalism at the end of the novel. Most interpret Underhill's use of "federal" as a term synonymous with "national," a slippage that has led his final statements to be read as a generic or, for some, an ironic expression of patriotism, rather than an argument for a specific form of national unity and identity.[44] Such interpretations seem overly simplistic given the intense debates over the meaning and practice of federalism at this time, and this problematic equation of "national" and "federal" is emblematic of the critical misreading of U.S. nationalism that this book attempts to correct. By foregrounding the significance of federalism within *The Algerine Captive*, I want to conclude this chapter by rethinking the nationalist function of novels in the early republic. Rather than providing citizens with a way to transcend their sense of differences within the nation or reimagine it, a novel like *The Algerine Captive* argues that differences are important and necessary for achieving national union. Taking seriously, then, Underhill's claim that reading his story will produce "FEDERAL" citizens, *The Algerine Captive* emerges as a novel that encourages readers to view the United States as a nation composed of distinct social, political, and geographic differences and provides them with the tools they need to interpret those differences in terms that are cohesive, rather than divisive. In this regard, my analysis of *The Algerine Captive* is closely aligned with the work of Nancy Armstrong and Len Tennenhouse, who have focused on the plural dimensions and sentiments of the novel to argue that *The*

Algerine Captive sets forth a "cosmopolitan" model of nationhood.[45] While Armstrong and Tennenhouse argue that the cosmopolitan dimensions of the novel raise ongoing questions about the coherence and cohesion of nationhood as a concept in the late eighteenth century, I argue that the cosmopolitan dimensions of *The Algerine Captive* were a means of affirming and reinforcing the federal national consciousness of the early United States.

The Algerine Captive illustrates this federal literacy through the character of Updike Underhill, who continually changes the way he interprets regional, cultural, and political differences over the course of the novel. Underhill begins the novel with a very homogeneous understanding of society. He has trouble understanding those who think and act differently from him, and he views such differences as a source of conflict. As he travels and encounters the variety of the nation, however, he changes the way he interprets these differences. Rather than viewing this variety as a source of instability and conflict, he learns to interpret the nation's differences in compatible terms, coexisting with his own beliefs and practices without compromising or disrupting them. Much like Mary Rowlandson, Underhill eventually develops a revised understanding of community that is defined by concurrent sentiments and experiences, rather than uniform practices and beliefs, and this revised conception of community—composed of compatible differences rather than absolute similarities—is what allows him to claim his federal citizenship at the novel's end. And as readers, in turn, follow Underhill's narrative, they likewise learn to reread the nation's diversity as a source of future promise and stability.

Examining the plural dimensions of *The Algerine Captive* must begin with the novel's form. Critics have often commented on the novel's "patchwork" structure, which presents Underhill's travels through a range of genres and styles, shifting from picaresque travel narrative to regional satire to sentimental captivity and back again. While early criticism dismissed this eclecticism as an aesthetic flaw, more recent work interprets the novel's variety as a critique of the nation's own diverse and disordered status, presenting readers with a disordered and non-cohesive narrative in order to criticize the disordered conditions of the United States. By characterizing diversity as a problem that needed to be resolved in the early republic, however, such assessments misinterpret the federal dimensions of early U.S. nationalism, which encouraged citizens to view the nation in precisely these heterogeneous terms.[46]

Instead of criticizing a lack of unity in the United States, the varied form and content of *The Algerine Captive* ultimately become a means of producing it. Through its hodgepodge account of Underhill's miscellaneous adventures at home and abroad, *The Algerine Captive* presents its readers with a range of experiences, beliefs, and perspectives, and, rather than selecting a primary experience or frame of reference, the novel encourages its readers to recognize the merits and limitations of each. By the end of the novel, the reader, much like Underhill, can no longer view the world through a single, homogeneous perspective. Instead, *The Algerine Captive* trains readers to recognize how a single individual can understand and respect many different views without necessarily altering their own core beliefs. In doing so, the novel makes it possible to imagine a nation where many interests, beliefs, and practices can be represented without compromising the stability and unity of the whole. In contrast, though, to a work such as *The Narrative of Mrs. Mary Rowlandson*, which similarly promotes a more tolerant view of differences, *The Algerine Captive* takes this concurrent logic farther by arguing that this diversified perspective is not just beneficial, but necessary for maintaining a stable and productive federal union. Only after learning to interpret differences equitably is Underhill able to return and make his home in the United States, where he can at last lay claim to his identity as a "worthy FEDERAL citizen." In this case, rather than defining the federal nation as a function of the different people, places, and practices that make up the United States, *The Algerine Captive* argues that the federal union is produced and made possible by the critical perspectives of its citizens.

Underhill begins the novel with a fixed understanding of his own national identity, which he assumes that he shares with all U.S. citizens. As the descendant of "one of the first emigrants to New England," Underhill presents himself as a quintessential Yankee who, like his ancestors, is marked by an "ardent love of liberty, civil and religious" (11). Having been told that the "high road to fame" lies in a classical education, he spends his early years "laboring incessantly at Greek and Latin," believing that these efforts will make him a respected American citizen who is "as much run after as the great Mr. Whitfield" and "equal to the Adamses in oratory ... or a Witherspoon in divinity" (25–26). As a result of this training, Underhill interprets everyone and everything he encounters in relation to this classical frame of reference. Instead of solidifying his identity as a successful American citizen, however, his single-minded perspective leaves him unable to earn a successful living or develop connections with other citizens in the United States.

On completing his studies, Underhill returns home where he tries to earn a living as a farmer, only to discover that he lacks the proper language or experience for working the land. "Poring so intensely on Homer and Virgil had so completely filled my brain with the heathen mythology, that I imagined a Hamadryade in every sapling, a Naiad in every puddle," he writes, reporting that "I gave Greek names to all our farming tools, and cheered the cattle with hexameter verse" (29). Unable to work or even read his father's farm correctly, Underhill is also unable to assist his fellow laborers. He describes an unfortunate scene when "my father's hired men, after a tedious day's labor in the woods, inspecting our stores for refreshment, instead of the customary bread and cheese and brandy, found Homer's Iliad, Virgil's Delphini, and Schrevelius's Lexicon, in the basket" (29). Here, Underhill's refusal to depart from his classical perspective not only hinders his own productivity; it limits the output of the entire farm.

Underhill's limited view of citizenship also continually prevents him from connecting with his countrymen. The novel presents several humorous scenes where Underhill's desire to interpret everything in relation to classical texts separates him from his local community. When his companions are discussing racehorses, for instance, Underhill "ventured to descant upon Xanthus, the immortal courser of Achilles," only to discover "they had never heard of 'squire Achilles or his horse, but they offered to bet, two to one, that Bajazet, the old Roan, or the deacon's mare, Pumpkin and Milk, would beat him" (29). Here, the novel clearly satirizes Underhill's pedantry, but there is more at stake than poking fun at his pretentions. Even though his fellow citizens do not understand Underhill's reference to Achilles, they still try to be inclusive by offering to add "Xanthus" to their betting pool. Rather than explaining the misunderstanding and joining in their game, however, Underhill dismisses his countrymen as fools and separates himself from their society, writing that "their conversation I could not relish; mine they could not comprehend." Even though he has a chance to explain and reconcile these varied views, he refuses to expand his worldview to accommodate different systems of meaning. For Underhill, the world must be interpreted either in his terms or not at all.

Underhill's strict adherence to this singular frame of reference has particularly destructive consequences when he becomes a schoolmaster. Drawing on the classical model of his own education, Underhill runs his schoolhouse according to an autocratic system of order, with his students "seated in awful silence around [him], [his] armchair and the birchen scepter of authority" (32). While this model corresponds to Underhill's vision of civic and educational order, it does not translate very well regarding the needs or expectations of this rural community. Unwilling to submit to Underhill's absolute rule, his students eventually revolt, "usurping [his] throne" (32) and burning down the school in the process.

This moment—which, as Underhill describes it, "shook my government to the center"—marks an important turning point in the novel. Following the collapse of the schoolhouse, Underhill begins to abandon his habit of viewing the nation through a single-minded, homogeneous perspective. Instead of interpreting the world exclusively through a classical frame, he begins to seek out and incorporate other views and experiences. By presenting this shift in focus as the result of a political rebellion or change in government, the novel suggests that developing a more tolerant and diversified perspective is not just a matter of personal improvement but a means of creating a more stable political order as well, one where stability derives from the representation of multiple perspectives, rather than the viewpoint of a single authority.

For the rest of volume 1, Underhill moves around the country in search of a successful place to settle, and, with each move, he becomes more willing and able to acknowledge and incorporate differences. On relocating to a new town and receiving a challenge for a duel, for example, Underhill is uncertain about how to respond. Instead of relying on his own interpretation, he decides to show the letter to someone with more local experience, which, in this case, is a man "born in South Carolina [who] understood the whole business" (49). The South Carolinian scoffs, "You have been bred in a Yankee land.... I must indoctrinate you." Following a quick lesson regarding the local expectations associated with a duel, Underhill finally acts in a way that his countrymen can accept and understand, which, in this case means merely "accepting the invitation" and, "shak[ing] hands" with his opponent, and "pronounc[ing], on our honours, that we would drop the affair" (50).

Underhill's willingness to expand his initial perspective and accommodate the views of others has an immediate effect. While he had previously been rejected as an incomprehensible outsider, his ability to understand and respond to local customs of dueling brings him the acceptance and respect he has been seeking. "My acceptance of the challenge, however unintentional, established my reputation among the bucks and belles. The former pronounced me a man of spunk and spirit; and the latter were proud of my arm in an evening rural walk on the paved street," he writes. To his gratification, Underhill also discovers that his ability to engage with these local customs brings greater acceptance for his own classical views and interests. "I verily believe that, if I had spouted a whole *Iliad* in the ball room no one would have ventured to interrupt me, for I had proved myself a MAN OF HONOUR" (51), he reports, acknowledging that his efforts to be more understanding about the beliefs and practices of others contributes to a plural mindset that benefits his own distinctive interests and views.

Underhill soon learns that an appreciation for local differences and variety can bring him professional success as well. Having failed as a farmer and a schoolmaster, Underhill resumes his studies to pursue a career in medicine, but he struggles to earn a living when he moves to a town that is already occupied by several doctors. He soon discovers, however, that these doctors succeed by clearly distinguishing themselves from one another. In this town, for instance, Underhill describes the practices of "a learned, a Cheap, a Safe, and a Musical Doctor" (64), who each provide a distinctive style of medical treatment. The "learned doctor" is known for his fastidious measurement of medicines. The "cheap doctor," who is known for prescribing "large doses of the most powerful drugs," is valued for the efficiency of his methods, which "always speedily cured—or killed" (65). The "safe doctor," who "dealt altogether in simples," is known for innocuous treatments that, "if [they] did no good, never did any harm," while the "musical doctor," who "had more practice than all other three," was known for his ability to treat patients through his "entertaining" behavior and gifted use of "prayer" (66). Even though all of these doctors provide medical care, by carefully differentiating their practices from one another and providing their customers with a variety of options, they can all succeed in a crowded market.

Critical assessments of these physicians have generally focused on their ridiculous methods, characterizing the doctors as "charlatans" whose "ignorant, unscrupulous, and mercenary" actions are meant to critique the rampant exploitation and opportunism that followed the end of the Revolution.[47] With the single exception of the "learned doctor" who knows nothing about medicine, however, these doctors do not engage in any deliberate deceptions. Even though their various treatments are silly and largely ineffective, the "cheap," "musical," and "safe" doctors accurately represent the styles of treatment they provide. In fact, the novel suggests that people choose one doctor over another precisely because they represent the specific character of their treatments so clearly, no matter how ineffective they may be. Rather than criticizing the honesty of their tactics, the novel ultimately seems more interested in emphasizing the *variety* these physicians represent.

The novel continues to emphasize the value of variety as it traces Underhill's path to professional success. Underhill initially struggles to succeed as a doctor precisely because he is unable to differentiate himself from his peers. Instead of becoming known for a particular medical skill or style, Underhill works as an assistant to the "learned doctor," a decision that prevents him from establishing the distinctive reputation he needs to succeed in a market that is defined by variety. As the learned doctor's assistant, Underhill is largely ignored by his potential clients, who dismiss him as "a young man of moderate talents whom the learned doctor might make something of, in a course of years" (70). Recognizing that difference and variety are crucial to his professional success, Underhill decides to move south where his skills will be more distinctive and valued. "I had often heard the southern states spoken of, as the high road to fortune. I was told that the inhabitants were immensely opulent, paid high fees with profusion, and were extremely partial to the characteristic industry of their New England brethren" (74), writes Underhill, whose comments indicate how he now views the nation in relation to an economy of differences—in this case, regional differences. While his individual qualities and experiences are of little value in the northern states where he cannot distinguish himself from his fellow physicians, in the South Underhill believes he can easily distinguish himself as a physician on the basis of his regional identity where he will be recognized immediately as the "Northern" doctor.

Such perceptions of regional differences and the distinctive value of regional goods and services were important for building federal unity in the early republic. As Peter Onuf writes, "[the] notion of a contingent and therefore consciously constructed union was predicated on [the] perception of the fluidity and dynamism of interdependent [state] interests."[48] By promoting the value and difference of regional goods and services, citizens would become more comfortable recognizing the variety of the nation, while also developing closer bonds by exchanging those goods and services and establishing interdependent relationships. John Jay summarized this logic in Federalist No. 2, writing that "Providence has in a particular manner blessed [us] with a variety of soils and productions . . . [while] a succession of navigable waters forms a kind of chain round its borders, as if to tie it all together . . . [providing] highways for the easy communication of friendly aids and the mutual transportation and exchange of their various commodities."[49] By transporting his Yankee characteristics southward, Underhill clearly hopes to capitalize on this federal logic by attracting patients with his regionally resonant expertise.

Just as Underhill seems poised to succeed, however, the promise of marketing his regional differences fails him. Instead of translating his New England industriousness into social and economic success, Underhill's move to the South leaves him impoverished and demoralized. "I attempted to obtain practice in the town of F——, in Virginia, but in vain," he writes. "The very decorum, prudence, and economy, which would have enhanced my character at home, were here construed into poverty of spirit. To obtain medical practice, it was expedient, to sport, bet, drink, swear, &c. with my patients. My purse forbad the former; my habits of life the latter" (83). Rather than earning him respect or profit, Underhill's sober and hardworking habits are met with disdain. Furthermore, though Underhill had previously gained some measure of acceptance by adapting to the customs of his local community, in this case he decides that the values and practices of the South are so far removed from his own that he cannot tolerate them without fundamentally compromising his own "habits of life."

Underhill's experiences with southern regional differences disrupt the trajectory of the novel. Up to this point, his ability to respect and accommodate differences—whether regional, social, or professional—has had productive consequences. In the South, however, Underhill confronts the limits of such toleration, particularly when he encounters the practice of slavery. After watching a minister beat his slaves and then deliver a lengthy sermon on virtue, Underhill is repelled by the violence and hypocrisy of his southern neighbors, and he grows concerned about his complicity by residing in the midst of it. "[A] certain staple of New England I had with me called conscience made my situation, even in the passive part I bore in it, so awkward and uneasy that I could not refrain from observing to my friend my surprise at the parson's conduct," he writes (80). To his dismay, he discovers that his friend, who was also originally from New England, does not share his outrage and instead aligns himself with the minister's racist actions and sentiments. "My friend was so happily influenced by the habits of these illiberal, enlightened people that he could not even comprehend the tendency of my remark . . . and observed, with warmth, that the parson had served the villain right, and that, if it had been his slave, he would have killed the black rascal" (80). By learning to tolerate the southern practice of slavery, this former New Englander had transformed into a person that Underhill can no longer recognize or comprehend.

Underhill's experiences in the southern states thus present him with a troubling dilemma. He can learn to tolerate the distinctive practices of the South and violate his own "habits of life," or he can refuse to accept those practices and become unable to make friends or earn a living. Either way, the South emerges as a place where Underhill cannot settle without compromising his citizenship either morally or financially, and by dramatizing this dilemma, the novel raises questions about the limits of variety in the federal nation. On the one hand, learning to interpret differences with equity and tolerance can have productive effects, as Underhill discovers when he abandons his narrow, classical perspective and learns to accommodate local differences. On the other hand, learning to tolerate different values and practices can also transform and compromise a person's values and actions, making variety a threat to national identity and unity.

The dilemma Underhill faces in the South epitomizes a central dilemma for the early United States—how could citizens support the diversity of the federal union when the nation's diversity included practices that contradicted its values of liberty, equality, and pluralism? As a state-sponsored practice that varied throughout the nation while simultaneously denying the rights of the nation's black residents, slavery marked the limits of federal nationalism. Delegates to the Continental Congress recognized the contradiction between the United States' rhetoric of liberty and equality and the practice of slavery, with James Madison noting that governmental support for slavery was "inconsistent with the principles of the Revolution, and dishonourable to the American character."[50] The close connection between slavery and the economies of the southern states, however, made discussions of the issue extremely divisive and, at various moments, nearly ended the Constitutional Convention. To avoid a permanent break, delegates decided not to legislate slavery at the national level, designating slavery as a matter for the states to manage individually, a resolution known as the "federal consensus" due to its reliance on the federal logic of plural sovereignty. As Don Fehrenbacher writes, "From the earliest years of the Republic... southerners were accustomed to maintaining and northerners to agreeing that, with a few exceptions... slavery was a state responsibility wholly beyond the reach of federal power."[51] By the end of the Constitutional Convention, the only shared national policy regarding slavery was an agreement to end the importation of slaves in 1808, pushing slavery off the national agenda for several decades.

Permitting slavery on the basis of state sovereignty provided a convenient logic for recognizing slavery as a legitimate practice in the federal United States, but concerns over the ethical inconsistencies of slavery and federal nationalism remained. In the northern states, antislavery activists continued to publicize the discrepancies between the federal principles of liberty, equality, and pluralism and state-sanctioned slavery. "In America, a slave is the standing monument of the tyranny and inconsistency of human governments," wrote one antislavery advocate, who emphasized the role of the states in fostering these contradictions. "He is declared by the united voice of America to be by nature free and intitled to privilege of acquiring and enjoying property and yet by laws passed and inforced in these States, retained in slavery and dispossessed of all property and security of acquiring any."[52] "The great principle (of government) is and ever will remain in force *that men are by nature created free* ... and [therefore] it is obligatory in the United States to prevent the citizens thereof [from] injuring the inhabitants of Africa," asserted a 1793 antislavery pamphlet, once again subsuming the rights of the states to the rights of African Americans.[53] Meanwhile, proponents of slavery countered these arguments by insisting that state support for slavery was not a contradiction of federal values but a legitimate expression of federal sovereignty. As Oliver Ellsworth argued, "The morality or wisdom of slavery are considerations belonging to the states themselves.... The states are the best judges of their particular interest. The old confederation had not meddled with this point, and [I do] not see any greater necessity for bringing it within the policy of the new one."[54] At the heart of these debates were the terms of the nation's federal pluralism. Was the United States a federal nation that equally represented and protected its different residents? Or was it a federal nation that equally represented and protected the interests of its different states?

Although Royall Tyler never voiced a definitive opinion on slavery, his writings and political affiliations suggest he was sympathetic to the abolitionist cause. Later in life, as a federal judge on the Vermont supreme court, Tyler issued an important antislavery decision by ruling that bills of sale were invalid for slaves taken into Vermont, a decision based on his reasoning that "the construction of our state constitution ... does not admit the idea of slavery."[55] Significantly, Tyler rejected the legality of slavery in Vermont using the same arguments for local sovereignty that the southern states used to defend their support of slavery.

As his later decision indicates, Tyler was surely aware of the complex contradictions at stake in a federal system that was rooted in the principles of equality and diversity yet nevertheless permitted the institution of slavery as a matter of state sovereignty—a contradiction that brings us back to Underhill's dilemma at the end of volume 1.

Unable to resolve the difficulties he encounters in the South, Underhill opts to abandon the federal nation altogether. "I quit my home, for all parts of the union I considered my home," he writes, and he sets sail for Europe where he hopes to obtain the "reputation," "property," and "freedom" his own country failed to provide (84). By thus quitting the nation in all its "parts," Underhill seems to reject the federal vision that the novel initially sets forth. Although he is willing to accommodate a certain level of national differences and, for a time, succeeds due to his varied and expansive perspective, he is unwilling to tolerate a federal nation that permits and protects slavery as part of its national variety. Through Underhill's abrupt and definitive departure, the first half of the novel suggests that there are clear limits to the degree of social and political differences that a federal nation can support.

From Algerine Captive to Federal Citizen

Given Underhill's decision to abandon the nation at the end of volume 1, *The Algerine Captive* raises serious questions about the extent to which federalism could manage the United States' regional differences. In the end, though, the novel refuses to abandon federal pluralism entirely. In volume 2, the novel continues to explore the productive consequences of recognizing and engaging with differences—this time in an international framework—when Underhill is captured by Barbary pirates and sold into servitude in Algiers. Speaking now from the perspective of a "degraded" slave rather than a free observer, Underhill continues to voice his opposition to slavery, declaring it to be a "detestable commerce" that "deprives [our] fellow creatures of freedom ... the unalienable birth right of man" (126, 106). This time, however, he can support his claims from his own experience, a position that eventually leads him to reaffirm federalism as a viable political model as long as it protects racial, ethnic, and cultural differences rather than regional sovereignties. "Grant me ... once more to taste the freedom of my native country," he writes shortly after being captured, "... and I will fly to our fellow citizens in the southern states ... [and] on my knees, conjure them, in the name of humanity to abolish a traffic that causes it to bleed in every pore" (106).

This tactic of dramatizing the horrors of Algerine captivity to criticize U.S. slavery was a common trope in early American Barbary captivity narratives.

"For many American authors writing about Algerine captivity, the fate of their 'enslaved' brethren in far away North Africa offered an opportunity to reflect on some of the evils of the institution of slavery closer to home," writes Peskin.⁵⁶ At the same time, notes Baepler, while Barbary slave narratives offered U.S. writers a useful means of "reveal[ing] the hypocrisy of the American slave system," their depictions of black masters and white slaves could also have the opposite effect, reinforcing racist hierarchies by pitting sympathetic and virtuous white slaves against the "barbarous" behavior of their black masters.⁵⁷

At first glance, *The Algerine Captive* seems to follow this pattern of criticizing slavery and reinforcing racial hierarchies by denouncing Underhill's abusive treatment while, at the same time, asserting his superiority over his savage Moorish captors. This hierarchical framework, however, proves to be short lived, and the novel's refusal to endorse Underhill's racial and cultural superiority marks the novel's interest in recuperating its federal values. As critics and, indeed, Tyler's own reviewers have often noted, the novel undergoes a significant shift over the course of Underhill's captivity.⁵⁸ The more he observes and interacts with the people of Algiers, the more he comes to tolerate and respect many aspects of their society. Tyler's contemporary reviewers took the novel to task for "favour[ing] the Musselman" and "too feebly defend[ing] that religion which he professes to revere."⁵⁹ These reactions to the novel's more open-minded and balanced representation of religious and cultural differences are important, as they illustrate the novel's shift in emphasis by prompting a reflective and instructional, rather than overtly critical, response to the cultural differences of Algiers. Shortly after his capture, for instance, Underhill reports that many of his initial assumptions about Algiers, such as his belief that all the men have multiple wives and show little regard for family, prove to be a "vulgar error," and he is increasingly "struck with their great resemblance" to the values and manners he associates with his own Christian beliefs (122). Motivated by a desire to "improve the understanding of my reader with what I really know" (173), Underhill gradually shifts the focus of his captivity narrative to provide readers with an instructional primer on the history, customs, and values of Algiers, rather than a denunciation of its cultural differences. In doing so, the novel abandons the sentimental conventions of the traditional captivity narrative to adopt, as Baepler describes it, an ethnographic style, transforming *The Algerine Captive* into a very different kind of captivity narrative as Underhill becomes "captivated" by the cultural differences of Algiers.⁶⁰

The shift in focus clearly emerges when Underhill agrees to meet with a "Mahometan priest" who wishes to debate matters of faith. At first glance, the stage seems set for a classic conflict between East and West as Underhill enters the room with confidence, ready to defend "the sacred truths of our holy religion against the insidious attack of the mussulman priest" (131). The Mollah greets him with equal assurance, likewise convinced of his ability to persuade "the Christian purified by Calvin" that the teachings of Muhammad also represent "sacred truths" (131). The scene that follows, however, fails to produce the expected clash. Instead of presenting Christianity and Islam as fundamentally at odds with one another, the dialogue characterizes these two religions as different yet compatible expressions of belief. As the two men converse, Underhill presents a series of points intended to "prove" the superiority of Christianity, namely, that it is "divinely inspired," "supported by miracles," and blessed by "wonderful increase." To each of these statements, the Mollah responds with a similar assertion, countering Underhill's arguments with the repeated claim, "so is ours." "Your argument I allow to be forcible," he tells Underhill, "but grant us also the use of it" (132).

In highlighting these similarities, the Mollah never completely equates the two religions. Throughout the dialogue, he stresses that Christianity and Islam are distinct systems of belief defined by different texts, prophets, histories, and doctrines. Instead of characterizing these differences as points of contention, however, the Mollah encourages Underhill to see Christianity and Islam in compatible terms, as alternate expressions of similar beliefs. The dialogue ends with the Mollah urging Underhill to read the Koran. "Read, then, this spotless book," he states. "There you will learn to love those of our faith and not hate those of any other.... In a word, you will learn the unity of god which, notwithstanding the cavil of your divines, your prophet, like ours, came into the world to establish and every man of reason must believe" (135–36). By arguing that the experience of reading the Koran will produce feelings of unity rather than division, the Mollah makes a striking point. Throughout the eighteenth century, early American writers tended to characterize the Islamic world as "heretical" and "barbarous," representing the antithesis of American governance and ideals—a view that persists today.[61] In sharp contrast to this oppositional relationship, the dialogue between the Mollah and Underhill suggests that engaging with the "heretical" texts and practices of Islam can actually produce relationships of tolerance and cooperation. By the end of the scene, Underhill feels pressured not to convert but to broaden his religious views to include a wider range of ideas and practices, thus expanding his sense of what "every man of reason" can and should find acceptable (135). The equitable, back-and-forth structure of the dialogue exemplifies this instructive and complementary argument, encouraging readers to learn about and reflect on the potentially acceptable differences of Islam, rather than simply rejecting them outright.

The instructional form and tone of volume 2, as a whole, prompts this equitable comparative response from readers, inviting them to interpret Algerine cultural differences from a more impartial and open-minded perspective. "I have interspersed reflections which I hope will be received by the learned with candour," he writes, encouraging his readers to find ways to acknowledge and tolerate "the history, government, religion, habits, and manners" of those whom they might initially perceive as a "ferocious race," rather than rejecting them outright (194).[62] Underhill's decision to include the transcript of a "Mahometan Sermon" offers a particularly apt illustration of how the novel portrays Algiers as a site of useful and potentially compatible differences. Instead of describing the sermon from his own perspective, Underhill presents it as a formal transcript of the officiant's speech. "I present [the sermon] to the candid reader as a curious specimen of their pulpit eloquence," he writes, "perhaps, conveying a more satisfactory idea of their creed than I have already attempted" (191). By characterizing the sermon as "specimen" to be reviewed by the "candid reader," Underhill provides a framework that encourages readers to take an open-minded, almost scientific approach to this statement of Mahometan beliefs. Describing this sermon as a "dignified" example of "pulpit eloquence" further encourages U.S. readers to view its content in equitable terms since eloquence was highly valued in the early nation, considered to be the "instrument and embodiment of a new Anglo-American republican authority."[63] By characterizing this expression of the Mahometan creed as a noteworthy example of eloquence, Underhill presents a document that readers might initially expect to be a site of radical difference in terms that push readers to recognize it as a form that any U.S. citizen should admire.

For Underhill, there is much to be gained by developing this new perspective on differences. First, his willingness to converse and interact with his captors, particularly regarding the practice of medicine, eventually earns him increased freedom and mobility. "After a marked and assiduous attention of some months," he remarks, "... I acquired the confidence of my superiors so far, that I was sometimes sent abroad to the city" (148). The more he interacts with and observes the people around him, the more he becomes admired and respected, allowing him not only to practice the medical skills he had been unable to capitalize on in the United States, but to travel widely throughout Algiers, to diminishing his sense of enslavement. "My reputation increased ... and I [was] able to acquire much useful information upon subjects of domestic concern, impervious to travelers," he writes. "I received a new and better suit of clothes ... [and] was received by Hadgi Mulladin [a wealthy gentleman] ... with great civility" (151–52).

In addition to his increased personal freedom, Underhill discovers that there are political and social benefits for studying the different practices of his Algerine captors as well. He comes to admire, for instance, some of the legal practices he encounters in Algiers, noting how "in the Algerine mode of distributive justice, instant decision relieved the anxiety and saved the purses of the parties." He contrasts this with the American system where "the lengthy bill of cost, [and] the law's delay... had taught [him] to view the judicial proceedings of our country with a jaundiced eye" (189). By informing his readers of this difference, he hopes his account might lead to positive changes back home: "I present it to my fellow citizens," he writes, "[that], if it is generally pleasing, it might be introduced among us" (190). Such exchanges work in both directions, as Underhill highlights how his "foreign" medical skills were valued in Algiers. "Applications vulgarly common in the United States were viewed [there] with admiration," he writes. "Sometimes, the physicians themselves would condescend to consult me ... [and] I often had the gratification of observing that they administered my prescriptions with success" (148–49). In both cases, Underhill's experiences in Algiers demonstrate the productive consequences of engaging with cultural differences. More than simply promoting peaceful coexistence, a tolerance for differences can foster productive and unifying forms of exchange.

Which brings us back to the novel's conclusion. Having learned, at last, to tolerate a wider range of cultural diversity and recognize the value of exchanging information across regional and national boundaries, Underhill returns to his "native country"—a place where he had previously been unable to find a place to settle—where he proclaims his desire to "contribute cheerfully to the support of our excellent government" and "secure to myself the enviable character of a useful physician, a good father, and a worthy FEDERAL citizen" (225). As I mentioned earlier, Underhill's emphasis on identifying himself not just as a citizen but a "federal" citizen is important considering the controversial and volatile status of this term throughout the 1790s. James Madison addressed the complicated ideas associated with this term in his discussion of the differences between the words "national" and "federal" in Federalist No. 39.

> If we try the Constitution by its last relation to the authority by which amendments are to be made, we find it neither wholly *national* nor wholly *federal*. Were it wholly national, the supreme and ultimate authority would reside in the *majority* of the people of the Union.... Were it wholly federal, on the other hand, the concurrence of each State in the Union would be essential to every alteration that would be binding on all. The mode provided by the plan of the convention is not founded on either of these principles. In requiring more than a majority, and particularly in computing the proportion by *States*, not by *citizens*, it departs from the national and advances towards the *federal* character; in rendering the concurrence of less than the whole number of States sufficient, it loses again the *federal* and partakes of the *national* character. The proposed Constitution, therefore ... is, in strictness, neither a national nor a federal Constitution, but a composition of both (emphasis in original).[64]

By proclaiming his desire to become "a worthy FEDERAL citizen" and his hope that his novel will promote the nation's "federal strength," Underhill is not simply asserting his commitment to the nation. Instead, he is carefully asserting his commitment to a particular *form* of nationhood—one that requires an expansive appreciation for differences. More than simply asserting support for federal nationalism, however, *The Algerine Captive* also provides citizens with a strategy for producing a workable federal union by teaching its audience how to read and interpret differences differently. Through Updike Underhill, the novel presents readers with a character who abandons one particular manner of reading and eventually lays claim to his identity as a federal citizen by adopting another manner of reading, one that is rooted in an equitable and tolerant interpretation of differences. Confident in his new interpretive outlook, Underhill concludes his novel by encouraging his own readers to follow his example and revise their own approaches for reading the nation's differences. As Underhill describes it, "if they peruse these pages with attention," citizens will ultimately learn how to read the nation in ways that "unit[e] our federal strength" (225).

For as much as *The Algerine Captive* promotes a federal literacy, the novel still leaves readers to contend with problematic variations within its borders. While the ability to read differences equitably allows Underhill to become the federal citizen he wants to be, his revised federal outlook must still contend with the issue of slavery, an issue that he conspicuously ignores when he returns home. Although the novel does not offer a clear resolution to this problem, it does gesture toward a potential solution by representing federal unity as the product of an individual interpretation, rather than political representation. In the end, the novel seems more invested in securing the unity of the nation by producing federally literate citizens than in defining federal states. In this regard (and in keeping with Tyler's known political affiliations), the novel adopts a Federalist Party stance to the concept of federal unity, deemphasizing the authority and autonomy of the different states in order to imagine the nation as a cooperative union of diverse, yet compatible, individuals. Within this model, different beliefs and practices can still be tolerated within the federal union, but they must be aligned with a broader sense of national consensus, rather than a strict respect for regional rights and particularities. Tyler's novel thus presents readers with a new federal outlook, where the nation can be imagined not simply as "we the people" or "we the states" but, rather, as "we the peoples"—neither wholly federal nor wholly national, but, as Madison described it, "a composition of both." This new framework, which promotes and celebrates differences while also emphasizing that citizens need training and guidance to contend effectively with those differences, sets the stage for situating these federal literary practices in the context of the westward expansion, a transition that would begin to push the limits of federal pluralism to a breaking point.

CHAPTER 5

★ ★ ★ ★ ★ ★ ★ ★ ★ ★ ★ ★

Federalism Redux

Reading the Literary West

> Every link of the golden and, we hope, perpetual chain of the union will be grasped as firmly by the citizens of the West, as of the Atlantic.
>
> ——TIMOTHY FLINT, "Present Population and Future Prospects of the Western Country"

Expansion tested and transformed the federal union. Between 1800 and 1830, the United States more than doubled in size, growing from a nation composed of sixteen states and 864,746 square miles to twenty-four states and 1,749,462 square miles. Though the United States had always been a diverse nation, this expansion magnified its variety on an unprecedented scale, introducing new topography, climates, and waterways that brought different industries, agricultural practices, and infrastructural networks to the nation. As the United States incorporated territory that was formerly under French and Spanish colonial rule, the nation also had to expand its Anglocentric cultural identity to include a wider range of languages, ethnicities, religious beliefs, cultural practices, and governing structures, not to mention an equally diverse range of Native American communities. Expansion also raised new questions about the status of African American residents as citizens argued over the practice of slavery in the new territories.

As the United States celebrated its fiftieth year of national independence in 1826, citizens looked back to the nation's plural origins with pride, while also contemplating how different the federal union had become.[1] In contrast to the early federal union, which represented an Anglocentric nation that was centered on the East Coast and dominated by northern and southern regional politics, the United States now represented a transcontinental federal nation that was shaped by the political and cultural influences of France, Spain, and other European and Native American nations and whose regional dynamics now included a vibrant and active West. The United States of the early nineteenth century was also a federal union that was increasingly dominated by internal divisions. In the early republic, expressions of state interests and authority had largely been celebrated as a means of supporting and unifying the nation, but in the early nineteenth century, such expressions became controversial as arguments over slavery, taxation, and Indian policies exacerbated tensions between the authority of the states and the central government. As U.S. citizens looked to the future, the plural dimensions of the nation no longer seemed as productive and unifying as they once had been.

At the end of the eighteenth century, captivity narratives such as Rowlandson's *True History* and Royall Tyler's *Algerine Captive* offered an optimistic view of the nation's ability to contend with expansion by training citizens to read religious, ethnic, cultural, regional, and gender differences in equitable and concurrent terms. In the aftermath of the Louisiana Purchase, however, this optimism faded, and, instead of facing expansion with confidence, citizens worried that the nation was becoming too large and diverse to remain unified. Jefferson highlighted these concerns in his second inaugural address when he acknowledged the "candid apprehension that the enlargement of our territory would endanger its union." Rather than responding to these concerns with a definitive answer, Jefferson responded with an open-ended question. "But who can limit the extent to which the federative principle may operate effectively?" he asked, challenging U.S. citizens to find ways to make federalism work in an ever-expanding nation.[2]

Jefferson's rhetorical question provides a useful frame for thinking about U.S. literature and culture in the context of expansion. Throughout the early nineteenth century, citizens were continually exploring the limits of federal nationalism, and studies of this period emphasize how citizens experimented with new ways for imagining this expansive republic. Hsuan Hsu, for instance, argues that Americans developed specific "spatial scales" to help them identify with the changing size and scope of the nation, while Lloyd Pratt explores how writers turned to heterogeneous and pluralized representations of time.[3] Without question, this process of trying to imagine the nation as "a panoply of changing and contested spaces" was fraught with anxiety, and recent work underscores how nineteenth-century U.S. literature exhibits, as Anne Baker describes it, "a sense of unease" about the prospect of representing the nation at all.[4] Dana Luciano and Ivy Wilson's recent collection, *Unsettled States*, exemplifies this emphasis on the uncertain and "unsettled" dimensions of U.S. literature and nationalism during this period as writers struggled to make sense of "the cacophony of analytic, affective, national, and temporal claims" that defined the nation's varied and variable space.[5]

Scholars have often turned to empire as the central critical framework for interpreting these uneasy articulations of plural nationhood, arguing that these unsettled expressions are a direct result of U.S. imperial efforts to subjugate and control these new territories. Instead of examining nineteenth-century expansion exclusively through the ideology of manifest destiny, work by Edward Watts, Stephanie LeMenager, and Andy Doolen has pushed this scholarship in new directions by arguing that U.S. writers and readers had a more complicated and critical relationship with imperialism in the decades prior to the 1848 Mexican-American War.[6] Anxious to avoid associating the United States with the oppressive, exploitive practices of European imperialism, western writers looked for alternative ways to represent U.S. expansion in terms that resisted, criticized, or revised these traditional imperial dynamics.[7] This is not to say, of course, that U.S. expansion before 1848 was not imperial—it certainly was. Writers of the early nineteenth century, however, made a concerted effort to reframe the nation's imperial practices in alternative or resistant terms, characterizing the nation, as Doolen writes, as an "empire in deferral."[8]

This chapter similarly explores how western writers represented expansion in deferred or alternative imperial terms in the early nineteenth century. While Doolen and LeManager look outward to explore how western writers sought to reframe the imperial dimensions of westward expansion through their depictions of western spaces such as deserts, oceans, rivers, mountains, and borderlands, I want to show how western writers also revised the nation's imperial dynamics by looking backward, returning to the federal rhetoric and literacy of the early republic to revive its plural dynamics in the literary culture of the West. During the 1830s and 1840s, the western states and territories were a hotbed of literary activism, particularly in the Ohio valley region where the explosive growth of new presses, newspapers, and magazines gave rise to a vibrant regional literary culture that distinguished the West from the eastern and southern states. "There is already marked, and it is every year more fully developed, a distinctive character of the western people," wrote Timothy Flint, who, along with many others, pushed for the development of a distinctive western literary culture that would "catch the slight but perceptible shades of difference and the visible peculiarities of national character which our peculiar origin, physical circumstances, and moral condition have imposed upon us."[9]

At first glance, Flint's literary visions might seem exclusively regional, but his emphasis on conveying the West's "visible peculiarities of national character" reveals the federal dimensions of this western literary imagination. Just as the writers and readers of the early United States continually emphasized that the nation was a union composed of many parts, these western writers and readers worked hard to represent their distinctive region as part of a composite national whole. Anxious that the literary and national culture of the United States was becoming dominated by the eastern and southern states, westerners argued that the literature of the United States needed to represent all its regional communities distinctly and equitably, and, furthermore, that such strong regional literatures could help unify the nation. The literature of the United States should "make a survey coextensive with the whole republic," wrote James Hall, editor of the *Western Monthly Magazine*, "... thus appears its tendency to add strength and permanence to the union of these states, implanting in them a living persuasion of reciprocal interests and rallying their patriotism."[10] Under the leadership of writers such as Hall and Flint, the literary culture of the antebellum West pushed readers, both locally and nationally, to recognize the West as a distinctive part of an increasingly plural nation, providing them with the tools to read the regional distinctions of the West and the rest of the nation in unified terms. By thus fostering these literary practices, asserted one writer, western literature will "aid in giving interpretation and reality to our federative motto '*E pluribus unum*.'"[11]

The revival of these federal literary dynamics eased national anxieties about expansion by allowing citizens to interpret it as consistent with their founding model of plural nationhood. Western writers continually evoked the federal metaphors of the early United States to frame expansion in terms that were familiar and unifying, as evident in Flint's reference to "the golden and perpetual chain of union" cited in the epigraph for this chapter. By describing this chain as something "grasped firmly by the citizens of the West, as of the Atlantic," Flint portrays the western territories as a familiar and strengthening extension of the nation's original federal structure, rather than a radical break from it.[12]

This western revival of federal nationalism was not just a repetition of the literary styles and tactics of the past, however. The literary culture of the antebellum West revised this federal nationalism in key ways, particularly its emphasis on mediating conflict. Rather than simply representing variety, western magazines such as Flint's *Western Monthly Review* and Hall's *Western Monthly Magazine* made a concerted effort to represent opposing views and experiences. As Hall described it, western literary culture was designed to "offer a field for ... [a] friendly conflict of opinions" so that citizens could learn not just to recognize the nation's differences but to contend with these conflicts productively.[13] This emphasis on using federal literacy to mediate conflict was a direct response to the increasingly tense relationship between the states and the central government in the early nineteenth century, which was exacerbated by issues involving slavery, tariffs, and Indian removal. As the states battled one another and the central government for the right to govern their own localities and gain a majority interest in the federal Congress, these three issues repeatedly brought the federal union to points of crisis, beginning with the Missouri Compromise of 1820, which was swiftly followed by the divisive Nullification and Indian removal debates. At the heart of these disputes were serious questions about how to manage the plural dynamics of the federal union in the context of expansion. Did the states need to be more tightly managed and controlled by the central government to maintain a stable union? Or was the federal union better served by protecting the rights of the states to manage their own local affairs?

As citizens debated these issues, there was a great deal of uncertainty about how to interpret expressions of local or regional pride and authority. In some cases, these assertions were closely aligned with feelings of national loyalty and affiliation, but in other cases, assertions of regional pride and interests were interpreted negatively, as an attack on the nation. A new term—"sectionalism"—arose to describe instances when the states seemed to privilege their local or regional interests over those of the nation, and the emergence of this term illuminates the growing complexities of regional representation as citizens struggled to determine the national implications of any local or regional expressions.[14]

The revival of federal literary culture in the West was supposed to help address these interpretive challenges by reminding citizens that regional and national sentiments could still be closely affiliated with one another and, moreover, that citizens could learn to contend with the conflicts between the states in productive and unifying terms. Focusing specifically on the federal literary tactics of the *Western Monthly Review*, the *Western Monthly Magazine*, and the array of social clubs, schools, and societies that thrived in the antebellum West, this chapter explores how this western literary culture trained readers to represent and engage productively with conflict, giving them tools to navigate the increasingly divisive regional dynamics of the federal nation.

This emphasis on contending with regional conflicts introduces the second distinctive feature of this western federal nationalism—the effort to institutionalize it. During the eighteenth century, federal literacy had been produced and practiced on a relatively informal basis. There were no institutionalized means to promote the nation's federal structure and principles. Instead, the federal dimensions of U.S. literature largely developed on its own terms, without the guiding influence of a particular group or cultural agenda. In contrast, the literary culture of the antebellum West was specifically designed to promote federal nationalism. Writers such as Flint, Drake, Hall, and their contemporaries were very up-front about structuring western literary culture to reflect "a real federative *esprit de corps*, corresponding in all respects with the nature of our government."[15] This federal emphasis not only determined the form and function of the West's literary periodicals, it also led to the establishment of social clubs, literary societies, subscription libraries, professional associations, and forums for speech and debate, which were intended to foster federal nationalism and sensibilities on a much larger and more official scale, producing, as Christopher Castiglia writes, a "federal affect" as citizens were able to imagine their everyday cultural experiences as a "metaphorical simulacra of the government."[16]

To explore the numerous ways that this antebellum western literary culture both revived and revised the federal literacy and federal literary nationalism of the late eighteenth century, this chapter has three sections. The first examines Timothy Flint's pioneering work with the *Western Monthly Review*, a magazine that set the stage for the revival of federal literary nationalism in the West. The second section explores the institutional development of federal nationalism in more detail by examining the literary culture of antebellum Cincinnati and the arguments of one of its leading proponents, Daniel Drake, who sought to designate the West as the new center for the nation's federal principles. The final section takes a look at the work of James Hall, another prominent western writer and editor of the *Western Monthly Magazine*. Like Flint and Drake, Hall pushed for the development of a more institutionalized federal culture that could represent the nation's diversity and enable citizens to contend productively with that diversity. Hall, however, was more aggressive in expanding the cultural and ethnic dimensions of the nation's federal imagination, an issue he primarily promoted through his fiction. Although Hall made an effort to include French and Spanish cultural communities in the federal nation in these works, his principles of federal tolerance ultimately break down when it comes to representing Native Americans, and this section concludes by examining the contradictions and inconsistencies that emerge when Hall tries to incorporate Native Americans within his federal literary framework, complexities that illustrate the racial limits of federal nationalism that would ultimately mark the end of this literary imagination.

A Bird's-Eye View of the Nation: Timothy Flint and the *Western Monthly Review*

Timothy Flint led the way in reviving federal literary culture in the antebellum West. Originally from Massachusetts, Flint attended Harvard University to become a minister, and he first went west as a missionary in 1815, traveling extensively throughout Ohio, Indiana, Kentucky, Arkansas, Louisiana, and Missouri. These experiences led him to abandon the ministry in 1818, when he embarked on a new career documenting the history, culture, and geography of the West. His first publication, *Recollections of the Last Ten Years* (1826) was a best-selling account of his western travels, and he followed it with *A Condensed Geography and History of the Western States* (1828), which he later expanded into a two-volume edition, *The History and Geography of the Mississippi Valley* (1832). This book established Flint's reputation as a leading expert on the western states, and he continued to publish works of western history and geography throughout his career, including *The Indian Wars of the West* (1833) and the *Biographical Memoir of Daniel Boone* (1833). Flint was also a popular novelist, whose works included *Francis Berrian* (1826), *The Life and Adventures of Arthur Clenning* (1828), *George Mason* (1829), *The Lost Child* (1830), and *The Shoshonee Valley* (1830).[17]

Flint was also the founding editor of the *Western Monthly Review*, one of the most successful western literary magazines of the antebellum period. Published in Cincinnati, the *Western Monthly Review* ran from May 1827 to June 1830, and Flint's efforts to revive and revise the nation's federal literary culture are on clearest display in this work. Flint established the magazine to address what he felt was a serious representational problem with the nation's print culture. Although the West had numerous writers and a distinctive regional community, he was troubled that there was no medium to accurately represent it. As he wrote in the inaugural issue, "At the census of 1830, the Mississippi valley will contain more than four millions of inhabitants. We are physically and from our peculiar modes of existence a scribbling and forth-putting people. Little as they have dreamed of the fact in the Atlantic country, we have our thousand orators and poets. [Yet] we have not a solitary journal expressly constituted to be the echo of public literary opinion." Flint's dismay over this lack of representation shows his interest in promoting a federal literary culture. For Flint, the United States needed to represent all of its regional communities on equal terms, which is why he stresses the importance of establishing "a review of our own . . . to do as much justice to a work written here as elsewhere." Flint was particularly concerned about the influence of eastern writers and reviewers who misrepresented and disparaged western life and literature. "We have seen and we therefore know . . . with what a curl of the lip and the crook of a nose an Atlantic reviewer contemplates the idea of a work written west of the Alleghany mountains," wrote Flint. He condemned the narrow focus of the Atlantic literary establishment, which "imagine[d] that nothing good can be written beyond a circle of three and a half miles diameter of which circle they are the centre."[18]

As far as Flint was concerned, these representational problems had significant political stakes. Because the nation's "reviews and journals in a great measure control public opinion," Flint argued that the unjust and imbalanced character of the nation's literary sphere would reproduce itself in the political sphere, transforming the nation from a "republic of letters" into a "shameless tyranny" controlled by the authority of the East.[19] In this regard, the lack of a western literary magazine was not just a regional deficiency. It was a national problem.

Calling on the nation to be "essentially just, both in politics and in literature," Flint argued that reviving the nation's federal literary culture would ensure the unity and stability of the United States in the context of its ongoing expansion.[20] Just as the nation's eighteenth-century residents turned to print to transform their differences into a stable and coherent union, Flint believed that print could continue to unify a nation whose differences were constantly expanding. The success of this literary nationalism, however, depended on representing these differences equally and comprehensively, without privileging one region over another. "The republic of letters ought to have no bounds but the range of intellect," Flint stated in the opening issue, ". . . and that wherever a vigorous intellect opens itself to the inspirations of nature, be it on the Ohio, the Mississippi, Red River or even near the borders of the Arkansas, it will operate the same results as it would in Boston."[21] In the absence of any medium to represent the literature of the West justly or equitably, Flint intended the *Western Monthly Review* to help return the nation's literary and political culture to these federal ideals.

To this end, Flint devoted the first year of the *Western Monthly Review* to representing and celebrating the distinctive characteristics of the West, providing a "fair sample" of the region taken from "above, below, and on all sides."[22] Articles covered western plants and wildlife, geography, geology, and detailed reports on western agriculture and industries, particularly regarding the construction of canals and steamboat enterprises. The magazine also published detailed state histories for Kentucky, Ohio, Louisiana, Tennessee, and Illinois, as well as articles about local politics, school systems, the arts, and western scientific and medical advancements, not to mention a steady stream of western literature. Flint took great pride in the comprehensive nature of this western coverage, writing in 1827, "We can easily enjoy in anticipation, the eagerness with which the future historian will repair to [this magazine] as a synopsis of most of what has been said and written in the Western Country touching its own natural, moral, and civil history."[23]

By the end of the magazine's first year, however, Flint grew concerned about this dominant western focus. Although representing the West was important to his federal outlook, he worried that readers might misinterpret the magazine's exclusive western content as a self-serving effort to privilege the West over the nation's other communities. He voiced these concerns directly in a June 1828 article where he raises the issue of "our *esprit du corps*, sectional feeling, or nationality . . . concerning the peculiar characteristics of western writers." "As regards our sectional feeling, of which we hear so much said abroad and in Congress," stated Flint, "we remark that so far as such feeling includes *amor patriae* and is not narrow but loves the whole country and looks with singleness of eye and affection to the whole Union."[24]

Flint's allusion to these "sectional feelings" refers specifically to the debates surrounding the Tariff of 1828, which dominated national politics for much of that year. As the southern states attacked Congress for passing a law that seemed to benefit the northern states while penalizing the South, the tariff prompted heated discussions about whether the federal government was representing the interests of the states equitably.[25] On both sides of this controversy, northerners and southerners accused each other of placing their own local interests over those of the nation, prompting the derisive accusations of "sectionalism" that Flint was anxious to avoid. The tariff debates were well covered in the western states, and as divisions between the North, the South, and the central government intensified, westerners became increasingly wary of articulating their own statements of regional pride or authority for fear of exacerbating these "sectional" tensions. Flint's effort to clarify the *Western Monthly Review*'s regional focus reflects his desire to assure readers that the magazine was not trying to privilege the West or attack the federal government. By insisting that the magazine's western focus was "not narrow" but, instead, "looks with singleness of eye and affection to the whole Union," Flint deliberately evokes the rhetoric of early federal nationalism, which encouraged citizens to interpret the nation's regional distinctions as a sign of national unity and affiliation. In doing so, Flint seeks not so much to deny the "sectional" focus of the magazine but to change the way his readers interpreted its regional content and recognize that "sectional feelings" can also include "amore patriae."

To better illustrate how these regional and national affiliations could coexist and reinforce one another, Flint completely restructured the form and content of his magazine, announcing in the November 1828 issue that the magazine would enter a new "stage of existence." Instead of focusing specifically on the West, Flint stated that the *Western Monthly Review* would now provide readers with a representative overview of the nation's many views and opinions. "Being, as this place is, nearly the geographic centre of the United States and not far remote from the centre of the population, our situation is extremely convenient for receiving information, books, and pamphlets from all over the country," noted Flint, who explained that the magazine would try to represent these many perspectives by providing a critical digest of reviews published in other magazines. "American reviews shall be abstracted and the summary given, and in giving the sum and abstract of these reviews, we shall always take leave to add our own opinion upon the ability and impartiality of the review," stated Flint. By thus providing summaries and responses to the nation's various literary productions and opinions, this new structure allowed the *Western Monthly Review* to situate the West more clearly within the nation's plural dimensions, rather than simply representing the West on its own. "Such a work," concluded

Flint, "as far as our knowledge extends, will be unique and alone in the annals of periodicals [as] every reading man in the community who has not literary leisure for the perusal of the reviews of books *in extenso* will here be able to take a bird's-eye view of them all."[26]

This emphasis on providing a "bird's-eye" view of the nation's literary reviews "in extenso" illustrates the *Western Monthly Review*'s shift from regional representation to federal literacy. Although the magazine still represented western perspectives, interests, and opinions, readers now had to consider this western content in relation to the nation's other views and interests, a process that required them to interpret all the nation's local and regional expressions as part of a diverse national whole. As readers gained experience recognizing and interpreting the nation in these diverse and dual terms, Flint hoped to produce citizens who were more grounded in and supportive of a plural conception of union. No longer afflicted by the "strained optics" of a single frame of reference, the *Western Monthly Review* encouraged readers to recognize the United States as a nation defined by the views of "twelve millions of men" rather than just "half a dozen existences."[27]

Flint followed this "new arrangement" of providing reviews of the nation's reviews for the rest of the magazine's run.[28] The reviews he selected were usually evenly divided between "Atlantick" and southern periodicals, with occasional selections from French and British publications.[29] In some issues, he published his summaries and responses in a brief digest format, addressing four or five different reviews in a single article. In other issues, he responded to his selected reviews individually through a detailed critical essay.[30] Scholars have often characterized Flint's reviews of these reviews as evidence of the "derivative" quality of the *Western Monthly Review*, arguing that Flint simply reprinted articles from other magazines to fill space.[31] While he often struggled to find contributors, Flint's engagement with these reviews cannot simply be dismissed as filler material. At times, he did include lengthy excerpts from the original reviews, but his own review articles were never word-for-word reprints. Instead, he carefully provided his own summaries and critical responses, producing a new review article that offered two distinct perspectives, that of the original author and Flint's own response, exemplifying the plural reading experience that he wanted to foreground.

Flint's responses to these reviews varied widely, and this variety was crucial to the magazine's federalizing tactics. Sometimes, Flint agreed wholeheartedly with the critical opinions expressed in other publications, as in his assessment of the Boston-based *Ladies Magazine*, which he praises as a "sound, sensible, and judicious magazine," or his review of the *Southern Agriculturalist*, whose articles are "all on matters of the first utility and importance and are written with neatness and uncommon vigor."[32] More often, though, Flint devoted his attention to instances where he disagreed with another magazine or critic. In these cases, Flint clearly stated his terms of disagreement while also acknowledging the value of considering a different view. In his December 1828 review of the "*Southern Review*, No. 4," for instance, Flint challenges a reviewer's claim that recent work by Washington Irving is "polished, courtly, and stately," presenting his own opinion that Irving's work shows "an elaborateness, a stately pomp . . . and affectation of courtliness and state that are to us exceedingly disgusting." He also disagreed with the political focus of the *Southern Review*, writing that "they do not appear to disguise that they are partizans," and he criticized this position by noting, "We have another opinion." Although he disagrees with the content of the *Southern Review* on many points, however, he concludes his review by asserting his tolerance and respect for these different opinions, writing, "If this *Southern Review* has its prejudices, we feel persuaded that they are honest ones and that they declare what they really think and feel touching the books upon which they pass judgment." For Flint, as long as writers honestly present the views and interests of their own communities, he affirms that their ideas should be represented and treated with respect. Furthermore, Flint argues that such differences can be instructive. Instead of getting angry or adversarial about his disagreements with the *Southern Review*, Flint reports that he has learned from engaging with these differences, noting, "We have read few of their reviews which have not given us new and valuable thoughts on the subjects reviewed."[33]

Flint's emphasis on disagreement and tolerance likewise emerges in his response to a review of the popular French novel *Paul and Virginia*. Although the original critic found numerous faults with the novel, dismissing it as a "sickening love story," Flint vehemently disagrees with this assessment, attacking this critic's opinion as a "vile, flippant malignity without the least particle of wit or taste."[34] Despite the harsh and definitive terms of his critique, however, Flint encourages his readers to consider both opinions and seek out others before coming to a conclusion about the novel, writing that "we only ask the reader to examine and compare the above with many of the reviews and notices of books that he has recently read."[35] Flint's account of these two competing assessments of *Paul and Virginia* models the kind of critical engagement he expects from all U.S. readers. Although he clearly believes in the value of his own response, he stops short of denying any value or consideration to the opposing view. Instead, by introducing readers to two divergent perspectives and inviting them to consider both as legitimate responses, Flint emphasizes that the United States will always be defined by varied and even opposing perspectives that can never be reduced to a single, definitive voice. Rather than allowing readers to become unsettled or upset by these ever-present differences, Flint models an alternative response by encouraging his readers to recognize the value of considering these varied views, rather than simply devolving into conflict. By producing these experiences, this new structure of the magazine provided a literary training ground that taught citizens how to engage with the nation's differences productively and recognize the plural dimensions of the nation as a manageable fact rather than a threat.

Flint's focus on the role and responsibilities of U.S. readers gets at the heart of his efforts to revive not just federal nationalism but federal literacy. Although he was committed to representing the regional variety of the United States, he was ultimately more interested in teaching his readers how to respond to that variety. From the beginning of the magazine, Flint criticized the passive qualities of U.S. readers, noting that "there is but one in ten thousand of our readers who is not either too diffident, too indolent, or too unused to the pain of making up a judgment or too much engaged to do it."[36] Throughout the *Western Monthly Review*'s run, Flint challenged his readers to reverse that course and take a more active role in the nation's literary culture. As far as Flint was concerned, all U.S. periodicals needed to share this commitment to representing the nation's variety and encouraging citizens to position themselves within it, and he regularly called on his fellow editors to showcase "the rivalry and opposition and clashing of interests which exist in our provincial capitals" and encourage readers to move "out of the orbit of [their] little universe." "A genuine American classical literature would result from such a system as this, which would be fraught with incalculable benefits," asserted Flint, inspiring "a new march of the mind" that will alleviate "bigotry, fury, and party rage that surround us on every side."[37]

Flint's reference to this "bigotry, fury, and party rage," which appeared in a February 1829 article titled "Impediments of American Literature," alludes once again to 1828 tariff debates, which intensified following the publication of John C. Calhoun's *South Carolina Exposition and Protest* in December 1828. In this pamphlet, Calhoun engaged in a detailed discussion of federalism and the principle of divided sovereignty that laid the foundation for Nullification, exacerbating tensions between the states and the federal government.[38] Within this increasingly adversarial environment, Flint's model of federal literacy offered citizens a chance to restore a balanced and productive relationship between the nation's parts and whole. As Flint described it, the best way to "forge a national character" is for citizens to "set down beside each other" and learn about the "sentiments, feelings, and thoughts that country, kindred, and home indelibly combine with the web of our existence." When residents from different parts of the country are provided with opportunities to encounter and learn about one another, he argued, "They begin to rub off mutual prejudices. One takes a step and then the other. They meet halfway and embrace, and the society, thus newly organized and constituted, is more liberal, enlarged, unprejudiced, and of course more affectionate and pleasant, than a society of people of *unique* birth and character, who bring all their early prejudices as a common stock, to be transmitted as an inheritance in perpetuity."[39] In describing the unifying consequences of encountering the nation's differences, Flint's comments echo Madison's famous argument that a diverse nation can be more unified than a smaller, homogeneous nation in the Federalist No. 10. Like Madison, Flint suggests that the solution to U.S. sectional divisions is not to find ways to limit or control the distinctive interests of the states. Instead, national unity and stability depend on highlighting those diverse interests and training citizens how to work with them.

While print culture provided a powerful means of enabling citizens to engage with the nation's differences in productive terms, Flint pushed his readers to find additional ways to foster this federal outlook and literacy, particularly through the nation's educational structures. Between November 1828 and January 1829, Flint published a three-part essay arguing for the establishment of a "National University" that would teach citizens how to contend with the nation's variety productively. The anonymous author of this proposal begins by insisting that national identities and affiliations are not innate, and that all citizens must be taught how to embrace the political structure of their home communities. "There is nothing more true, nor are there many truths more important than that the general education of a country ought to be in harmony with the government of the country," asserts the author. "Is the government a monarchy and do you wish to render it permanent? Inculcate on youth, even from their infancy, monarchical principles. Is it an aristocracy? Let the youth, while at school, be impressed with it. . . . In like manner, under a federal representative government, let the early and uniform inculcation of sentiments and principles . . . make a part of education." According to this logic, ensuring the strength and stability of the United States depends on finding ways to teach federal "sentiments and principles" to its citizens. "Federalize, therefore, as much as possible, the mind of the whole American youth," asserts the author, "and nothing can dissolve the integrity of the union."[40]

This process of "federalizing the mind" describes the practice of federal literacy at the heart of this study, where a plural sense of unity and affiliation is produced, not by government structures or policies, but by the interpretive practices of citizens. The crucial difference here, however, is the argument for establishing formal institutional structures to produce this federal mindset, as opposed to relying on individual reading practices. Castiglia has explored how, during the early nineteenth century, citizens increasingly turned to institutional structures such as schools, professional associations, social clubs, and civic societies to "interiorize federal law into the affective orders of social feelings," and this proposal for a national university illuminates this interest in developing more standardized institutional measures for supporting the federal union.[41] As the author of this proposal affirms, "In this way will be engendered, on a wider scale of a more durable character and with higher powers than could be otherwise united in it a real federative *esprit de corps*."[42]

The proposal for the "National University" lays out an educational plan that follows the literary tactics of the *Western Monthly Review* by teaching citizens how to recognize and value the nation's many differences while fostering a sense of collective unity and identity. To this end, the proposed university will enroll "youth from all the different states and sections of the Union" and encourage them to cultivate and exhibit their regional identities and affiliations, such that "the alumni that go forth from it will feel all the attachment to state rights and sovereignties." The author clearly states that, by fostering these strong regional sentiments, the national university will intentionally produce conflict. "In the combat of intellect which it will necessarily awaken," he writes, "the North will contend for superiority over the South, the East for superiority over the West and the converse, and each section and state for ascendancy over every other." These conflicts, however, are a crucial part of the university's federal education because they teach students how to contend with regional discord in unifying terms. "Nor will a conflict like this, among generous youth, engender alienation of feeling," reports the author. "On the contrary, [these conflicts] will add strength and durability to their ties of friendship and mutual regard" by training citizens to develop a "mutually sustaining" and "enlightened regard" for one another's varied skills and knowledge.[43] These unifying bonds, however, can only be produced when citizens have opportunities to encounter and interact with their respective differences. Such bonds cannot be produced when citizens isolate themselves and focus solely on their local concerns.

Despite the unifying promise of such a university, the article concludes by encouraging readers to find even more ways to foster this federal mindset. "Multiply, therefore, as much as practicable national measures, institutions, and arrangements, and by framing them all on a federative model, give symmetry to the whole," urges the author, who pushes for the establishment of multiple institutional bodies to promote federal knowledge and literacy, writing that "such a combination of means cannot fail to be powerful and must strengthen in a high degree, the general tie that binds to their common centre the states of the Union."[44] The more citizens can find ways to reproduce federal structures and sentiments in their daily experiences, the stronger the federal nation will be.

Flint wholeheartedly endorsed this call for establishing new forms of institutional support for federal nationalism. He added an editorial note to the last installment of the "National University" series where he pushed citizens to take its call to multiply these federal institutional structures to heart, noting that "if such a system could be established, we are fully impressed, that a stronger cord to bind the many members of our wide republic in sacred, inviolate, and indissoluble union could not be imagined."⁴⁵ Flint's decision to redesign the *Western Monthly Review* to provide a "bird's-eye view" of the nation's opinions was his own effort to create a more formalized structure for promoting the nation's federal principles, and throughout the magazine's run, he pushed readers to establish other institutional means for promoting a federal consciousness. At one point, he even proposed establishing a federal literary "congress" where "the well-known writers and editors of the different states and divisions of our country ... should meet annually at Philadelphia to pass upon the books and other literary productions of the past year and give counsels for the unborn productions of the coming year."⁴⁶ Although this proposal was not entirely serious, Flint's arguments illuminate his belief that the United States needed more formal and visible structures for promoting federal literacy to mediate the pressures posed by expansion. "We deem that such a censurate might do something towards breaking down sectional and building up in its stead a national literature," asserted Flint, who insisted that such institutional forms of support needed to provide citizens with opportunities to encounter the nation's differences in terms of conflict and opposition. As he wrote in 1828, "We shall be unworthy of our family alliance if we do not immediately institute a friendly rivalry in these respects which will be equally honorable and useful for each of the parties."⁴⁷ Even though such conflicts would always be present in a diverse federal union, establishing institutional frameworks for promoting federal literacy could ensure that citizens would learn how to interpret and negotiate such differences effectively.

The *Western Monthly Review* ended rather abruptly in June 1830 when ill health forced Flint to return to New England, but his arguments laid the groundwork for the emergence of an increasingly institutionalized system of federal literacy and education in the West during the 1830s. Building on Flint's ideas and the example set by the *Western Monthly Review*, residents in the West began to establish cultural institutions involving schools, social clubs, and professional organizations that enabled readers to contend productively with the nation's variety, in addition to maintaining a vibrant literary sphere. The growth of these federal cultural institutions made it possible for citizens to reconsider the limits of federal nationalism and imagine the possibility of including citizens who were not part of the Anglo-American majority.

Federalizing the Mind:
The Institutional Federalism of Antebellum Cincinnati

The federal nationalism and literacy promoted by the *Western Monthly Review* thrived in the cultural environment of antebellum Cincinnati, which, by the early 1820s, was the largest and most prosperous city in the West. Fueled by cotton, wheat, meatpacking, manufacturing, and steamboat industries, Cincinnati exemplified what Daniel Aaron describes as the new "urban west" as rural, subsistence-oriented communities transformed into interconnected cities that were inextricably involved with the national economy.[48] Located at the center of a number of major transportation networks, Cincinnati could facilitate the circulation of ideas, goods, and practices from the eastern to the western states and vice versa, and this status as a prominent regional crossroads made the city ideally suited for developing institutional practices that promoted a federal outlook. Castiglia has explored the emergence of these institutionalized forms of national consciousness in the nineteenth century, arguing that this institutionalism created "modes of vigilant and habitual self-management" that encouraged citizens to assume particular kinds of "social responsibility and distribute socially accepted behavior." In the case of Cincinnati, civil institutions such as schools, professional associations, reading rooms, social clubs, and lyceums all helped promote a collective mindset or "social interior" that supported the plural structure and principles of the federal nation.[49]

In terms of public education, Cincinnati led the way in establishing curricular standards that were meant to promote federal literacy. Primary school lessons were required to make "ample provision" for educating students about "the peculiar forms of their National and State Constitutions" and provide "broad, liberal, and solid knowledge" about all the state communities.[50] Cincinnati also fostered this federal knowledge in its institutions of higher learning. The city was home to three colleges (Cincinnati College, Woodward College, and St. Xavier College), three theological seminaries (the Lane Theological Seminary, the St. Francis Xavier Theological Seminary, and the Western Baptist Theological Seminary), a law school (Cincinnati Law School) and a medical school (Medical College of Ohio), as well as several schools for women, including the Cincinnati Female Academy, the Cincinnati Female Institution, and the Western Female Academy.[51] Reports of these institutions emphasized how Cincinnati's location enabled students to acquire knowledge about the nation's variety and interconnected regional relationships. "It must be obvious to everyone acquainted with the Western Country that Cincinnati is a very eligible situation for a seat of learning [as] its location on the Ohio river renders the communication with distant parts of the nation easy and frequent," noted one observer, a situation that enabled these institutions to educate students about the nation's diverse plural dynamics.[52]

This federal education also took place in the many reading rooms, libraries, and museums of antebellum Cincinnati. The Cincinnati Reading Room, established in 1818, provided residents with access to "the most valuable newspapers and literary journals of the United States," and its open policy toward visitors, who could use the reading room free of charge for the duration of their stay, promoted Cincinnati's reputation as a city that was committed to the active and open exchange of ideas, as did more specialized reading rooms sponsored by the Ohio Mechanics Institute and the Western Academy of Natural Sciences.[53] The city also maintained several prominent libraries and museums, including the Cincinnati Library, the Apprentices' Library, Letton's Museum, and the Cincinnati Museum, which likewise enabled patrons to access a wide variety of local and national materials and attend lectures from local and visiting academics that fostered "a public discourse" on the nation's various "objects and advantages."[54]

Efforts to institutionalize the practice of federal literary nationalism were most apparent in Cincinnati's numerous social clubs and intellectual and professional societies. Such organizations were common in the United States during the early nineteenth century, but Cincinnati saw an unprecedented level of growth. "Indeed, the formation of societies became almost a craze," observes Aaron, who reports that between 1820 and 1840, more than one hundred clubs, societies, and associations devoted to literature, fine arts, music, theater, education, and science were established in Cincinnati.[55] While these organizations each had their own specific focus or purpose, most were committed to fostering local pride and national affiliation. In their 1826 review of Cincinnati's cultural, political, and economic conditions, Benjamin Drake and E. D. Mansfield praised these social organizations, which were "admirably calculated to promote intercourse, good feeling, and taste for intellectual pleasures" while simultaneously "aiding in the diffusion of Literature and Science and establishing and fostering useful public institutions."[56]

The two largest professional associations in Cincinnati were the Western Literary Institute and the Western Academy of Natural Sciences, which promoted a federal sensibility through their diverse participants.[57] Both organizations maintained open membership policies. The Western Literary Institute welcomed anyone committed to "the diffusion of knowledge in regard to education," which included professional educators and administrators, writers, editors, scientists, historians, ministers, and local businessmen, and the Western Academy of Natural Sciences was likewise open to any "friends of science," including professional scientists with training in medicine, botany, geology, paleontology, and ornithology, as well as laymen with varying degrees of education.[58] These organizations took great pride in their diverse membership because it reflected the plural conditions of the nation and enabled them to circulate information and ideas throughout their communities in comprehensive terms. The Western Literary Institute took particular pride in its diverse membership, characterizing itself as "a crucible of amalgamation" where different perspectives could be examined and combined with other ideas to help develop an effective educational system for the West.[59] The Western Literary Institute published the varied opinions expressed at these meetings in their annual *Transactions* to ensure that their collective "knowledge, [would be] disseminated among the people and rendered accessible to every human being within our borders."[60]

An active lyceum culture also thrived in antebellum Cincinnati, which likewise fostered a productive engagement with variety. Cincinnati had two prominent lyceums, the Cincinnati Lyceum and the Ohio Medical Lyceum, and the Ohio Mechanics Institute also regularly sponsored lyceum events. Although lyceums would become sites of commercial entertainment later in the nineteenth century, during the 1820s and 1830s they were primarily invested in providing opportunities for public discussion and debate.[61] Lyceum events typically began with a lecture by an invited speaker, but the bulk of the evening was devoted to a heated discussion of the speaker's ideas. As Angela Ray observes, "lyceum members practiced engaging in controversy but in a controlled, restricted setting," and, by facilitating the exchange of different opinions in an environment that was collegial and publicly acceptable, lyceums provided yet another mechanism for promoting the kind of critical engagement needed to sustain a federal union.[62] The subjects and speakers for these events were widely covered in local newspapers, and the Cincinnati lyceums regularly featured controversial topics that were meant to produce varied and contesting opinions, such as female education, banking reform, U.S. expansion into Mexico, constitutional law and interpretation, and new medical treatments. Although these lyceum events always produced disagreement, newspaper coverage typically expressed appreciation for encouraging citizens to consider and reflect on these multiple views. "Such discussions are salutary and refreshing," wrote one journalist, "and we hope that others . . . may be induced to exert their talents in the same manner for the public good."[63]

The literary clubs and societies of Cincinnati likewise sponsored this federal culture of debate. As with most clubs in Cincinnati, membership in these literary clubs was open and diverse, and discussions often focused on political and social issues rather than just literary debate. Edward Deering Mansfield, a western writer and editor who was actively involved in Cincinnati's literary scene, described these varied conversations. Within these "little circles of ladies and gentlemen," noted Mansfield, "I have heard many of the questions which have since occupied the public mind talked over with an ability and fullness of information which is seldom possessed by larger and more authoritative bodies." Mansfield was particularly struck by the way these literary clubs enabled the productive exchange of different views, and he cited the regular meetings of two competing newspaper editors, Moses Dawson, a staunch Jacksonian who edited the *Cincinnati Advertiser*, and Charles Hammond, editor of the *Cincinnati Gazette*, who was "a firm Federalist of the old school." The two met regularly with other writers at a local saloon where they would discuss the issues covered in their respective periodicals, engaging in heated and, often, contentious debates while nevertheless remaining "jovial companions."[64] As in the case of the lyceums, these literary societies provided a forum for representing differences in an environment that could promote friendship and tolerance, and such environments became a hallmark of the Cincinnati literary scene.

Cincinnati's most famous literary clubs were the Semi-Colon Club and the Buck-Eye Club, established in 1829 and 1833, respectively. Both clubs operated informally, without any bylaws or fixed leadership, and they were meant to serve as literary salons where members could share their writing, discuss recent literary works, and debate the current state of western and national literature. Although membership was open to all, these clubs were dominated by professional writers and editors, and they were extremely influential in fostering western literature and promoting the careers of writers such as Timothy Flint, Caroline Hentz, Daniel Drake, James Hall, and, most famously, Harriet Beecher Stowe.[65]

Although the Semi-Colon Club and the Buck-Eye Club were invested in western literature, these clubs had very different visions of what western literary culture should look like. The Semi-Colon Club, which was largely composed of transplanted New Englanders, argued that western literary culture needed to assimilate rather than innovate by following the cultural standards and aesthetics of the eastern literary establishment. Lyman Beecher, one of the club's founding members, was particularly vocal in pushing this agenda, arguing that "the institutions which have blessed the East are to bless the West," and he encouraged Semi-Colon members to promote "a holy, fraternal fellowship between the East and West, which shall secure our preservation."[66] Although there was still room for regional pluralism in this model, the Semi-Colon Club encouraged western writers to downplay their distinctions and follow the aesthetic standards modeled by the East Coast.

Not all members of the Semi-Colon Club embraced these views, however. Over time, many of the club's founding members, including Timothy Flint, Daniel Drake, and James Hall, criticized these efforts to model the West after the East, condemning this perspective for "assigning a degree of moral purity and elevation to the one and of darkness and degradation to the other not justified by the actual condition of either."[67] To counter this East Coast–centered vision of literary nationalism, Drake took the lead in establishing a new literary society, the Buck-Eye Club, which was dedicated to developing an independent western literary culture. Founded in 1832, the Buck-Eye Club was named after the distinctive emblem of Ohio to foreground its western focus, and although the club was originally meant to be a literary forum, it soon became involved with western boosterism on a much broader scale. The club held annual "Buck-Eye

Celebrations" that commemorated western events and encouraged westerners to take pride in their local identities. At a Buck-Eye event honoring Cincinnati's forty-fifth anniversary, for instance, Drake encouraged "every native of the valley of the Ohio [t]o feel proud of the appellation, which, from the infancy of our settlements, has been conferred upon him; for the Buckeye has many qualities which may be regarded as typical of a noble character." This emphasis on fostering a strong sense of regional pride and identity, however, was always accompanied by an equal emphasis on nationalism. Buck-Eye events opened with a national salute or a toast, followed by a song or a poem that evoked national sentiments, often by referencing George Washington and the nation's early "revolutionary patriots." For Drake, his western advocacy was closely linked to fostering nationalist sentiments and devotion. As he stated on numerous occasions, "My Buckeyism belongs to the *country*," assuring his audiences that his statements of local pride and affiliation simultaneously served the interests of the nation.[68]

Drake's emphasis on the close connection between national and regional sentiments echoes the rhetoric of the early republic, where, as Waldstreicher notes, citizens often engaged in "local expression[s] of national feelings."[69] Drake, however, went a step farther, not just reviving these federal sentiments but revising them to imagine a much more expansive and inclusive plural union. Instead of looking back to the original thirteen states as the model for its federal character, Drake argued that the West provided a better foundation for imagining a stable and productive future for the federal nation.

Drake was ideally suited to transform these federal dynamics because he had a hand in nearly all of the West's leading cultural institutions. Drake served as a member and, in most cases, leader of almost every major social organization in Cincinnati, including the Western Literary Institute, the Western Academy of Sciences, the Cincinnati Lyceum, and both the Semi-Colon and Buck-Eye Clubs. An esteemed writer, Drake published articles on western literature, science, and culture in local and national periodicals, and he was a regular speaker at lyceum sessions and society meetings throughout the Ohio valley region. He was also a respected scientist and practicing physician who helped establish the Medical College of Ohio and the Departments of Medicine at Miami University and Cincinnati College, in addition to founding and editing the *Western Journal of the Medical and Physical Sciences*. Drake's exceptional range of accomplishments and experiences, combined with his commitment to public service, earned him the nickname "Franklin of the West," and, much as Benjamin Franklin had done in the early United States, Drake worked hard to promote a plural model of nationhood that could simultaneously serve local interests and foster a comprehensive union.

Drake's efforts to revive and revise the federal dynamics of the early United States are evident in his two major essays, "Remarks on the Importance of Promoting Literary and Social Concert in the Valley of the Mississippi" (1833) and "Discourse on the History, Character, and Prospects of the West" (1834). In both works, he praises federalism as an ideal structure for unifying a diverse nation, writing that "this complex political organization, [is] the only one, perhaps, that could enable the inhabitants of an *extensive* territory to establish union and, at the same time, to enjoy the blessings of laws adapted to their respective wants." He acknowledges, however, that this political structure is prone to instability. "Like everything complicated," he writes, federalism "is liable to decomposition," and he goes on to suggest that the federal structure of the United States is currently in a state of crisis that the western states have the potential to resolve. "At a period when such a catastrophe is spoken of by all and apprehended by many, it cannot be unprofitable for the people of the different states to consider what they may do to avert it. As a citizen of the valley of the Mississippi, addressing those who dwell in the same region, I propose to say something on the means of prevention which lie within *our* reach . . . which is precisely that which would most effectively perpetuate the UNION." By characterizing the West as a means of resolving the tensions that were currently undermining the federal union, Drake redeems federalism as a viable model for the United States while simultaneously reorienting its federal foundation. Instead of aligning the United States with the federal model set by the original thirteen states, Drake argues that the nation needs to reimagine its plural unity in terms that reflect the diversity of the West. He invokes the traditional image of the federal edifice, arguing that the original structure of the United States was unstable because the eastern states were too limited in their geography, industries, and demography to create "a physical tie of paramount influence" that could link all the states together. Comparing the original federal union to an unstable arch, Drake characterized the West as a counterweight that could stabilize its precarious and imbalanced structure. "But happily, there also rests on the arch a weight, which, unremoved, must forever preserve it," he asserts. "This weight is the superstructure of the trans-alpine states and territories, which stretch from the western foot of the Alleghenies to the wilds of the Missouri, in prospect even to the Chippewan mountains and from the Lakes to the gulf of Mexico in natural association."[70] Drake's use of this metaphor of the federal edifice exemplifies his efforts to both revive and revise the federal dimensions of the early republic by reasserting the value of the nation's composite structure, while also revising that structure to position the West as its new foundation.

Drake identifies two specific reasons that the West can play this unifying and redemptive role. The first, which is the primary focus of "Remarks on the

Importance of Promoting Literary and Social Concert in the Valley of the Mississippi," concerns the physical space of the West. In this essay, Drake provides a comprehensive overview of the West's diverse geography, arguing that its many different landscapes, climates, and waterways allow the residents of the West to produce and circulate a varied range of goods for all the states, forging unifying bonds of exchange and interdependence among them. Unlike the original states of the Eastern Seaboard, whose landscapes and industries had limited value or use for the rest of the nation, Drake argued that the western states could produce and distribute goods needed by all the states, creating "such natural connections and dependencies ... as must forever set the spirit of disunion at defiance."[71] This argument echoes the logic of the American System that dominated the nationalist ideology of the United States at this time.[72] Drake, however, insisted that the unity of this interconnected system was contingent on the western states. "The cement of future adhesion among all the states exudes, to speak figuratively, from the soil of the West," asserted Drake. "To borrow a metaphor from my own profession, it is the interior of the sovereign body politic, embracing the vital organs which distribute nourishment through the outer parts."[73] Here, Drake again evokes a traditional federal metaphor, that of the body, to describe the nation's plural union, revising it to position the West as the central foundation for this union. In Drake's image of the federal body politic, the West is not simply one part of a composite union, it is the central component that unites and sustains all the parts of the federal union.

Drake also identifies the West's cultural diversity as another factor that allowed this region to serve as a supportive foundation for the federal union. He presents this argument in "Discourse on the History, Character, and Prospects of the West," where he identifies cultural diversity as one of the West's most definitive features, noting that "the millions who already flourish in the valleys of the Mississippi and the lakes are chiefly emigrants. They have entered it on every side and are derived, not only from all the original states of the Union but from western and even central Europe, bringing with them various national particularities."[74] Here, Drake specifically emphasizes the non-Anglo and non-U.S. dimensions of the West's emigrant population, which includes "various national particularities" that are not necessarily connected to "the original states of the Union." He draws particular attention to the region's French and Spanish residents, arguing that "its French and Spanish population [has] opened to the inhabitants of the Valley a new source of intellectual improvement ... [and] made thousands acquainted with the manners and customs and character of a people different from ourselves." For Drake, the presence of people who differ from the nation's Anglocentric norms plays an important educational role that strengthens the nation's plural unity. As he describes it, "day after day is brought into the West the enterprising and ambitious from other realms, and each has been a schoolmaster to our native population, presenting them with strange manners and customs, arts, opinions, and prejudices not seen before," such that "without leaving our native woods, we have seen specimens well fitted to enlarge our conceptions of character."[75] By describing these emigrant communities as "schoolmasters," Drake grants legitimacy and authority to their cultural differences, arguing that their "strange manners [and] customs" can impart useful knowledge and skills to strengthen and improve the nation's expansive and plural character. He stopped short of insisting that residents of the West should adopt the different traditions and beliefs of these diverse cultural communities. Instead, he simply highlights the value of representing and learning about them, arguing that this appreciation will enhance the stability and unity of the federal nation.

This argument—that the non-Anglo residents of the West could represent and strengthen the nation's federal identity—marks a radical shift in the plural dynamics of U.S. federal nationalism. Although the United States was founded on the representation of its differences, this plural nationalism typically excluded people who did not fit Anglo-American cultural norms, as I have tried to emphasize throughout this study. By reorienting the federal nation so that its stability and unity were contingent on the diverse conditions of the West, Drake argued that the United States needed to change its plural dynamics to represent the non-Anglo residents who now constituted much of its western population. There were still limits, of course, to Drake's expansive federal vision. Although he pushed citizens to include residents with French, Spanish, and other European cultural backgrounds as part of the nation's federal variety, he did not extend this federal imagination to include the rights of African American or Native American communities. Despite these limitations, Drake's arguments nevertheless represented a more inclusive form of federal unity than had previously existed in the United States. Rather than representing a radical alteration of the nation's federal identity, however, Drake characterized this shift as a logical continuation of the nation's federal principles. His continual references to the federal metaphors of the early republic exemplify his efforts to connect his new federal vision to the plural values of the past. He concludes his arguments for expanding the cultural dynamics of the United States in "Discourse" by comparing the nation to the Milky Way, "whose image . . . combines the stars of the sky into one broad and sparkling firmament."[76] As it did in the early United States, this image allows Drake to characterize the nation as a strong and admirable union composed of many parts. Unlike the early republic, however, Drake uses this metaphor to represent a much wider range of cultural and ethnic differences than had previously been included as part of this composite union.

Drake's celebratory and stabilizing view of the nation's cultural differences coincided with the rise of a strong nativist movement in the early 1830s that both rejected and feared this inclusive federal vision. Lyman Beecher, Drake's former associate in the Semi-Colon Club, was the primary spokesman for this nativist movement in the West, and in 1835 he published a pamphlet titled *A Plea for the West* that set forth the "dangers" posed by "the rapid influx of foreign emigrants, the greater part unacquainted with our institutions [and] unaccustomed to self-government." Characterizing these immigrants as "masses of ignorance ... most dangerous to liberty," Beecher encouraged westerners to restrict or outright reject any cultural practices that did not conform with the Anglo-American Protestant standards set by "the conditions of the East," particularly the practice of Catholicism. For Beecher, incorporating people who did not share the same cultural values, beliefs, and political experiences that defined the early United States was equivalent to "a birthright abandoned," and he called on his fellow westerners to reaffirm "our alliance of blood and political institutions and common interests" and limit the expression of any cultural traditions that "threaten our permanent prosperity and liberty."[77]

The contrast between Beecher's and Drake's arguments illuminates two distinct and opposing visions of federal nationalism in the age of expansion. On the one side was a vision firmly rooted in the nation's past that continued to promote a racially and culturally exclusive model of pluralism that privileges the values, practices, and products of the original thirteen states. On the other side was a vision that was rooted in the nation's new states and territories, expanding the plural dynamics of the original federal union to incorporate a much greater range of geographic, economic, and cultural and ethnic differences. As Watts has argued, these two competing visions of federal nationalism dominated western literary culture for the next thirty years, and over the course of the nineteenth century, western writers became increasingly comfortable with rejecting East Coast standards and emphasizing their regional distinctiveness and their right to represent the West in distinct and independent terms.[78] Not everyone, however, was as comfortable embracing and promoting Drake's arguments for expanding the cultural and ethnic dimensions of the federal union, and these arguments became an increasing point of contention throughout the 1830s, 1840s, and 1850s.

Other western writers responded to Drake's arguments with varying degrees of support. While many readily embraced his emphasis on representing the West as a distinct and central part of a decidedly plural union, they were often less inclined to promote his expansive cultural vision. William Davis Gallagher, a journalist, editor, and poet who closely followed in the footsteps of Flint and Drake, marks a notable case in point. Much like Drake, Gallagher was deeply involved in promoting the West in numerous forums in antebellum Cincinnati. Gallagher served as the editor for nearly all of the major western magazines that followed Flint's *Western Monthly Review*, including the *Cincinnati Mirror*, the *Hesperian*, and the *Cincinnati Gazette*, and he also compiled the first comprehensive anthology of western poetry and prose, *Selections from the Poetical Literature of the West* (1841). In these publications, Gallagher worked hard to represent the variety of the West, not just to promote his home region but to foster a plural sense of national unity by distinguishing the West "as a young and rising province of our Great Republic of Letters."[79] Despite his emphasis on promoting western variety and national pluralism, however, Gallagher's work did not draw any attention to the ethnic and cultural diversity of the West, and his publications focus almost exclusively on Anglo-American perspectives and experiences. Gallagher's lack of attention to the West's cultural diversity is somewhat surprising considering his involvement with other radical political causes involving labor rights, feminism, and abolition during his career.[80] His continual struggles to earn a living and keep his magazines afloat, however, might explain his reluctance to promote a more ethnically and culturally diverse model of regional nationalism, particularly in light of the growing strength of the nativist movement in the 1840s. While promoting regional pride and pluralism was a successful literary strategy that found a supportive audience in the 1830s and 1840s, promoting cultural and ethnic pluralism did not.

A few western writers did try to promote a more culturally inclusive model of federal union and literacy, however. Benjamin Drake, Daniel Drake's younger brother, actually took his brother's arguments for cultural diversity even further by attempting to represent Native Americans as legitimate residents of the West who deserved just recognition from the United States. A noted historian who also served as the editor of the *Cincinnati Chronicle*, Benjamin Drake wrote two important biographies of Native American leaders, *The Life and Adventures of Black Hawk* (1838) and *Life of Tecumseh and of His Brother the Prophet* (1841). In both works, Drake tried to provide a more balanced and equitable representation of these leaders and their native communities by providing "a careful review of their history."[81] Although, at times, Drake's portrayal of native individuals, beliefs, and customs is overly simplistic and romanticized, his writings made a concerted effort to revise the racist and discriminatory assumptions that informed most accounts of native culture at this time. As Watts writes, "his intent is more than an accurate recreation of their lives; each attempts to correct a misrepresentation of the region's Natives" in order to "inculcate a more general multivocality and to represent a diversity of regional presences" in the West.[82] By giving careful and detailed attention to native beliefs, customs, and perspectives, Drake ultimately sought to recognize "the original, natural right of the Indians to the occupancy and possession of their lands" and "awaken the public mind to a sense of the wrongs inflicted upon the Indians and to arouse the Christian statemen of this land to the adoption of a more liberal, upright, and benevolent policy towards them."[83] Here, we see Drake's emphasis on promoting a more expansive and inclusive practice of federal nationalism as he encouraged his readers to extend equal rights and representation to these native communities within the United States, a critical reinterpretation of Native Americans and U.S. Indian policy that, according to Drake, would restore "national honor" to the United States.[84]

In making these arguments, Benjamin Drake always expressed his indebtedness to the work of another western writer, James Hall, whom Drake praised for his careful attention "to the study of aboriginal history" and "valuable assistance" in sharing his knowledge about these communities.[85] Alongside Flint and Daniel Drake, Hall was one of the most prolific and influential writers of the antebellum West who likewise promoted a western-oriented model of federal pluralism and literacy, particularly through his role as editor for his own western periodical, the *Western Monthly Magazine*, which ran, under various titles, from 1830 to 1837. Much like the Drake brothers, Hall also specifically advocated for expanding the nation's federal pluralism to include non-Anglo residents and cultural practices. In arguing for a more diverse and inclusive federal culture, however, Hall primarily turned to a different literary genre—that of fiction—to help readers imagine the nation's plural union in non-Anglo terms. Through short stories, both his own and those that he published in his magazine, Hall invoked the nation's federal principles to encourage readers to imagine the United States as a nation defined by a much wider range of ethnic and cultural differences, particularly regarding its French and Spanish cultural heritage. Like Benjamin Drake, Hall also tried to imagine a nation that could represent and acknowledge Native American communities as part of its federal identity. The place of Native Americans within the federal nation, however, would ultimately prove to be the breaking point of Hall's federal nationalism, and by studying the complexities and contradictions that emerge in Hall's accounts of the nation's cultural and ethnic diversity, we can begin to see the racial limits of federal nationalism that would eventually lead to the disintegration of this literary and cultural imagination in the 1850s and 1860s.

Pushing the Limits of Federal Literacy: The Literary Imagination of James Hall

James Hall stands equally with Timothy Flint and Daniel Drake in reviving and revising federal nationalism in the antebellum West. All three men were close friends and collaborators, and their efforts to develop a more institutionalized federal imagination, particularly through the establishment of a strong regional literary culture, dovetailed throughout their careers. Like Flint and Drake, Hall was not a native westerner. Born in Philadelphia in 1793, Hall was well connected to the New England literary establishment. His mother, Sarah Ewing Hall, was a poet and essayist, and his brother, John, was one of the editors for the influential *Port-Folio* magazine where Hall published some of his early work. After briefly serving in the army during the War of 1812, Hall decided to pursue a career in law and completed his degree in 1818. In the spring of 1820, however, he took an extended sightseeing trip through Illinois, Ohio, and Kentucky that convinced him to settle permanently in the West later that year. Hall published his first full-length work, a chronicle of his western travels titled *Letters from the West*, in 1822, successfully launching his western literary career, although he would continue to work as a lawyer and, later, as a federal circuit judge throughout his life.[86]

Hall's next literary project exemplified his lifelong interest in promoting both a strong western literary culture and a federal literary imagination. Beginning in 1828, Hall set to work compiling and editing the first western literary annual, the *Western Souvenir*, which he published with great fanfare in 1829. These annuals, which were extremely popular in the antebellum United States, were decorative gift books that were designed to provide readers with a comprehensive portrait of the nation's literary works for a given year.[87] Although their contents were supposed to be representative, these books were typically dominated by New England and mid-Atlantic writers, and by publishing an annual that was exclusively devoted to western literature, Hall sought to correct this imbalance. Critics praised "the efforts of Judge Hall ... to advance the literature of the West," characterizing his collection as "equal in every respect to those of the Atlantic cities," and his efforts to ensure that western literature would be represented as an equal participant within the literary culture of the United States set the stage for the federal focus of all his subsequent literary work.[88]

Much like Flint's, Hall's efforts to promote a federal literary culture in the West were initially concentrated in his magazine work. Hall established the *Illinois Monthly Magazine* in Vandalia in 1830; despite its state-centered name, Hall intended this publication to provide readers with a representative and comprehensive portrait of the West as a whole. "Every topic connected with the arts, the industry, or the resources of this flourishing state or of the western country will come within the scope of this work," Hall stated in the first issue, and he eventually changed its name to the *Western Monthly Magazine* when he moved to Cincinnati in 1832 so as to "give it a more general circulation and to identify its character with that of the western country at large."[89]

Hall intended the *Western Monthly Magazine* to fill the gap created by the closure of Flint's *Western Monthly Review*, and he carefully structured his magazine to imitate Flint's federal tactics and ethos, particularly by representing the distinctive characteristics of the West and encouraging readers to situate the region as part of a larger, plural nation. "The leading features of our humble attempt will be to disseminate knowledge, to cultivate a taste for letters, and to give correct delineations of this country to our distant friends," stated Hall, and, much like Flint and Drake, he believed that representing and circulating this regional information was a means of strengthening national union. "By circulating intelligence, each would be informed of what the other is doing," which, in turn, "give[s] impulse to national character," he affirmed.[90] Rather than focusing on his individual efforts to provide this comprehensive "intelligence" to readers, Hall was much more aggressive in asserting the federal influence of the nation's print culture, writ large. "Our republican institutions and our mild laws do much toward the formation of national character but the press does more," argued Hall, who published more than twenty articles about the current status of U.S. print culture in the *Western Monthly Magazine* that encouraged his fellow editors to promote federal nationalism and literacy on a unified, institutional scale, "implanting in them a living persuasion of reciprocal interests and rallying their patriotism around the standard of kindred feelings."[91]

Like Flint, Hall structured his magazine to represent differences equitably and clearly showcase conflict. Articles published in the *Western Monthly Magazine* regularly featured opposing critical views about topics such as literature, education, road and canal development, emigration, southern and eastern regional values, and U.S. Indian policy, and he often printed letters from his readers that expressed varied positions regarding these arguments. He described this editorial policy in an 1833 address to his readers, where he stated his intention to publish "a great variety of topics" while also promising his contributors that they were free to express any ideas or opinions they wished. "We extend the invitation to all who are capable of writing in any department of literature. Ladies and gentlemen will be alike welcome; they may select their own topics and treat them in their own manner. . . . The rich and varied emanations of genius, the matured results of patient thought, and the stores of profound research will be equally acceptable."[92] By stating that all writers were "alike welcome" and that their "varied emanations" would be "equally acceptable," Hall's editorial policy modeled the interpretive approach he wanted his readers to take with regard to recognizing the nation's differences and treating those differences equitably.[93] Acknowledging that this policy would inevitably produce disagreements, he took pride in the magazine's ability to foster disputes so that readers could learn how to handle them productively. "If the curs bark at our chariot, let them bark—the more noise it makes the better," asserted Hall, who took pains to represent each side of these conflicts with equal tolerance and respect.[94] By showcasing these conflicts, Hall's goal was to highlight not the arguments themselves but his magazine's response to them. "Above all, we shall keep our own temper, unruffled, and be as pleasant, as witty, and as wise as we can. We desire to live in charity with all the world," stated Hall.[95] By continually encouraging readers to respond to conflicts by considering the "equal strength" and "equal worth" of all opinions, the *Western Monthly Magazine* modeled the interpretive approach that Hall wanted to foster in all the nation's readers, an approach that lent stability and support to a plural union.[96]

Following Drake, Hall also used the *Western Monthly Magazine* to expand the plural dimensions of the United States. Hall's efforts to challenge the nation's Anglo-Protestant cultural norms drew national attention in his famous opposition to Lyman Beecher's nativist pamphlet, *A Plea for the West*. Hall published two separate essays that criticized Beecher's arguments in the May and June issues of the *Western Monthly Magazine* for 1835, and, in both works, he condemned Beecher's "labored arguments against the Catholics and the emigrants from foreign countries" as "founded in ignorance, error, and gross prejudice."[97] Rather than engaging in a discussion of the legitimacy or value of Catholic beliefs, Hall focused instead on the federal principles of pluralism and equal representation to argue that Catholics, as well as other emigrants, had every right to be recognized as citizens of the United States. He criticized Beecher for "seeking to rob a large body of unoffending citizens of those rights which are guaranteed to them by the constitution of our country."[98] By invoking these constitutional rights, which included the nation's commitment to pluralism and the free exercise of religion, Hall reminds readers that the federal United States has always represented and protected such differences. Even though Catholic beliefs and practices differed from those of the Protestant majority, these residents were not "foreigners opposed to the principles of our government," as Beecher claimed. Instead, Hall argued that these differences represented legitimate expressions of federal citizenship. The Catholics, emphasizes Hall, "*do* mingle with us as American citizens and come under the full action of our republican institutions." He concluded his arguments by reminding readers that such differences have always been a part of a federal nation and, furthermore, that they have continually strengthened its unity. "The Roman Catholics," writes Hall, are "a body in which have numbered many of the patriots of the revolution, and of those who, at a later period, have participated in the councils of the nation or have bared their breasts in battle to the enemies of our country, and among whom are found thousands of reputable, industrious citizens."[99] By thus reminding his readers that the nation has always been well served and supported by people who were not a part of the dominant Anglo-Protestant culture, Hall reaffirms the United States' heterogeneous cultural origins and encourages citizens to embrace cultural and religious diversity as both an admirable part of the nation's past and an important part of its future.

Although Hall was clearly opposed to Beecher's nativist arguments, he also made sure that the *Western Monthly Magazine* represented multiple opinions and perspectives on this issue. Hall received numerous letters expressing both support and opposition for his views and for Beecher's arguments, and he published many of these responses in the magazine, taking care to represent views from all sides. By showcasing these varied opinions, Hall shifted the magazine's focus away from the details of these arguments to foreground the spirit of tolerance and equity that he hoped to promote in his readers. Many of the letters he published commented specifically on the magazine's open-minded approach. "Despising alike the trickery and fanaticism of the bigot," one reader praised Hall's editorial style for "the even tenor of his ways, rendering equal justice to all." Another reader declared his appreciation for "the principles of free, temperate discussion and criticism" in the magazine. "I did not entirely agree with you in your review of Beecher's *Plea*, nor in your views of the Roman Catholic movements," he wrote, "but I had no notion of having all the talk on one side—so you wrote, and so I read, and we both felt the better for it."[100] By highlighting such letters, Hall emphasized his central purpose for the magazine, which was to present multiple perspectives equally and, most importantly, to show the positive consequences of this equitable approach.

Implicit in Hall's critique of Beecher's anti-Catholic sentiments is an argument for transforming the cultural dimensions of the United States. Most Catholics in the United States were non-Anglo residents whose cultural identities were usually linked to France or Spain, which meant that Hall's push for greater religious tolerance in the United States was, simultaneously, a push for greater cultural tolerance. Hall stopped short, however, of promoting the non-Anglo dimensions of his arguments directly, a decision that reflects the tensions surrounding the cultural and racial boundaries of federal citizenship at this time. For Hall, encouraging his readers to embrace religious diversity was easier than pushing them to accept non-Anglo immigrants and residents as part of the federal nation, which accounts for the implicit character of his arguments. As Watts writes, "Hall's essay reveals that his conflict with Beecher involved more than simply questions of faith: at stake were issues of identity, nation, and citizenship," although he typically had to present his revisions of these categories with "restraint."[101]

Throughout the run of his magazine, Hall would continue to promote a culturally diverse model of federal nationhood that included non-Anglo communities, but he would rarely do so explicitly. Instead Hall turned primarily to fiction to imagine the nation's federal pluralism in more expansive and inclusive terms. In fiction, writers had more freedom to introduce controversial ideas because of its "imaginative" dimensions, and the fiction Hall published in the *Western Monthly Magazine* regularly pushed citizens to imagine the United States in terms that were less Protestant and less white. The stories published in the *Western Monthly Magazine* were remarkably diverse in their form and focus, including sentimental tales of love and courtship; stories of western exploration, emigration and settlement; captivity narratives; ghost stories; and lighthearted local sketches of country balls, rifle matches, and river expeditions. Many of these stories encouraged readers to adopt a plural mindset for interpreting the nation, either by poking fun at people who would only view the world through a single-minded frame of reference, exemplified by stories such as "The Intestate" and "Isabelle and Her Sister Kate and Their Cousin," or by showing the benefits of embracing people with different ideas, beliefs, or backgrounds, as in "The Village Musician" or "James Kirkwood."[102] Quite a few of these stories, however, specifically pushed readers to recognize and value the West's cultural diversity by drawing attention to the region's French and Spanish residents, heritage, and neighbors. Watts and Doolen have examined how western writers often tried to incorporate French, Spanish, and other transnational characters and practices into U.S. national consciousness during the late 1820s through the 1840s, focusing specifically on the ways these narratives of cross-cultural encounter and comparison were often used to criticize and revise U.S. political practices and cultural norms.[103] As Doolen writes, "these flows of transnational individuals and groups expose and deconstruct the hegemonic practices of the state," and Watts focuses specifically on the way these transcultural narratives encouraged citizens to reimagine the United States as a nation that "tolerated and even championed interculturalism and other forms of cultural plurality."[104] Much of the fiction published in the *Western Monthly Magazine* follows these models. Works such as "La Rouge or the Red Tavern," for instance, invited readers to recall the nation's French cultural past and recognize, first, that French settlers had always been strong supporters of U.S. national principles and, second, that these settlers may have represented and enacted those principles better than their Anglo-American compatriots. Other stories such as "The Spectre Hunter," which tells the story of the ghost of a Spanish settler who haunts the Ohio valley, or "The Intestate," which recalls a traveler's efforts to negotiate the cultural diversity of New Orleans, similarly draw on these different cultural experiences and perspectives to encourage readers to develop a more inclusive understanding of the people and practices "comprised within that one endearing word—*home*."[105] Such stories also represented these experiences of transcultural diversity and engagement almost exclusively in the nation's past, rather than the present. Although readers were encouraged to recognize the French and Spanish dimensions of the United States as important and instructive, this cultural diversity was almost always cast in vanishing terms, which is why it was so crucial to commemorate them in writing so that citizens could continue to benefit from these diverse perspectives as their opportunities to experience them directly diminished.

Which brings us to Hall's own fiction. Hall published numerous stories in the *Western Monthly Magazine*, and his fiction also appeared in other periodicals and anthologies, as well as his own short story collections, which included *Legends of the West* (1832), *The Soldier's Bride and Other Tales* (1832), *Sketches of the West* (1835), and *Tales of the Border* (1835). Much of this fiction engages with the French or Spanish cultural heritage of the West, and he uses these experiences to promote a more expansive, inclusive, and non-Anglo federal nationalism. His relationship to portraying the nation's cultural diversity in vanishing terms, however, is more complicated and ambivalent than in most fiction from this period. In some cases, he absolutely follows the example of his peers by representing the nation's cultural diversity as part of a distant past that must be commemorated, rather than preserved, as in his short story "The Legend of Carondelet." In other stories, however, such as "The French Village" or "Michel de Coucy," he seems to protest this disappearance, encouraging readers to preserve the nation's cultural diversity and ensure that this diversity remains a visible and vibrant part of its character in the present. Hall's shifting positions on this issue illuminate the anxieties and complexities involved in imagining the federal union that was more culturally inclusive.

One of Hall's earliest efforts to promote a more culturally diverse and inclusive model of federal nationalism in fiction can be found in "The Legend of Carondelet," which he published in the *Illinois Monthly Magazine* in 1830. The tale begins in New England in the 1780s where we meet Timothy Eleazar Tompkinson, "the hopeful heir of a worthy mariner," who has lived his whole life under the watchful care of his aunt, "the worthy Miss Fidelity Tompkinson."[106] Industrious, practical, and plain spoken, Timothy Eleazar is the quintessential Yankee whose identity is reinforced by the constant repetition of his regionally resonant Protestant name.[107]

When his father dies unexpectedly, Timothy Eleazar moves west and settles in the Missouri Territory where he must immediately contend with its Spanish and French culture. At this point, the narrator interrupts the story to remind readers of the cultural diversity of the region, which is no longer readily apparent. "Here I must leave my hero for the present and ask the gentle reader to accompany me to the pleasant village of Carondelet, or as it is more commonly called,

Vuide Poche, on the margin of the Mississippi . . . now dwindled to an abscure and ruinous hamlet."[108] The narrator's reference to the two different names of this village—one formal (Carondelet) and the other colloquial (Vuide Poche)—evokes the dual Spanish and French culture of the region, "Carondelet" being the name of a Spanish colonial governor for the Louisiana Territory and "Vuide Poche" highlighting its French cultural claims. Much like its colloquial French name, which means "empty pockets," the village of Vuide Poche is presented to readers as an empty space whose diverse cultural history is no longer evident, a gap that the story seeks to fill.

In Vuide Poche, Timothy Eleazar encounters a cultural space that, at first, seems completely foreign to him. On arriving in town, he meets Monsieur Dunois, "a round-faced, laughing Frenchman . . . [with] that mahogany tinge of complexion which belongs to this region," a description that draws a clear ethnic distinction between the two men. The story continues to emphasize their cultural differences with the following comic dialogue.

> Pray sir, said Timothy Eleazar, with his best college bow, can you direct me to a tavern?
>
> Tavern! *vat* you call? *Eh? Oh la! d'auberge*—no, *Monsieur, dere* is no tavern in *Vuide Poche.*
>
> This is awkward enough—what shall I do? My horse must be fed, and I am almost starved.
>
> *Eh bien!* You will have some *ros bif,* and somebody for eat your *cheval? N'est ce pas?*
>
> I need food and lodging and know not where to go.
>
> *Fude! Vat* is *fude,* Marie? Ah ha! *Aliment. Sacre! Monsieur* is *hungry! Loge!* Here is *ver* good place, *chez moi.* You shall stay *vid* me. *Ver* good *loge* here, and plenty for eat you, *et votre cheval.*[109]

This stylized juxtaposition of the college-bowing Timothy Eleazar and "zee ver French" Dunois highlights their cultural differences in exaggerated terms. Antebellum fiction often used these regional stereotypes as a comic shorthand for asserting and comparing regional identities by pitting the industrious Yankee over the indolent southerner, for example, or the clever and humorous westerner over the short-sighted, uptight New Englander.[110] Hall's story engages with these stereotypes but avoids presenting them in hierarchical or adversarial terms. Even though Timothy Eleazar and M. Dunois initially have trouble understanding one another, the two men eventually interact on friendly and equitable terms, and, as the story continues, Timothy Eleazar finds that he can adapt to this new French cultural environment quite easily. He soon adopts "the free and social habits of the French," and, by the end of the story, the narrator reports that

Timothy Eleazar now speaks French fluently and is "as garrulous as any of his townsmen." His physical appearance even changes as he "grew swarthy as his neighbors, and, as he wore a *capot* and smoked a short pipe, no one would have suspected that he was not a native."[111]

Timothy Eleazar's ability to assimilate to this French cultural community is aided by the fact that Vuide Poche turns out to be more similar to the United States than he initially thinks. Despite clear differences in language, religious beliefs, and professional pursuits, the French culture of Vuide Poche shares many of the political values and characteristics of New England. Consider the following description, which is worth quoting at length:

> The inhabitants presented, I suppose, a fair specimen of the French peasantry, as they existed in France, previous to the first revolution.... Though subject, at the date of our tale, to a foreign king, they were as good republicans as if they had been trained up in one of our own colonies. They knew the restraints and distinctions of a monarchy only by report, practicing the most rigid equality among themselves, and never troubling their heads to enquire how things were ordered elsewhere. The French commandants and priests who ruled in their numerous colonies, had always the knack of giving a parental character to their sway, and governed with so much mildness that the people never thought of questioning either the source or extent of their authority; while the English invariably alienate the affections of their colonists by oppression. The inhabitants of Vuide Poche were all plebians; a few, who traded with the Indians, had amassed some little property; the remainder were hunters and boatmen—men who traversed the great prairies of the west and traced the largest rivers to their sources.[112]

This description draws clear distinctions between the Protestant, English-speaking world of New England, whose residents support themselves through farming, seafaring, and manufacturing, and the French-speaking Catholics of the West who are hunters, fishers, and trappers. Despite these differences, the French colonial West also emerges as a space that shares the same political values as the United States. The residents of Vuide Poche, for instance, are as "good republicans, as if they had been trained up in one of our own colonies." Like their American neighbors, these western "republicans" value social and political equality and reject a hierarchical social order ("they were all plebians"). Although they are technically subject to the French Crown, French westerners are disconnected from this mode of governance and maintain a strong sense of local autonomy and authority. In some ways, the colonial government of the West—described as "mild" and "parental"—is even presented as superior to that of the British colonies, which "alienate[d]" its residents through oppression. Based on this description, the West emerges as a space that is culturally distinct from the early United States in terms of its language, religion, and economic practices, but politically and culturally aligned with its founding principles. By the end of this passage, readers are led to believe that the French colonial West was just as "American" as its New England counterparts.

This idyllic image of an independent, republican French frontier is, of course, a fiction. Just as the dialogue between Timothy Eleazar and M. Dunois presents an exaggerated portrait of these regional differences, this description also presents a falsely stylized picture of this "American" French colonial West. Focusing on the inaccuracies of this description, however, misses its rhetorical point. As Watts has argued, "the French came to be an effective rhetorical weapon to combat exclusionary and discriminatory narratives" in the 1820s and 1830s, and by inviting readers to look back and imagine the West as a proto-American political space, Hall likewise uses French colonial culture as a trope to promote a more inclusive model of federal nationalism.[113] Even though this non-Anglo, Catholic, monarchical, French culture might initially seem completely different from, if not outright opposed to, U.S. national ideals and identity, Hall's story encourages readers to recognize this French cultural community as a space that can be a legitimate and equal part of the nation.

In the end, Timothy Eleazar is able to settle and assimilate successfully in the West precisely because of these similarities. "All this chimed so well with the feelings of Mr. Timothy Eleazar Tompkinson," the narrator reports, "that he resolved forthwith to engraft himself upon this vigorous and cheerful stock."[114] The use of the verb "engraft," which involves creating a new identity out of different but compatible parts, emphasizes the federal dimensions of Hall's narrative. By representing the French colonial West in terms that are compatible with U.S. national values, Timothy Eleazar's status as a swarthy, French-speaking, *capot*-wearing westerner does not preclude his status as an "American." Indeed, the story continually refers to him as an "American," even as he becomes less associated with the white, Anglo-Protestant culture of New England.

Although Timothy Eleazar emerges as the celebrated hero of "The Legend of Carondelet," the story stops short of insisting that his newly adopted French cultural identity is the best or only way to represent himself as an American. Instead, the story argues that regional variety must continue to be a definitive feature of the nation by concluding not with the assimilated figure of Timothy Eleazar but with "the worthy Miss Fidelity Tompkinson." "No one would have suspected that he was not a native," continues the narrator, "had it not been for his aunt, the worthy Miss Fidelity Tompkinson . . . who absolutely refused, through life, to eat *gumbo-soup*, to speak French, or to pay any reverence to that respectable man, the priest."[115] By ending with the return of Aunt Fidelity, "The Legend of Carondelet" argues that the United States is not a nation that can be represented by just one set of regional experiences or identities. Although Timothy Eleazar was eager to embrace the French characteristics and culture of the West, his aunt refuses follow his example. Despite this refusal, she is still able to live comfortably in Vuide Poche, where she is accepted as a steadfast New Englander and never pressured to assimilate.

This final image of the Tompkinson household—occupied both by the *capot*-wearing Timothy and gumbo-eschewing Aunt Fidelity—presents readers with a compelling model of federal unity. As Timothy Eleazar transitions from an American defined by his New England cultural identity to an American defined by his French cultural identity, the story shows how a different ethnic history and culture can be incorporated into the nation in productive and positive terms. Meanwhile, Aunt Fidelity's refusal to change her identity despite the altered cultural dimensions of her new home also suggests that the people of the United States do not need to share the same cultural histories, identities, or experiences in order to live in unified terms. Citizens from all parts of the United States and all parts of the world can retain a sense of national unity, even if they don't eat the same foods, share the same histories, or even speak the same language.

Although this story pushes readers to adopt a more diverse cultural understanding of the West and, by extension, the nation, "The Legend of Carondelet" also places some constraints on its diverse cultural vision. The story grants legitimacy and recognition to French culture, but this is still an Anglocentric narrative because the value and equity of the nation's French cultural dynamics only become apparent when they are adopted by a white New Englander. The language, customs, and character of the French may have a lot to offer the United States, but they require Anglo-American authorization to be considered legitimate. This story also perpetuates the view that the cultural diversity of the nation should be located in the past. The narrator continually reminds readers that the events of the story took place many years ago and these experiences of cross-cultural engagement have "now dwindled" into obscurity. By recalling this period, Hall insists that the nation's diverse cultural history still has value in the present but suggests that it is better to value these experiences through celebratory memories, rather than trying to retain or recreate them in the present.

Hall pushed back against this vanishing trope, however, in some of his other fiction, arguing that the diverse cultural dimensions of the West needed to be better preserved and protected and not just remembered as a fading aspect of the nation's character. In "The French Village," which Hall published in his commemorative literary annual, the *Western Souvenir*, he once again reminds readers that the nation was not exclusively defined by its Anglo-American residents as he describes a town "composed partly of emigrants from France and partly of *natives*—not Indians—but *bona fide* French born in America." Here,

Hall again characterizes French culture as compatible with U.S. values of liberty, equality, and property, such that, when the United States incorporates this French village into the nation, its residents immediately feel at home as they join a "government which had afforded them protection without constraining their freedom." In this case, Hall pushes his arguments for a diverse cultural nationalism further by suggesting that the future stability and integrity of the United States will be compromised if citizens fail to preserve the nation's French cultural history. When U.S. settlers and soldiers arrive in the newly acquired territories of the West and start appropriating and transforming French traditions and landmarks in the village, the story criticizes their "destructive" and "deforming" consequences, which eventually cause many of the original residents to leave, "shak[ing] their heads and declar[ing] that this was no longer the country for them."[116] As far as Hall is concerned, failing to represent and protect U.S. French cultural heritage has lasting and damaging effects for the nation's federal identity and unity, which encourages readers to take steps to counteract its disappearance.

In other stories, Hall uses the cultural diversity of the West to remind readers that a federal nation requires citizens to adopt a particular interpretive mindset to succeed. An 1831 story published in the *Illinois Monthly Magazine* titled "Michel de Coucy" represents the West as a space that is equally defined by its French and Spanish cultural history. The story is set along the banks of the Mississippi where the French control the eastern side of the river and the Spanish control the western. By all accounts, these French and Spanish residents get along well, working alongside one another in the "business of buying and selling," a relationship exemplified by the story's two main characters.[117] On one side of the river is Michel de Coucy, a Mississippi boatman who is described as "genuinely French" (339); on the other side is Pedro Garcia, a "black whiskered" Spaniard who had "amassed a large fortune, nobody knew how" (342). When de Coucy finds himself in debt, "the distressed Frenchman applied to the Spaniard for a loan" (342), and the men agree to a six-month term, signing a contract composed in Spanish with the aid of a translator and a Spanish notary, a productive illustration of cross-cultural collaboration.

This relationship breaks down, however, when de Coucy cannot repay the loan and Garcia takes his case to the magistrate in the local French village. At this point, the story presents readers with two different approaches for interpreting and responding to cultural differences. When Garcia arrives at the magistrate's office with his notarized agreement, the magistrate refuses to accept it because of Garcia's Spanish identity. "The laws of France," he informs Garcia, "are made for the benefit of the French people, and the honor of their King, and not for Spaniards, and my duty is to administer those laws to my fellow subjects, not to foreigners" (343). Here, the magistrate decides to restrict the rights and protections of French law solely to French citizens, excluding anyone who does not fit this identity, even if they conduct business in French territory. Implicit here is his own sense of national superiority as he notes his "astonishment that a subject of Spain should think of suing a subject of the Grand Monarque" (343). Garcia next approaches the French military forces, where he again encounters a culturally exclusive view. First, the commandant refuses to acknowledge the validity of the loan agreement because it is written in Spanish. "*Diable!* How shall I know this to be a bond seeing that it is written in an unknown tongue?" (343). When Garcia points out that they can easily find a translator, the commandant still refuses to consider the document, stating that "*officially* I am not presumed to know any other language but my own" (343). As the French authorities refuse to consider any documents or arguments that do not fit French cultural, legal, or political norms, the story shows the damaging and nonproductive effects of trying to maintain a homogeneous national culture, particularly in territories that contain and support residents with different cultural backgrounds.

This cultural intolerance and discrimination eventually has violent effects when Garcia abandons his legal actions and kidnaps de Coucy's daughter, threatening to "sell her to the Sioux or the English or the Long Knives" unless he agrees to pay his debt (347). Shocked by this action and indignant at the wrongs suffered on both sides, de Coucy and Garcia agree to return to court one more time to try resolving the dispute peacefully. This time, however, they present their case in a different interpretive environment. Instead of going to the local authorities, the men travel to Fort Chartres, which was the seat of government for all the French settlements in Illinois (348). Within this centralized location, the men encounter a judge who takes a more inclusive and equitable view of the case. Unlike the previous authorities, who would only consider the French side of the argument, this new judge asks all the people involved with the case to participate. Both Garcia and de Coucy are present to testify, as is the original Spanish notary, and the new judge states his intention to consider "the decisions of . . . the civil officers on both sides of the river." Also present at the proceedings are assorted members of both families and residents from their respective French and Spanish villages. Oddly enough, the story reports that "several aged chiefs of the Kaskaskia tribe" are also in attendance, where they observe the varied testimony "in grave and solemn expectation" (349). Presented with a more complete and representative view of "both sides" of this case, the head commandant interprets this dispute differently than his predecessors. Unlike his predecessors, who would only consider evidence written in French or presented by French subjects, the head commandant recognizes the validity of both French and Spanish claims as he considers their arguments. He examines the Spanish loan agreement without questioning its validity, and he also considers the legal assessments of the previous French magistrate and lieutenant, as well as the testimony of both Garcia and de Coucy before making his final decision. As a result of this inclusive and equitable approach, he delivers a ruling that everyone finds acceptable, namely, that de Coucy's daughter "should be safely returned to her parents, that Michel should pay to Pedro the principal borrowed, without interest, [and] the latter withheld as a fine for the violence committed in the French territory" (349). Everyone retires from the hearing "well satisfied" with this decision, including the Indians who watched the proceedings. After the commandant delivers his pronouncement, they approach the judge to express their satisfaction with the hearing, telling him, "Father we came to see you do justice; we opened our ears and our hearts are satisfied.... It is all very good. We bid you farewell" (349).

In "Michel de Coucy," Hall thus continues to promote a more diverse and inclusive model of federal nationalism, but this story makes a bolder statement by modeling the interpretive practices that are needed to create this unified and stable cultural environment. By juxtaposing these two different responses from the French government, "Michel de Coucy" shows the dangers of privileging one cultural identity over another and interpreting and governing a diverse community through the lens of a single, homogeneous cultural framework. Only by ensuring that the views and policies of different cultural communities will be represented equally "on both sides" and approached with "open ears" will a government be able to preserve unity and justice in a diverse nation. Furthermore, this story points out that this kind of perspective cannot always be achieved at the local level. A larger governing structure is needed to make sure that the views and experiences of a diverse community can be represented justly.

Which brings us to the presence of the Native Americans at the end of the story. The appearance of the Kaskaskia chiefs at the final resolution of this French and Spanish conflict seems odd since they are not involved in the dispute and do not figure as important characters anywhere else in the story. Their interest, however, in observing the way that a centralized governing authority evaluates a legal claim made by a person outside of the dominant culture makes sense when considering the status of Native Americans in the western United States in the 1830s. At the time "Michel de Coucy" was published in May 1831, the Supreme Court had recently issued its decision in the *Cherokee Nation v. Georgia* case, which was made public in March of that same year. In this case, the Cherokee had accused the state of Georgia of violating their national sovereignty by passing laws that "go directly to annihilate the Cherokees as a political society," particularly regarding their efforts to claim Cherokee lands despite existing treaty agreements.[118] While the Cherokee insisted on the legitimacy of their sovereign claims, citing the rights and recognition granted to the Cherokee Nation by the United States within these many treaty agreements, the Supreme Court ultimately refused to consider their arguments by ruling that the Cherokee Nation had no legitimate standing to bring the case due to their status as "domestic, dependent nations."[119] By refusing to consider the validity of the U.S.-Cherokee treaty agreements or the sovereignty of the Cherokee in a U.S. court of law, the Supreme Court's decision mirrors, to some degree, Garcia's frustration at being unable to obtain a fair and equitable hearing as a Spaniard in the French colonial government, despite the fact that the two men had engaged in legal and documented forms of recognition and exchange. In contrast to the *Cherokee Nation v. Georgia* case, "Michel de Coucy" imagines a different interpretive process for considering the rights and arguments of people who were not part of the nation's majority, with more productive and positive effects. In doing so, the conclusion of "Michel de Coucy" offers both a critical condemnation of the United States' exclusive and discriminatory interpretive practices and a revised model for considering U.S. policies toward Native Americans in the future. Just as the French government responds favorably to Garcia's claim after considering his case on all sides, "Michel de Coucy" argues that the U.S. government likewise needed to attend to Native American claims with the same equity, respect, and consideration.[120]

Despite this optimistic and inclusive outlook, Native Americans ultimately mark the breaking point of this western revival of federal nationalism. For as much as western activists such as James Hall, Daniel Drake, and Timothy Flint pushed U.S. citizens to embrace a more diverse understanding of U.S. nationalism and imagine a federal nation that was much more regionally, culturally, politically, and ethnically diverse than the United States had ever attempted to represent before, this federal logic could not easily account for Native Americans. Native Americans, of course, were not asking to be incorporated into the United States as citizens, and they always maintained their claims of sovereignty when petitioning for their lands. In doing so, these Native American communities simply asked the United States to live up to their own principles of federal tolerance and equity when they evaluated native claims, something that the U.S. government under the Jackson administration was ultimately unwilling to do.

Hall's position on Native Americans is notoriously hard to pin down, and his conflicted views illuminate the racial limits of his federal nationalism. Hall devoted a lot of attention to Native American history, legends, and U.S. Indian policy in the *Western Monthly Magazine*. Unlike the tolerant, equitable approach he brought to other topics, however, much of this coverage perpetuated negative and demeaning stereotypes. Articles in the magazine often characterized Native Americans as primitive "savages" who were "formidable and dangerous neighbors to the whites."[121] Other articles presented a more sympathetic view but portrayed the Indians in condescending terms, such as an 1831 article that praises a "pious and excellent" speech of a Kickapoo chief, describing him as an "uneducated man of the forest" who is "much attached to the whites."[122] Such depictions stand in sharp contrast to Hall's efforts to promote a more equitable view of cultural differences in the rest of his magazine, and, on occasion, he seemed aware of these discrepancies and tried to correct them. In his 1833 review of B. B. Thatcher's *Indian Biography*, for instance, Hall criticizes those who portray Native Americans "with strong prejudices" and praises Thatcher's efforts to "appreciate the character of the aborigines justly," encouraging all U.S. writers to follow his example and take a more "comprehensive and impartial approach" when representing them.[123] Such comments echo the principles of tolerance and equity that define the rest of Hall's magazine, while also illuminating the contradictions of Hall's federal pluralism since his magazine perpetuates many of the "strong prejudices" he criticizes here.

Hall's contradictory vision of federal nationalism is particularly evident in his four-part essay "On the Intercourse of the American People with the Indians," which he published in the *Illinois Monthly Magazine* between May and August 1831. In the first two installments, Hall condemns U.S. Indian policies as a violation of the nation's federal laws and values, asserting that "the details of our negotiations with them and of our legislation with respect to them are full of the strangest contradictions." He provides an extensive list of these inconsistencies, noting how "we admit their purely alloidal title to their lands ... yet we restrain them from selling their land to anyone but ourselves ... we treat them as with free states, but we plant our agents, our military posts among them ... we acknowledge them to be free both as nations and as individuals, yet we claim the power to punish ... aggressions committed in their boundaries," and so on.[124] Dismissing these contradictory policies as "ruinous" and "unprincipled," he calls on citizens to develop policies that are more consistent with the nation's equitable ideals and pluralist identity. "It becomes us now as a great enlightened people to devise a system more consistent with our national dignity and better adapted to advance the interests of the respective parties," writes Hall, whose arguments here exemplify the principles of plural equity that he models throughout the *Western Monthly Magazine* (1:353).

By extending these arguments to include native people and communities, Hall proposes a radical expansion of the nation's federal imagination by insisting that the federal structure and principles of the United States require citizens to recognize the rights and the sovereignty of native peoples. Hall takes this criticism even further by accusing the United States of deliberately promoting racist attitudes and stereotypes to justify their efforts to deny Native American rights and sovereignty, arguing that greed has taken precedence over preserving the nation's federal ideals. "Our system is not only inefficient, but it is positively mischievous," writes Hall, who describes how the United States masks its "mercenary" actions by "asserting that the Indians are savages, not capable of civilization, not to be trusted, not to be dealt with as rational beings" (3:467). Hall implicates the nation's print culture in these exclusionary practices for "continually administering nourishment to the prejudices of the Indians and keeping alive the distinctions that separate them from us" (3:469). For Hall, resolving the nation's federal inconsistencies required significant changes in national legislation and the public sphere, and he ultimately turned to federal literacy as the ideal approach for transforming the "ruinous tendency of the policy now pursued" and restoring the integrity of the nation's federal character (1:352).

In order to develop Indian policies that supported the nation's federal principles, Hall argued that citizens needed to change the way they represented and interpreted Native American people. Recognizing that U.S. Indian policy was founded on the assumption that Native Americans were hostile, primitive people who lacked a cohesive culture and government, Hall asked citizens to consider the possibility that "we assume a position that is not supported by the facts" (1:353). "Why are they ferocious, ignorant and brutal, while we, their neighbors, are civilized and polished?" he asked, pushing citizens to question their interpretive practices and reevaluate Native Americans on the basis of verifiable knowledge and experience, rather than developing policies rooted "entirely in a speculative point of view" (1:353–54). Hall also encouraged his readers to "consult also the character, dignity, and advantage of our own people and government," which will help them develop a more expansive, equitable, and consistent approach for managing these differences. Such an approach, he concludes, would lead them to "look at the Indians as rational beings and their tribes as social communities, having inherent and indefensible rights" (1:353). Here, Hall is clearly describing a practice of federal literacy as he encourages citizens to draw on the principles and structures of their government as they reevaluate their perceptions of Native Americans. Such an approach, he argues, will inevitably prompt citizens to interpret Native Americans in equitable terms and develop policies that "break down the barrier that separates them from us . . . and extend to them the benefits, immunities, and privileges which we enjoy ourselves" (3:470). Creating such policies, however, is contingent on changing the nation's interpretive practices so that citizens can recognize Indians as "neighbors" rather than "barbarous" enemies (1:354).

Despite the strength of these arguments, Hall ultimately failed to live up to them. After pushing his readers to use their federal literacy to interpret Native Americans in equitable terms, Hall concluded his essay by reasserting the racist and prejudicial views he just criticized. In contrast, for instance, to his earlier claims that Native Americans should be recognized as "rational beings" with "inherent and defensible rights," he later denies the validity of this interpretation by arguing that native people lack the knowledge, skills, and experience for such recognition. "It is very clear that the north American Indians have, at this time, no regularly organized governments . . . no foreign intercourse, no revenue, nor any laws for the protection of life, liberty, and property," writes Hall, who characterizes the Indians as "too ignorant to farm and too weak to support local government . . . commerce, agriculture, arts, education, or any means of social comfort or intellectual improvement" (4:510, 512). Although he previously suggested that the federal character of the United States required citizens to recognize and respect native cultures and sovereignty, he later argues that Native Americans are only worth representing if they assimilate to Anglo-American cultural norms. For Hall, Native Americans should only be granted rights if "they would learn our language, see our customs, [and] imbibe our opinions . . . until by degrees their appearance would be assimilated to ours." "To come at once to the point," he argues, "we believe that it is the duty of our government to take Indians directly under its own control as subjects" (4:514, 512).

This radical reversal in Hall's arguments is disconcerting. Although he begins his essay by proposing a bold expansion of the nation's federal principles, he concludes the same essay by reaffirming the racial and cultural exclusions that have traditionally defined U.S. federal nationalism. His insistence that Native Americans must assimilate to Anglo-American cultural norms is particularly disruptive since it marks a significant change from his efforts to promote the nation's cultural diversity in his fiction. In "The Legend of Carondelet," for instance, the swarthy French westerners did not have to assimilate to the standards of New England to be treated as Americans. Likewise, in "Michel de Coucy," Garcia did not have to abandon his Spanish language or character and assimilate to French cultural norms to make his arguments heard or respected. In the case of Native Americans, however, Hall was not willing to recognize or accommodate their racial and cultural differences, even though he clearly recognizes that the logic of federal nationalism should require him to do so.

Hall would continue to exhibit these contradictions in his writings about Native Americans throughout his career. During the 1830s, Hall worked closely with the secretary of Indian affairs, Thomas McKinney, to produce a three-volume collection of Native American portraits and biographies titled *History of the Indian Tribes of North America*, with accompanying lithographs by Charles Bird King. This work exemplifies Hall's conflicted federal politics by encouraging readers to recognize and value the cultures and contributions of Native American leaders while also perpetuating racist assumptions and stereotypes by depicting Native Americans as a vanishing people whose culture and influence will soon "have passed away."[125]

Hall's difficulties in reconciling his federal principles with his views of racial difference are particularly evident in his representations of the "Indian Hater," which was a popular trope in western fiction. This figure was usually a white backwoodsman who killed Indians to avenge the murder of his own friends or relatives, and Hall wrote both an essay and a short story that explored how this trope was deeply connected to public perceptions of Indian savagery and violence.[126] "Is it to be wondered at," asked Hall, "that a man should fear and detest an Indian who has always been accustomed to hear him described only as a midnight prowler, watching to murder the mother as she bends over her helpless children?"[127] For Hall, the figure of the "Indian Hater" provided writers with an opportunity to perpetuate or challenge these stereotypes, either by depicting the "Indian Hater" as a righteous and sympathetic crusader against Indian savagery or criticizing the "Indian Hater" as a violent, indefensible murderer. He explored these competing interpretations in his own short story titled "The Indian Hater," which he published in the *Western Souvenir*. For most of the story, the narrator presents his Indian Hater, a man named Samuel Monson, as a murderous villain whose actions are repeatedly described as excessively violent, racist, and unjustified. After Monson brutally murders the narrator's young Indian guide, he denounces him as a "Wretch—Miscreant—Murderer!" inviting readers to share his condemnation, while also fostering sympathy for the innocent Indians that Monson kills. At the end of the story, however, Hall turns the tables when Monson describes the reason he became an Indian Hater. Monson then provides a graphic portrait of Indian brutality as he describes how "a gang of yelling savages" invaded his home and "roared and laughed and mocked us" as they burned his wife and children to death.[128] This information reaffirms traditional stereotypes about native savagery and transforms Monson into a sympathetic figure whose murderous actions can now be understood and, perhaps, seem justified. Hall stops short of endorsing one interpretation over the other, however, and the narrative ends abruptly after Monson finishes his account and sends the narrator away, telling him "Go! Pursue your own way and leave me to mine." We never get the narrator's final thoughts as to whether he still views Monson as an unjustified killer or as a sympathetic victim, and Hall leaves it to the readers to come to their own decision about how to interpret Monson and the Indians in light of this new information.

In the end, "The Indian Hater" illustrates Hall's own uncertainty about how to handle the politics of racial difference in a nation that was struggling to be more federally inclusive. Did the United States need to expand its federal pluralism to accommodate a greater range of racial and cultural differences? Or would such inclusions and expansions produce a national community that would be defined by racial divisions and violence? Could the United States retain its federal unity if its plural dimensions were no longer restricted to white, Anglo-American cultural norms? Over the course of the 1830s, figuring out how to reconcile the federal principles and pluralism of the nation with its racial diversity became increasingly difficult, and as the racial limits of this federal nationalism came into clearer and troubling focus, race would eventually mark the breaking point of the federal union.

EPILOGUE

✯ ✯ ✯ ✯ ✯ ✯ ✯ ✯ ✯ ✯ ✯ ✯

The Failure of Federal Literacy

> Our treaties of relationship are based upon the principles of the federal constitution.
> ——"General Council Message," *Cherokee Phoenix*
>
> America is as much our country as it is yours.
> ——DAVID WALKER, *Appeal to the Coloured Citizens of the World*

Race marks the breaking point of federal nationalism in the early United States. For a nation that was always composed of an expansive array of differences, federalism enabled the United States to operate as a unified community while still managing to respect, support, and protect its definitive and incontestable diversity. As this study has demonstrated, print was instrumental in allowing this federal union to succeed, and literary forms such as the almanac, magazines, satire, and captivity narratives made it possible for citizens to represent and interpret the variety of the nation in terms that were equitable and cohesive. As the United States expanded, however, it got harder for citizens to read the nation's ever-multiplying differences in these compatible and interconnected terms. Efforts to revive a federal literary culture in the western states brought these challenges into clear focus as writers such as James Hall struggled to reconcile the federal principles of the nation with the region's policies involving Native Americans. Although Hall recognized that the principles of federal nationalism—which celebrated pluralism and encouraged citizens to represent and interpret the nation's differences equitably—should logically be extended to recognize the sovereignty and claims of indigenous people, his perception of racial differences left him unable to put those principles into practice. His racism, in short, took priority over his federalism.

Throughout the 1830s, it became abundantly clear that the United States' principles of federal pluralism would not accommodate the nation's racial differences. For as much as the federal imagination and literary culture of the United States expanded to make room for a wider range of cultural, ethnic, geographic, linguistic, and economic differences in the early nineteenth century, the federal rights and principles of the nation were increasingly restricted to the state and regional affiliations of its white residents. Two issues—the divisive debates over the practice and expansion of slavery and the equally controversial policies of Indian removal—brought the racial limits of U.S. federal nationalism into clearer public focus. In both cases, the United States made a concerted effort to exclude African Americans and Native Americans from the federal nation, either by restricting their individual rights and activities in ways that removed them from the nation's cultural and political spheres or, quite literally, by removing them from the physical space of the nation, exemplified by its Indian removal policies and efforts to resettle free blacks in the African colony of Liberia.

These exclusionary practices were not new. The United States had a long history of placing restrictions on its federal pluralism, not only with respect to racial differences but also regarding the rights and roles of women. And, as this study has examined, the United States also has a long history of writers who challenged these restrictions, including Benjamin Banneker, Judith Sargent Murray, Royall Tyler, and others who drew on the principles and practices of federalism to criticize the contradictions inherent in the nation's federal practices and argue for their own rights to be included as equal members of the federal union. In the 1830s, African American and Native American writers continued to deploy these same federal literary tactics to argue against slavery, African American colonization, and Indian removal, most notably in works such as the *Cherokee Phoenix*, the first Native American newspaper that was published by the Cherokee Nation from 1828 to 1834, and David Walker's *Appeal to the Coloured Citizens of the World, but in Particular and Very Expressly, to Those of the United States of America*, which was published as a pamphlet in 1829. Much like Banneker, Murray, and Tyler, these works appeal to the plural dimensions of the federal union and its principles of equitable tolerance to argue for their equal recognition by the United States. They also identify the contradictions between the United States' federal principles and their current discriminatory practices, contradictions that, they argue, will ultimately have destructive effects.

More than simply criticizing the United States for failing to enact its plural values and federal ideals, however, the writings in the *Cherokee Phoenix* and Walker's *Appeal* also work very hard to redeem federalism as an effective and productive model of nationalism. Although the federal unity and coherence of the United States were compromised by the practices of slavery, Indian removal, and other racially discriminatory policies, the *Cherokee Phoenix* and Walker's *Appeal* insist that federalism is still a viable and valuable mode of plural nationalism that can produce a constructive union. The success and integrity of such a union, however, depends on eliminating the nation's racist modes of interpretation. The *Cherokee Phoenix* and Walker's *Appeal* both argue that the federal nation cannot coexist with racist strategies of interpretation. The United States could be a nation that was defined by race or a nation that was defined by federalism, but it could not be a nation that incorporated both of these interpretive frameworks.

We, Too, the People: The Federal Literacy of the *Cherokee Phoenix*

Established in 1828, the *Cherokee Phoenix* was the primary voice for asserting Cherokee national sovereignty. Asserting that sovereignty, however, required complicated strategies of representation. On the one hand, members of the Cherokee Nation wanted to assert their sovereignty on their own terms by describing their distinctive people, practices, and government. On the other, the Cherokee also recognized that they needed to present their sovereignty in terms that were acceptable to the United States. The editor of the *Cherokee Phoenix*, Elias Boudinot, who had been educated at a missionary boarding school in New England, was well aware of the importance of representing Cherokee sovereignty in both indigenous and assimilationist terms, and his prospectus for the newspaper reflects this dual focus. He addresses the newspaper to both Cherokee and U.S. readers and promises to provide them with "the laws and public documents of the nation" and an "account of the manners and customs of the Cherokees and their progress in Education, Religion, and the arts of civilized life."[1] By printing Cherokee laws, documents, and articles about Cherokee manners and customs, the *Cherokee Phoenix* clearly sought to represent the nation on its own, independent terms. By simultaneously framing these laws, documents, and manners as evidence of Cherokee progress in "the arts of civilized life," however, the *Cherokee Phoenix* also sought to illustrate how the Cherokee were following the standards of "civilized" nationalism set by the United States.

This effort to negotiate dual audiences and rhetorical strategies is a common practice in Native American forms of writing and literacy. As Hilary Wyss observes, native writers were "fluent in the cultures and conventions" of the United States and also "fully committed to Native community as an ongoing political and cultural concern," a position that led them to produce works that "self-consciously manipulated print" in order to serve these often contradictory ends.[2] This need to represent the Cherokee Nation as both distinct and independent from yet also closely aligned with the United States explains why the

Cherokee turned to the logic and rhetoric of federalism to voice their arguments for sovereignty. Since federalism represents differences in positive, compatible, and collaborative terms, this model of nationhood provided a useful way for the Cherokee to align themselves with U.S. principles of nationalism while still articulating a distinct and independent national identity. By adopting federal principles and structures, the Cherokee Nation could mimic U.S. nationalism while still asserting the authority of their indigenous voices, values, and practices.

The bilingual structure of the *Cherokee Phoenix* exemplifies its federal literary tactics. The newspaper was printed in both English and Cherokee, using the newly devised Cherokee syllabary that had been formally adopted by the Cherokee Nation in 1825.[3] By printing the newspaper in the Cherokee language, Boudinot was able to represent indigenous Cherokee voices in terms that also supported U.S. standards of "civilized" nationalism. His decision to use a bilingual format, however, magnified the newspaper's ability to represent the Cherokee nation in distinct but equitable terms to U.S. readers. "The columns of the *Cherokee Phoenix* will be filled, partly with English, and partly with Cherokee print and all matter which is of common interest will be given in both languages in parallel columns," asserted Boudinot.[4] On the one hand, this parallel representation of English and Cherokee text drew a clear distinction between U.S. and Cherokee culture since their languages look very different from one another. On the other, these parallel translations also enabled readers to recognize that, even with these differences, the two nations could still understand and engage with one another. Although they might not always agree, the bilingual structure of the newspaper created a framework where citizens of the Cherokee Nation and the United States could begin to interpret one another in equitable rather than oppositional or exclusionary terms.[5]

The articles that Boudinot printed in English and Cherokee were carefully chosen to promote these equitable interpretations. The first three issues of the newspaper, for example, feature a bilingual edition of the Cherokee Constitution. Written and ratified in 1827, the Cherokee Constitution had been carefully designed to imitate the U.S. Constitution, using the same rhetoric and structure and defining the Cherokee Nation as a federal government composed of three distinct branches of government whose citizens were protected by a bill of rights. By printing the Constitution in English and Cherokee, the *Cherokee Phoenix* was able to make those similarities visible to U.S. readers, while simultaneously demonstrating that the Cherokee Constitution was a Cherokee document designed for Cherokee use. Consider, for instance, the preamble to the Cherokee Constitution, which was reprinted in English as follows: "We, the representatives of the people of the Cherokee Nation, in Convention assembled, in order to establish justice, ensure tranquility, promote our common welfare, and secure to ourselves and our posterity the blessings of liberty; acknowledging with humility and gratitude the goodness of the sovereign Ruler of the Universe, in offering us an opportunity so favorable to the design, and imploring His aid and direction in its accomplishment, do ordain and establish this Constitution for the Government of the Cherokee Nation."[6] In the *Cherokee Phoenix*, the English-language version of the Constitution was printed to the left of the Cherokee-language version of the text, and this bilingual structure transforms the Cherokee Constitution from a document that U.S. readers could not understand into an expression of sovereignty that seems to be equal to their own. Not only does this preamble convey the same national sentiments as the U.S. Constitution, it uses the same phrasing and rhetoric to articulate them. Of course, in highlighting these similarities, the English translation also makes it easier for U.S. readers to identify points of difference. In the case of the preamble, the Cherokee Constitution's emphasis on "acknowledging with humility and gratitude the goodness of the sovereign Ruler of the Universe" would have stood out since the U.S. Constitution does not include any references to religious faith and divine influence in its opening statement. While this difference clearly distinguishes the Cherokee Constitution from the U.S. Constitution, however, it does not provide U.S. readers with grounds for denying Cherokee national sovereignty. Opponents of Cherokee sovereignty often cited a lack of religious belief as a reason to deny their national claims, arguing that a "savage race of heathens" could not constitute a civilized nation.[7] By defining the Cherokee Nation as a nation rooted in the acknowledgment of divine aid and influence, the preamble encourages U.S. readers to interpret this document as a distinct assertion of sovereignty that nevertheless corresponds with U.S. standards for nationhood.

The *Cherokee Phoenix* goes on to reprint all six articles of the Cherokee Constitution in English and Cherokee, a format that continues to encourage readers to interpret the Cherokee Nation in different but equitable terms. Some portions of the Cherokee Constitution mimic the language of the U.S. Constitution almost exactly, such as the Cherokee Constitution's inclusion of a "necessary and proper" clause stating that "the General Council shall have power to make all laws and regulations, which they shall deem necessary and proper for the good of the Nation" or the stipulation that the executive office be restricted to "a natural born citizen" and "neither shall any person be eligible to that office, who shall not have attained the age of thirty-five years."[8] The Cherokee Constitution even concludes with a "Bill of Rights" that carefully follows the language and policies expressed in the U.S. Constitution, noting that Cherokee citizens will be guaranteed "the free exercise of religious worship" and the "right of a trial by jury," and that "no person shall for the same offence be twice put in jeopardy, nor shall any person's property be taken or applied to public use without his consent."⁹ By emphasizing these similarities, the English translations of the Cherokee Constitution portray the Cherokee Nation as an equal expression of U.S. national values and structures.

At other moments, though, the bilingual structure draws attention to significant differences between these nations. These points of distinction, however, are always presented in terms that are equitable and compatible. Article II, for instance, explains that the Cherokee Nation will be organized as a union of eight "districts" represented by a "National Committee" and a "General Council." Although this terminology differs from that of the U.S. government, which is organized into "states" and represented by a "Senate" and "House of Representatives," these differences are clearly equivalent. A more significant difference emerges in Article I, where the Cherokee Constitution states that the lands of the Cherokee Nation "are, and shall remain, the common property of the Nation." This assertion of communal ownership would have stood out sharply to U.S. readers, particularly since the U.S. Constitution makes a point of prioritizing private property ownership as a right that is protected by the Fifth Amendment. Nevertheless, a closer look at the U.S. Constitution reveals that the United States also has experience with collective ownership through its federal lands, which were owned and managed by the government, a condition outlined in Article IV where "Congress shall have Power to dispose of and make all needful Rules and Regulations respecting the Territory or other Property belonging to the United States." Compared to the United States, the collective ownership of land in the Cherokee Nation represents a difference of scale, rather than substance, allowing readers to interpret this as an equitable form of difference. Another distinction emerges in Article IV, where, once again, the Cherokee government establishes a closer relationship with religious practices than the United States does. For most of this article, the Cherokee Constitution mimics the U.S. Constitution by guaranteeing "the free exercise of religious worship" and supporting the separation of church and state, such that "no minister of the Gospel, or public preacher, of any religious persuasion whilst he continues in the exercises of his pastoral functions, shall be eligible to the office of Principal Chief, or a seat on either house of the General Council." A key difference emerges, however, when the Cherokee Constitution states, "No person who denies the being of a God, or a future state of rewards and punishment shall hold any office in the civil department of this Nation." This requirement clearly differentiates the Cherokee Nation from the United States, which has no religious requirement for holding office. Once again, however, this difference serves to strengthen rather than weaken Cherokee claims of sovereignty for U.S. readers, because, as mentioned earlier, the United States often cited religious beliefs and practices as a necessary condition for recognizing Cherokee nationhood. Although the Cherokee Nation's religious policies are different from those of the United States, this difference reinforces their claim to nationhood rather than undermining it.

By thus encouraging U.S. citizens to read the Cherokee Nation as a different but equitable expression of U.S. nationalism, the *Cherokee Phoenix* uses the same tactics of federal literacy that I have been exploring throughout the study. In the case of the *Cherokee Phoenix*, however, these federal tactics are being used to very different nationalist ends. Instead of encouraging U.S. readers to accept the Cherokee as part of their own nation, the federal literacy of the *Cherokee Phoenix* enables U.S. readers to legitimize Cherokee sovereignty by interpreting their acceptance as an expression of their own federal values. In other words, within the pages of the *Cherokee Phoenix*, accepting the Cherokee Nation provides another way for U.S. readers to support their own federal nationalism.

The *Cherokee Phoenix*'s bilingual publication of Cherokee laws illustrates the newspaper's innovative use of this federal literacy more clearly. From March through July 1828, the *Cherokee Phoenix* opened each issue by printing selected "laws of the Cherokee Nation" in English and Cherokee, and, in this case, Boudinot was much more direct in identifying U.S. readers as his primary audience for this bilingual format. Acknowledging that these laws "have already been circulated in this Nation in a pamphlet form," Boudinot directs them specifically to "our readers at a distance" who, he notes, "will perhaps be gratified to see the first commencement of written laws among the Cherokees."[10]

The bilingual representation of these laws once again encourages these distant readers to read the Cherokee Nation in different but equitable terms. On the one hand, the Cherokee-language versions of these laws emphasize that the Cherokee Nation is distinct and separate from the United States, governed by laws that have been composed by a different government in a different language for a different people. On the other, the English translations of these laws encourage U.S. readers to recognize that these laws, while separate and distinct from their own, nevertheless represent equitable expressions of national order and sovereignty. Covering a range of criminal and civil issues, the laws translated in the *Cherokee Phoenix* would have looked very familiar to U.S. readers, including prohibitions on theft, public violence, and murder, restrictions on gambling and the sale of liquor, and laws concerning the practice of law enforcement, as well as the legal codes for acquiring business licenses, collecting taxes, and maintaining roads and infrastructure, all of which closely mirror U.S. laws and policies. By illuminating these parallels, the *Cherokee Phoenix* sought to mediate the differences posed by the Cherokee-language versions of these laws by assuring U.S. readers that the Cherokee Nation was governed in a manner similar to their own. This experience of reading the Cherokee laws in distinct but equitable terms would have resonated with a U.S. audience who drew on these same interpretive tactics to make sense of their own plural nation. As a result of these parallels, reading the Cherokee laws in different but equitable terms allows U.S. readers to exercise their own federal principles. Through its bilingual structure, then, the *Cherokee Phoenix* makes recognizing Cherokee sovereignty a valid practice of U.S. federal nationalism. Rather than threatening or undermining U.S. sovereignty, Cherokee sovereignty serves to reinforce it.

Although these literary tactics were intended to represent the Cherokee Nation in terms that were acceptable to U.S. readers, reaction to this approach was not favorable. Rather than interpreting the Cherokee Constitution and Cherokee laws as equitable assertions of sovereignty, U.S. readers largely viewed these documents as an aggressive attack on the United States. The *Cherokee Phoenix* covered this negative response, noting that "many influential men of the adjoining States and elsewhere, particularly members of Congress . . . have raised the cry, that an 'Indian tribe in the heart of the Union has assumed an attitude of independence, by forming a constitution and ought to be opposed.'"[11] One of the leading voices of this opposition was John Forsyth, the governor of Georgia, and Boudinot regularly reprinted his speeches in the *Cherokee Phoenix* to illuminate the terms of this opposition. Characterizing the Cherokee Nation as "a Government exercising authority independent of ours and denationalizing our citizens in order to strengthen itself in opposition to our will," Forsyth's comments illustrate how the Cherokee's arguments for equality failed to have their intended effects.[12] Instead of recognizing the Cherokee Nation as a government that was equitably aligned with the United States, Forsyth interprets the Cherokee Nation as an oppositional force whose existence threatens the identity and authority of the United States. For Forsyth and those opposed to Cherokee nationhood, the problem with the Cherokee Nation was not so much with its specific government, laws, or practices. The problem was their belief that the Cherokee Nation was privileging their national rights and authority over the rights and authority of the states. As Forsyth describes it, the Cherokee "government, professing to be independent, is set up in defiance of the authority of the States of Georgia, Tennessee, Alabama, and North Carolina upon territory and within the jurisdiction of these States," and it is this "defiance" of state authority that transforms their claims into a "denationalizing" force.[13]

At stake in these arguments about Cherokee sovereignty are two very different appeals to federal nationalism. By asking the United States to accept the Cherokee Nation as a different but equitable expression of U.S. nationalism, the Cherokee appealed to the values of federal pluralism and tolerance that were required for imagining and maintaining the United States. Because the Cherokee modeled their nation so closely on the federal structure and values of the

United States, this strategy made it very difficult, rhetorically, for U.S. citizens to reject Cherokee sovereignty without simultaneously undermining their own national values and authority. In order to counter the federal dynamics of the Cherokee arguments, opponents of Cherokee sovereignty thus had to invoke a different interpretation of the nation's federal structure and values. Rather than appealing broadly to the nation's ability to tolerate and accommodate a wide range of differences, opponents of Cherokee sovereignty sought to clarify the specific kinds of "differences" that the United States was authorized to represent. For opponents of Cherokee sovereignty, U.S. federalism was meant to represent the interests and authority of the states, not its people. By thus reorienting and restricting the nation's federal principles to reflect the pluralism of the states rather than pluralism writ large, residents of the United States could reject the Cherokee arguments without negating their own support for federal nationalism. As Governor Forsyth asserted, "extending the State laws over the Indians within our territory is founded [in] accord with those of the present administration of the Federal Government."[14]

As the United States intensified its efforts to deny Cherokee sovereignty by privileging the authority of the states, the *Cherokee Phoenix* shifted its tactics of argument. Instead of asserting Cherokee sovereignty by using Cherokee voices and documents, the newspaper drastically reduced its bilingual content and began citing U.S. documents instead. "The jurisdiction, then, of our nation over its soil is settled by the laws, treaties, and constitution of the United States, and has been exercised from time out of memory," stated a memorial reprinted in the *Cherokee Phoenix* in April 1830. The newspaper proceeded to publish numerous articles that now cited the language of specific treaties to show how the United States had a long history of acknowledging Cherokee sovereignty, as articulated in the 1785 Treaty of Hopewell, the 1791 Treaty of Holston, the 1798 and 1805 Treaties of Tellico, the 1816 Treaty of the Chickasaw Council, and three different Treaties of Washington that were authorized in 1816, 1819, and 1828.[15] "We have the faith and pledge of the United States, repeated over and over again, in treaties made at various times," argued another memorial. "By these treaties, our rights as a separate people are distinctly acknowledged, and guaranties given that they shall be secured and protected."[16]

By invoking the authority of these treaties, the Cherokee effectively recast the Cherokee Nation as the product of U.S. laws and policies rather than their own. In doing so, the Cherokee continued to align their nation with the federal principles of the United States, but their relationship to those federal principles was now quite different. Whereas before, the *Cherokee Phoenix* appealed to the United States' federal values of pluralism and equity to support their claims to sovereignty, the newspaper now appealed to the federal distinctions between state and national power. This shift in focus is evident in the *Cherokee Phoenix*'s repeated references to the treaty-making powers in the U.S. Constitution. An 1829 article titled "Present Crisis in the Condition of the American Indians" reports that "the Constitution of the United States (Art. VI) has these words. 'All treaties made under the authority of the United States, shall be the supreme law of the land: and the judges in every State shall be bound thereby, anything in the laws or Constitution of any State to the contrary notwithstanding.'"[17] Although the federal United States granted authority to its constituent states, the U.S. Constitution specifically limited state powers in the case of negotiating and authorizing national treaties. By defining the Cherokee Nation through U.S. treaties, the Cherokee assertions of sovereignty were now contingent on affirming the power of the central government over the states. As the Cherokee National Council wrote in a memorial published in the *Cherokee Phoenix* on April 14, 1830, "The sacredness of Treaties made under the authority of the United States are paramount and Supreme, stronger than the laws and constitution of any state."[18] With these pronouncements, the Cherokee reoriented their engagement with U.S. federal nationalism to downplay, rather than celebrate, the nation's pluralism. According to the federal powers outlined in the U.S. Constitution, the states had no right to determine or contest Cherokee sovereignty if it was asserted in a national treaty. Instead, Cherokee sovereignty was authorized simply and solely by the authority of the central U.S. government, without any reference to its numerous constituencies or, for that matter, the voices of the Cherokee themselves.

Although defining Cherokee sovereignty as the product of the U.S. government might seem to undermine Cherokee agency and authority, these new critical tactics actually strengthened their position by portraying the Cherokee as the superior exemplars of U.S. federal nationalism. Instead of defying the authority of the United States, Cherokee sovereignty could now be read as a means of authorizing and respecting the federal powers articulated in the U.S. Constitution and enacted by U.S. treaties, in contrast to the states who seek to ignore and disrespect the terms of these documents. Within this new framework, the Cherokee effectively switched critical positions with the United States, so that the Cherokee now emerge as the nation that is committed to upholding and enacting the principles of U.S. federalism, in contrast to the states who seek to deny their sovereignty. As Boudinot wrote in an 1831 editorial, "As respects the Cherokees, their duty is plain—they cannot err.... They are surrounded with guarantees which this Republic has voluntarily made for their protection and which once formed a sufficient security against oppression. If those guarantees must now be violated with impunity for purposes altogether selfish, the sin will not be at our door, but at the door of our *oppressor*."[19] Here, Boudinot clearly positions the Cherokee in a superior position to the states regarding U.S. nationalism. "Surrounded" by U.S. "guarantees," the Cherokee are more aligned with U.S. laws and principles than the states who seek to "violate" them. For Boudinot, the consequences of this critical reversal are high, extending well beyond the issue of Cherokee sovereignty to damage the political strength and stability of the United States. "The integrity of the Union is at stake," asserts Boudinot, who insists that as long as the states continue to privilege their own "selfish" interests, the future of the nation will be in jeopardy. "If such proceedings are sanctioned by the majority of the people of the United States, the Union is but a tottering fabric, which will soon fall and crumble into atoms," projected Boudinot, recasting the exercise of state power as a threat to the federal union rather than an appropriate and supportive expression of it.[20]

With these arguments, the *Cherokee Phoenix* ultimately asks U.S. readers to reconsider the ways that they define and enact the plural dynamics of the federal nation. Although the United States was, quite literally, defined by the representation of its multiple states, the Cherokee remind U.S. readers that, at times, their federal government placed limits on state authority to ensure that the nation could exercise its principles of plural equity in other forms. Defining the United States solely through the interests of its constituent states was dangerous because it prevented the nation from recognizing other forms of difference that were equally important to the stability and integrity of the federal union. By representing the Cherokee Nation as the superior practitioners of U.S. federal nationalism, the *Cherokee Phoenix* encouraged U.S. readers to follow a different model of federal pluralism where, instead of prioritizing the representation of different states, the nation privileged the equitable representation of different cultural communities and practices.

From a rhetorical standpoint, the Cherokee's federal tactics should have been very convincing. Although the form of their federal arguments shifted as they moved from relying on their own voices to assert their sovereignty to those of the United States, these tactics continually represented the Cherokee as a nation that was deeply committed to the federal structure and values of the United States, a position that required U.S. readers to interpret the Cherokee as familiar and friendly allies, rather than a dangerous and alien threat. As the *Cherokee Phoenix* reported in 1829, "Our treaties of relationship are based upon the principles of the federal constitution.... Much, therefore, depends on our unity of sentiment and firmness of action, in maintaining those sacred rights."[21] Furthermore, by aligning the Cherokee Nation so closely with the principles of federal nationalism, it was difficult for U.S. readers to challenge or dismiss their arguments without undermining their own national claims. In order to create a logic for denying the Cherokee arguments, their opponents needed to find a definitive mark of difference that would discredit their claims of similarity and prevent U.S. citizens from reading their arguments in equitable and compatible terms, a distinction that was ultimately supplied by race.

As James P. Rhonda writes, debates over Cherokee sovereignty quickly became a matter of "redefining national space in racial terms."[22] Rather than contending with the Cherokee's own arguments for sovereignty, their opponents quickly dismissed them on the grounds of racial difference, arguing, as Governor Forsyth wrote in 1830, that the Cherokee "were a race not admitted to be equal to the rest of the community."[23] Other U.S. leaders echoed this position, such as Lewis Cass, the U.S. superintendent of Indian affairs who dismissed the Cherokee as "too ignorant and barbarous to establish and maintain a government."[24] Andrew Jackson likewise viewed the Indians as an inferior race who must be treated in terms that were separate from the United States, characterizing them as a people with "neither the intelligence, the industry, the moral habits, nor the desire for improvement" who currently are living "in the midst of another and superior race without appreciating the causes of their inferiority or seeking to control them."[25] These arguments of racial inferiority would provide the logic for removing the Cherokee and other indigenous communities from the United States completely, a policy that illustrates an aggressive effort to define the nation in racially exclusive terms. Although the United States had always been defined through points of racial exclusion, as Benjamin Banneker so clearly articulated in the 1790s, arguments for Indian removal intensified efforts to define the United States as a nation that only represented white citizens, marking the racial limits of U.S. federal nationalism in definitive terms.

In the end, the *Cherokee Phoenix* and other Cherokee writers did little to address the racial dimensions of U.S. arguments in advocating for their national sovereignty or resisting removal. Rather than engaging directly with the issue of race or aggressively countering the racist assumptions of their U.S. opponents, Cherokee writers more often chose to keep their arguments in the realm of political and legal rhetoric, appealing, again and again, to U.S. federal laws and principles to assert their equality and authority, only to have those arguments repeatedly fail. In 1829, the same year that the *Cherokee Phoenix* shifted its federal tactics to rely more heavily on the authority of the central U.S. government and downplay the interests of the states, David Walker, a dynamic African American activist from Boston, would publish his own arguments for challenging the racially exclusive practices of the United States. Rather than sidestepping the issue of race, Walker confronted the racial limits of U.S. federalism directly, picking up and magnifying the arguments begun by Banneker nearly fifty years earlier to argue that racism and federalism were fundamentally incompatible systems of representation, an argument that foretold the eventual dissolution of the federal union.

Rereading Federal Literacy: Walker's *Appeal*

Advocates for African American rights and equality likewise turned to the logic and rhetoric of federalism during the 1830s, drawing on the federal principles of pluralism and equity to criticize the institution of slavery and argue that black residents should be represented as equal citizens in the United States. These arguments coincided with southern efforts to expand and protect the practice of slavery through the authority of states' rights, which were bolstered by arguments involving the Missouri Compromise and the ongoing Nullification debates. As leaders of the southern and some of the western states invoked the federal powers of the states to promote policies of racial exclusion and oppression, African American advocates, much like the Cherokee, had to find ways to argue for racial equity and pluralism in the United States without reinforcing the logic that empowered the states.

One of the boldest and most innovative engagements with U.S. federalism emerges in the work of David Walker. Born free in North Carolina in 1796, Walker eventually moved to Boston where he became an activist for African American rights and abolition in the mid-1820s. In 1826 Walker cofounded the Massachusetts General Colored Association, an organization that was opposed to slavery and all forms of racial discrimination. The following year, he became a writer for the *Freedom's Journal*, the first paper owned and operated by African Americans, where he contributed to its efforts not just to oppose slavery but to represent African Americans as equal citizens in the United States.[26] Walker is best known, however, for his pamphlet, *Walker's Appeal, in Four Articles; Together with a Preamble, to the Coloured Citizens of the World*, which was published in September 1829. In this document, Walker identifies and condemns the racial limits of U.S. federal nationalism by contrasting the "wretched, degraded, and abject" status of African Americans with the principles of pluralism, equality, and liberty set forth in the nation's founding documents. For Walker, the racist laws and policies of the United States posed an unconscionable contradiction to the nation's federal values and identity, and he calls on all of his "beloved brethren," black and white, to correct this incongruity by granting equal rights and citizenship to all residents, regardless of race. "Remember, Americans, that we must and shall be free and enlightened as you are," asserted Walker, who warns his readers that failure to ensure racial equality will have violent and destructive effects. "Will you wait until we shall, under God, obtain our liberty by the crushing arm of power? Will it not be dreadful for you? . . . And wo, wo [*sic*] will be to you if we have to obtain our freedom by fighting."[27]

The intense anger of Walker's *Appeal*, combined with his calls for rebellion and resistance, had incendiary effects. Readers were alarmed by the militancy of Walker's *Appeal*, which prompted widespread fear about the possibility of an armed revolt. The work was highly censored in the South, where it was condemned for "expressing sentiments totally subversive of all subordination in our slaves."[28] Antislavery activists also distanced themselves from it, with the editor of Boston's *Columbian Centinel* describing it as "one of the most wicked and inflammatory productions ever issued from the press."[29] "[A] good end does not justify wicked means," wrote William Lloyd Garrison, who objected to Walker's call for aggressive resistance and rebellion, although he would later come to embrace it as an important rallying point for the abolitionist cause.[30]

Despite its aggressive critical tone, Walker's *Appeal* is ultimately a strong defense of U.S. federal principles and governing structures. Although he harshly criticizes current U.S. policies and practices, Walker expresses strong support for the nation's federal values of pluralism and equality. As Sean Wilentz and others have noted, "even in his bitterest passages, Walker did not repudiate ... republican principles or his native country," and he regularly invoked the U.S. Constitution and the Declaration of Independence throughout the *Appeal*, praising these documents for their efforts to establish "a new government" that would represent and protect the rights of "all men" rather than just "some of you."[31] While Walker clearly affirms the value of the nation's federal structure and principles, however, he objects to the current U.S. practice and interpretation of federalism, which excludes the nation's black residents from its rights and protections. For Walker, these racist views and policies are fundamentally incompatible with federalism, and he argues that if the United States defined itself as a nation founded on pluralism and the equal representation of differences, then it could not restrict or delimit that pluralism on the basis of race. By pushing the United States to revise its conception of pluralism and recognize blacks as equal citizens, Walker's arguments are very similar to those of the Cherokee, who likewise argued that the United States needed to embrace new models of pluralism that privileged the equal representation of its diverse people over the equal representation of its diverse states. Unlike the Cherokee, however, Walker is much more explicit and aggressive in challenging the racism that informed the current practice of federalism in the United States.

Walker highlights the contradictions between the racist policies of the United States and its federal ideology by structuring his *Appeal* to mimic the U.S. Constitution. Like the U.S. Constitution, Walker presents the *Appeal* as a formal account of the structures that govern the experiences of African Americans in the United States. The *Appeal* opens with a preamble that asserts the collective identity, status, and expectations of African Americans in the United States, followed by four "Articles" that identify and explain the specific institutional features that determine their rights, status, and experiences in the federal nation. Despite the structural similarities between these two documents, the content of the *Appeal* immediately makes it clear that the collective experiences of African Americans do not correspond with the identities, rights, or experiences represented by the U.S. Constitution. Consider, for instance, the content of Walker's preamble, which states that "we (coloured people of these United States), are the most degraded, wretched, and abject set of beings that ever lived since the world began; and I pray God that none like us ever may live again until time shall be no more."[32] Here, Walker clearly imitates the language of the U.S. Constitution to show how the United States has failed to extend its constitutional rights to black residents. In contrast to the preamble of the U.S. Constitution, which defines the United States as a nation devoted to providing unity, justice, peace, security, welfare, and liberty for all its united people, Walker's preamble describes how the collective experiences of the nation's black residents are defined by degradation, abuse, and misery. By illuminating these sharp contrasts between the experiences of the nation's black and white residents, Walker identifies the racial exclusions inherent in the current practice of U.S. federal nationalism where African Americans are not granted the same rights or protections under the U.S. Constitution as white residents.

Walker next invites his readers to examine the specific causes for these exclusions and inequalities. "My object is, if possible, to awaken in the breasts of my afflicted, degraded and slumbering brethren, a spirit of inquiry and investigation respecting our miseries and wretchedness in this *Republican Land of Liberty*" (2), writes Walker, who once again criticizes the contradiction between the abusive experiences of African Americans and the U.S. principles of just representation and liberty. By encouraging his readers to recognize and investigate the specific reasons why black residents have been exempted from the nation's rights and privileges, Walker hopes to identify ways to correct these injustices, allowing the United States to become the "republican land of liberty" that it currently fails to be. Walker ultimately identifies four specific "source[s] from which our miseries are derived" (3), which he presents to his readers in the form of "Articles." Article I is devoted to "Our Wretchedness in Consequence of Slavery" (7), Article II to "Our Wretchedness in Consequence of Ignorance" (19), Article III to "Our Wretchedness in Consequence of the Preachers of the Religion of Jesus Christ" (35), and Article IV to "Our Wretchedness in Consequence of the Colonizing Plan" (45). By using this article structure, Walker once again mimics the U.S. Constitution to expose the racial shortcomings of the nation's founding document. In contrast to the Articles in the U.S. Constitution, which identify and explain the institutional features that enact and protect the rights of U.S. citizens, Walker's articles identify and explain the cultural and institutional factors that deny equal rights or protection for black residents in the United States—a contrast that illuminates the contradictions between U.S. national ideology and its practice the extent to which African Americans are denied access and representation by the federal Constitution.

Each of the articles in Walker's *Appeal* provides detailed descriptions of the way these factors contribute to African American inequality in the United States. Within these discussions, however, Walker clearly identifies racism as the underlying cause for these institutional forms of oppression. Again and again, Walker cites the prevailing assumptions that "we (coloured people) and our children are *brutes*," that blacks are "ignorant, impudent, and restless disturber[s] of the peace," and that blacks constitute "an *inferior* and *distinct race* of beings" to explain the nation's discriminatory and exclusionary policies (2, 19). More importantly, Walker argues that these racist beliefs have been embedded in U.S. nationalism from the very beginning, a connection he traces through the writings of Thomas Jefferson. Walker quotes extensively from Jefferson's *Notes on the State of Virginia* throughout the *Appeal*, citing Jefferson's claims that "blacks . . . are inferior to the whites, both in the endowments of our bodies and our minds," that "the unfortunate difference of colour and perhaps of faculty is a powerful obstacle to the[ir] emancipation," that "it is not their *condition* then, but *nature*, which has produced the distinction" (10, 27, 15). For Walker, Jefferson's racist statements have had pervasive influence on the policies and practices of the United States. "Mr. Jefferson's remarks respecting us, have sunk deep into the hearts of millions of the whites" (28), he writes, granting legitimacy to the nation's efforts to exclude African Americans as equal members of the federal nation. "Have not Americans instituted laws to hinder us from obtaining our freedom? . . . Have not the Americans instituted laws to prohibit a man of color from obtaining or holding any office whatever under the government of the United States of America?" asks Walker, who attributes these policies directly to "Mr. Jefferson's arguments respecting us" (15–16).[33]

For as much as Walker opposes Jefferson's racist views, he supports the principles of equality and just representation that Jefferson expresses in his other political writings. Like Benjamin Banneker forty years earlier, Walker affirms the value and validity of Jefferson's claim that "all men are created equal, that they are endowed by their Creator with certain unalienable rights," and he praises Jefferson as "one of as great characters as ever lived among the whites" for his efforts to establish a nation committed to these principles (15). The fact that Jefferson could establish a nation founded on equality while simultaneously denying that equality to its African American residents, however, exemplifies the racial limits of his national vision. "It is indeed surprising, that a man of such great learning, combined with such excellent natural parts, should speak so of a set of men in chains" (10), writes Walker, highlighting both the inconsistencies of Jefferson's nationalist and racist views and Jefferson's apparent blindness to these contradictions. Jefferson's status, however, as a respected author of the United States' national principles grants legitimacy to the racial limits he places on the nation's expressions of "equality." As Walker writes, the prevailing claims of African American inferiority, "having emanated from Mr. Jefferson ... ha[ve] in truth injured us more, and ha[ve] been as great a barrier to our emancipation as any thing that has ever been advanced against us" (27). Through Jefferson, racism has become so ingrained with the government policies and culture of the United States that citizens can no longer see the contradictions between the nation's equitable principles and its inequitable practices.

By exposing the contradictions between U.S. racism and U.S. nationalism, Walker's *Appeal* ultimately constitutes both a defense and a revision of the nation's federal principles. Throughout the *Appeal*, Walker clearly values the principles of equality, pluralism, and just representation expressed in the Declaration of Independence and the U.S. Constitution. What he objects to, however, is the way U.S. citizens have failed to live up to those principles in their treatment of the nation's African American residents. Although the citizens of the United States would like to believe—as Jefferson did—that their racist views are compatible with the principles of equality, pluralism, and just representation on which the nation was founded, Walker argues that these contradictions will ultimately undermine and erode the union. In this regard, Walker argues that the racist views of U.S. leaders and citizens are not just damaging to African Americans. They also threaten the stability and integrity of the United States. The persistent belief that blacks can be "treat[ed] like brutes" has "carried th[e] country to the brink of a precipice," writes Walker, who characterizes the belief "that our Creator made us to be an inheritance to them" as a notion that is "ten thousand times more injurious to this country than all the other evils put together; and which will be the final overthrow of its government unless something is speedily done" (39–40).

By thus representing racism as a threat to the nation, Walker pushes citizens to embrace a new understanding of the federal United States. In order to be a stable, unified nation that lives up to its national principles, the United States must also be a nation that embraces, represents, and respects racial differences. "Remember, Americans, that we must and shall be as free and enlightened as you are," asserts Walker, arguing for a nation that represents its white and black residents equally. "I speak, Americans, for your own good," continues Walker. "Set us free and treat us like men, and there will be no danger for we will love and respect them and protect our country—but we cannot conscientiously do these things until they treat us like men" (69–70). By transforming the United States into a nation that represents all of its citizens, black and white, equally, the United States will be able to live up to the principles of pluralism, equity, and just representation articulated in their founding documents, ensuring the success and stability of the United States.[34] "Treat us like men and there is no danger but we will all live in peace and happiness together," insists Walker. "What a happy country this will be" (70). Failing to grant this equality, however, will have damaging and destabilizing effects for the federal union. "But Americans, I declare to you, while you keep us and our children in bondage and treat us like brutes . . . we cannot be your friends," cautions Walker. "Unless you speedily alter your course, you and your Country are gone!!!" (70, 39).

Although Walker argues for expanding the federal pluralism of the United States to include race, he avoids using the term "federalism" explicitly in his arguments. Instead, when he refers to the national structure or government of the United States, he uses "republican" rather than "federalism" to describe it, a matter of phrasing that allows him to emphasize the representative dimensions of the government in more neutral terms. Much like the Cherokee, Walker's reluctance to use this term was strategic since "federalism" was a term invoked by the states to defend and protect the practice of slavery. In fact, he specifically points to the states and their appeals to federalism as an example of the contradictory and destabilizing dimensions of the current U.S. federal practices since they use these arguments to support racist policies and legislation. In Article IV, Walker provides a list of the abusive and contradictory federal practices of the state governments, noting that "a law has recently passed the Legislature of the *republican* state (Georgia) prohibiting all free or slave persons of colour from learning to read or write," which he follows with descriptions of other laws passed in Virginia, Ohio, Florida, South Carolina, and Kentucky that similarly "restrict[ed] the rights of free Negroes" (53–54). For Walker, promoting and privileging states' rights was not an effective expression of the nation's federal pluralism. Instead, such arguments perpetuated a damaging practice of federalism by using this political philosophy to support a racially exclusive vision of the nation.

Walker's efforts to redefine the nation's plural nationalism in terms of race were motivated, not just by the destabilizing actions of the states, but also by the growing influence of the American Colonization Society, which argued for resettling the nation's free blacks in Africa. Although colonization had long been posed as a possible solution to the racial differences and divisions in the United States, this movement gained momentum in the 1820s and 1830s, and Walker devoted the entire concluding article of the *Appeal* to exposing the racist logic of these arguments. He begins by quoting from the speeches of two leading proponents of colonization, Henry Clay and Elias B. Caldwell, who argued that Africa offered a more "suitable establishment" for blacks to experience "the blessings of our arts, our civilization, and our religion" (46). Walker, however, sarcastically paraphrases the racist implications of these arguments, which suggest "from their condition and the unconquerable prejudices resulting from their colour, [African Americans] never could amalgamate with the free whites of this country. It [is] desirable, therefore . . . to drain them off" (46). Although proponents of colonization ostensibly supported African American liberty and equality, Walker attacked these arguments for perpetuating a racially exclusive definition of the United States. By granting liberty and equality to African Americans only under the condition of removing them from the nation, arguments for colonization continued to characterize the United States as a nation where equal rights and privileges were restricted to white residents. For Walker, these arguments were problematic, not just because they continued to place racial limits on U.S. citizenship, but also because they failed to recognize the very real presence and significance of African Americans within the nation. Walker insists that free blacks deserve to be represented within the United States because they have always played a foundational role in establishing and maintaining it. "This country is as much ours as it is the whites, whether they will admit it now or not, they will see and believe it by and by" (55), writes Walker, who argues that efforts to deny the presence and contributions of black residents misrepresent the nation's history and identity. Walker goes even further by arguing that African Americans have been particularly responsible for the nation's economic success and stability. "America is more our country than it is the whites [because] we have enriched it with our *blood and tears*. The greatest riches in all America have arisen from our blood and tears—and will they drive us from our property and homes, which we have earned with our *blood*?" (65). For Walker, African Americans have a right to be represented equally within the United States precisely because their work has secured the nation's prosperity and success.

Walker's claim that African Americans have a legitimate stake and ownership in the United States introduces a new approach to his arguments for racial equality. Throughout the *Appeal*, Walker has primarily argued for African American equality by criticizing the contradictions between the national principles of the United States and the racist interpretation and application of those principles by its white citizens and leaders. With these concluding arguments, however, Walker shifts his attention from the ways that whites have defined the country to the way that blacks have defined the country. From this position, Walker argues that African Americans do not deserve liberty, equal rights, and representation just because the United States is supposed to be committed to these principles. African Americans deserve these rights because they have been crucial for defining the nation.

This new focus in Walker's argument once again shows his engagement with the politics of federal representation. At the heart of Walker's argument is an effort to redefine—or, rather, to justly represent—the plural dynamics of the nation. By highlighting the role that African Americans have played in defining the United States, Walker reminds his readers that the United States has always been composed of many different races and ethnicities, and, moreover, that this racial diversity has been instrumental in shaping the nation's history and success. The United States, however, has consistently failed to represent the racial diversity of its history and identity, perpetuating a false perception of the nation's plural composition. Arguments for colonization threaten to continue this misrepresentation by granting African Americans equality while continuing to deny and erase the nation's racial pluralism. For Walker, the United States must begin to represent itself as a racially diverse nation if it wants to have a stable and credible future. "Let no man of us budge one step" (65), he writes, requiring citizens to account for the black residents who have always been a part of the union. For Walker, failing to include race as part of the nation's composite identity will ultimately compromise its federal integrity and stability. "My color will yet root some of you out of the very face of the earth," asserts Walker, who encourages the nation to incorporate this "color" into the federal nation to avoid prompting conflict over this issue of representation (72).

Walker's push to represent the United States as a multiracial federal nation is ultimately a call for a new practice of national reading and interpretation. By asking his audience to recognize that "this country is as much ours as it is the whites," Walker asks them to reread the history and identity of the United States and replace a racially exclusive interpretation of the nation with a racially inclusive interpretation. As Apap has observed, Walker's *Appeal* "rejects the white American interpretation of history by illuminating its racial and logical fault lines."[35] Looking back, the entire *Appeal* is actually structured as a series of critical rereadings that are meant to illuminate a critical problem with the nation's interpretive practices. One by one, Walker presents his audience with a selection of the nation's definitive texts—the U.S. Constitution, *Notes on the State of Virginia*, various state laws, the Declaration of Independence—and asks them to reread these works from the perspective of the nation's African American residents. This process of rereading is, in turn, a process of recognizing that the United States has been long been defined by racially exclusive practices of interpretation that transform documents that are supposed to signify the nation's values of plurality, equity, and just representation into works that actually betray these values. He concludes his *Appeal* by asking his audience to reread the language of the Declaration of Independence and recognize how the United States has misinterpreted and misapplied its assertions of equality. "See your Declaration, Americans!!" he demands. "Do you understand your own language? Hear your language, proclaimed to the world, July 4, 1776—'We hold these truths to be self-evident—that ALL MEN ARE CREATED EQUAL'... Compare your own language, extracted from your Declaration of Independence, with the cruelties and murders inflicted by your cruel and unmerciful fathers and yourself on our fathers and on us—men who have never given your fathers or you the least provocation" (75). By contrasting the language of the Declaration with the nation's racist policies and practices, Walker shows how U.S. citizens have refused to extend these principles of equality to African Americans, an interpretive choice that completely discredits the significance of this document and the nation it is supposed to represent. Rather than reading the United States as a nation founded on equality, Walker asks his audience to read the United States as a nation that *fails* to represent this equality. In doing so, Walker's *Appeal* enacts a practice of federal literacy that exposes rather than celebrates the United States' equitable commitment to pluralism.

By thus exposing the United States as a nation that falsely represents its own federal principles, Walker argues that African Americans have legitimate grounds for a militant rebellion. "Hear your language further!" he writes, referring back to the text of the Declaration of Independence to note that "'when a long train of abuses and usurpation, pursuing invariably the same object, evinces a design to reduce them under absolute despotism, it is their *right*, it is their *duty*, to throw off such a government and to provide new guards for their security'" (75). Rather than completely rejecting the principles of pluralism, equality, and liberty on which the United States was founded, however, Walker pushes his readers to find a way to revive and restore these principles to the United States' current practices of federal nationalism. Doing so, however, requires transforming the national interpretation of race. The future of the federal nation depends on developing and promoting these new practices of reading and interpretation. Failing to read the nation in racially inclusive terms will foreclose any future for the federal nation at all.

In the years leading up to the Civil War, many other writers would similarly appeal to these federal principles and strategies of reading to argue for a more inclusive model of federal pluralism and equality. Frederick Douglass drew on these federal tactics to condemn the practice of slavery and the nation's racially discriminatory laws and policies in much of his work, most famously in his 1852 speech "What, to a Slave, Is the 4th of July?" Native American writers and opponents of U.S. Indian removal policies likewise continued to draw on the logic and rhetoric of U.S. federalism to assert their rights and sovereignty, exemplified by the work of writers such as William Apess, whose 1833 essay "An Indian's Looking-Glass to the White Man" follows Walker's work by asking U.S. readers to consider the inconsistencies of their racist views and their national, as well as their Christian, values, while his 1835 book, *Indian Nullification*, presents an even more strident critical engagement with the principles of federalism for the purpose of indigenous resistance.³⁶ Jeremiah Evarts, a white activist and editor of the *Panoplist* magazine, also used federal arguments and tactics to oppose U.S. Indian removal policies in his famous "William Penn" essays, many of which were reprinted in the *Cherokee Phoenix*, arguing that "the character of our government, and our country, may be deeply involved."³⁷ Kelly Wisecup has recently argued that many Native American writers did more than simply address these "failures of logic and illegality" in U.S. federal policies, examining how John Ridge, another important Cherokee activist, structured his writings to reorient national practices of reading and interpretation. By thus requiring "that readers participate in the process of reinterpreting" both native and U.S.-authored texts, argues Wisecup, Ridge's writing forced his readers to come "to their own understandings of Cherokee sovereignty," a move that builds on the tactics of federal literacy to foster new forms of federal resistance.³⁸

Women also drew on these federal tactics to argue for expanding their own rights and representation in the nation, most famously in the "Declarations of Rights and Sentiments" that was presented at the 1848 Seneca Falls convention, a document that was closely modeled on the Declaration of Independence, as well as the principles expressed in the U.S. Constitution in order to highlight its exclusions and prompt a more equitable and inclusive interpretation of its language.³⁹ These various efforts to revive the principles of the nation's federal pluralism and extend those principles to those excluded from that pluralism presented U.S. readers with powerful arguments that should have been very difficult to challenge without simultaneously denying the logic and value of the nation's own federal identity. The failure of these arguments to gain any significant traction to alter the nation's discriminatory and exclusionary policies, however, ultimately marks both the limitations and the disintegration of this plural model of union. For as much as the United States, aided by its print culture, tried to find ways to represent its diverse constituent differences in unified terms, this unity could not be preserved or sustained when it came to representing the nation in terms of its racial or gender differences, at least insofar as the federal nation was imagined in the late eighteenth and early nineteenth centuries.

While this study must conclude by reporting the failure of the nation's federal literary tactics, there is much to be learned from recalling this history. Although the federal pluralism imagined within the early United States proved to be unsustainable, this model of nationalism provides a promising framework for representing diversity in unified, collaborative, and concurrent terms. Rather than simply criticizing the United States for its failure to realize these federal ideals, this study argues, much as writers like Banneker, Murray, Flint, Drake, Hall, Walker, Boudinot, and others did, that the United States should find ways to revive and revise these practices and principles of federalism. Doing so, however, remains contingent on continually rethinking and reinterpreting the ways we read the terms of the nation's pluralism. Returning to Patrick Henry's compelling question, "The question turns on that poor little thing—the expression, 'We, the people,'" we are continually in the process of determining just what, exactly, "we" might mean.

NOTES

✶ ✶ ✶ ✶ ✶ ✶ ✶ ✶ ✶ ✶ ✶ ✶

INTRODUCTION
Drawing Together by Drawing Apart

1. *Geography: An Amusement*, outer box.
2. Rush, "Thoughts upon a Mode of Education," 115–16. For more on the relationship between nationalism, literacy, and the rhetoric of diffusion in the early republic, see Warner, "Nationalism and the Problem of Republican Literature," 122–32.
3. Beeman, *Varieties of Political Experience*, 3.
4. Adams, "Letter to Samuel Osgood," 342.
5. Witherspoon, "Part of a Speech to Congress," 151. For more on the philosophical and colonial development of early U.S. federalism, see LaCroix, *Ideological Origins*; White, *Backcountry and the City*; Yirush, *Settlers, Liberty, and Empire*.
6. For more on the classical origins of federalism, see Coby, "Aristotle's Three Cities."
7. For a thorough discussion of federalism by these Enlightenment-era thinkers, see Hope, *Virtue by Consensus*.
8. See Gellner, *Nations and Nationalism*; Breuilly, *Nationalism and the State*; Hechter, *Containing Nationalism*.
9. Madison, Federalist No. 10, 78.
10. Patterson and Dougall, *Eagle and the Shield*, 84.
11. For more on early federal iconography, see Olson, *Emblems of American Community*.
12. Lepore, *A Is for American*, 15. See also Waldstreicher, *In the Midst*, for more on the federal dimensions of early national celebrations.
13. This list represents an overview of some of the dominant arguments concerning early American literary culture by Cathy Davidson, Michelle Burnham, Michael Warner, Christopher Looby, and Sandra Gustafson, among many others. For an overview of these "unifying" arguments and the relationship of literature and nationalism in the history of early American literary studies, see Fluck, "From Aesthetics to Political Criticism."
14. Brown, *Pilgrim and the Bee*, 32.
15. Ibid., x. Chartier offers a particularly useful discussion of the relationship between studies of form and reader response in *Forms and Meanings*.

16. Davidson offers a useful discussion of the merits of incorporating reader-response approaches to the study of early American literature, as well as the archival methods needed for such studies in "Toward a History."

17. See Castiglia, *Interior States*; Frank, *Constituent Moments*; Larkin, *American School of Empire*; Loughran, *Republic in Print*; Slauter, *State as a Work of Art*; Smith-Rosenberg, *This Violent Empire*.

18. Smith-Rosenberg, *This Violent Empire*, 38.

19. Loughran, *Republic in Print*, xx.

20. Brückner and Hsu, *American Literary Geographies*, 16. For other work that exemplifies this spatial turn in early American Studies, see Brückner, *Geographic Revolution in Early America*; Hsu, *Geography and the Production of Space*; Bauer, *Cultural Geography*; Blum, *View from the Masthead*; Baker, *Heartless Immensity*.

21. Kaplan, "'Left Alone with America,'" 11. See also Larkin, *American School of Empire*; Go, *Patterns of Empire*; Rifkin, *Manifesting America*; Watts, *American Colony*; Greene, *Peripheries and Center*.

22. Larkin, *American School of Empire*, 11.

23. See Byrd, *Transit of Empire*; Doyle, *Freedom's Empire*; Rifkin, *Manifesting America*; Stoler, *Haunted by Empire*.

24. Stoler, *Haunted by Empire*, 13.

25. Scholarship that addresses the literary forms and practices of literacy associated with writers located "outside" of the cultural majority of the early United States informs my approach to this topic, most notably Wyss, *English Letters and Indian Literacies*; Round, *Removable Type*; and the essays collected in Cohen and Stein, *Early African American Print Culture*.

26. Adams, *Memoirs*, 5:401.

27. For a historical overview of the transformation of federalism in the United States, see Joseph Zimmerman, *Contemporary American Federalism*.

28. For a further discussion of the plural dynamics of the term "United States," see Santin et al., "Is or Are."

29. DeWispelare provides a useful overview of this aesthetics of "copiousness" in "What We Want in Elegance." See also Olivia Smith, *Politics of Language*, and Sorenson, *Grammar of Empire*, for more on these plural aesthetics, particularly in the context of linguistics and the politics of the British Empire.

30. Cosmopolitanism and federalism are closely linked by offering a positive approach for interpreting and negotiating plurality in the eighteenth century. For analysis of the discourse of cosmopolitanism and its relationship to early U.S. nationalism, see the essays collected in Nicolaisen and Spahn, *Cosmopolitanism and Nationhood*; Ziesche, *Cosmopolitan Patriots*.

CHAPTER 1

The United States Are Thirteen

1. For an overview of the Greek origins of federalism, see Buckler, "Federalism"; J. A. O. Larson, *Greek Federal States*.

2. Althusius's early theories of federalism can be found in *Politica Methodice Digesta*; Grotius presents his views on divided sovereignty in *De Jure Belli ac Pacis*. For Pufendorf's arguments about a "system of states" see *De Statu Imperii*.

3. Pufendorf, *Of the Law of Nature and Nations*, 681–82.

4. Montesquieu, *Spirit of Laws*.

5. Ibid.

6. Go, *Patterns of Empire*, 45; Watts, *American Colony*; Onuf, *Jefferson's Empire*; Larkin, *American School of Empire*; Greene, *Peripheries and Center*.

7. "Vision of the Paradise," *United States Magazine*, March 1779, quoted in Onuf, *Jefferson's Empire*, 58.

8. For discussions of empire and its relationship to diversity, see Hardt and Negri, *Empire*; Abernathy, *Dynamics of Global Dominance*; Larkin, *American School of Empire*.

9. Hamilton, Federalist No. 11, 84.

10. Madison, Federalist No. 51, 322.

11. Pownall, *Administration of the Colonies*, 306.

12. Adams, "Letter to Samuel Osgood," 302.

13. For more on the federal background and education of early U.S. politicians, see LaCroix, *Ideological Origins of American Federalism*, 68–104; Onuf and Onuf, *Federal Union, Modern World*, 5–7.

14. White, *Backcountry and the City*, 10. Work by White and Yirush has led the way in reperiodizing U.S. federalism as a political discourse with origins in the colonial period.

15. Articles of Confederation of the United Colonies.

16. Yirush examines how the colonial structure of government created a "nascent federalism" in the British American colonies in *Settlers, Liberty, and Empire*, 18.

17. The Albany Plan of Union.

18. For analysis of the relationship between the 1707 Act of Union and the conditions of the British American colonies, see LaCroix, *Ideological Origins of American Federalism*, 87–88; Yirush, *Settlers, Liberty, and Empire*, 29–50.

19. Franklin, "Reasons and Motives," 2.

20. Articles of Confederation.

21. "Proceedings of Commissioners to Remedy Defects of the Federal Government."

22. Madison, "Record of the Convention," 18.

23. For a useful discussion of the Great Compromise and the Virginia and New Jersey Plans that contributed to it, see Yazawa, *Contested Conventions*.

24. Hamilton, Federalist No. 23, 148, 151.

25. Agrippa, "Letter IV," 166.

26. Brutus, "Letter I." Other notable, though pseudonymous, Anti-Federalist writers include Centinel, whose letters were published in the *Philadelphia Independent Gazetteer* and the *Philadelphia Freeman's Journal* between October 1787 and January 1788; Agrippa, whose letters were published in the *Massachusetts Gazette* between November 1787 and January 1788; Cato, whose letters were published in the *New York Journal* between October 1787 and December 1787; and Federal Farmer, whose letters were published as a pamphlet in October 1787.

27. Patrick Henry, "Address," 391.

28. For a thorough analysis of Federalist and Anti-Federalist ideology, particularly the variations within each partisan position, see Cornell, *Other Founders*.

29. Madison, Federalist No. 39, 242.

30. McPherson claims that "before 1861 the two words 'United States' were rendered as a plural noun: 'the United States are a republic.' The war marked a transition of the United States to a singular noun." *Battle Cry of Freedom*, 859. Subsequent studies have shown, however, that the plural use of the United States was not quite as standardized as McPherson suggests. Still, this plural usage was much more common in the late eighteenth and early nineteenth centuries, and the Supreme Court consistently used the United States as a plural term during this time. See Myers, "Supreme Court Usage"; Santin et al., "Is or Are."

31. John Adams, Alexander Hamilton, Richard Henry Lee, Thomas Jefferson, Charles Pinkney, and George Washington all used the term in both singular and plural forms, depending on context.

32. Noah Webster, *Grammatical Institute*, 137.

33. Olson, *Benjamin Franklin's Vision*, 124.

34. Morse, *Geography Made Easy* (1796), 96. Morse's first use of the term "federal Americans" appears in *American Universal Geography*, 207.

35. Morse, *Geography Made Easy* (1796), 96.

36. Noah Webster, "On the Education of Youth."

37. Brückner, "Lessons in Geography," 313–14.

38. Morse, *Geography Made Easy* (1796), v.

39. Morse, *American Geography*, 120.

40. Ibid., 219.

41. Morse, *Geography Made Easy* (1809), 100.

42. The following population descriptions and data are drawn from Morse's *American Geography*, 218, 250.

43. For more on the relationship between coverture and U.S. representation, see Jan Lewis, "'Of Every Age.'"

44. Morse, *American Universal Geography*, 210–12.

45. For representative examples of maps without state boundaries, see the various editions of Morse's *Geography Made Easy* and *American Universal Geography*, as well as Faden, *United States of North America*; Wallis, *United States of America*.

46. See Short, *Representing the Republic*. Brückner also touches on the diversity of views regarding the representation of the early United States in his essay "The Plurality of Early American Cartography."

47. For an example of a map with state boundaries clearly outlined, see Bowles's *New Pocket Map*.

48. For background on the history and design of Buell's map, see Cohen, "Abel Buell."

49. See Shankle, *State Names*.

50. For more on border conflicts between states in the early United States, see Spero, *Frontier Country*.

51. Waldstreicher, *In the Midst*, 14, 249.

52. DeForest, *History of the Indians*, 440, 476.

53. Brückner, *Geographic Revolution*, 48.

54. See G. Malcolm Lewis, "Maps, Mapmaking, and Map Use."

55. Hopkinson, "Account," 16.

56. Olson, *Emblems of American Community*, 73.

57. "Resolution for the U.S. Flag."

58. For more on the history of the flag's design, see Leepson, *Flag*, 17–18.

59. For a discussion of these allegorical images, see Derek H. Davis, *Religion and the Continental Congress*, 138–39.

60. Cigrand, *Story of the Great Seal*, 156–57.

61. Patterson and Dougall, *Eagle and the Shield*, 84.

62. For more on early U.S. currency, see Newman, *Early Paper Money of America*.

63. See Doolitle, "New Display."

64. For a more extended discussion of federal images in popular culture, see Olson, *Emblems of American Community*, 133–40.

65. Slauter, *State as a Work of Art*, 85. See also his chapter titled "Making a Government of Laws," 39–86.

66. These images of the federal edifice, represented as a series of columns being added as each state ratified the Constitution, were featured in the *Massachusetts Centinel* between January and August 1788.

67. For a thorough analysis of the role that public celebrations played in imagining and supporting the federal United States, see Waldstreicher, *In the Midst*.

68. Hopkinson, "Account," 3.

69. Ibid., 2.

70. For a full list of the professions featured in this procession, see Hopkinson, "Account," 4–14.

71. Ibid., 22.

72. See Waldstreicher's chapter titled "The Constitution of Federal Feeling" in *In the Midst*, 53–107.

73. For more on the care and attention given to the structure of the federal processions, see Waldstreicher, *In the Midst*, 90–92.

74. Hopkinson, "Account," 23.

75. Ibid., 18.

76. Ibid., 22.

77. Cornell, *Other Founders*, 222. For a thorough overview of the many different publications and reprintings of the ratification debates and convention proceedings, see Hutson, "Creation of the Constitution."

78. For more on the connection between reading and writing and federal principles, see Merrill and Wilentz, "Introduction," 50–53.

79. Hopkinson, "New Roof"; Hopkinson, "Raising."

80. Hopkinson, "New Roof," 42.

81. Hopkinson, "Raising," 95.

82. "Farmer and His Thirteen Sons," 82.

83. "Story of the Thirteen Partners," 134.

84. "Farmer and His Thirteen Sons," 81.

85. "Story of the Thirteen Partners," 135, 136.

86. "Continental Medley," 560.

CHAPTER 2
Reading Parts and Wholes

1. Horrocks, *Popular Print and Popular Medicine*, 6.

2. Santoro, "After the Old," 56; Raymond, "To Reach Men's Minds," 370. For more information about the diverse audiences of almanacs and their profitability, see Horrocks, *Popular Print and Popular Medicine*, 5–7; Spero, "Revolution in Popular Publications," 44; Stowell, *Early American Almanacs*, ix–x.

3. Some of the almanacs including information about the federal documents and structure of the United States include *The North American Calendar, Bickerstaff's New England Almanack, The New England Almanack, Thomas's Massachusetts, Connecticut, Rhode Island, New Hampshire, and Vermont Almanack, The South-Carolina and Georgia Almanack, The New Jersey Almanack, Father Tammany's Almanac, Gaine's Universal Register: A Pocket Almanack, Poor Will's Almanac, The Palladium of Knowledge, Fleet's Pocket Almanac, The Pennsylvania Almanac, Bickerstaff's Boston Almanack, The Federal Almanac, Green's Register for the State of Connecticut, Hall's Massachusetts Almanac*, and *Hutchin's Improved*.

4. *Bickerstaff's Boston Almanack* (1789), 2.

5. *Bickerstaff's Boston Almanack* (1789); *The Continental Almanac* (1785).

6. *The Columbian Almanac* (1791).

7. Brückner's discussion of the ways that early American primers taught citizens to "read and comprehend the social order" provides a useful model for considering the educational function of almanacs. See *Geographic Revolution*, 108–9. Santoro also discusses how some almanacs educated readers about the federal government in "After the Old," 60.

8. These quantities and statistics are drawn from a survey of the almanacs listed in the *Early American Imprints* database, cross-checked against the listings in Milton Drake's bibliography *Almanacs of the United States*.

9. See White, *Backcountry and the City*; Yirush, *Settlers, Liberty, and Empire*.

10. See Gardner, *Rise and Fall*; Pasley, *Tyranny of Printers*; Gustafson, *Eloquence Is Power*.

11. See Waldstreicher, *In the Midst*, 45–50; Santoro, "After the Old," 55; Horrocks, *Popular Print and Popular Medicine*, 1.

12. Brown, *Pilgrim and the Bee*, 53.

13. Scholars typically identify the sixteenth and seventeenth centuries as the "golden age" of the English almanac. For more on the history of English almanacs, see Perkins, *Visions of the Future*.

14. Horrocks discusses the growing rate of American almanacs in his introduction to *Popular Print and Popular Medicine*. These specific figures for 1760 and 1790 are compiled from an analysis of listings for almanacs in Early American Imprints (https://www.readex.com/content/early-american-imprints) and Early English Books Online (https://eebo.chadwyck.com/home).

15. Perkins and Spero offer useful discussions of the history of almanac production in England, particularly regarding its highly controlled and centralized processes of production. See Perkins, *Visions of the Future*, 18–23; Spero, "Revolution in Popular Publications," 47.

16. Some of these specialized almanacs include *The Ladies Diary or Woman's Almanack*, *The Ladies and Gentlemen's Diary or Royal Almanack*, and *Poor Robin's Almanack*. Horrocks briefly discusses the different audiences for English almanacs in *Popular Print and Popular Medicine*, 6–8.

17. Spero, "Revolution in Popular Publications," 47.

18. See *The South-Carolina and Georgia Almanack* (1776), as well as sample recipes and advice printed in *The United States Almanac* for 1790 and 1793 and *The New-England Farmer's Almanack* for 1794.

19. Stowell, *Early American Almanacs*, 273.

20. John Tobler was an experienced almanac maker, having established a successful almanac series in his home country of Switzerland—the *Appenzeller Kalender*—in the early 1720s before moving to the United States in 1737, where he compiled and published several successful almanacs. After his death in 1765, his sons continued to compile and publish almanacs under his name throughout the late eighteenth century. For more on Tobler's career, see Robbins, "John Tobler's Description."

21. *The Pennsylvania Town and Country-Man's Almanack* (1777).

22. "Making Common Salt," 26–30, and "Remedies for a Bruise," 30, in *The Pennsylvania Town and Country-Man's Almanack* (1777). Other editions include articles addressing "The Uncertainty of Judging According to Appearance," "Civility and Manners," and a "Remedy for Lameness."

23. *The Pennsylvania Town and Country-Man's Almanack* (1777), 31–37. For a sense of these formatting and content issues, see the full run of John Tobler's *The Pennsylvania Town and Country-Man's Almanack* during the early national period (1774–77).

24. *The South-Carolina and Georgia Almanack* (1777).

25. See the following articles in *The South-Carolina and Georgia Almanack* (1777): "Declaration of Independence," 18–20; "Defeat at Sullivan's Island," 21–22; "The Impossibility of Pleasing Everybody," 22; domestic advice, 23–31.

26. For a sense of these formatting and content issues, see the full run of John Tobler's *The South-Carolina and Georgia Almanack* (also known as *The South-Carolina Almanack* and *The Georgia and South-Carolina Almanack*) during the early national period (1774–80).

27. See, for example, *The South-Carolina and Georgia Almanac* (1777), 23–31.

28. Ibid., 27–28.

29. Raymond discusses such indirect means of supporting colonial resistance, which included recipes for sugar substitutes and directions for making saltpeter and gunpowder at home. Examples of indirect support for colonial resistance can be found in Benjamin West's *Bickerstaff* almanacs for the Boston region, David Rittenhouse's *Virginia Almanack*, John Nathan Hutchins's New York–based *Hutchins Improved*, and Benjamin Franklin's Philadelphia-based *Poor Richard Improved*. See Raymond, "To Reach Men's Minds," 375, 391.

30. Spero, "Revolution in Popular Publications," 60.

31. Raymond, "To Reach Men's Minds," 371.

32. Loughran, *Republic in Print*, 23.

33. Tiedemann, "Interconnected Communities," 6.

34. Spero, "Revolution in Popular Publications," 47, 53, 60.

35. Ibid., 43. Loughran likewise emphasizes the fragmented quality of early print culture, noting how the nation's regional diversity created an environment where writers produced fictional rhetorics of unity to mask their disconnected status in her chapter "Virtual Nation: State-Based Identity and Federalist Fantasy," in *Republic in Print*, 161–222.

36. The sense of federal space produced by early American almanacs is informed by Frederic Jameson's concept of "cognitive mapping," which he defines in *Postmodernism* as a process by which individuals learn to situate themselves within a larger totality. See also Herman, *Narrative Theory*, and Certeau, *Practice of Everyday Life*.

37. Brown, *Pilgrim and the Bee*, 53.

38. McCarthy, "Redeeming the Almanac," 2.

39. Washington kept more extensive almanac diaries than Jefferson, which he regularly maintained from 1765 to 1775. See McCarthy, *Accidental Diarist*, 259. McCarthy also provides more detail about the history of this practice of interleaving diary pages within almanacs, 11–54.

40. For examples of these conventional notes and records in almanac diaries, see McCarthy, *Accidental Diarist*, 17–22.

41. See Lovejoy's interleaved almanac diaries in Nathaniel Lovejoy Diaries. These diaries include various Boston almanacs printed by Nathaniel Ames, Benjamin West, Samuel Stearns, Nathaniel Low, and the *Bickerstaff* almanacs.

42. See Moore's interleaved almanac diaries in John Moore Diaries.

43. See Peirce, Jonathan Peirce Diary.

44. Moore, John Moore Diaries; Washington, "Diaries."

45. See McCarthy, *Accidental Diarist* 18–20, as well as Washington, "Diaries."

46. Waldstreicher explores how these new national chronologies helped unite provincial audiences in "a sacred history and national future." See *In the Midst*, 49. See also Santoro, "After the Old," 60.

47. Spero, "Revolution in Popular Publications," 66.

48. For examples of almanac diaries that record this personalized family information, see the following manuscript collections at the American Antiquarian Society: Samuel Bridge Diaries, 1777–98; Samuel Man Diary, 1777, 1781–83; Belcher Noyes Diaries, 1775–76, 1782; Jonathan Sayward Diaries, 1760–99.

49. See Carter, Diary, which is interleaved in the *Virginia Almanack* for 1774.

50. There was some variation in the phrasing of this statement. Almanacs featured phrasing such as "year of independence," "year of independency," and, in some cases immediately after the end of the Revolution, even "year of our redemption."

51. See Stanton, John Stanton Papers, 1774–94.

52. See Noyes, Belcher Noyes Diaries, 1775–76, 1782. Noyes's 1775 diary is interleaved in *An Astronomical Diary*, which is part of the manuscript collection.

53. See Man, Samuel Man Diary, 1777; 1781–83. Man's 1777 diary is interleaved in Benjamin West's *New England Almanack's for Providence, Rhode Island*. See also Pownell, William Powell Diary, 1777, which is interleaved in *Bickerstaff's Almanack*.

54. Other almanac diaries that record events from the American Revolution include the Caleb Gibbs Diary of 1778 and the Rodney Family Diaries, *1779–1809*, both in the American Antiquarian Society manuscript collections.

55. For references to these specific court schedules, see the following almanacs: *Father Abraham's Almanack* (Boston, 1774–1805); *Poor Will's Almanack* (Philadelphia, 1774–1803); *Hutchin's Improved* (New York, 1774–79); *The Maryland, Delaware, Pennsylvania, Virginia, and North-Carolina Almanack* (Baltimore, 1780–95).

56. Freidman provides a useful history of the different state court systems in the early nation, noting that the organization of the courts, the authority of judges, and the practice of law could vary considerably from state to state. *History of American Law*, 111.

57. See Bridge, Samuel Bridge Diaries.

58. Berkowitz and Clay discuss how the different state systems worked together in "State Courts."

59. For more extensive discussions of visual language, see McGann, *Textual Condition*; Kress, *Literacy*.

60. Landow, *Hypertext 2.0*, 60.

61. For Brown's useful discussion of this "indexical" literacy, which, as he argues, can help illustrate "how time was felt and how texts were valued by readers in early New England," see *Pilgrim and the Bee*, 50–60.

62. For discussions of the concept of "reading pathways," see Walsh, "Reading Visual and Multimodal Texts"; Kostelnick and Hasset, *Shaping Information*, particularly chapters 1 and 5.

63. For background on "heteroglossia," see Bakhtin, *Dialogic Imagination*. For the multivoiced, hybrid, and performative dimensions of postcolonial and marginalized literature, see Bhabha, *Location of Culture*. For "minor" literature, see Deleuze and Guattari, *Kafka* and *Thousand Plateaus*.

64. McCarthy, "Redeeming the Almanac," 1.

65. For a thorough discussion of multimodal texts and the experience of multimodal reading, see Kress and Van Leeuwen, *Multimodal Discourse*, and Kress, *Multimodality*.

66. Kostelnick and Hasset, *Shaping Information*, 181.

67. DeWispelare, "What We Want," 121–22. For more on these plural aesthetics, particularly in the context of linguistics and the politics of the British Empire, see also Olivia Smith, *Politics of Language*, and Sorenson, *Grammar of Empire*.

68. For helpful explanations of the astrological belief system and its representation in almanacs, particularly in relation to the "Man of Signs," see Capp, *Astrology and the Popular Press*, esp. 17–22, and Tomlin, "'Astrology's from Heaven."

69. Capp explores the decline of astrology as a credible belief system, as well as its changing significance, in *Astrology and the Popular Press*, 238–40.

70. Slauter offers a comprehensive analysis of this federal iconography, with respect to images of the body and the constellations, in his chapter titled "Making a Government of Laws" in *State as a Work of Art*.

71. Tomlin, "'Astrology's from Heaven," 289.

72. For more on Banneker's mixed-race heritage and the situation of his family, see Bedini, *Life of Benjamin Banneker*, 3–25.

73. Banneker, "Copy of a Letter," 9.

74. For more on Banneker's early life and accomplishments, see Bedini, *Life of Benjamin Banneker*, 22–48, and Cerami, *Benjamin Banneker*, 45–66.

75. See Carroll, "Maryland Quakers and Slavery." See also Phillips, *Freedom's Port*, especially 38–40.

76. Cerami, *Benjamin Banneker*, 91. See also Franklin and Moss, *From Slavery to Freedom*, 64–78.

77. Banneker, "Copy of a Letter," 7.

78. For a history of the laws restricting the rights of African Americans in Maryland after the American Revolution, see Bogen, "Maryland Context of *Dred Scott*."

79. Ibid., 390.

80. For more on the status of African Americans and these discriminatory laws in the 1780s and 1790s, see Franklin and Moss, *From Slavery to Freedom*, 76–81.

81. Jefferson, *Notes*, 150–51. For more on the influence of *Notes on the State of Virginia* on U.S. racial policies and attitudes, see Forbes, "'Cause of This Blackness'"; Onuf, "'To Declare Them.'"

82. Banneker was particularly close to Andrew Ellicott's cousin, George, who taught him the principles of surveying and encouraged Banneker's almanac work. For more on Banneker's relationship with the Ellicotts, see Bedini, *Life of Benjamin Banneker*, 49–76, and Cerami, *Benjamin Banneker*, 67–81.

83. "Description of the City of Washington," 656. For more on the symbolic implications of the design for the "Federal City," see Luria, *Capital Speculations*; Arnebeck, *Through a Fiery Trial*.

84. Cerami, *Benjamin Banneker*, 143.

85. *Georgetown Weekly Ledger*, March 12, 1791, quoted in Bedini, *Life of Benjamin Banneker*, 122–23. For a deeper study of the politics associated with Banneker's role on the federal survey, see Bedini, "Survey of the Federal Territory."

86. This observation was recorded by George Ellicott's daughter, Martha Ellicott Tyson, who wrote the first extended biographies of Banneker. This quotation is cited in Bedini," Survey of the Federal Territory," 87.

87. *Benjamin Banneker's Pennsylvania, Delaware, Maryland, and Virginia Almanack* (1792), 2.

88. Rittenhouse, "On Negro Slavery," 33.

89. Andrews, "Benjamin Banneker's Revision," 219. See also Ray, "'In My Own Hand Writing.'"

90. Banneker, "Copy of a Letter," 7. Subsequent references will be given parenthetically within the text.

91. For more on the significance of Banneker's decision to provide a handwritten manuscript copy of his almanac, see Ray, "'In My Own Hand Writing.'"

92. For a more thorough analysis of Jefferson's response to Banneker, see Andrews, "Benjamin Banneker's Revision," 232–34; Bedini, *Life of Benjamin Banneker*, 158–59.

93. Buchanan, *Oration*, 10.

94. William Smith, "Pretensions of Thomas Jefferson," 10.

95. Selections of articles published in the Philadelphia edition of Banneker's *Almanack and Ephemeris* (1793) include "Peace and Goodwill to Men: Ah! Why Will Men Forget That They Are Brethren," "Abstract from the Speech of William Pitt on the Motion for the Abolition of the Slave Trade," "Extract from Wilkinson's Appeal to England on Behalf of the Abused Africans," and a poem titled "On Liberty."

96. A few samples of the articles published in the Baltimore edition of *Benjamin Banneker's Pennsylvania, Delaware, Maryland, and Virginia Almanack* (1793) include "The Progress of Vice: A Moral Tale," "The Bear, the Monkey, and the Pig: A Fable," and "Hints, by the Late Dr. Franklin."

CHAPTER 3
Reading Differences Differently

1. Washington, "Letter to the Printer," 3. For an extensive discussion of this rhetoric and ideology of diffusion, see Warner, *Letters of the Republic*, 118–50.
2. Kamrath, "Eyes Wide Shut," 521. For more on the diverse content of early U.S. magazines, see Gardner, *Rise and Fall*, and Smith-Rosenberg, *This Violent Empire*.
3. "On the Rise and Progress of Magazines," 257.
4. Ibid.; "On the Utility of Well-Regulated Magazines," 8.
5. "Literary Ware-House," 254. Prominent supporters of U.S. magazines included figures such as John Dickinson, Benjamin Rush, Ezra Stiles, Tench Coxe, and Francis Hopkinson, several of whom joined George Washington in asserting their support for the magazine in the July 1788 issue of the *American Museum*. For other magazine editorials that praise the variety of the magazine's contents, see "On the Advantages of Periodical Performances"; "On Periodical Publications"; "Dialogues of the Living"; "To the Editor of the Monthly Magazine."
6. Patterson and Dougall provide a useful history of the origins of the *e pluribus unum* motto, which was featured on the title pages for the annual editions of the *Gentleman's Magazine*. See *Eagle and the Shield*, 22–25.
7. Gardner, *Rise and Fall*, 36, 77.
8. For discussions of the popularity of satire in the early United States, see Lee, "Republican Rhymes"; Schulz, "John Trumbull"; Minor, "Shaved Monkeys."
9. See *American Museum*, May 1787, 433, as well as the index for the 1788 run of the magazine, which lists "Satire" as a subject heading in the table of contents (104).
10. Palmeri, *Satire in Narrative*, 1–2. Mikhail Bakhtin's work is instrumental in examining the dialogic form and possibilities of literary forms such as satire, theater, and the novel, most notably in *The Dialogic Imagination*.
11. For a Federalist reading of *The Foresters*, see Okker, "Jeremy Belknap's Serializing the Nation"; Gardner, *Rise and Fall*, 83–84. For *The Anarchiad*, see Dowling, "Joel Barlow and *The Anarchiad*"; for *M'Fingal*, see Cowie, *John Trumbull*, especially 192–93, and Howard, *Connecticut Wits*, 75–77.
12. Numerous critics have explored the Federalist dimensions of early U.S. magazines, most notably Dowling, who coined the term "literary federalism" to describe the close relationship between early American magazine culture and Federalist Party politics in the late eighteenth and early nineteenth centuries. In *Rise and Fall* Gardner explores the Federalist ideology of early periodical culture in his chapter titled "The American Magazine in the Early National Period," esp. 73–84. See also Smith-Rosenberg, *This Violent Empire*, 27–40.
13. Gardner, *Rise and Fall*, 74.
14. "On the Advantages of Periodical Magazines," 637.

15. Free presents the most detailed study of the history, contents, and the editorial and financial status of the *Columbian Magazine* in *The Columbian Magazine and American Literary Nationalism*. See also Mott's summary in *History of American Magazines*, 94–99.

16. "Preface," *Columbian Magazine*, quoted in Free, *Columbian Magazine*, 2.

17. Free, *Columbian Magazine*, 14.

18. See Free's chapter titled "American Ideals and British Genres" for a more detailed overview of the literary contents of the *Columbian Magazine*, especially regarding its novels and short fiction, in *Columbian Magazine*, 75–102.

19. In addition to the political connections of its editors, many of the *Columbian Magazine*'s regular contributors and subscribers had close connections to the Constitutional Convention. Several were even delegates, among them Benjamin Rush, Francis Hopkinson, and Charles Thompson. See Free, *Columbian Magazine*, 45–48.

20. "Genius of Foederate America."

21. Washington, "In Convention," 665.

22. McMaster and Stone, *Pennsylvania and the Federal Constitution*, 15. More detailed information about this controversy can be found in Free, *Columbian Magazine*, 2–22, as well as Butterfield, *Letters of Benjamin Rush*, 1:450.

23. Eitner, "Jeremy Belknap's *The Foresters*," 157. Belknap's career as a historian and editor, as well as his role as a minister in New Hampshire and Massachusetts, is covered more thoroughly in Lawson, *American Plutarch*. See also Free's discussion of Belknap in *Columbian Magazine*, 28–33.

24. Belknap, *The Foresters*, June 1787, 453.

25. For scholarship that reads *The Foresters* as a work that endorses Federalist Party politics, see Gardner, *Rise and Fall*, 81–84; Okker, "Jeremy Belknap's Serializing the Nation," 42–44; Kirsch, "Jeremy Belknap," 49–50.

26. The popularity of *The Foresters* led Belknap to expand and republish the serialized edition as a full-length book in 1792, adding new chapters that carried the history of the colonies through the end of the Revolution and the establishment of national independence. The first book-length edition of *The Foresters* was published in Boston in 1792, with a second edition, considerably enlarged and revised, appearing in 1796. In the context of national debates about federalism, it was the first, shorter edition that was most directly involved in responding to and influencing debates about newly proposed federal government, and my analysis of *The Foresters* is therefore drawn from the *Columbian Magazine*'s serial publication of the narrative. For a detailed assessment of the changes that took place in the different publications of *The Foresters*, see Eitner, "Jeremy Belknap's *The Foresters*."

27. References to having the freedom to live according to their "own way" occur throughout *The Foresters*. For the first reference to this phrase, see the installments published in July 1787, 515, and August 1787, 185.

28. See *The Foresters*, February 1788, 58.

29. Belknap, *The Foresters*, June 1787, 454.

30. Ibid., July 1787, 515, 517.

31. Ibid., November 1787, 738, 741.

32. Ibid., August 1787, 567.

33. Ibid., 568.

34. Ibid., October 1787, 707–8.
35. Ibid., July 1787, 517.
36. Agrippa, "Letter VIII," 171. The "Agrippa" letters were a leading voice of Anti-Federalist arguments during the state ratifying conventions, and they were published in the *Massachusetts Gazette* from November 1787 to January 1788.
37. Agrippa, "Letter VIII," 171.
38. Belknap, *The Foresters*, August 1787, 567.
39. Ibid., December 1787, 792.
40. Ibid., 793, 792.
41. Ibid., November 1787, 738.
42. Mason, "Objections to the Proposed Constitution," 36.
43. Agrippa, "Letter IV," 167.
44. Belknap, *The Foresters*, August 1787, 565, 566.
45. Ibid., 566–67.
46. "Letter of a Democratic Federalist," 153.
47. Mason, "Objections to the Proposed Constitution," 67.
48. Belknap, *The Foresters*, November 1787, 741.
49. Ibid., December 1787, 790.
50. Ibid., August 1787, 567–68.
51. Hamilton, Federalist No. 22, 289.
52. Belknap, *The Foresters*, December 1787, 791.
53. The first installment of *The Anarchiad* was published October 26, 1786, with subsequent installments appearing on November 2 and December 28, 1786; January 11, 25, February 22, March 15, 22, April 5, May 24, August 16, and September 13, 1787.
54. Howard provides a brief discussion of the *New-Haven Gazette* in *Connecticut Wits*. More detailed information about the magazine and the literary works and political coverage it offered can be found in the issues archived in the *American Periodicals Series* database at www.proquest.com/products-services/aps.html.
55. Barlow et al., *The Anarchiad*, 461. All text quotations are taken from Parrington's edition of *The Connecticut Wits* and will be cited parenthetically in the text.
56. Humphreys, "Oration on the Political Situation," 336–37.
57. As Dowling argues, *The Anarchiad* "recover[s] a sense of Federalism as an ideology born in crisis." See *Literary Federalism*, 19. For more detailed assessments of the Federalist politics and motives of *The Anarchiad*, see also Dowling, "Joel Barlow and *The Anarchiad*" Post, "Revolutionary Dialogics"; Howard, *Connecticut Wits*, 180–200.
58. Madison, "Record of the Convention," 14.
59. Palmeri, *Satire in Narrative*, 1. See also Culler, "Convention and Naturalization"; Bogel, *Difference Satire Makes*; Griffin, *Satire*; Everett Zimmerman, *Swift's Narrative Satires*; Burke, "Why Satire."
60. Madison, Federalist No. 49, 312.
61. Madison, Federalist No. 37, 227.
62. For more on the Revolutionary politics of *M'Fingal*, see Cowie, *John Trumbull*; Howard, *Connecticut Wits*; Blakemore, "World Turned Upside Down," 103–4.
63. Trumbull commented on the altered focus of the 1782 edition in a letter to the Marquis de Chastellux, where he noted that his goal in this later edition was to satirize

both the Tories and the patriots "with as much impartiality as possible." Cowie, *John Trumbull*, 192. For more on the changes made in the 1782 edition, see Cowie, *John Trumbull*, 188–200; Grasso, "Print, Poetry, and Politics."

64. Cowie examines the publication history and popularity of *M'Fingal* from the 1770s through the early 1800s in *John Trumbull*, 188–92.

65. Noah Webster, *Grammatical Institute*, 3–4, 106–7.

66. For more on the popularity and prevalence of *M'Fingal* during the constitutional debates, see Howard's chapter on John Trumbull in *Connecticut Wits*.

67. "Contents," May 1787, 384.

68. The *New-Haven Gazette* reprinted selections from *M'Fingal* in its August 24 and September 21, 1786, issues, and the *Massachusetts Centinel* published selections in its January 2 and January 26, 1788, issues. See Cowie, *John Trumbull*, 193–94.

69. Trumbull, *M'Fingal*, 22, 21. Subsequent references will be given parenthetically in the text. Irvin offers a helpful description of the way Congress represented itself in the early United States in *Clothed in Robes of Sovereignty*, 1–18.

70. Brutus, "Letter I," 18.

71. Madison, "Record of the Convention," 31.

72. Cowie discusses the use of "M'Fingalick" and "M'Fingalism" as popular terms in *John Trumbull*, 193–94.

73. Gardner, *Rise and Fall*, 103.

74. From *New-England Magazine* (1758), quoted in Gardner, *Rise and Fall*, 63. Gardner focuses specifically on the interactive demands that periodicals placed on their readers, see especially 22–23 and 63–64.

75. For a thorough discussion of the goals and purpose of this magazine, see Matthew Carey's "Preface," which was featured in the June 1787 issue of the *American Museum*.

76. See "Papers Reflecting the Late Private Transactions," 447–51.

77. "Documents Respecting the Battles," 79–87.

78. "Rural Concerns," 324–26.

79. "Account of Jemimah Wilkinson," 151.

80. "To the Printer," March 1787, 219–20.

81. "To the Printer," April 1787, 333–35.

82. "Albany Papers," 190–95.

83. Mott, *History of American Magazines*, 65.

84. *Gentleman and Lady's Town and Country Magazine*, May 1784, 2. For more on women and early U.S. magazines, see Branson, *These Fiery, Frenchified Dames*, 23–27.

85. Branson, *These Fiery, Frenchified Dames*, 23.

86. Skemp, *First Lady of Letters*, 347.

87. For biographical information about Judith Sargent Murray, see Skemp, *First Lady of Letters*; Harris, *Selected Writings*, xv–xliv.

88. For more on the representation of women in the U.S. Constitution, see Jan Lewis, "'Of Every Age.'"

89. Women who were unmarried or widowed occupied a more uncertain status regarding their representation, though most were assumed to be represented by their fathers, brothers, or sons. For more on the status of women and the ideology of coverture in the early United States, see Norton, *Liberty's Daughters*; Kerber, *Women of the Republic*; Dillon, *Gender of Freedom*.

90. Kerber discusses this criticism of the logic of coverture in the early republic in "Paradox of Women's Citizenship," 352.

91. Murray, "On the Equality," 10. Subsequent references will be given parenthetically within the text.

92. For more on Murray's engagement with the concept of republican motherhood, see Skemp, *First Lady of Letters*, 178–210.

93. Murray, *Gleaner*, "No. I," 17.

94. Baym, "Introduction," xiii.

95. Murray, *Gleaner*, "No. XXXIV," 286.

96. Ibid., "No. IV," 35. Disiderio also explores the way the *Gleaner* essays emphasize networks of interaction as a means of fostering union, arguing that Murray's work "imagines a complex system of exchange between Americans in an effort to maintain cohesion and unity." Disiderio, "Periodical," 19.

97. The Gleaner specifically engages with the federal structure of the United States in "No. XXVI" and "No. XXVII," which are often published together as a complete essay titled "Sketch of the Present Situation in America, 1794." Disiderio also examines the connections between Murray's discussion of federalism and the form of the *Gleaner* essays.

98. Murray, *Gleaner*, "No. XXVII," 215, 218; "No. XXVI," 210.

99. Ibid., "No. XXVII," 214, 222, 218.

CHAPTER 4
Concurrent Sentimentality

1. Rowlandson, *True History*, 50. Subsequent references will be given parenthetically within the text.

2. Goodman examines how Rowlandson readily returns to the values and customs of her English colonial community despite the different behaviors and ideas she relied upon during her captivity. See "'Money Answers All Things,'" 5.

3. Kollock, *True Narrative*, 110.

4. Gay, *Genuine and Correct Account*, 102.

5. Fletcher, *Narrative of the Captivity*, 72.

6. See Logan, "Cross-Cultural Conversations," for a useful overview of the way critics have focused on the "transcultural" dimensions of captivity narratives. For the lack of conversion or assimilation in captivity narratives, see Goodman, "'Money Answers All Things,'" 5–6; Derounian-Stoloda, "Captivity and the Literary Imagination"; Toulouse, *Captive's Position*.

7. Rawls uses the term "overlapping consensus" to describe the way decisions and, ultimately, laws are made and justified within modern, pluralistic systems of government. Arguing that absolute, uniform agreement cannot be achieved in modern, organized societies, Rawls suggests that collective decisions and positions can be established by drawing on a range of different interests and logical arguments, which, while different, can nevertheless be directed to arrive at shared points of agreement. By referring to this agreement as an "overlapping" consensus, Rawls's model accounts for existence of real and continuing differences within a pluralist society while also acknowledging the unity that also emerges within them. See Rawls, "Idea of an Overlapping Consensus," as well as *Theory of Justice* and *Political Liberalism*.

8. LaCroix, *Ideological Origins of American Federalism*, 96.

9. See Williams's introduction to *Liberty's Captives* for a discussion of the close connection between captivity narratives and the discourse of liberty and independence (1–16).

10. For foundational studies regarding the relationship of captivity narratives to the discourse of sentiment and modern formulations of liberal citizenship, see Burnham, *Captivity and Sentiment*; Armstrong and Tennenhouse, *Imaginary Puritan*.

11. Sieminski, "Puritan Captivity Narrative," 44.

12. Davidson, *Revolution and the Word*, 64.

13. Franklin, *Examination of Doctor Benjamin Franklin*, 14–15. Examples of this "part to whole" rhetoric can be found in the writings of Richard Bland of Virginia, James Otis of Massachusetts, Daniel Dulany of Maryland, and John Dickinson of Pennsylvania, who all published pamphlets and essays about the relationship of the colonies to the mother country during this period, with Dickinson's *Letters from a Farmer in Pennsylvania* being one of the most widely known. For more on these writings, see LaCroix's chapter titled "Dividing Lawmaking Power" in *Ideological Origins of American Federalism*, esp. 46–67.

14. Franklin, *Examination of Doctor Benjamin Franklin*, 13.

15. See Loyal Patriot, *Some Observations*, 22.

16. *Pennsylvania Gazette*, April 19, 1786, 3. Peskin addresses how the Barbary captivity crisis raised questions about the viability of the federal republic in *Captives and Countrymen*, 99–100.

17. "Washington's Farewell Address" was originally printed in the *American Daily Advertiser* on September 19, 1796, and was widely reprinted in other U.S. newspapers throughout the year.

18. Salisbury, "Mary Rowlandson," 49. See also Derounian-Stoloda, "Publication," 255–57; Burnham, *Captivity and Sentiment*, 13–14; Mott, *Story of Best Sellers*, 303.

19. "Preface to the Reader," 11.

20. Sieminski examines the different images used in the frontispiece for Rowlandson's narrative, particularly their similarity to depictions of the Boston Massacre. See "Puritan Captivity Narrative," 38–43. See also Burnham's chapter titled "Captivity, Cultural Contact, and Commodification" in *Captivity and Sentiment*, esp. 10–14.

21. Burnham and Sieminski both examine the "ideological usefulness" of Rowlandson's text in the context of the colonial revolution. See Burnham, *Captivity and Sentiment*, 49; Sieminski, "Puritan Captivity Narrative," 44.

22. Hosmer, *Life of Thomas Hutchinson*, 372.

23. Ibid., 412.

24. LaCroix, *Ideological Origins of American Federalism*, 103.

25. Bradford, *Speeches of the Governors*, 354.

26. Fritz, *American Sovereigns*, 194, 6.

27. Hamilton, "Hamilton's Opinion."

28. Quoted in Sean Wilentz, *Rise of American Democracy*, 65.

29. Ibid., 64.

30. Logan, "Mary Rowlandson's Captivity," 274.

31. Gay, *Genuine and Correct Account*, 10; Kollock, *True Narrative*, 115.

32. For a thorough analysis of Maria Kittle's narrative, see Rex, "Revising the Nation"; Burnham, *Captivity and Sentiment*, 92–96.

33. For feminist readings of *A Surprising Account*, see Kolodny, "Turning the Lens"; Pratt, "Pleasure of Being Lost."

34. The biblical reference here is to Matthew 35:25, "For I was hungry and you gave me something to eat, I was thirsty and you gave me something to drink, I was a stranger and you invited me in."

35. Shuffelton, introduction to *Mixed Race*, 10. See also Cairney, "Need for Strangeness"; Simpson, "From White into Red."

36. *Wonderful Escape of Dr. Knight*, 37, 36.

37. Boone's narrative originally appeared in John Filson's *Discovery*, 66.

38. Anderson, "Red Crosscurrents," 24. Anderson provides a detailed analysis of the "cross-cultural" engagements in Dickinson's work that lead to an altered and increasingly positive understanding of the relationship between white and native communities.

39. Dickinson, *God's Protecting Providence*, 47, 63.

40. Logan, "Cross-Cultural Conversations," 473.

41. *Surprising Account*, 40.

42. Decalves, *New Travels to the Westward*, 30, 26.

43. Royall Tyler, *Algerine Captive*, 225. Subsequent references will be given parenthetically within the text. Underhill's emphasis on the nation's international authority can be linked to the push for a national naval force. Peskin examines the novel's engagement with the politics of U.S. military development in *Captives and Countrymen*, 130–33.

44. For scholarship that interprets Underhill's reference to "federalism" as an expression of generic nationalist sentiments, see Gardner, *Master Plots*, 36–50; Schöpp, "Liberty's Sons and Daughters," 291–307; Dennis, "Legitimizing the Novel," 71–80. Margulis and Proietti likewise read the novel's ending as an attempt to recover a sense of unified American patriotism, albeit a conflicted one, as does Watts. See Margulis, "Spies, Pirates, and White Slaves," 25–29; Proietti, "Sailing across the Color Line," 331–32; Watts, *Writing and Postcolonialism*, 73–94. Only Davidson comments specifically on the novel's use of the term "federal," and, even then, it is only in passing, noting that the "'federalism' here recommended is open-minded, pluralistic, democratic, and utterly opposed to oligarchy or autocracy, to one people's dominating over one another." Davidson, *Revolution and the Word*, 303.

45. Armstrong and Tennenhouse, "Problem of Population."

46. For examples of this older model of interpretation regarding *The Algerine Captive*, see Tanselle, *Royall Tyler*, 140–79, and Dennis, "Legitimizing the Novel," 71–80. More recently, Davidson argues that the novel's multiple styles, locations, and perspectives present "a mirror version of America" that "extend[s] and exaggerate[s] the same hierarchies dividing the American political and social scene," *Revolution and the Word*, 302, a perspective echoed by Gardner, *Master Plots*, 40–46, 73–80; Watts, *Writing and Postcolonialism*, 73–94; Proietti, "Sailing across the Color Line," 526–27.

47. See Tanselle, *Royall Tyler*, 163; Margulis, "Spies, Pirates, and White Slaves," 17, 21–22; Wood, "Alien's Act of Sedition," 327.

48. Onuf, "Federalism," 27.

49. Jay, Federalist No. 2, 32. This federal emphasis on transregional interaction found particular expression in government plans for transportation networks during this time, which John Larson explores in *Internal Improvement*.

50. Madison, "Debates of the Federal Convention," 3:1389.
51. Fehrenbacher, *Slaveholding Republic*, 10. For more on the "federal consensus," see Wiecek, *Sources of Anti-Slavery Constitutionalism*, and Fehrenbacher's introduction to *Slaveholding Republic*, 3–14.
52. Rice, "Slavery Inconsistent," 14–15. For more on antislavery rhetoric and the revolutionary rhetoric of equality, see David Brion Davis, *Problem of Slavery*; MacLeod, *Slavery*.
53. Miflin, *Serious Expostulation*, 12.
54. Madison, "Debates of the Federal Convention," 3:1389.
55. Royall Tyler, "Selectmen v. Jacob," 200. Tanselle discusses Tyler's 1802 decision in *Royall Tyler*, 41–42.
56. Peskin, *Captives and Countrymen*, 72.
57. Baepler, *White Slaves*, 29.
58. For discussions of this shift in focus, see Margulis, "Spies, Pirates, and White Slaves," 2–6; Wood, "Alien's Act of Sedition," 325–26.
59. Davidson, *Revolution and the Word*, 208.
60. Baepler, *White Slaves, African Masters*, 46–47.
61. Marr explores how Islam was typically represented as the antithesis of American values and principles in U.S. popular culture, such that "while Islam signified antichristian imposture, America promised Christian purity; while Islam meant barbaric despotism, America cherished enlightened democracy." Marr, *Cultural Roots of American Islamicism*, 10.
62. In noting this shift, it is important to emphasize that Underhill's "authentic portrait" of Algiers is a representation. Tyler never set foot in Algiers, and scholars have noted that his material for the Algerine portion of the novel is drawn from a variety of secondhand sources, most notably Foss, *Journal*; Carey, *Short Account of Algiers*; Markoe, *Algerine Spy in Pennsylvania*; Stevens, *Historical and Geographical Account*.
63. Fliegelman, *Declaring Independence*, 54. See also Gustafson, *Eloquence Is Power*; Looby, *Voicing America*.
64. Madison, Federalist No. 39, 240.

CHAPTER 5
Federalism Redux

1. For an excellent discussion of the commemorative and critical dimensions of this "Jubilee" year marking the fiftieth anniversary of independence, see Burstein, *America's Jubilee*.
2. Jefferson, "Second Inaugural Address."
3. Hsu, *Geography*, 3; Pratt, *Archives of American Time*.
4. Hsu, *Geography*, 7; Baker, *Heartless Immensity*, 1.
5. Luciano, introduction to Luciano and Wilson, *Unsettled States*, 3, 5.
6. See Watts, *American Colony*; LeMenager, *Manifest and Other Destinies*; Doolen, *Territories of Empire*.
7. Rather than focusing on how the West was involved with the logic and rhetoric of imperial exceptionalism, Watts argues that western writers engaged in forms of postcolonial resistance, representing the West in terms that would criticize and counteract

the imperial influences and policies set by the eastern states. See Watts, *American Colony* and *In This Remote Country*.

8. Doolen, *Territories of Empire*, 4–5.

9. Flint, "National Character," 133.

10. Hall, "Conditions and Influence," 398.

11. "Thoughts on a National University," part 2, 372.

12. Flint, *Condensed Geography*, 205.

13. Hall, "New Year," 52.

14. For more on the emergence of the term "sectionalism" in the context of regional divisions in the United States in the early nineteenth century, see Onuf, "Federalism."

15. "Thoughts on a National University," part 2, 371.

16. Castiglia, *Interior States*, 3. For a more extended discussion of Castiglia's arguments about institutionalism in the nineteenth-century United States and the production of this "federal affect," see the chapter titled "'Matters of Internal Concern': Federal Affect and the Melancholy Citizen," esp. 17–30.

17. For biographical background on Timothy Flint, see Kirkpatrick, *Timothy Flint*; Venable, chapter 11 in *Beginnings of Literary Culture*; Folsom, *Timothy Flint*.

18. Flint, "Editor's Address," May 1827, 9, 10, 16.

19. Flint, "Impediments of American Literature," 482.

20. Ibid., 484.

21. Flint, "Editor's Address," May 1827, 18.

22. Flint, "Progress of the West," 26. Scholars have often commented on the breadth and depth of the *Western Monthly Review*'s western coverage. See Folsom, *Timothy Flint*, 64–65; Chielens, *American Literary Magazines*, 448–49; Watts, *American Colony*, 124–29.

23. "Advertisement to *Western Monthly Review*," iii.

24. Flint, "Writers of the Western Country," 12.

25. For critical background on the 1828 tariff controversy, see Ellis, *Union at Risk*; McDonald, *States' Rights and the Union*; Brooks, *Webster-Hayne Debate*.

26. Flint, "To the Public," 367, 368.

27. Ibid, 368.

28. Ibid.

29. Flint chose to include British and French reviews as part of his comprehensive critical digest because he felt these works continued to play an important role in defining the national character of U.S. literature. The focus on French reviews would have been relevant for many in the West due to the former French colonial status of several states in this region, particularly Louisiana, and his decision to include British reviews likewise reveals the extent to which U.S. national literature was still heavily dependent on British views and assessments.

30. For examples of Flint's use of the short digest format, see "Notices," March 1828, 691–94; "Notices of Works Lately Published," 304; "Notices," October 1828, 290; "Notices of Periodical Works," 535–36. For longer reviews of single periodicals or articles, representative examples include "Paul and Virginia," October 1828, 281–86; "Southern Review, No. 4," 405–18; "Pandect," 460–63; "Requiem," 592.

31. See Chielens, *American Literary Magazines*, 447–50.

32. Flint, "Notices of Periodical Works," 535; "Notices," October 1828, 290.

33. Flint, "Southern Review, No. 4," 405, 406.

34. Flint, "Paul and Virginia," 282, 285. The French novel *Paul et Virginia* by Jacques-Henri Bernardin de Saint-Pierre was originally written in 1788 and translated into English by Helen Maria Williams in 1795. The novel was a huge hit in the United States and was continually reprinted throughout the early nineteenth century.

35. Ibid., 285.

36. Flint, "Editor's Address," May 1827, 11.

37. Flint, "Impediments of American Literature," 484, 486.

38. For more on Calhoun's arguments for Nullification and national and congressional debates, see Niven, *John C. Calhoun*; Freehling, *Prelude to Civil War*.

39. Flint, "National Character," 133–34.

40. "Thoughts on a National University," part 2, 373.

41. Castiglia, *Interior States*, 20.

42. "Thoughts on a National University," part 2, 371.

43. Ibid., 369–70.

44. Ibid.

45. Flint, "To Our Readers," 480.

46. Flint, "Impediments of American Literature," 485.

47. Flint, "Present Population," 334.

48. Aaron, *Cincinnati*, 7.

49. Castiglia, *Interior States*, 4, 7.

50. Picket, "Opening Address," 36.

51. For more on Cincinnati's institutions of higher learning, see Drake and Mansfield, *Cincinnati in 1826*, 39–43.

52. *Cincinnati Directory* (1819), quoted in Aaron, *Cincinnati*, 207.

53. Aaron, *Cincinnati*, 44.

54. Drake and Mansfield offer a detailed discussion of Cincinnati museums and libraries in *Cincinnati in 1826*, 44–47. See also Aaron, *Cincinnati*, 130–38.

55. Aaron, *Cincinnati*, 113. As Kelley observes, these social clubs and organizations "sanctioned and supported intellectual engagement and productivity" using informal collaborative practices, which made them particularly effective for defining local and national identities and setting standards for civil society. Kelley, *Learning to Stand and Speak*, 4–5.

56. Drake and Mansfield, *Cincinnati in 1826*, 90.

57. The full name of the Western Literary Institute is the Western Literary Institute and the College of Professional Teachers. For more on the history and structure of these organizations, see Eckelberry, "Western Literary Institute"; Hendrickson, "Western Academy."

58. See statement in the organization's original constitution, published in *Transactions of the Ninth and Tenth Annual Meetings*.

59. Aaron, *Cincinnati*, 222–23.

60. "Transactions of the Fourth Annual Meetings," 260.

61. See Aaron, *Cincinnati*, 131–37.

62. Ray, *Lyceum and Public Culture*, 131–35.

63. "Introductory Discourse," 165.

64. Mansfield, *Personal Memories*, 263, 174, 175.

65. For more on the history of the Semi-Colon Club and its members, see Tucker, "Semi-Colon Club." See also Venable, *Beginnings of Literary Culture*, 418–20; Aaron, *Cincinnati*, 268–70.

66. Beecher, *Plea for the West*, 46.

67. Hall, "Plea for the West," 321.

68. "Buckeye Dinner," 152, 148, 151.

69. Waldstreicher, *In the Midst*, 18.

70. Daniel Drake, "Remarks," 342, 343.

71. Ibid., 347.

72. See Van Atta, "Western Lands."

73. Daniel Drake, "Remarks," 347.

74. Ibid., 349. For a more detailed account of the history of European immigration in the West, see Rohrbough, *Trans-Appalachian Frontier*, 63–172, 323–27.

75. Daniel Drake, "Discourse," 357.

76. Ibid., 367.

77. Beecher, *Plea for the West*, 51, 40, 46, 32, 52.

78. Watts reads this western regionalism in postcolonial rather than federal terms, although these ideological frameworks are not necessarily antithetical. See *American Colony* and *In This Remote Country*.

79. Gallagher, "Sketches and Response," 211.

80. For more on Gallagher's life and radical politics, see Venable, *Beginnings of Literary Culture*, 486–70; Watts, *American Colony*, 148–53.

81. Benjamin Drake, *Life and Adventures of Black Hawk*, 48. Drake also notes his emphasis on providing a "full and faithful history" of Tecumseh's native community in *Life of Tecumseh*, 59.

82. Watts, *American Colony*, 102.

83. Benjamin Drake, *Life of Tecumseh*, 230; *Life and Adventures of Black Hawk*, 6.

84. Benjamin Drake, *Life and Adventures of Black Hawk*, 7.

85. Benjamin Drake, *Life of Tecumseh*, 229; *Life and Adventures of Black Hawk*, 7.

86. Hall's eldest brother, John Hall, served as chief editor of the *Port-Folio* from 1816 to 1827. For Hall's connection to the *Port-Folio* magazine, see Randall, "Authors of the *Port Folio*." For more on Hall's biography, see Venable, *Beginnings of Literary Culture*, 361–85; Watts, *American Colony*, 129–30.

87. See also Ralph Thompson, *American Literary Annuals*, and Faxon, *Literary Annuals and Gift Books*.

88. "Western Souvenir," 40. *The Western Souvenir* featured more than fifty stories and poems by western writers, including five of Hall's own short stories and works by Timothy Flint, Benjamin Drake, and Morgan Neville.

89. Hall, "Preface," 3; Hall, "Editor's Message," 93. I will refer to Hall's magazine solely as the *Western Monthly Magazine* in this chapter because it was principally known by this name, although my citations will reflect the specific title for each reference.

90. Hall, "Preface," 2–3.

91. Hall, "To the Reader," 2.

92. Hall, "Budget," 190–91.

93. For more on the magazine's varied content, see Hall's overview of his contributors in "Editor's Message," 95.

94. Hall, "Editor's Message," 95.

95. Hall, "New Year," 52.

96. Hall, "Essay on Criticism," 16.

97. Hall's critical review of "A Plea for the West" appeared in May 1835 and his essay "The Catholic Question" in June 1835. Hall, "Plea for the West," 323.

98. Hall, "Plea for the West," 325.

99. Ibid., 323.

100. Hall, "Editorial Remarks," 242, 241.

101. Watts, *In This Remote Country*, 182, 207.

102. "The Intestate" appears in *Illinois Monthly Magazine*, February 1831, 193–202; "The Village Musician" appears in *Illinois Monthly Magazine*, January 1831, 158–72; "Isabelle and Her Sister Kate and Their Cousin" appears in *Western Monthly Magazine*, February 1834, 72–75; "James Kirkwood" appears in *Western Monthly* Magazine, August 1834, 423–29.

103. See Watts, *In This Remote Country*; Doolen, *Territories of Empire*, especially chaps. 3 and 4.

104. Doolen, *Territories of Empire*, 6; Watts, *In This Remote Country*, 14.

105. "The Intestate," 201. See also Russell, "The Spectre Hunter."

106. Hall, "Legend of Carondelet," 98.

107. Tandy discusses how names were used to connote certain regional types, particularly the biblical and Protestant names of the Yankee type in *Crackerjack Philosophers*.

108. Hall, "Legend of Carondelet," 100–101.

109. Ibid., 103–4.

110. For more on the history of French cultural stereotypes in U.S. literature and culture, see Chew's introduction to *National Stereotypes in Perspective*, 1–54, and Featherstone's analysis of the way regional identities are imagined through forms of exaggeration, performance, and conflict in *Localism, Globalism, and Cultural Identity*, 54–55.

111. Hall, "Legend of Carondelet," 109.

112. Ibid., 101.

113. Watts, *In This Remote Country*, 13.

114. Hall, "Legend of Carondelet," 104.

115. Ibid., 109.

116. Hall, "French Village," 123, 130, 137.

117. Hall, "Michel de Coucy," 342. Subsequent references will be given parenthetically within the text.

118. *Cherokee Nation v. Georgia*, 30 U.S. 5 Pet. 11 (1831).

119. For discussions of the *Cherokee Nation v. Georgia* decision, particularly the interpretive bias and exclusions at work, see McLoughan, *Cherokee Renascence*; Newmyer, "John Marshall's Last Campaign."

120. While "Michel de Coucy" seems to comment specifically on the Cherokee appeals to the U.S. Supreme Court, we might also consider this story in relation to disputes over treaty agreements that led to the Black Hawk War. In 1828 trouble was brewing as Black Hawk led a band of Sauk across the Mississippi from Iowa to reclaim

land in Illinois in protest against a problematic land settlement negotiated by the 1804 Treaty of St. Louis. When "Michel de Coucy" was written, this conflict was in its earliest stages, and readers in the western United States, surrounded by memories of armed conflicts over treaty agreements and new possibilities for legal conflicts, would have noted this story, which identifies the courts as a peaceful and effective way to resolve Native American conflicts, provided, of course, that the U.S. government would extend them just and equal representation. For more on the Black Hawk War, see Jung, *Black Hawk War of 1832*.

121. Other articles in the *Western Monthly Magazine* that exhibit similar stereotypical depictions of Native American violence include Peck, "Historical Sketch," 74; "Sketch of the Life of General Harrison," 116.

122. Hall, "Kickapoo Sermon," 473. For other similar depictions, see "Young Warriors"; "Reminiscence of the Scioto Valley"; "Wood River Massacre"; "History of Ohio, Ch. III"; "History of Ohio, Ch. V"; "Historical and Scientific Sketches of Michigan."

123. Hall, "Indian Biography," 48.

124. Hall, "On the Intercourse," 1:352. Subsequent references will be given parenthetically within the text, by part number and page number.

125. McKenney and Hall, *History of the Indian Tribes*, 10.

126. Hall, "Indian Hating," 403–8; Hall, "Indian Hater."

127. Hall, "Indian Hating," 404.

128. Hall, "Indian Hater," 10, 11.

EPILOGUE
The Failure of Federal Literacy

1. Boudinot, "Prospectus," 3.

2. Wyss, *English Letters and Indian Literacies*, 6, 18. Round also explores this issue of duality and rhetorical manipulation in *Removable Type*.

3. The Cherokee syllabary was developed by a Cherokee silversmith named Sequoyah between 1810 and 1820. For more on the history of the syllabary and its influence on Cherokee print culture, see Cushman, *Cherokee Syllabary*.

4. Boudinot, "Prospectus," 3.

5. Wyss's distinctions between "Readerly" and "Writerly" Indians, which address the ways that Native American writers represented themselves in order to meet white expectations and ideals for Native American identities and culture ("Readerly") and how they represented themselves in ways to argue for native authority, sovereignty, and equality ("Writerly") offers a useful framework for considering the critical dynamics of the bilingual structure of the Cherokee Phoenix. See *English Letters and Indian Literacies*, 6–10.

6. "Constitution of the Cherokee Nation," 1.

7. Lumpkin, *Removal*, 150.

8. "Constitution of the Cherokee Nation," 1.

9. Ibid. Restrictions on the office of the principal chief can be found in Article IV, sec. 2. The "necessary and proper" clause appears in Article III, sec. 16, and the Cherokee "Bill of Rights" appears in Article VI.

10. Boudinot, "Cherokee Laws," 1.

11. Boudinot, "Communications: Cherokee Constitution," 2.
12. Boudinot, "Georgia and the Cherokees," 2.
13. Ibid.
14. Boudinot, "Gov. Forsyth's Message," 2.
15. "Indians Memorial of the Cherokee Legislature," 3. A survey of the electronic archive of the *Cherokee Phoenix* available through Western Carolina University reveals that, between 1828 and 1834, the newspaper published 10 articles citing language from the Treaty of Hopewell, 15 articles citing language from the Treaty of Holston, 26 articles citing language from the Treaties of Tellico, 16 articles citing language from the Treaty of the Chickasaw Council, and 25 articles citing language from the Treaties of Washington.
16. "The Cherokee Indians, Concluded," 1.
17. "Present Crisis," 1.
18. "Indians Memorial of the Cherokee Legislature," 2.
19. Boudinot, "To the Public," 1.
20. Boudinot, "From the Editor," 1.
21. "General Council Message," 2.
22. Rhonda, "'We Have a Country,'" 746.
23. Quoted in Harry L. Watson, *Liberty and Power*, 110.
24. Cass, "Documents and Proceedings."
25. Jackson, "Fifth Annual Message to Congress," 1021–22.
26. For Walker's biography and activism, see Hinks, *To Awaken My Afflicted Brethren*.
27. Walker, *Appeal*, 70.
28. McRae, "James F. McRae to Gov. John Owen," 323.
29. Quoted in Wilentz, "Mysteries of David Walker," vii.
30. Garrison, "Walker's Appeal," 6. For more on the public reception of Walker's *Appeal*, see Hinks, *To Awaken My Afflicted Brethren*, 116–72.
31. Wilentz, "Mysteries of David Walker," xvii; Walker, *Appeal*, 75, 72. Apap also addresses Walker's support for the political philosophy and ideas underlying the United States. See "'Let No Man of Us,'" 338–40.
32. Walker, *Appeal*, 1. Subsequent citations will be given parenthetically within the text.
33. For additional studies of Walker's engagement with Jefferson's arguments in *Notes on the State of Virginia*, see Peter Thompson, "David Walker's Nationalism"; Jarret, "'To Refute Mr. Jefferson's Arguments.'"
34. Apap explores Walker's efforts to promote a revised sense of federal pluralism, noting how "Walker argued for the ways that a different, racially heterogenous America might develop." Apap, "'Let No Man of Us,'" 342.
35. Ibid., 341.
36. See Apess's arguments in "An Indian's Looking-Glass for the White Man" and critical studies of his rhetorical strategies in Gura, "Son of the Forest"; Lopenzina, *Through an Indian's Looking-Glass*. For Apess's strategic use of the principles of federalism in *Indian Nullification*, see Dahl, "Nullifying Settler Colonialism"; Gaul, "Dialogue and Public Discourse."
37. Evarts, "Present Crisis," 4. See also the twenty-four "William Penn" essays protesting U.S. Indian removal policies, which were published in magazines throughout

the United States, including the *Cherokee Phoenix*. For critical background, see Prucha, *Cherokee Removal*.

38. Wisecup, "Practicing Sovereignty," 32, 33.

39. For studies of the rhetorical strategies in the "Declaration of Rights and Sentiments," see Martha Solomon Watson, "Dynamics of Intertextuality"; David Henry, "Garrison at Philadelphia."

BIBLIOGRAPHY

Aaron, Daniel. *Cincinnati: Queen City of the West: 1819–1838*. Columbus: Ohio State University, 1992.
Abernathy, David. *The Dynamics of Global Dominance: European Overseas Empires, 1415–1980*. New Haven, Conn.: Yale University Press, 2002.
"Account of Jemimah Wilkinson." *American Museum*, February 1787, 151–53.
Adams, John. "Letter to Samuel Osgood, 14 November 1775." In *Letters of Delegates to Congress, 1774–1789*, vol. 2, edited by Paul H. Smith, Gerard W. Gawalt, Rosemary Fry Plakas, and Eugene R. Sheridan, 342. Washington, D.C.: Library of Congress, 1976–96.
Adams, John Quincy. *Memoirs of John Quincy Adams*, vol. 5, edited by Charles Francis Adams. Philadelphia: J. B. Lippincott, 1875.
"Advertisement to the First Volume of the *Western Monthly Review*." *Western Monthly Review*, May 1827.
Agrippa. "Letter IV," December 3, 1787. In Lewis, *Anti-Federalists versus Federalists*, 166–67.
———. "Letter VIII," December 25, 1787. In Lewis, *Anti-Federalists versus Federalists*, 170–72.
"The Albany Papers." *American Museum*, February 1789, 190–95.
The Albany Plan of Union. 1754. The Avalon Project: Documents in Law, History, and Diplomacy. October 10, 2010. http://avalon.law.yale.edu/18th_century/albany.asp.
Althusius, Johannes. *Politica Methodice Digesta, Atque Exemplis Sacris et Profanis Illustrata*. Translated by Frederick S. Carney. 1603; Indianapolis: Liberty Fund, 1995.
Anderson, Eric Gary. "Red Crosscurrents: Performative Spaces and Indian Cultural Authority in the Florida Atlantic Captivity Narrative of Jonathan Dickinson." *Mississippi Quarterly* 65, no. 1 (Winter 2012): 17–32.
Andrews, William. "Benjamin Banneker's Revision of Thomas Jefferson: Conscience vs. Science in the Early American Anti-Slavery Debate." In *Genius in Bondage: Literature of the Early Black Atlantic*, edited by Vincent Caretta and Philip Gould, 218–40. Lexington: University Press of Kentucky, 2001.

Apap, Christopher. "'Let No Man of Us Budge One Step': David Walker and the Rhetoric of African American Emplacement." *Early American Literature* 46, no. 2 (2011): 319–50.

Apess, William. *Indian Nullification of the Unconstitutional Laws of Massachusetts*. In *On Our Own Ground: The Complete Writings of William Apess, A Pequot*. edited by Barry O'Connell, 163–274. 1835; Amherst: University of Massachusetts Press, 1992.

———. "An Indian's Looking-Glass for the White Man." In *On Our Own Ground: The Complete Writings of William Apess, a Pequot*, edited by Barry O'Connell, 155–61. 1833; Amherst: University of Massachusetts Press, 1992.

Armstrong, Nancy, and Leonard Tennenhouse. *The Imaginary Puritan: Literature, Intellectual Labor, and the Origins of Personal Life*. Berkeley: University of California Press, 1994.

———. "The Problem of Population and the Form of the American Novel." *American Literary History* 20, no. 4 (Winter 2008): 667–85.

Arnebeck, Bob. *Through a Fiery Trial: Building Washington DC, 1790–1800*. New York: Madison, 1991.

Articles of Confederation. March 1, 1781. The Avalon Project: Documents in Law, History, and Diplomacy. October 10, 2010. http://avalon.law.yale.edu/18th_century/artconf.asp.

The Articles of Confederation of the United Colonies of New England. May 19, 1643. The Avalon Project: Documents in Law, History, and Diplomacy. October 10, 2010. http://avalon.law.yale.edu/17th_century/art1613.asp.

Bacigalupo, M., and P. Castagneto, eds. *America and the Mediterranean: Proceedings of the Sixteenth Biennial International Conference, Genova, November 8–11, 2001*. Torino: Otto Editore, 2001.

Baepler, Paul, ed. *White Slaves, African Masters: An Anthology of Barbary Captivity Narratives*. Chicago: University of Chicago Press, 1999.

Baker, Anne. *Heartless Immensity: Literature, Culture, and Geography in Antebellum America*. Ann Arbor: University of Michigan Press, 2006.

Bakhtin, Mikhail. *The Dialogic Imagination: Four Essays*. Austin: University of Texas Press, 1981.

Banneker, Benjamin. *Banneker's Almanack and Ephemeris for the Year of Our Lord, 1793*. Philadelphia: Joseph Crukshank, 1793.

———. *Benjamin Banneker's Pennsylvania, Delaware, Maryland, and Virginia Almanack*. Baltimore: William Goddard & James Angell, 1792.

———. *Benjamin Banneker's Pennsylvania, Delaware, Maryland, and Virginia Almanack*. Baltimore: William Goddard & James Angell, 1793.

———. "A Copy of a Letter from Benjamin Banneker to the Secretary of State with His Answer." Philadelphia: Daniel Lawrence, 1792.

Barlow, Joel, David Humphreys, John Trumbull, and Lemuel Hopkins. *The Anarchiad* (1786–87). In *The Connecticut Wits*, edited by V. I. Parrington, 428–74. Hamden, Conn.: Archon, 1968.

Bauer, Ralph. *The Cultural Geography of Colonial American Literature*. Cambridge: Cambridge University Press, 2009.

Baym, Nina. "Introduction" to *The Gleaner* by Judith Sargent Murray. Schenectady, N.Y.: Union College Press, 1992, iii–xx.

Bedini, Silvio A. *The Life of Benjamin Banneker*. New York: Charles Scribner's Sons, 1972.

———. "The Survey of the Federal Territory: Andrew Ellicott and Benjamin Banneker." *Washington History* 3, no. 1 (Spring/Summer 1991): 76–95.
Beecher, Lyman. *A Plea for the West*. Cincinnati: Truman & Smith, 1835.
Beeman, Richard. *The Varieties of Political Experience in Eighteenth-Century America*. Philadelphia: University of Pennsylvania Press, 2004.
Belknap, Jeremy. *The Foresters*. Pts. 1–9. *Columbian Magazine*, June 1787, 453–56; July 1787, 514–17; August 1787, 565–69; September 1787, 618–22; October 1787, 706–10; November 1787, 737–41; December 1787, 790–93; February 1788, 58–60; April 1788, 183–86.
Benson, Thomas, ed. *Rhetoric and Political Culture in Nineteenth-Century America*. East Lansing: Michigan State University Press, 1997.
Berkowitz, Daniel, and Karen Clay. "State Courts." In *The Evolution of a Nation: How Geography and Law Shaped the American States*. Princeton, N.J.: Princeton University Press, 2012, 133–68.
Bhabha, Homi. *The Location of Culture*. New York: Routledge, 1994.
Bickerstaff's Boston Almanack, or, The Federal Calendar, for the Year of Our Redemption, 1788. Boston: E. Russell, 1787.
Bickerstaff's Boston Almanack, or Federal Calendar, for 1789. Boston: E. Russell, 1788.
Blakemore, Steven. "The World Turned Upside Down: Scottish 'Second Sight' and Ironic Inversion in Trumbull's *M'Fingal*." In *Literature, Intertextuality, and the American Revolution: From* Common Sense *to "Rip Van Winkle*." Madison, N.J.: Fairleigh Dickinson University Press, 2012, 27–48.
Blatchford, John. *Narrative of the Remarkable Occurrences in the Life of John Blatchford* (1788). In Williams, *Liberty's Captives*, 52–66.
Blum, Hester. *The View from the Masthead: Maritime Imagination and Antebellum Sea Narratives*. Chapel Hill: University of North Carolina Press, 2008.
Bogel, Frederick. *The Difference Satire Makes: Rhetoric and Reading from Johnson to Byron*. Ithaca, N.Y.: Cornell University Press, 2001.
Bogen, David Silken. "The Maryland Context of *Dred Scott*: The Decline in the Legal Status of Maryland Free Blacks, 1776–1810." *American Journal of Legal History* 34, no. 4 (October 1990): 381–411.
Boudinot, Elias. "Cherokee Laws." *Cherokee Phoenix*, March 13, 1828.
———. "Communications: Cherokee Constitution." *Cherokee Phoenix*, April 24, 1828.
———. "From the Editor." *Cherokee Phoenix*, January 8, 1831.
———. "Georgia and the Cherokees." *Cherokee Phoenix*, November 26, 1828.
———. "Gov. Forsyth's Message." *Cherokee Phoenix*, November 25, 1829.
———. "Prospectus." *Cherokee Phoenix*, February 28, 1828.
———. "To the Public," *Cherokee Phoenix*, November 12, 1831.
Bowles, Carington. *New Pocket Map of North America, Divided into Its Provinces, Colonies, States, &c*. London: Carington Bowles, 1784.
Bradford, Alden, ed. *Speeches of the Governors of Massachusetts from 1765–1775*. Boston: Russell & Gardner, 1818.
Branson, Susan. *These Fiery, Frenchified Dames: Women and Political Culture in Early National Philadelphia*. Philadelphia: University of Pennsylvania Press, 2001.
Breuilly, John. *Nationalism and the State*. Manchester: Manchester University Press, 1982.

Bridge, Samuel. *Samuel Bridge Diaries, 1777–98*. Mss. Octavo vol. B, no. 271272. American Antiquarian Society, Worcester, Massachusetts.

Brooks, Stefan Marc. *The Webster-Hayne Debate: An Inquiry in the Nature of Union*. Lanham, Md.: University Press of America, 2009.

Brown, Matthew. *The Pilgrim and the Bee: Reading Rituals and Print Culture in Early New England*. Philadelphia: University of Pennsylvania Press, 2007.

Brückner, Martin. *The Geographic Revolution in Early America: Maps, Literacy, and National Identity*. Chapel Hill: University of North Carolina Press, 2006.

———. "Lessons in Geography: Maps, Spellers, and Other Grammars in the Early Republic." *American Quarterly* 51, no. 2 (1999): 311–43.

———. "The Plurality of Early American Cartography." In *Early American Cartographies*, edited by Martin Brückner. Chapel Hill: University of North Carolina Press, 2011, 1–32.

Brückner, Martin, and Hsuan L. Hsu, eds. *American Literary Geographies: Spatial Practice and Cultural Production, 1500–1900*. Newark: University of Delaware Press, 2007.

Brutus. "Letter I." *New York Journal*, October 18, 1787.

Buchanan, George. *An Oration upon the Moral and Political Evil of Slavery*. Baltimore: Philip Edwards, 1793.

"The Buckeye Dinner." *Western Monthly Review*, March 1834, 145–57.

Buckler, John. "Federalism: Greek and American." *Journal of Liberal Arts* 2 (1995): 5–16.

Buell, Abel. *New and Correct Map of the United States of North America*. New Haven, Conn.: Abel Buell, 1784.

Burke, Kenneth. "Why Satire, with a Plan for Writing One." *Michigan Quarterly Review* 13 (Winter 1974): 307–37.

Burnham, Michelle. *Captivity and Sentiment: Cultural Exchange in American Literature, 1682–1861*. Dartmouth, N.H.: University Press of New England, 1997.

Burstein, Andrew. *America's Jubilee: How in 1826 a Generation Remembered Fifty Years of Independence*. New York: Knopf, 2001.

Butterfield, L. H., ed. *Letters of Benjamin Rush*, vol. 1. Princeton, N.J.: Princeton University Press, 1951.

Byrd, Jodi A. *The Transit of Empire: Indigenous Critiques of Colonialism*. Minneapolis: University of Minnesota Press, 2011.

Cairney, Christopher. "The Need for Strangeness: Captivity Narratives and Issues of Race and Gender in Early America." In *Close Encounters of an Other Kind: New Perspectives on Race, Ethnicity, and American Studies*, edited by Roy Goldblatt, Jopi Nyman, and John Stotesbury. Joensuu, Finland: University of Joensuu, 2005, 216–22.

Capp, Bernard. *Astrology and the Popular Press: English Almanacs, 1500–1800*. London: Faber & Faber, 1979.

Carey, Matthew. *A Short Account of Algiers*. Philadelphia: Matthew Carey, 1794.

Carroll, Kenneth. "Maryland Quakers and Slavery." *Quaker History* 72, no. 1 (Spring 1983): 27–42.

Carter, Robert Wormeley. Diary, 1774. Reserve 1773 06, no. 271323. American Antiquarian Society, Worcester, Massachusetts.

Cass, Lewis. "Documents and Proceedings relating to ... the Emigration, Preservation, and Improvement of the Aborigines of America." *North American Review*, January 1830, 62–120.

Castiglia, Christopher. *Interior States: Institutional Consciousness and the Inner Life of Democracy in the Antebellum United States.* Durham, N.C.: Duke University Press, 2008.

Cato. "Letter III." *New York Journal,* October 25, 1787.

Centinel. "Letter V." *Philadelphia Independent,* December 4, 1787. Reprinted in Lewis, *Anti-Federalists versus Federalists,* 144–46.

Cerami, Charles. *Benjamin Banneker: Surveyor, Astronomer, Publisher, Patriot.* New York: John Wiley & Sons, 2002.

Certeau, Michel de. *The Practice of Everyday Life.* Berkeley: University of California Press, 1984.

Chartier, Roger. *Forms and Meanings: Texts, Performances, and Audiences from Codex to Computer.* Philadelphia: University of Pennsylvania Press, 1985.

"The Cherokee Indians, Concluded." *Cherokee Phoenix,* August 12, 1829.

Cherokee Nation v. Georgia. 1831. *Legal Information Institute, Cornell University Law School.* February 12, 2011. https://www.law.cornell.edu/supremecourt/text/30/1.

Chew, William L. *National Stereotypes in Perspective: Americans in France, Frenchmen in America.* Amsterdam: Rodopi, 2001.

Chielens, Edward E. *American Literary Magazines: The Eighteenth and Nineteenth Centuries.* New York: Greenwood, 1986.

Cigrand, Bernard. J. *The Story of the Great Seal of the United States or A History of American Emblems.* Chicago: Cameron, Amberg, 1892.

Coby, Patrick. "Aristotle's Three Cities and the Problem of Faction." *Journal of Politics* 50, no. 4 (November 1988): 896–919.

Cohen, Lara Langer, and Jordan Alexander Stein. *Early African American Print Culture.* Philadelphia: University of Pennsylvania Press, 2014.

Cohen, Paul. "Abel Buell, of Connecticut, Prints America's First Map of the United States, 1784." *New England Quarterly* 86, no. 3 (September 2013): 357–97.

"Constitution of the Cherokee Nation." *Cherokee Phoenix,* February 21, 1828.

"Contents." *American Museum,* May 1787, 384.

"Contents." *American Museum,* January 1788, 104.

The Continental Almanac, for the Year of Our Lord, 1785. Philadelphia: Francis Bailey, 1784.

"The Continental Medley." *Columbian Magazine,* July 1787, 560.

Cornell, Saul. *The Other Founders: Anti-Federalism and the Dissenting Tradition in America, 1788–1828.* Chapel Hill: University of North Carolina Press, 1999.

Cowie, Alexander. *John Trumbull: Connecticut Wit.* Westport, Conn.: Greenwood, 1936.

Culler, Jonathan. "Convention and Naturalization." In *Structuralist Poetics: Structuralism, Linguistics and the Study of Literature.* Ithaca, N.Y.: Cornell University Press, 1975, 130–60.

Cushman, Ellen. *The Cherokee Syllabary: Writing the People's Perseverance.* Norman: University of Oklahoma Press, 2011.

Dahl, Adam. "Nullifying Settler Colonialism: William Apess and the Paradox of Settler Sovereignty." *Polity* 48, no. 2 (April 2016): 279–304.

Davidson, Cathy. *Revolution and the Word: The Rise of the Novel in America.* New York: Oxford University Press, 1984.

———. "Toward a History of Books and Readers." In *Reading in America,* edited by Cathy Davidson. Baltimore: Johns Hopkins University Press, 1989, 1–26.

Davis, David Brion. *The Problem of Slavery in the Age of Revolution*. New York: Oxford University Press, 1999.
Davis, Derek H. *Religion and the Continental Congress, 1774–1789*. Oxford: Oxford University Press, 2000.
Decalves, Alonso. *New Travels to the Westward*. Boston: John W. Folsom, 1788.
DeForest, John. *History of the Indians of Connecticut: From the Earliest Known Period to 1850*. Hartford, Conn.: Wm. Jas. Hamersley, 1851.
Deleuze, Gilles, and Felix Guattari. *Kafka: Toward a Minor Literature*. Minneapolis: University of Minnesota Press, 1975.
———. *A Thousand Plateaus: Capitalism and Schizophrenia*. Minneapolis: University of Minnesota Press, 1980.
Democratic Federalist. "Letter, 23 October 1787." In Lewis, *Anti-Federalists versus Federalists*, 152–57.
Dennis, Larry R. "Legitimizing the Novel: Royall Tyler's *The Algerine Captive*." *Early American Literature* 9 (1974): 71–80.
Derounian-Stodola, Kathryn. "Captivity and the Literary Imagination." In *The Cambridge Companion to Nineteenth-Century American Women's Writing*, edited by Dale M. Bauer and Philip Gould. New York: Cambridge University Press, 2001, 105–21.
———. "The Publication, Promotion, and Distribution of Mary Rowlandson's Indian Captivity Narrative in the Seventeenth Century." *Early American Literature* 23 (1988): 239–61.
———, ed. *Women's Indian Captivity Narratives*. New York: Penguin, 1998.
"Description of the City of Washington." *New York Magazine, or Literary Repository*, November 1791, 656–58.
DeWispelare, Daniel. "'What We Want in Elegance, We Gain in Copiousness': Eighteenth-Century English and the Empire of Tongues." *The Eighteenth Century* 57, no. 1 (2016): 121–40.
"Dialogues of the Living: Dialogue II." *Monthly Magazine and American Review*, February 1800, 96–99.
Dickinson, Jonathan. *God's Protecting Providence*. Philadelphia: Joseph Cruckshank, 1791.
Dillon, Elizabeth Maddock. *The Gender of Freedom: Fictions of Liberalism and the Literary Public Sphere*. Stanford, Calif.: Stanford University Press, 2004.
Disiderio, Jennifer. "The Periodical as Monitorial and Interactive Space in Judith Sargent Murray's 'The Gleaner.'" *American Periodicals* 18, no. 1 (2008): 1–25.
"Documents Respecting the Battles of Lexington and Concord." *American Museum*, January 1787, 79–87.
Doolen, Andy. *Territories of Empire: U.S. Writing from the Louisiana Purchase to Mexican Independence*. Oxford: Oxford University Press, 2014.
Doolitle, Amos. "A New Display of the United States of America." New Haven, Conn.: Amos Doolittle, 1799.
Dowling, William C. "Joel Barlow and *The Anarchiad*." *Early American Literature* 25, no. 1 (1990): 18–33.
———. *Literary Federalism in the Age of Jefferson*. Columbia: University of South Carolina Press, 1999.

Doyle, Laura. *Freedom's Empire: Race and the Rise of the Novel in Atlantic Modernity, 1640–1940.* Durham, N.C.: Duke University Press, 2007.
Drake, Benjamin. *The Life and Adventures of Black Hawk.* Cincinnati: George Conclin, 1838.
——. *Life of Tecumseh.* Cincinnati: E. Morgan, 1841.
Drake, Benjamin, and E. D. Mansfield. *Cincinnati in 1826.* Cincinnati: Morgan, Lodge & Fisher, 1827.
Drake, Daniel. "Discourse on the History, Character, and Prospects of the West" (1834). In Watts and Rachels, *First West,* 353–67.
——. "Remarks on the Importance of Promoting Literary and Social Concert in the Valley of the Mississippi" (1833). In Watts and Rachels, *First West,* 341–52.
Drake, Milton. *Almanacs of the United States.* New York: Scarecrow, 1962.
Eckelberry, R. H. "The Western Literary Institute and College of Professional Teachers." *Educational Research Bulletin* 4, no. 16 (November 1925): 333–38.
Eitner, Walter H. "Jeremy Belknap's *The Foresters*: A Thrice-Told Tale." *Early American Literature* 14, no. 2 (1979): 156–62.
Elkins, Stanley, and Eric McKitrick. *The Age of Federalism.* New York: Oxford University Press, 1993.
Ellis, Richard. *The Union at Risk: Jacksonian Democracy, States' Rights, and Nullification.* New York: Oxford University Press, 1989.
Engell, John. "Narrative Irony and National Character in Royall Tyler's *The Algerine Captive.*" *Studies in American Fiction* 17, no. 1 (Spring 1989): 19–32.
Evarts, Jeremiah. "Present Crisis in the Condition of the American Indians." In *Essays on the Present Crisis in the Condition of the American Indians.* Boston: Perkins & Marvin, 1829, 1–7.
Faden, William. *The United States of North America, with the British & Spanish Territories according to the Treaty of 1784.* London, 1785.
"The Farmer and His Thirteen Sons." *American Museum,* July 1789, 80–82.
Father Abraham's Pocket Almanack, for the Year 1777. Philadelphia: John Dunlap, 1777.
Faxon, Frederick. *Literary Annuals and Gift Books: A Bibliography, 1823–1903.* Middlesex, U.K.: Private Libraries Association, 1973.
Featherstone, Mike. *Localism, Globalism, and Cultural Identity.* Durham, N.C.: Duke University Press, 1996.
Fehrenbacher, Don E. *The Slaveholding Republic: An Account of the United States Government's Relations to Slavery.* Completed and edited by Ward M. McAfee. New York: Oxford University Press, 2001.
Filson, John. *The Discovery, Settlement, and Present State of Kentucke* (1784). In Watts and Rachels, *First West,* 59–72.
Fletcher, Ebeneezer. *A Narrative of the Captivity and Sufferings of Mr. Ebeneezer Fletcher of Newipswitch . . .* (1798). In Williams, *Liberty's Captives,* 70–81.
Fliegelman, Jay. *Declaring Independence: Jefferson, Natural Language, and the Culture of Performance.* Stanford, Calif.: Stanford University Press, 1993.
Flint, Timothy. *A Condensed Geography and History of the Western States.* Cincinnati: E. H. Flint, 1828.
——. "Editor's Address." *Western Monthly Review,* May 1827, 9–20.

———. "Editor's Address." *Western Monthly Review*, June 1828, 9–11.
———. "Impediments of American Literature." *Western Monthly Review*, February 1829, 481–86.
———. "An Introductory Discourse Delivered before the Mechanics' Institute and Chillicothe Lyceum." *Western Monthly Magazine*, March 1834, 165–66.
———. "National Character of the Western People." *Western Monthly Review*, June 1827, 133–39.
———. "Notices." *Western Monthly Review*, March 1828, 691–94.
———. "Notices." *Western Monthly Review*, October 1828, 290.
———. "Notices of Periodical Works." *Western Monthly Review*, February 1829, 535.
———. "Notices of Works Lately Published." *Western Monthly Review*, October 1828, 304.
———. "The Pandect." *Western Monthly Review*, January 1829, 460–63.
———. "Paul and Virginia." *Western Monthly Review*, October 1828, 281–86.
———. "Present Population and Future Prospects of the Western Country." *Western Monthly Review*, October 1827, 329–34.
———. "Progress of the West." *Western Monthly Review*, May 1827, 25–27.
———. "The Requiem." *Western Monthly Review*, March 1829, 592.
———. "Sketch of the Geographical Rout of a Great Railway." *Western Monthly Review*, July 1829, 19–24.
———. "Southern Review, No. 4: November 1828." *Western Monthly Review*, December 1828, 405–19.
———. "To Correspondents." *Western Monthly Review*, September 1827, 308–10.
———. "To Our Readers." *Western Monthly Review*, January 1829, 480.
———. "To the Public." *Western Monthly Review*, November 1828, 367–68.
———. "Writers of the Western Country." *Western Monthly Review*, June 1828, 11–21.
Fluck, Winfried. "From Aesthetics to Political Criticism: Theories of the Early American Novel." In Schmidt and Fleischman, *Early America Re-explored*, 225–68.
Folsom, James K. *Timothy Flint*. New York: Twayne, 1965.
Forbes, Robert Pierce. "'The Cause of This Blackness': The Early American Republic and the Construction of Race." *American Nineteenth Century History* 13, no. 1 (March 2012): 65–94.
Foss, John. *Journal of the Captivity and Sufferings of John Foss*. Newburyport, Mass.: Angier March, 1793.
Frank, Jason. *Constituent Moments: Enacting the People in Postrevolutionary America*. Durham, N.C.: Duke University Press, 2010.
Franklin, Benjamin. *The Examination of Doctor Benjamin Franklin, Before an August Assembly, Relating to the Appeal of the Stamp Act*. Philadelphia: Hall & Sellers, 1766.
———. "Reasons and Motives for The Albany Plan of Union." In *Works of Benjamin Franklin in Philosophy, Politics, and Morals*, edited by William Temple Franklin. Philadelphia: William Duane, 1809, 1–22.
Franklin, John Hope, and Alfred A. Moss. *From Slavery to Freedom: A History of African Americans*. 7th ed. New York: McGraw-Hill, 1994.
Free, William J. *The Columbian Magazine and American Literary Nationalism*. The Hague: Mouton, 1968.

Freehling, William W. *Prelude to Civil War: The Nullification Crisis in South Carolina, 1816–1836*. New York: Oxford University Press, 1965.
Freidman, Lawrence. *A History of American Law*. New York: Simon & Schuster, 1973.
Fritz, Christian. *American Sovereigns: The People and America's Constitutional Tradition before the Civil War*. New York: Cambridge University Press, 2007.
Gallagher, William Davis. "Sketches and Response." *Western Literary Journal and Monthly Review*, August 1836, 210–14.
Gardner, Jared. *Master Plots: Race and the Founding of an American Literature*. Baltimore: Johns Hopkins University Press, 1998.
———. *The Rise and Fall of Early American Magazine Culture*. Chicago: University of Illinois Press, 2012.
Garrison, William Lloyd. "Walker's Appeal." *Liberator*, January 8, 1831, 6.
Gaul, Theresa Strouth. "Dialogue and Public Discourse in William Apess's Indian Nullification." *American Transcendental Quarterly* 15, no. 4 (December 2001): 275–92.
Gay, Bunker. *A Genuine and Correct Account of the Captivity, Sufferings, and Deliverance of Mrs. Jemima Howe* (1792). In Derounian-Stodola, *Women's Indian Captivity Narratives*, 96–104.
Gellner, Ernest. *Nations and Nationalism*. Ithaca, N.Y.: Cornell University Press, 1983.
"General Council Message." *Cherokee Phoenix*, October 21, 1829.
"The Genius of Foederate America." *Columbian Magazine*, January 1789.
Geography: An Amusement, or, A Complete Set of Geographical Cards. Burlington, N.J.: Riley, 1805.
Gibbs, Caleb. Caleb Gibbs Diary, 1778. Mss. Octovo vol. G, no. 271526. American Antiquarian Society, Worcester, Massachusetts.
Go, Julian. *Patterns of Empire: The British and American Empires, 1688 to the Present*. Cambridge: Cambridge University Press, 2011.
Goodman, Nan. "'Money Answers All Things': Rethinking Economic and Cultural Exchange in the Captivity Narrative of Mary Rowlandson." *American Literary History* 22, no. 1 (2010): 1–25.
Grasso, Christopher. "Print, Poetry, and Politics: John Trumbull and the Transformation of Public Discourse in Revolutionary America." *Early American Literature* 30, no. 1 (1995): 5–31.
Greene, Jack P. "The Background of the Articles of Confederation." *Publius* 12, no. 4 (Autumn 1982): 15–44.
———. *Peripheries and Center: Constitutional Development in the Extended Polities of the British Empire and the United States, 1607–1789*. Athens: University of Georgia Press, 1986.
Griffin, Dustin. *Satire: A Critical Re-Introduction*. Lexington: University Press of Kentucky, 1994.
Grotius, Hugo. *De Jure Belli ac Pacis* (1625). Translated by A. C. Campbell. Kitchener, Ont.: Bartoche, 2001.
Gura, Philip. "Son of the Forest: William Apess and the Fight for Indigenous Rights." *New England Review* 35, no. 4 (2015): 72–81.
Gustafson, Sandra. *Eloquence Is Power: Oratory in Early America*. Chapel Hill: University of North Carolina Press, 2000.

Hall, James. "The Budget." *Western Monthly Magazine*, April 1833, 190–91.
———. "The Catholic Question." *Western Monthly Magazine*, June 1835, 375–88.
———. "The Conditions and Influence of the American Periodical Press." *Western Monthly Magazine*, August 1834, 393–407.
———. "Editorial Remarks." *Western Monthly Magazine*, April 1836, 239–43.
———. "The Editor's Message." *Western Monthly Magazine*, February 1835, 91–95.
———. "An Essay on Criticism." *Western Monthly Magazine*, January 1836, 10–24.
———. "The French Village" (1828). In Watts, *Indian Hater*, 121–38.
———. *History of the Indian Tribes of North America*. Philadelphia: E. C. Biddle, 1836–1844.
———. "Indian Biography." *Western Monthly Magazine*, January 1833, 47–48.
———. "The Indian Hater" (1828). In Watts, *Indian Hater*, 1–12.
———. "Indian Hating." *Western Monthly Magazine*, September 1833, 403–8.
———. "A Kickapoo Sermon." *Illinois Monthly Magazine*, July 1831, 473–76.
———. "The Legend of Carondelet." *Illinois Monthly Magazine*, December 1830, 97–109.
———. "Literature and Religion." *Western Monthly Magazine*, December 1833, 545–50.
———. "Michel de Coucy." *Illinois Monthly Magazine*, May 1831, 337–50.
———. "The New Year." *Western Monthly Magazine*, January 1834, 46–51.
———. "On the Formation of a National Character." *Western Monthly Magazine*, August 1833, 348–55.
———. "On the Intercourse and Prospects of the American People with the Indians." Pts. 1–4. *Illinois Monthly Magazine*, pt. 1, May 1831, 352–68; pt. 2, June 1831, 385–446; pt. 3, July 1831, 463–71; pt. 4, August 1831, 509–16.
———. "Periodical Literature." *Western Monthly Magazine*, February 1834, 57–71.
———. "A Plea for the West." *Western Monthly Magazine*, May 1835, 320–28.
———. "Preface." *Illinois Monthly Magazine*, October 1830, 1–4.
———. "To the Reader." *Western Monthly Magazine*, January 1833, 1–5.
———, ed. *Western Souvenir: Christmas and New Year's Gift*. Cincinnati: N. & G. Guilford, 1828.
———. "The Young Warriors." *Illinois Monthly Magazine*, September 1831, 571–73.
Hamilton, Alexander. Federalist No. 11. In Rossiter, *Federalist Papers*, 79–86.
———. Federalist No. 22. In Rossiter, *Federalist Papers*, 139–48.
———. Federalist No. 23. In Rossiter, *Federalist Papers*, 148–53.
———. "Hamilton's Opinion as to the Constitutionality of the Bank of the United States." 1791. The Avalon Project: Documents in Law, History, and Diplomacy. November 11, 2010. http://avalon.law.yale.edu/18th_century/bank-ah.asp.
Hardt, Michael, and Antonio Negri. *Empire*. Cambridge, Mass.: Harvard University Press, 2000.
Harris, Sharon, ed. *Selected Writings of Judith Sargent Murray*. New York: Oxford University Press, 1995.
Hechter, Michael. *Containing Nationalism*. New York: Oxford University Press, 2001.
Hendrickson, Walter B. "The Western Academy of Natural Sciences of Cincinnati." *Isis* 37, no. 3–4 (July 1947): 138–45.
Henry, David. "Garrison at Philadelphia: The 'Declaration of Sentiments' as Instrumental Rhetoric." In Benson, *Rhetoric and Political Culture*, 113–29.

Henry, Patrick. "Address to the Virginia Ratifying Convention," June 5, 1788. In *Roots of the Republic: American Founding Documents Interpreted*, edited by Stephen Schecter. New York: Rowman & Littlefield, 1991, 391–94.
Herman, David. *Narrative Theory and the Cognitive Sciences*. Stanford, Calif.: CLSI, 2003.
Hinks, Peter P. *To Awaken My Afflicted Brethren: David Walker and the Problem of Antebellum Slave Resistance*. University Park: Pennsylvania State University Press, 1997.
"Historical and Scientific Sketches of Michigan." *Western Monthly Magazine*, October 1835, 239–54.
"History of Ohio, Ch. III." *Western Monthly Magazine*, July 1833, 309–21.
"History of Ohio, Ch. V." *Western Monthly Magazine*, November 1833, 489–99.
Hope, Vincent. *Virtue by Consensus: The Moral Philosophy of Hutcheson, Hume, and Adam Smith*. New York: Oxford University Press, 1990.
Hopkinson, Francis. *Account of the Grand Federal Procession*. Philadelphia: Matthew Carey, 1788.
———. "The New Roof." *American Museum*, August 1788, 40–44.
———. "The Raising: A Song for the Federal Procession." *American Museum*, July 1788, 95.
Horrocks, Thomas. *Popular Print and Popular Medicine*. Amherst: University of Massachusetts Press, 2008.
Hosmer, James Kendall. *The Life of Thomas Hutchinson, Royal Governor of the Province of Massachusetts Bay*. New York: Houghton Mifflin, 1896.
Howard, Leon. *The Connecticut Wits*. Chicago: University of Chicago Press, 1943.
Hsu, Hsuan. *Geography and the Production of Space in Nineteenth-Century American Literature*. New York: Cambridge University Press, 2010.
Humphreys, David. "An Oration on the Political Situation of the United States." In *The Miscellaneous Works of David Humphreys*, edited by William K. Bottoroff. Gainesville, Fla.: Scholars Facsimiles and Reprints, 1968, 335–42.
Hutson, James H. "The Creation of the Constitution: The Integrity of the Documentary Record." In *Interpreting the Constitution: The Debate over Original Intent*, edited by Jack N. Rakove. Boston: Northeastern University Press, 1990, 151–78.
"Indians Memorial of the Cherokee Legislature." *Cherokee Phoenix*, April 14, 1830, 1–3.
"The Intestate." *Illinois Monthly Magazine*, February 2, 1831, 193–202.
"An Introductory Discourse Delivered before the Mechanics' Institute and Chillicothe Lyceum." *Western Monthly Magazine*, March 1834, 165.
Irvin, Benjamin H. *Clothed in Robes of Sovereignty: The Continental Congress and the People Out of Doors*. New York: Oxford University Press, 2014.
"Isabelle and Her Sister Kate and Their Cousin." *Western Monthly Magazine*, February 1834, 72–75.
Jackson, Andrew. "Fifth Annual Message to Congress, Dec. 3, 1833." In *A Compilation of Message and Papers of the Presidents*, edited by James D. Richardson, vol. 3. New York: Bureau of National Literature and Art, 1896–99, 1021–22.
Jameson, Frederic. *Postmodernism: The Cultural Logic of Late Capitalism*. New York: Verso, 1991.
"James Kirkwood." *Western Monthly Magazine*, August 1834, 423–29.
Jarret, Gene Andrew. "'To Refute Mr. Jefferson's Arguments Respecting Us': Thomas Jefferson, David Walker, and the Politics of Early African American Literature." *Early American Literature* 46, no. 2 (2011): 291–318.

Jay, John. Federalist No. 2. In Rossiter, *Federalist Papers*, 31–35.
Jefferson, Thomas. *Notes on the State of Virginia*. 1785; New York: Penguin Classics, 1999.
———. "Second Inaugural Address, March 4, 1805." The Avalon Project: Documents in Law, History, and Diplomacy. October 12, 2010. http://avalon.law.yale.edu/19th_century/jefinau2.asp.
———. "Thomas Jefferson to John Holmes, April 22, 1820." Thomas Jefferson Papers, Library of Congress. https://www.loc.gov/resource/mtj1.051_1238_1239/?st=gallery.
Jung, Patrick. *The Black Hawk War of 1832*. Norman: University of Oklahoma Press, 2008.
Kamrath, Mark. "Eyes Wide Shut and the Cultural Poetics of Eighteenth-Century American Periodical Literature." *Early American Literature* 37, no. 3 (2002): 497–536.
Kaplan, Amy. "'Left Alone with America': The Absence of Empire in the Study of American Culture." In *Cultures of United States Imperialism*, edited by Amy Kaplan and Donald Pease. Durham, N.C.: Duke University Press, 1993, 3–21.
Kelley, Mary. *Learning to Stand and Speak: Women, Education, and Public Life*. Chapel Hill: University of North Carolina Press, 2006.
Kerber, Linda. "The Paradox of Women's Citizenship in the Early Republic: The Case of *Martin vs. Massachusetts*, 1805." *American Historical Review* 97, no. 2 (April 1992): 349–78.
———. *Women of the Republic: Intellect and Ideology in Revolutionary America*. Chapel Hill: University of North Carolina Press, 1997.
Kirkpatrick, John Ervin. *Timothy Flint: Pioneer, Missionary, Author, Editor, 1780–1840*. Cleveland: Arthur H. Clark, 1911.
Kirsch, George B. "Jeremy Belknap: Man of Letters in the Young Republic." *New England Quarterly* 54, no. 1 (March 1981): 33–53.
Kollock, Shepard. *A True Narrative of the Sufferings of Mary Kinan* (1795). In Derounian-Stodola, *Women's Indian Captivity Narratives*, 109–16.
Kolodny, Annette. "Turning the Lens on 'The Panther Captivity': A Feminist Exercise in Practical Criticism." In *Writing and Sexual Difference*, edited by Elizabeth Abel. Chicago: University of Chicago Press, 1982, 159–79.
Kostelnick, Charles, and Michael Hasset. *Shaping Information: The Rhetoric of Visual Conventions*. Carbondale: Southern Illinois University Press, 2003.
Kress, Gunther. *Literacy in the New Media Age*. New York: Routledge, 2003.
———. *Multimodality: A Semiotic Approach to Contemporary Communication*. New York: Routledge, 2009.
Kress, Gunther, and Theo Van Leeuwen. *Multimodal Discourse: The Modes and Media of Contemporary Communication*. New York: Bloomsbury, 2001.
LaCroix, Allison. *The Ideological Origins of American Federalism*. Cambridge, Mass.: Harvard University Press, 2010.
Landow, George. *Hypertext 2.0: The Convergence of Contemporary Critical Theory and Technology*. Baltimore: Johns Hopkins University Press, 1997.
Larkin, Edward. *The American School of Empire*. Cambridge: Cambridge University Press, 2016.
"La Rouge, or The Red Tavern." *Western Monthly Review*, July 1835, 44–57.
Larson, Edward J., and Michael P. Winship. "Introduction." *The Constitutional Convention*. New York: Modern Library, 2005, 1–10.

Larson, J. A. O. *Greek Federal States: The Institutions and History.* Oxford: Clarendon Press, 1968.
Larson, John. *Internal Improvement: National Public Works and the Promise of Popular Government in the Early United States.* Chapel Hill: University of North Carolina Press, 2001.
Lawson, Russell M. *The American Plutarch: Jeremy Belknap and the Historian's Dialogue with the Past.* New York: Praeger, 1998.
Lee, Judith Yaross. "Republican Rhymes: Constitutional Controversy and the Democratization of The Verse Satire, 1786–1799." *Studies in American Humor* 6 (1988): 30–39.
Leepson, Marc. *Flag: An American Biography.* New York: St. Martin's, 2005.
LeMenager, Stephanie. *Manifest and Other Destinies: Territorial Fictions of the Nineteenth-Century United States.* Lincoln: University of Nebraska Press, 2004.
Lepore, Jill. *A Is for American: Letters and Other Characters in the Newly United States.* New York: Random House, 2002.
"Letter of a Democratic Federalist." October 23, 1787. In Lewis, *Anti-Federalists versus Federalists*, 152–58.
Lewis, G. Malcolm. "Maps, Mapmaking, and Map Use by Native North Americans." In *Traditional Cartography in the Americas*, edited by David Woodward and G. Malcolm Lewis. Chicago: University of Chicago Press, 1998, 51–182.
Lewis, Jan. "'Of Every Age, Sex, and Condition': The Representation of Women in the Constitution." *Journal of the Early Republic* 15, no. 3: 359–87.
Lewis, John, ed. *Anti-Federalists versus Federalists: Selected Documents.* San Francisco: Chandler, 1967.
"A Literary Ware-House." *Monthly Magazine and American Review*, April 1800, 254.
Logan, Lisa. "Cross-Cultural Conversations: The Captivity Narrative." *A Companion to the Literatures of Colonial America*, edited by Susan Castillo and Ivy Schweitzer. Hoboken, N.J.: Blackwell, 2005, 466–79.
———. "Mary Rowlandson's Captivity and the 'Place' of the Woman Subject." *Early American Literature* 28, no. 3 (1993): 255–77.
Looby, Christopher. *Voicing America: Language, Literary Form, and the Origins of the United States.* Chicago: University of Chicago Press, 1996.
Lopenzina, Drew. *Through an Indian's Looking-Glass: A Cultural Biography of William Apess, Pequot.* Boston: University of Massachusetts Press, 2017.
Loughran, Trish. *The Republic in Print: Print Culture in the Age of U.S. Nation Building, 1770–1870.* New York: Columbia University Press, 2009.
Lovejoy, Nathaniel. Nathaniel Lovejoy Diaries, 1762–1809. Mss. Octavo vol. L, no. 271794. American Antiquarian Society, Worcester, Massachusetts.
Lowe, Lisa. *The Intimacies of Four Continents.* Durham, N.C.: Duke University Press, 2015.
Loyal Patriot. *Some Observations in Consequence, in Three Parts, Occasioned by the Stamp Act.* Philadelphia, 1768.
Luciano, Dana, and Ivy Wilson, eds. *Unsettled States: Nineteenth-Century American Literary Studies.* New York: New York University Press, 2014.
Lumpkin, Wilson. *The Removal of the Cherokee Indians from Georgia.* New York: Dodd, Mead, 1907.

Luria, Sarah. *Capital Speculations: Writing and Building Washington, D.C.* Durham, N.H.: University Press of New England, 2006.
MacLeod, Duncan J. *Slavery, Race, and the American Revolution.* London: Cambridge University Press, 1974.
Madison, James. "Debates of the Federal Convention." In *The Papers of James Madison*, vol. 3, edited by Henry D. Gilpin. New York: J. & H. G. Langley, 1841.
———. Federalist No. 10. In Rossiter, *Federalist Papers*, 71–79.
———. Federalist No. 39. In Rossiter, *Federalist Papers*, 236–43.
———. Federalist No. 49. In Rossiter, *Federalist Papers*, 310–14.
———. Federalist No. 51. In Rossiter, *Federalist Papers*, 317–22.
———. Federalist No. 57. In Rossiter, *Federalist Papers*, 348–53.
———. "Record of the Convention." In *The Constitutional Convention: A Narrative History from the Notes of James Madison*, edited by Edward J. Larson and Michael P. Winship. New York: Modern Library, 2005, 13–156.
Man, Samuel. Samuel Man Diary, 1777, 1781–83. Mss. Octavo vol. M, no. 271802. American Antiquarian Society, Worcester, Massachusetts.
Mansfield, Edward Deering. *Personal Memories: Social, Political, and Literary, with Sketches of Many Noted People, 1803–1843.* Cincinnati: Robert Clarke, 1879.
Margulis, Jennifer. "Spies, Pirates, and White Slaves: Encounters with the Algerines in Three Early American Novels." *Eighteenth-Century Novel* 1 (2001): 1–36.
Markoe, Peter. *The Algerine Spy in Pennsylvania.* Edited by Timothy Marr. 1789; Yardley, Penn.: Westholme, 2008.
Marr, Timothy. *The Cultural Roots of American Islamicism.* New York: Cambridge University Press, 2006.
Mason, George. "Objections to the Proposed Constitution." October 1787. In Lewis, *Anti-Federalists versus Federalists*, 65–68.
McCarthy, Molly. *The Accidental Diarist: A History of the Daily Planner in America.* Chicago: University of Chicago Press, 2013.
———. "Redeeming the Almanac: Learning to Appreciate the iPhone of Early America." *Common-Place: A Common Place, an Uncommon Voice* 11, no. 1 (2010), http://www.common-place-archives.org/vol-11/no-01/.
McDonald, Forrest. *States' Rights and the Union: Imperium in Imperio, 1776–1876.* Lawrence: University Press of Kansas, 2000.
McGann, Jerome. *The Textual Condition.* Princeton, N.J.: Princeton University Press, 1991.
McKenney, Thomas, and James Hall. *History of the Indian Tribes of North America.* Philadelphia: E. C. Biddle, 1836–44.
McLoughan, William. *Cherokee Renascence in the New Republic.* Princeton, N.J.: Princeton University Press, 1986.
McMaster, John Bach, and Frederick D. Stone, eds. *Pennsylvania and the Federal Constitution, 1787–1788.* Philadelphia: Historical Society of Pennsylvania, 1888.
McPherson, James M. *Battle Cry of Freedom: The Civil War Era.* New York: Oxford University Press, 1988.
McRae, James. "James F. McRae to Gov. John Owen, Aug. 7, 1830." Reprinted in Clement Eaton, "A Dangerous Pamphlet in the Old South." *Journal of Southern History* 2, no. 3 (August 1836): 323–34.

Merrill, Michael, and Sean Wilentz. "Introduction." *The Key of Liberty: The Life and Democratic Writings of William Manning*. Cambridge, Mass.: Harvard University Press, 1993, 3–80.

Miflin, Warner. *A Serious Expostulation with the Members of the House of Representatives of the United States*. Philadelphia: Daniel Lawrence, 1793.

Minor, Dennis. "Shaved Monkeys, Sleepy Students, and Dangerous Kegs: Revolutionary War Humor and Satire." In *George Washington in and as Culture*. New York: AMS, 2001, 99–106.

Montesquieu, Charles-Louis de Secondat, Baron de La Brède et de. *The Spirit of Laws*, Book 9. Translated by Thomas Nugent. The Constitution Society. October 10, 2010. http://www.constitution.org/cm/sol_09.htm.

Moore, John. John Moore Diaries, 1788–1815. Mss. Octavo vol. M, no. 271866. American Antiquarian Society, Worcester, Massachusetts.

Morse, Jedidiah. *American Geography, or, A View of the Present Situation of the United States of America*. Elizabethtown, N.J.: Shepard Kollock, 1789.

———. *The American Universal Geography*. Boston: Thomas & Andrews, 1793.

———. *Geography Made Easy*. Boston: Thomas & Andrews, 1796.

———. *Geography Made Easy*. Boston: Thomas & Andrews, 1809.

Mott, Frank Luther. *A History of American Magazines: 1741–1850*. Vol. 1. Cambridge, Mass.: Harvard University Press, 1930.

———. *The Story of Best Sellers in the United States*. New York: Macmillan, 1947.

Murray, Judith Sargent. *The Gleaner*. Edited by Nina Baym. Schenectady, N.Y.: Union College Press, 1992.

———. "On the Equality of the Sexes" (1790). In *Selected Writings of Judith Sargent Murray*, edited by Sharon Harris. New York: Oxford University Press, 1995, 3–14.

Myers, Minor. "Supreme Court Usage: The Making of an Is." *Green Bag 2D*, 11 (Summer 2008): 457–65.

The New-England Almanack, or, Lady's and Gentleman's Diary, for the Year of Our Lord Christ 1783. Providence: John Carter, 1782.

Newman, Eric P. *The Early Paper Money of America*. Iola, Wisc.: Krause, 2008.

Newmyer, R. Kent. "Chief Justice John Marshall's Last Campaign: Georgia, Jackson, and the Cherokee Cases." *Journal of Supreme Court History* 24, no. 1 (1999): 76–94.

Nicolaisen, Peter, and Hannah Spahn, eds. *Cosmopolitanism and Nationhood in the Age of Jefferson*. Heidelberg: Universitätsverlag, 2013.

Niven, John. *John C. Calhoun and the Price of Union*. Baton Rouge: Louisiana State University Press, 1988.

Norton, Mary Beth. *Liberty's Daughters: The Revolutionary Experience of American Women, 1750–1800*. Ithaca, N.Y.: Cornell University Press, 1996.

Noyes, Belcher. Belcher Noyes Diaries, 1775–76, 1782. Mss. Octavo vol. N, no. 271911. American Antiquarian Society, Worcester, Massachusetts.

Okker, Patricia. "Jeremy Belknap's Serializing the Nation." In *Social Stories: The Magazine Novel in Nineteenth-Century America*. Charlottesville: University of Virginia Press, 2003, 29–54.

Olson, Lester. *Benjamin Franklin's Vision of American Community*. Columbia: University of South Carolina Press, 2004.

———. *Emblems of American Community in the Revolutionary Era*. Washington, D.C.: Smithsonian Institution Press, 1991.
"On Periodical Publications." *Massachusetts Magazine*, April 1795, 3–4.
"On the Advantages of Periodical Performances." *New-York Magazine*, November 1791, 635–37.
"On the Means of Preserving Public Liberty." *New-York Magazine*, January 1790, 23–25.
"On the Rise and Progress of Magazines." *New-York Magazine*, May 1790, 256–58.
"On the Utility of Well-Regulated Magazines." *Massachusetts Magazine*, January 1789, 7–9.
Onuf, Peter. "Federalism, Republicanism, and the Origins of American Sectionalism." In *All Over the Map: Rethinking American Regions*, edited by Edward Ayers. Baltimore: Johns Hopkins University Press, 1996, 11–37.
———. *Jefferson's Empire: The Language of American Nationhood*. Charlottesville: University of Virginia Press, 2000.
———. "'To Declare Them a Free and Independent People': Race, Slavery, and National Identity in Jefferson's Thought." *Journal of the Early Republic* 18, no. 1 (Spring 1998): 1–46.
Onuf, Peter, and Nicholas Onuf. *Federal Union, Modern World: The Law of Nations in the Age of Revolutions, 1776–1814*. Madison, Wisc.: Madison House Publishers, 1993.
Palmeri, Frank. *Satire in Narrative*. Austin: University of Texas Press, 1990.
"Papers Reflecting the Late Private Transactions with the Oneida Indians." *American Museum*, May 1788, 447–51.
Pasley, Jeffrey. *The Tyranny of Printers: Newspaper Politics in the Early American Republic*. Charlottesville: University of Virginia Press, 2002.
Patterson, Richard S., and Richardson Dougall. *The Eagle and the Shield: A History of the Great Seal of the United States*. Washington, D.C.: Department of State, 1978.
Peck, J. M. "An Historical Sketch." *Western Monthly Magazine*, February 1833, 73–83.
Peirce, Jonathan. Jonathan Peirce Diary, 1791. Mss. Octavo vol. P, no. 271961. American Antiquarian Society, Worcester, Massachusetts.
The Pennsylvania Town and Country-Man's Almanack, for the Year of Our Lord 1777. Wilmington, Del.: James Adams, 1776.
Perkins, Maureen. *Visions of the Future: Almanacs, Time, and Cultural Change, 1775–1870*. New York: Oxford University Press, 1996.
Peskin, Lawrence A. *Captives and Countrymen: Barbary Slavery and the American Public, 1785–1816*. Baltimore: Johns Hopkins University Press, 2009.
Phillips, Christopher. *Freedom's Port: The African American Community of Baltimore, 1790–1860*. Chicago: University of Illinois Press, 1997.
Picket, Albert. "Opening Address." *Transactions of the Eighth Annual Meeting of the Western Literary Institute*. Cincinnati: James R. Allbach, 1836, 35–43.
Poor Richard Improved: Being an Almanack and Ephemeris . . . for the Year of Our Lord 1791. Philadelphia: Hall & Sellers, 1790.
Poor Will's Almanack, for the Year of Our Lord, 1788. Philadelphia: Joseph Crukshank, 1787.
Post, Constance J. "Revolutionary Dialogics in American Mock-Epic Poetry." *Studies in American Humor* 6 (1988): 40–51.

Powell, William. William Powell Diary, 1777. Mss. Octavo vol. P, no. 271998. American Antiquarian Society, Worcester, Massachusetts.

Pownall, Thomas. *The Administration of the Colonies* (1764). In *Great Britain and the American Colonies*, edited by Jack P. Green. Columbia: University of South Carolina Press, 1970.

Pratt, Amy. "The Pleasure of Being Lost: 'The Panther Captivity' and the Metaphysics of Commerce." *Mosaic* 34, no. 1 (March 2001): 1–18.

Pratt, Lloyd. *Archives of American Time: Literature and Modernity in the Nineteenth Century*. Philadelphia: University of Pennsylvania Press, 2010.

"Preface." *American Museum*, July 1788, v–vi.

"Preface," *Columbian Magazine*, September 1786, 3–4.

"Preface to the Reader." *A True History of the Captivity and Restoration of Mrs. Mary Rowlandson* (1682). In Derounian-Stodola, *Women's Indian Captivity Narratives*, 7–11.

"Present Crisis in the Condition of American Indians, No. VIII." *Cherokee Phoenix*, October 21, 1829, 1.

"Proceedings of Commissioners to Remedy Defects of the Federal Government." September 11, 1786. The Avalon Project: Documents in Law, History, and Diplomacy. October 10, 2010. http://avalon.law.yale.edu/18th_century/annapoli.asp.

Proietti, Salvatore. "Sailing across the Color Line: On Royall Tyler's *The Algerine Captive*." In Bacigalupo and Castagneto, *America and the Mediterranean*, 525–31.

Prucha, Francis Paul, ed. *Cherokee Removal: The William Penn Essays and Other Writings*. Knoxville: University of Tennessee Press, 1981.

Pufendorf, Samuel von. *De Statu Imperii*. Translated by Edmund Bohun. 1667; Indianapolis: Liberty Fund, 2007.

———. Of *the Law of Nature and Nations: or, A General System of the Most Important Principles of Morality, Jurisprudence, and Politics*. Translated by Basil Kennet. 5th ed. London, 1749.

Rakove, Jack N., ed. *Interpreting the Constitution: The Debate over Original Intent*. Boston: Northeastern University Press, 1990.

Randall, Randolph. "Authors of the *Port Folio* Revealed by the Hall Files." *American Literature*. 11.4 (Jan. 1940): 379–416.

Rawls, John. "The Idea of an Overlapping Consensus." *Oxford Journal of Legal Studies* 7, no. 1 (Spring 1987): 1–25.

———. *Political Liberalism*. New York: Columbia University Press, 1996.

———. *A Theory of Justice*. Cambridge, Mass.: Harvard University Press, 1971.

Ray, Angela. "'In My Own Hand Writing': Benjamin Banneker Addresses the Slaveholder of Monticello." *Rhetoric and Public Affairs* 1, no. 3 (1998): 387–405.

———. *The Lyceum and Public Culture in the Nineteenth-Century United States*. East Lansing: Michigan State University Press, 2005.

Raymond, Allen. "To Reach Men's Minds: Almanacs and the American Revolution." *New England Quarterly* 51, no. 3 (September 1978): 370–95.

"Reminiscence of the Scioto Valley." *Illinois Monthly Magazine*, May 1831, 370–73.

"Resolution for the U.S. Flag." *Journals of the Continental Congress*. Vol. 8. American Memory, Library of Congress. October 12, 2012. http://memory.loc.gov.

Rex, Cathy. "Revising the Nation: The Domesticated Nationalism of Ann Eliza Bleecker's *The History of Maria Kittle*." *Women's Studies* 42, no. 8 (December 2013): 956–97.

Rhonda, James P. "'We Have a Country': Race, Geography, and the Invention of Indian Territory." *Journal of the Early Republic* 19, no. 4 (Winter 1999): 739–55.

Rice, David. *Slavery Inconsistent with Justice and Good Policy*. Lexington, Ky.: John Bradford, 1792.

Rifkin, Mark. *Manifesting America: The Imperial Construction of U.S. National Space*. New York: Oxford University Press, 2009.

Rittenhouse, David. "On Negro Slavery and the Slave Trade." In *Benjamin Banneker's Pennsylvania, Delaware, Maryland, and Virginia Almanack*. Baltimore: William Goddard & James Angell, 1792, 33.

Robbins, Walter L. "John Tobler's Description of South Carolina." *South Carolina Historical Magazine* 71, no. 3 (July 1970): 141–61.

Rodney, Thomas, et al. Rodney Family Diaries, 1779–1809. Mss. Octavo vol. 4, no. 272051. American Antiquarian Society, Worcester, Massachusetts.

Rohrbough, Malcolm J. *The Trans-Appalachian Frontier*. New York: Oxford University Press, 1978.

Rossiter, Clinton, ed. *The Federalist Papers*. New York: Signet Classic, 2003.

Round, Phillip. *Removable Type: Histories of the Book in Indian Country, 1663–1880*. Chapel Hill: University of North Carolina Press, 2010.

Rowlandson, Mary. *A True History of the Captivity and Restoration of Mrs. Mary Rowlandson* (1682). In Derounian-Stodola, *Women's Indian Captivity Narratives*, 1–51.

"Rural Concerns: On the Hessian Fly." *American Museum*, April 1787, 324–26.

Rush, Benjamin. "Thoughts upon Female Education." *Universal Asylum and Columbian Magazine*, May 1790, 209–14.

Russell, John. "The Spectre Hunter." *Western Monthly Magazine*, October 1833, 458–66.

Salisbury, Neal. "Mary Rowlandson in a World of Removes." In *The Sovereignty and Goodness of God, with Related Documents*, edited by Neal Salisbury. New York: Bedford/St. Martin's, 1997.

Santin, Bryan, Daniel Murphy, and Matthew Wilkens. "Is or Are: The 'United States' in Nineteenth-Century Print Culture." *American Quarterly* 68, no. 1 (March 2016): 101–24.

Santoro, Lily. "After the Old; yet as agreeable . . . to the Newest: British and American Almanacs in the Era of American Independence." In *Books without Borders: The Cross-National Dimension in Print Culture*, edited by Mary Hammond and Robert Fraser. London: Palgrave Macmillan, 2008, 55–66.

Sayward, Jonathan. Jonathan Sayward Diaries, 1760–1799. Mss. Octavo vol. S, no. 272081. American Antiquarian Society, Worcester, Massachusetts.

Schmidt, Klaus H., and Fritz Fleischman, eds. *Early America Re-explored: New Readings in Colonial, Early National, and Antebellum Culture*. New York: Peter Lang, 2000.

Schöpp, Joseph C. "Liberty's Sons and Daughters: Susanna Haswell Rowson's and Royall Tyler's Algerine Captives." In Schmidt and Fleischman, *Early America Re-explored*, 291–307.

Schulz, Max F. "John Trumbull and Satirical Criticism of Literature." *Modern Language Notes* 73, no. 2 (1958): 85–90.

Shankle, George Earle. *State Names, Flags, Seals, Songs, Birds, Flowers, and Other Symbols.* Rev. ed. New York. H. W. Wilson, 1941.
Short, John R. *Representing the Republic: Mapping the United States.* London: Reaktion, 2001.
Shuffelton, Frank, ed. *A Mixed Race: Ethnicity in Early America.* New York; Oxford University Press, 1993.
Sieminski, Greg. "The Puritan Captivity Narrative and the Politics of the American Revolution." *American Quarterly* 42, no. 1 (March 1991): 35–56.
Simpson, Audra. "From White into Red: Captivity Narratives as Alchemies of Race and Citizenship." *American Quarterly* 60, no. 2 (June 2008): 251–57.
Skemp, Sheila. *First Lady of Letters: Judith Sargent Murray and the Struggle for Female Independence.* Philadelphia: University of Pennsylvania Press, 2009.
"Sketch of the Life of General Harrison." *Western Monthly Magazine,* March 1835, 113–29.
Slauter, Eric. *The State as a Work of Art: The Cultural Origins of the Constitution.* Chicago: University of Chicago Press, 2009.
Smith, Melancthon. *An Address to the People of the State of New York.* New York: Robert Hodge, June 1788.
Smith, Olivia. *The Politics of Language, 1789–1819.* Oxford: Oxford University Press, 2009.
Smith, William. "The Pretensions of Thomas Jefferson to the Presidency." Philadelphia: John Fenno, 1796.
Smith-Rosenberg, Carroll. *This Violent Empire: The Birth of an American National Identity.* Chapel Hill: University of North Carolina Press, 2010.
Sorenson, Janet. *The Grammar of Empire in Eighteenth-Century British Writing.* Cambridge: Cambridge University Press, 2000.
The South-Carolina and Georgia Almanack, for the Year of Our Lord 1777. Charlestown, S.C.: Robert Wells & Son, 1776.
Spero, Patrick. *Frontier Country: The Politics of War in Early Pennsylvania.* Philadelphia: University of Pennsylvania Press, 2016.
———. "The Revolution in Popular Publications: The Almanac and the New England Primer, 1750–1800." *Early American Studies* 8, no. 1 (Winter 2010): 41–74.
Stanton, John. John Stanton Papers, 1774–94. Mss. Octavo vol. S, no. 272125. American Antiquarian Society, Worcester, Massachusetts.
Stevens, James Wilson. *An Historical and Geographical Account of Algiers.* Philadelphia: Hogan & M'elroy, 1797.
Stoler, Ann Laura, ed. *Haunted by Empire: Geographies of Intimacy in North American History.* Durham, N.C.: Duke University Press, 2006.
"Story of the Thirteen Partners." *American Museum,* September 1790, 134–36.
Stowe, Calvin Ellis. *Report on Elementary Public Instruction.* Harrisburg, Penn.: Thompson & Clark, 1837.
Stowell, Marion. *Early American Almanacs: The Colonial Weekday Bible.* New York: Burt Franklin, 1977.
A Surprising Account of the Captivity and Escape of Philip M'Donald and Alexander M'Leod, of Virginia, from the Chickkemogga Indians. In Williams, *Liberty's Captives,* 34–41.
Tandy, Jeannette. *The Crackerjack Philosophers in American Humor and Satire.* Port Washington, N.Y.: Kennicat, 1925.

Tanselle, G. Thomas. *Royall Tyler*. Cambridge, Mass.: Harvard University Press, 1967.
Thompson, Peter. "David Walker's Nationalism—and Thomas Jefferson's." *Journal of the Early Republic* 37, no. 1 (Spring 2017): 47–80.
Thompson, Ralph. *American Literary Annuals and Gift Books, 1825–1865*. New York: H. W. Wilson, 1936.
"Thoughts on the Establishment of a National University." Pts. 1–3. *Western Monthly Review*, November 1828, 305–20; December 1828, 369–79; January 1829, 425–36.
Tiedemann, Joseph. "Interconnected Communities: The Middle Colonies on the Eve of the American Revolution." *Pennsylvania History* 76, no. 9 (2009): 1–41.
"To the Editor of the Monthly Magazine." *Monthly Magazine and American Review*, October 1800, 264–65.
"To the Printer." *American Museum*, March 1787, 218–23.
"To the Printer." *American Museum*, April 1787, 333–37.
Tomlin, T. J. "'Astrology's from Heaven Not from Hell': The Religious Significance of Early American Almanacs." *Early American Studies* 8, no. 2 (Spring 2012): 287–321.
Toulouse, Teresa A. *The Captive's Position: Female Narrative, Male Identity, and Royal Authority in Colonial New England*. Philadelphia: University of Pennsylvania Press, 2007.
Transactions of the Fourth Annual Meetings of The Western Literary Institute and College of Professional Teachers. *Western Monthly Magazine*, May 1835.
Transactions of the Ninth and Tenth Annual Meetings of The Western Literary Institute and College of Professional Teachers. Cincinnati: Kendall & Barnard, 1841.
Trumbull, John. *M'Fingal: An Epic Poem*. New York: American Book Exchange, 1881.
Tucker, Louis. "The Semi-Colon Club of Cincinnati." *Ohio History* 73, no. 1 (1964): 13–26.
Tyler, Moses Coit. *A History of American Literature during the Colonial Time*. New York: G. P. Putnam & Sons, 1897.
Tyler, Royall. *The Algerine Captive, or the Life and Adventures of Updike Underhill*. 1797; New York: Modern Library, 2002.
———. "Selectmen v. Jacob." In *Reports of Cases Argued and Determined in the Supreme Court of Judicature of the State of Vermont*, vol. 2. New York: I. Rileu, 1810, 192–201.
The United States Almanac, for the Year of Our Lord 1789. Elizabeth-Town, N.J.: Shepard Kollock, 1788.
The Universal Calendar, and the North-American's Almanack, for the Year of the Creation . . . 1788. Boston: Edes & Son, 1787.
Van Atta, John R. "Western Lands and the Political Economy of the American System." *Journal of the Early Republic* 21, no. 4 (Winter 2001): 633–67.
Van Campen, Moses. *A Narrative of the Escape of the Capture of Certain Americans at Westmoreland*. New London, Conn.: T. Green, 1784.
Venable, W. H. *Beginnings of Literary Culture in the Ohio Valley*. New York: Peter Smith, 1949.
"The Village Musician." *Illinois Monthly Magazine*, January 1831, 158–72.
The Virginia Almanack, for the Year of Our Lord, 1790. Richmond, Va.: John Dixon, 1789.
Waldstreicher, David. *In the Midst of Perpetual Fetes: The Making of American Nationalism*. Chapel Hill: University of North Carolina Press, 1997.

Walker, David. *Appeal to the Coloured Citizens of the World*. Edited by Sean Wilentz. 1829; New York: Hill & Wang, 1995.
Wallis, John. *The United States of America Laid Down from the Best Authorities, Agreeable to the Peace of 1783*. London, 1783.
Walsh, Maureen. "Reading Visual and Multimodal Texts: How Is Reading Different?" *Australian Journal of Language and Literacy* 29, no. 1 (2005): 24–37.
Warner, Michael. *Letters of the Republic: Publication and the Public Sphere in Eighteenth-Century America*. Cambridge, Mass.: Harvard University Press, 1990.
———. "Nationalism and the Problem of Republican Literature." In Warner, *Letters of the Republic*, 122–32.
Washington, George. "Diaries, 1748–1799." George Washington Papers. American Memory Collection, Library of Congress. August 16, 2017. https://www.loc.gov/collections/george-washington-papers.
———. "Farewell Address." 1796. The Avalon Project: Documents in Law, History, and Diplomacy. October 12, 2006. http://avalon.law.yale.edu/18th_century/washing.asp.
———. "In Convention, September 17, 1787." *Columbian Magazine*, September 1787, 659–66.
———. "Letter to the Printer of *The American Museum*." *American Museum*, July 1788, 3.
Watson, Harry L. *Liberty and Power: The Politics of Jacksonian America*. New York: Farrar, Strauss & Giroux, 1990.
Watson, Martha Solomon. "The Dynamics of Intertextuality: Re-Reading the Declaration of Independence." In Benson, *Rhetoric and Political Culture*, 91–111.
Watts, Edward. *An American Colony: Regionalism and the Roots of Midwestern Culture*. Columbus: Ohio University Press, 2002.
———. *In This Remote Country: French Colonial Culture in the Anglo-American Imagination*. Chapel Hill: University of North Carolina Press, 2006.
———, ed. *The Indian Hater and Other Stories by James Hall*. Kent, Ohio: Kent State University Press, 2009.
———. *Writing and Postcolonialism in the Early Republic*. Charlottesville: University Press of Virginia, 1998.
Watts, Edward, and David Rachels. *The First West: Writing from the American Frontier, 1776–1860*. New York: Oxford University Press, 2002,
Webster, Daniel. "Speech to the Senate, January 26, 1830." In *Speeches of Hayne and Webster in the United States Senate*. Boston: A. T. Hotchkiss & W. P. Fetridge, 1853.
Webster, Noah. *Grammatical Institute of the English Language, Part III*. Philadelphia: Young & M'Culloch, 1787.
———. "On the Education of Youth in America." In *A Collection of Essays and Fugitiv Writings on Moral, Historical, Political and Literary Subjects*. Boston, 1790.
"Western Monthly Review." *Philadelphia Album and Ladies Literary Gazette*, December 26, 1827, 36.
"Western Monthly Review." *Ariel*, January 12, 1828, 151.
"Western Souvenir." *Ladies Literary Portfolio*, January 14, 1829, 40.
White, Ed. *The Backcountry and the City: Colonization and Conflict in Early America*. Minneapolis: University of Minnesota Press, 2005.

Wiecek, William. *The Sources of Anti-Slavery Constitutionalism in America.* Ithaca, N.Y.: Cornell University Press, 1977.
Wilentz, Sean. "The Mysteries of David Walker." In *David Walker's Appeal,* edited by Sean Wilentz. New York: Hill & Wang, 1995, vii–xxiii.
———. *The Rise of American Democracy: Jefferson to Lincoln.* New York: W. W. Norton, 2005.
Williams, Daniel. *Liberty's Captives: Narratives of Confinement in the Print Culture of the Early Republic.* Athens: University of Georgia Press, 2006.
The Wilmington Almanack, or Ephemeris, for the Year of Our Lord 1782. Wilmington, Del.: James Adams, 1781.
Wisecup, Kelly. "Practicing Sovereignty: Colonial Temporalities, Cherokee Justice, and the 'Socrates' Writings of John Ridge." *Native American and Indigenous Studies* 4, no. 1 (Spring 2017): 30–60.
Witherspoon, John. "Part of a Speech to Congress, upon the Confederation." In *The Selected Writings of John Witherspoon,* edited by Thomas P. Miller. Carbondale: Southern Illinois University Press, 2015, 148–51.
The Wonderful Escape of Dr. Knight and John Slover from Captivity. Philadelphia: Francis Bailey, 1783.
"Wood River Massacre." *Western Monthly Magazine,* June 1833, 280–83.
Wood, Sarah. "An Alien's Act of Sedition: Structural Coherence and North African Attachments in Royall Tyler's *The Algerine Captive.*" In Bacigalupo and Castagneto, *America and the Mediterranean,* 325–32.
Wyss, Hilary. *English Letters and Indian Literacies: Reading, Writing, and New England Missionary Schools, 1750–1830.* Philadelphia: University of Pennsylvania Press, 2012.
Yazawa, Melvin. *Contested Conventions: The Struggle to Establish the Constitution and Save the Union, 1787–1789.* Baltimore: Johns Hopkins University Press, 2016.
Yirush, Craig. *Setters, Liberty, and Empire: The Roots of Early American Political Theory, 1675–1775.* New York: Cambridge University Press, 2011.
"The Young Warriors." *Illinois Monthly Magazine,* September 1831, 571–72.
Ziesche, Philipp. *Cosmopolitan Patriots: Americans in Paris in the Age of Revolution.* Charlottesville: University of Virginia Press, 2010.
Zimmerman, Everett. *Swift's Narrative Satires.* Ithaca, N.Y.: Cornell University Press, 1983.
Zimmerman, Joseph. *Contemporary American Federalism: The Growth of National Power.* Albany: State University of New York Press, 2008.

INDEX

Act of Union, 22, 145, 245n18
Adams, John, 46, 120, 130, 161, 246n31; federalism and, 3, 20–21; national motto and, 100; national seal and, 37
Adams, John Quincy, 11
Adventures of Col. Daniel Boon, 140, 156–57
Affecting History of the Dreadful Distresses of Frederic Manheim's Family, 156
African Americans, 14, 29–30; arguments for equality and rights, 89–97, 167, 220, 231, 234–39; arguments for federal inclusion, 10, 30, 89, 92, 94–96, 220, 236–40; colonization of, 220, 236–37; contributions to United States, 92, 237–38; federal exclusion and, 10, 14, 27, 29, 89–92, 94, 98, 196, 220, 231–39; Jefferson and, 91, 92, 94–96, 234–35; print culture and, 91, 92–94, 96–97, 231, 244n25; racism and, 16, 89, 92, 95, 166, 230, 231–37, 239; restricted rights and, 30, 89–91, 233–34, 236–37. *See also* Banneker, Benjamin; race; slavery; Walker, David
Agrippa, 108, 110, 245n26, 255n36
Albany Plan of Union, 4, 22–23, 128
Algerine Captive, The (Tyler), 15, 141; concurrent sentiments and, 143, 158, 160–61, 175; cosmopolitanism and, 160; critical assessments of, 141–42, 160, 259n46; cultural inclusion and, 143, 158; federal literacy and, 160–61, 163, 166, 173; federal nationalism and, 143, 158–61, 163–65, 168, 172–73, 175; formal structure, 160–61; homogeneous models of nationalism and, 161–63; representation of Algiers, 169–72, 260n62; representation of Islam, 169–70; representation of the South, 164–66; slavery and, 141, 166–69, 173
Alien and Sedition Acts, 25
almanacs, 6, 7, 9, 55–98, 99, 219; African Americans and, 14, 89, 91, 92–98; Anatomy Man and, 13, 85–88, *86*; astrology and, 7, 12, 13, 61, 85–88; audiences, 55, 61–62, 66–67, 86–87; calendar pages, 7, 60, 63–65, *63, 65*, 66, 69, 76, 79, 81, 83–85, *84*, 87, 93; chronologies, 74–76; court schedules, 13, 62, 64, 68, 76–78, *77*, 79, 83, 88, 93, 97; critical neglect of, 58–59; domestic advice, 58, 63–66, 75, 79–80; early history, 55, 60–61; English almanacs, 60–61, 88; federal content, 55–58, 68; federal literacy and, 7, 12, 14, 58, 59, 68, 79, 87–88; federal nationalism and, 7, 9–10, 13–15, 54–60, 68–79, 82–89, 91, 93–95, 98; formal structure, 7, 13, 58, 59–60, 68–70, 88, 93–94; gardening advice, 61–62, 64, 75, 79, 81; layout, 60, 62–64, 66, 68, 79–85; literary content, 62, 63–64, 66, 81, 93; local focus, 58–62, 64, 66–67, 70–71, 73, 75–79, 83, 88, 102; multimodality and, 81–82, 251n65; multiple uses of, 68–70, 80–83, 102; as personal diaries, 60, 68–69, 73–75, 76, 78–79, 81, 250n39; plural dimensions, 10, 59–61, 67, 71, 81–82, 88–89, 93–94, 102; political content, 55–58, 62, 65–66, 79, 92–94, 97; reader engagement and, 7, 56–59, 61–62, 66–71, 73–76, 78–85, 80–85, 87–89, 94, 96; regional variations of, 59, 61–67, 80, 88, 97; represen-

almanacs (*continued*)
  tations of time, 58, 60, 63, 68–69, 74–78, 81, 83–85; road tables, 7, 12, 60, 64, 68, 70–73, 72, 75, 78, 79, 81, 83, 88, 93, 97; sense of situatedness, 9, 14, 58, 67–74, 76–79, 83, 88, 102. *See also* Banneker, Benjamin
  —specific works: *Benjamin Banneker's Pennsylvania, Delaware, Maryland, and Virginia Almanack and Ephemeris*, 92–94; *Bickerstaff's Boston Almanack*, 56, 70; *Columbian Almanac*, 57; *Continental Almanac*, 56–57, 57; *Father Abraham's Almanack*, 62, 72, 73, 76–77; *New-England Almanack*, 62, 72, 73; *New-Jersey Almanac*, 62; *Pennsylvania Town and Country-Man's Almanack*, 62–66; *Poor Richard Improved*, 62, 69, 85, *86*, 249n29; *Poor Will's Almanack*, 74, 77, 248n3; *South-Carolina and Georgia Almanack*, 62, 64–66; *United States Almanack*, 62, 70, 79, 80; *Universal Calendar and North American's Almanack*, 83, 84; *Virginia Almanack*, 62, 69, 72, 73, 249n29; *Wilmington Almanack*, 85, 86
American Museum, 14, 53, 99, 100, 103; federal literacy and, 127–29; *M'Fingal* and, 101, 121; varied content of, 126–28
American Revolution, 36, 65–66, 82, 139, 202; African Americans and, 90; almanacs and, 74, 76; captivity narratives and, 139, 141, 145, 164; *M'Fingal* and, 120
Anarchiad, The, 14, 114–20; Connecticut Wits and, 114; constitutional debates and, 114, 116, 119–20; federal literacy and, 117–18, 120; Federalist party arguments and, 114–16; *New-Haven Gazette and Connecticut Magazine* and, 114–15; reader engagement and, 118–19; representations of variety, 115–17, 119–20; satiric dimensions, 114, 117–19; Shay's Rebellion and, 115
Anatomy Man, 13, 85, *86*, 87, 88
Anti-Federalist party, 24, 25, 105–6, 108, 110, 121, 242n26
Anti-Federalist writers: Agrippa, 108, 110, 245n26, 255n36; Brutus, 24, 245n26; Cato, 245n26; Centinel, 245n26; Federal Farmer, 245n26
Anti-slavery arguments, 90–92, 94, 96–97, 167, 198, 231–32. *See also* Banneker, Benjamin; captivity narratives; Walker, David

Apess, William, 239–40
Appeal to the Coloured Citizens of the World (Walker), 16, 231–40; American Colonization Society and, 236–37; arguments for racial equality, 220, 232–38; critical responses to, 231–32; critique of racism, 231, 232, 234–37, 239; Declaration of Independence and, 232, 235, 238, 239; defense of federal principles, 232, 234–35; federal contradictions and, 220, 231–37; federal exclusion and, 16, 232–34, 236–38; federal literacy and, 16, 238–39; formal structure of, 232–33; Jefferson and, 234–35; revision of federal principles, 232, 235–36, 237–38, 240; similarities to Cherokee arguments, 232, 236; states' rights and, 231, 236; U.S. Constitution and, 232–34, 238. *See also* African Americans
Articles of Confederation, 9, 22–23, 25, 26, 56, 58, 114, 116, 122

Bank of the United States, 25, 142, 150, 159
Banneker, Benjamin, 10, 89–98; almanacs and, 14, 60, 89, 91; arguments for African American equality, 89–90, 93–97; *Benjamin Banneker's Pennsylvania, Delaware, Maryland, and Virginia Almanack and Ephemeris*, 92–94; critique of racism, 90–95, 97; federal nationalism and, 89, 91–96, 98; Jefferson and, 90, 94–96; public responses to Banneker's almanacs, 96–97; survey of Washington, D.C., 91–92. *See also* African Americans; almanacs
Barlow, Joel, 14, 101, 104, 114, 115, 118
Beecher, Lyman, 192, 197, 202–3
Belknap, Jeremy, 14, 100, 105–6, 130, 254n23, 254n26. See also *Foresters, The*
Benjamin Banneker's Pennsylvania, Delaware, Maryland, and Virginia Almanack and Ephemeris, 92–94
Bickerstaff's Boston Almanack, 56, 70
Black Hawk, 198, 264–65n120
Blatchford, John, 140
Bleeker, Eliza, 153
Boone, Daniel, 156–57, 180
Boudinot, Elias, 10, 221–22, 225–26, 228–29, 240
Brutus, 24, 245n26
Buck-Eye Club, 192–93. *See also* western literary culture
Buell, Abel, 31–35. *See also* maps

Calhoun, John C., 185, 262n38
captivity narratives, 6, 10, 138–73; Barbary captivity narratives, 168–69; concurrent sentiments and, 139, 140, 14, 158, 175; critique of slavery, 141, 165–69; cross-cultural dimensions of, 139–40, 142, 154–58, 169–70, 172; exclusionary dimensions of, 143, 154–56, 158; federal literacy and, 141, 143, 151, 158, 160, 162–63, 166, 173; federal nationalism and, 7, 9, 12, 15, 54, 139–43, 146–53, 158–61, 165–69, 172; plural sovereignty and, 140–43, 145, 149–51, 167–68; race and, 143, 154–56, 165–66, 169; representations of Native Americans, 144, 155–58; representations of slavery, 141, 165–69, 173–74; representations of variety, 139–41, 143, 146–47, 149, 158, 160, 162–66, 168, 172–73; representations of women, 143, 151–54, 158
—specific works: *Adventures of Col. Daniel Boon*, 140, 156–57; *Affecting History of the Dreadful Distresses of Frederic Manheim's Family*, 156; *A Genuine and Correct Account of the Captivity, Sufferings, and Deliverance of Mrs. Jemima Howe*, 139, 153, 156; *God's Mercy Surmounting Man's Cruelty, Exemplified in the Captivity and Redemption of Elizabeth Hansen*, 156; *God's Protecting Providence*, 156–57; *The History of Maria Kittle*, 153; *A Narrative of the Captivity and Sufferings of Mr. Ebeneezer Fletcher of Newipswitch*, 139–40; *A Narrative of the Remarkable Occurrences in the Life of John Blatchford of Cape-Ann*, 140; *New Travels to the Westward*, 157; *The Redeemed Captive Returning to Zion*, 156; *A Surprising Account of the Captivity and Escape of Philip M'Donald and Alexander M'Leod*, 157; *A Surprising Account of the Discovery of a Young Woman Discovered in a Rocky Cave*, 153–54; *A True Narrative of the Sufferings of Mrs. Mary Kinnan*, 139, 153, 156; *The Wonderful Escape of Dr. Knight and John Slover from Captivity*, 156. See also *Algerine Captive, The*; *Narrative of Mrs. Mary Rowlandson, The*
Carey, Matthew, 101, 103, 121, 126
Catholics, 10, 197, 202–3, 207, 208
Cato, 245n26
Centinel, 245n26

Cherokee Nation, 220–29; arguments for sovereignty, 223–30, 240, 265n5; *Cherokee Nation v. Georgia*, 212–13; constitution of, 222–24, 226; language and syllabary, 222–23, 225, 265n3; laws, 221, 223, 225–26; print culture and, 219–22; similarities to United States, 222–25, 228–29; treaties with United States, 227–28, 266n15. See also Boudinot, Elias; *Cherokee Phoenix*
Cherokee Nation v. Georgia, 212–13
Cherokee Phoenix, 16, 220–30, 240; arguments for Cherokee sovereignty, 221–30; bilingual dimensions of, 222–26, 227; critique of racism, 16, 221, 230; dual audiences of, 221; federal contradictions and, 220; federal literacy and, 221–22, 225, 229, 240; federal nationalism and, 225–30; reader engagement and, 222–27, 229; response of U.S. readers, 226; rhetorical strategies, 221–23, 227, 229–30; states' rights and, 226–29. See also Boudinot, Elias; Cherokee Nation
Cincinnati, 179, 180, 188–93, 198, 200. See also western literary culture
Civil War, 10, 11, 16, 239
Clay, Henry, 236
Columbian Almanac, 57
Columbian Magazine, 14, 48, 49, 54, 94, 103–5; federal content, 104–5; *The Foresters* and, 100, 103–5, 111; Murray and, 129
concurrence, 142–43, 151, 161, 175, 240; concurrent sentiments, 15, 139–40, 158, 160; concurrent sovereignty, 140, 142, 257n7. See also captivity narratives
Congress, Continental, 4, 37, 41, 56, 65–66, 74, 122, 166; national currency and, 43; national flag and, 36; national seal and, 37–40. See also Congress, U.S.
Congress, U.S., 1, 11, 150, 181, 182, 226; bicameral structure of, 23; powers, 111, 150, 224; representing national variety, 119, 121, 123; state representation and, 13, 23, 29, 122, 128, 177. See also Congress, Continental
Connecticut, 21, 28, 29, 31–35, 43, 44, 91, 107
Connecticut Wits, 14, 114
Constitution, Cherokee, 222–24, 226
Constitution, U.S., 11, 26, 51, 56, 58, 91, 104, 202; African Americans and, 232–35; *The Anarchiad* and, 114, 116, 118; Cherokee Constitution and, 222–24, 226; federal principles

Constitution, U.S. (*continued*)
of, 9, 17, 23–25, 103, 106, 119, 142, 149–50, 172, 228, 235; *The Foresters* and, 101, 106, 109–11, 113; interpretations of, 24–25, 52, 105, 111, 113, 151; *M'Fingal* and, 121–22; ratification of, 24–25, 48, 52, 104–5, 128–29, 149; slavery and, 166–67; women and, 130, 240. See also *Appeal to the Coloured Citizens of the World*.
Constitutional Convention, 23–24, 101, 109, 111, 116, 118, 119, 121–22, 166–67, 254n19
Continental Almanac, 56–57, *57*
copia, aesthetics of, 12–13, 82
cosmopolitanism, 12–13, 160, 244n30
currency, 12, 115; national, 12–13, 43, *45*; state, 43, *44*

Decalves, Alonzo, 157
Declaration of Independence, 64–66, *65*, 75; Banneker and, 90, 95; Walker and, 232, 235, 238–39, 240
Dickinson, John, 3, 21, 258n13
"Discourse on the History, Character, and Prospects of the West" (D. Drake), 194–95
Doolittle, Amos, 43–44, *46*
Douglass, Frederick, 239
Drake, Benjamin, 190, 198–99
Drake, Daniel, 15, 178, 199, 200; Buck-Eye Club and, 192–93; federal nationalism and, 179, 192–93, 195–97, 199, 201, 202, 240; western cultural diversity and, 195–97, 213; western cultural institutions and, 193; western geography and, 195. *See also* western literary culture
—works: "Discourse on the History, Character, and Prospects of the West," 194–95; "Remarks on the Importance of Promoting Literary and Social Concert in the Valley of the Mississippi," 194–95

Ellicott, Andrew, 91–92
empire. *See* imperialism
Enlightenment ideology, 4, 21, 86
e pluribus unum, national motto, 2, 37, 38, 40, 57, 100, 177
exceptionalism, 9–10, 20, 260n7

"Farewell Address" (Washington), 142–43
Father Abraham's Almanack, 62, *72*, 73, 76–77

federal celebrations, 5, 49–52
Federal Farmer, 245n26
federal iconography, 5, 12, 13, 36–54, 56–58, 68, 71, 104, 112, 142; arrows, 5, 38, 41–43, 104; bees, 42, 43; body, 48, 85, 87, 115–16, 195; cakes, 5; candelabra, 41–43, 49; chain, 5, 42–43, *42*, 45–48, *46*, *47*, 52, 174, *177*; eagle, 5, 38–39, 40, 57; federal chariot, 56, *56*; federal edifice, 5, 48, *48*, 49, 52, 53, 56–57, *57*, 104, 194; harp, 5, 42, 43, *45*, 49, 104; rattlesnake, 36; stars, 5, 36–38, 41, *45*, 49, 52, 57, *57*, 87, 104, 196; stripes, 5, 36–38, 41, 49, 52, 57, 104, 124; sun, 56, 57. *See also* flag, U.S.; seal, national; seal, state
federalism: authority of central government, 15, 17, 18–19, 23–25, 101, 104–5, 108–13, 116–17, 121, 142, 149–51, 175, 177–78, 182, 228, 230; authority of constituent states, 15, 17–19, 23–25, 30, 76–78, 104–5, 108–11, 115–16, 149–51, 166–68, 175, 177–78, 182, 226–31, 236; British colonial background, 3–4, 17, 20–22, 58, 74, 89, 106, 128, 140–42, 145–46; contradictions of, 20, 27–28, 43, 91, 94–95, 129, 166–69, 214, 216, 220, 231–33, 235–37; divided sovereignty and, 4–5, 17–19, 21–22, 140–42, 145–46, 149–51, 185; empire and, 9–10, 18–21; institutional culture and, 178–79, 186–90, 193, 200, 233; paradoxical dimensions, 2, 17, 26, 28, 31, 43, 47, 52, 54, 89; political philosophy of, 3–4, 13, 17–20; racial limits and, 10, 16, 26–27, 89–98, 143, 165–67, 179, 196, 199, 213, 217–20, 230–31, 234–35, 237, 240; sectionalism and, 11, 23, 178, 181–82, 186, 188; western revival and revision of, 10, 15–16, 104, 109, 114, 150, 173, 176–81, 185, 193–95, 199, 213, 219, 232, 235, 239–40. *See also* Anti-Federalist party; Anti-Federalist writers; federal iconography; federal literacy; *Federalist Papers, The*; Federalist party; print culture, U.S.; variety, U.S.
Federalist Papers, The: No. 2, 165; No. 10, 5, 186; No. 11, 20; No. 22, 112; No. 23, 24; No. 39, 17, 25, 172; No. 49, 119, 120; No. 51, 20
Federalist party, 23–25, 101, 105–6, 112–16, 121, 151, 173, 191
federal literacy, 6–8, 12–16, 52–60, 87–88, 99–103, 106, 114, 123–26, 129, 133–34, 159–60, 173, 183, 186; Cherokee and, 220–21, 225; practices of interpretation and, 8, 12, 19, 23–25,

37, 50–52, 58–59, 68, 78; Walker and, 220–21, 239–40; western revival of, 177–79, 183, 185–89, 215–16. See also *Algerine Captive, The*; almanacs; *Anarchiad, The*; captivity narratives; *Foresters, The*; magazines; *M'Fingal*; *Narrative of Mrs. Mary Rowlandson, The*; satire

flag, U.S., 5, 31, 34–37, 42

Fletcher, Ebeneezer, 139–40

Flint, Timothy, 15, 176–88. See also *Western Monthly Review*

Foresters, The, 14, 100, 103–14; as allegory, 105–6, 111, 113–15; Anti-Federalist Party arguments and, 106, 108–10, 112; *Columbian Magazine* and, 100, 103–5, 111; Constitutional Convention and, 101, 109, 111–12; Federalist Party arguments and, 101, 106, 109–10, 112–13; federal literacy and, 14, 101, 106, 110–11, 113–14; satiric dimensions of, 101–3, 105–7, 113–14. See also Belknap, Jeremy

Franklin, Benjamin, 21, 56, 63, 142, 193; almanacs, 62; image of federal chain and, 42–43, *42*, 46, 48, 52; national motto and, 100; national seal and, 37

French colonial culture, 16, 207, 261n29; federal inclusion and, 16, 174, 196, 199, 205; stereotypes, 206–7, 264n110; U.S. cultural diversity and, 16, 195–96, 199, 204–5; western expansion and, 11, 174. See also Hall, James

"French Village, The" (Hall), 205, 209–10

Gallagher, William Davis, 197–98

Genuine and Correct Account of the Captivity, Sufferings, and Deliverance of Mrs. Jemima Howe, A (Howe), 139, 153, 156

geography, U.S., 26–28, 61–62, 194–95; federalism and, 9, 27–28, 30–36, 52, 194–95; games, 1, 3, 6; textbooks, 26–31; the West and, 179–80, 194–95. See also maps

God's Mercy Surmounting Man's Cruelty, Exemplified in the Captivity and Redemption of Elizabeth Hansen, 156

God's Protecting Providence, 156–57

Grand Federal Procession, 36, 49–51, 53

Great Britain, 23, 38, 43, 74, 118, 139; almanacs and, 60–61, 88; in *The Foresters*, 105–6; imperial structure, 3, 12, 19–20, 22, 82, 142; magazines and, 99, 100, 183, 261n29; management of British American colonies, 3, 21–22, 117, 142, 145–46, 207; sovereignty and, 140–42, 145, 149

Grotius, Hugo, 3, 18, 21

Hall, James, 10, 15, 177, 199–200; dispute with Beecher, 192, 202–3; as editor, 199, 200–205, 210, 213–16; expectations for readers, 177–87, 199–205, 208–10, 212–13, 215, 217; federal literacy and, 177–79, 199–216; federal nationalism and, 177–79, 199–205, 208, 210, 212–19; fiction and, 179, 199, 204–13, 216–18; Native Americans and, 179, 199, 212–19; race and, 179, 199, 213–18; representations of French colonial culture, 179, 199, 205–13, 216; representations of Spanish colonial culture, 179, 199, 204–6, 210–13, 216; western cultural diversity and, 176–77, 179, 199, 202–14, 216–18; western literary culture and, 177–79, 192, 199–205, 219. See also *Illinois Monthly Magazine*; western literary culture; *Western Monthly Magazine*

—works: "The French Village," 205, 209–10; *History of the Indian Tribes of North America*, 216–17; "The Indian Hater," 217–18; "The Legend of Carondelet" 205–9, 216; *Letters from the West*, 200; "Michel de Coucy," 205, 210–13, 216; "On the Intercourse of the American People with the Indians," 214–16; *Sketches of the West*, 205; *The Soldier's Bride and Other Tales*, 205; *Tales of the Border*, 205; *The Western Souvenir*, 200, 209, 217

Hamilton, Alexander, 20, 21, 23–24, 112, 150, 246n31

Henry, Patrick, 24, 241

History of Maria Kittle, The (Bleeker), 153

History of the Indian Tribes of North America (Hall), 216–17

Hopkinson, Francis, 52, 103, 104; Grand Federal Procession and, 49–51; national seal and, 37–38, *39*

Howe, Jemima, 139, 153, 156

Illinois Monthly Magazine, 200, 205, 214. See also Hall, James; western literary culture

imperialism, 18, 22, 82, 87; divided sovereignty and, 20, 22, 142; federalism and, 9–10, 18–21; United States and, 9, 176, 260n7. See also Great Britain

"Indian Hater, The" (Hall), 217–18
Indian removal, 16, 177–78, 200–201, 230, 239, 240

Jefferson, Thomas, 3, 10, 21, 100, 121, 246n31; Banneker and, 90, 92, 94–97; Declaration of Independence and, 90, 234–35; national seal and, 37; *Notes on the State of Virginia*, 91, 234; views on race, 91, 95–96, 234–35

Kinnan, Mary, 139, 153, 156
Kittle, Maria, 153

"Legend of Carondelet, The" (Hall), 205–9, 216
Letters from the West (Hall), 200
Locke, John, 3, 4, 18, 21
Louisiana Purchase, 175. *See also* western expansion

Madison, James, 3, 20–21, 119–20, 166; *Federalist* No. 10 and, 5, 20, 186; *Federalist* No. 39 and, 17, 24–25, 172–73
magazines, 6, 9, 14–15, 43, 58, 99–137, 176, 219; Anti-Federalist Party politics and, 105–6; compared with almanacs, 102; Federalist Party politics and, 101–2, 105, 114; federal literacy and, 10, 12, 99–101, 103, 126, 128–29, 177–78, 183, 188; federal nationalism and, 7, 13, 54, 100, 104–5, 128–29, 177, 179–80, 182, 188, 201, 203–4; literary content and, 100–101, 104, 199, 201–2, 204–13; reader engagement and, 102–3, 110, 126–29, 183, 185–86, 188, 201–2, 210; regional focus and, 180–83, 200; variety of contents, 7, 12, 13, 99–100, 103–4, 126, 135, 177, 181–83, 201–3; women and, 129–31, 137. *See also Anarchiad, The; Foresters, The; Illinois Monthly Magazine; M'Fingal; Western Monthly Magazine; Western Monthly Review*
Magna Carta, 142, 145
maps, 12, 13, 7, 30–36, *32–33*, 68, 71. *See also* geography
Mason, George, 23, 109, 111
Massachusetts Centinel, 48, 101, 121, 247n66
Massachusetts Magazine, 14, 100, 102, 103, 129; Murray and, 130, 131, 135. *See also* magazines
M'Fingal, 14, 101, 120–26; Anti-Federalist Party arguments and, 121; Constitutional Convention and, 121–22; Federalist Party arguments and, 121; federal literacy and, 101, 123–26; reader engagement and, 123–26; representation of variety, 121–22, 124–25; satire and, 102, 124–25, 133. *See also* magazines

"Michel de Coucy" (Hall), 205, 210–13, 216
Missouri Compromise, 178, 231
Montesquieu, Baron de, 3, 18, 21
Morse, Jedidiah, 26–31, 34–35, 130, 246n45
Murray, Judith Sargent, 10, 15, 129–37; federal literacy and, 133–34; federal nationalism and, 130–31, 135–37; *The Gleaner* and, 130, 135–37; reader engagement and, 130–32, 134–37; satire and, 130, 133, 134; women's roles in United States and, 129–30, 132–33, 135, 137. *See also* magazines; women

Narrative of Mrs. Mary Rowlandson, The, 15, 138–58; colonial reception of, 143–44; concurrent sentiments and, 139–43, 146, 149, 151; debates over sovereignty and, 141–42, 145–46, 149–51; early U.S. reception, 141, 144–46; federal literacy and, 175; federal nationalism and, 141–43, 146, 149–51; heterogeneous view of home, 138–39, 146–51, 154–55, 161; homogenous view of home, 138, 146–47, 149; Native Americans and, 146, 154–55; Rowlandson's interpretative practices, 146–49, 151, 155; women's roles and, 151–53
Narrative of the Captivity and Sufferings of Mr. Ebeneezer Fletcher of Newipswitch, 139–40
Narrative of the Remarkable Occurrences in the Life of John Blatchford of Cape-Ann, A, 140
Native Americans, 11, 29, 35–36; assimilation and, 216, 221–25; federal exclusion and, 29–30, 36, 179, 213, 216, 220; federal nationalism and, 10, 198–99, 212–16, 219; racism and, 154–58, 215–16, 219, 221–30, 239–40; representation in captivity narratives, 146, 154–58; stereotypes, 146, 213–14, 216; treaties with United States, 22, 212–14, 219, 227–29, 264–65n120, 266n15. *See also* Boudinot, Elias; Cherokee Nation; *Cherokee Phoenix*; Hall, James; Indian removal
nativism, 197–98, 202–3
New and Correct Map of the United States of North America (Buell), 31–35, *32–33*

New-England Almanack, 62, 72, 73
New-Haven Gazette and Connecticut Magazine, 101, 114, 121. *See also* magazines
New-Jersey Almanac, 62
New Travels to the Westward (Decalves), 157
Notes on the State of Virginia (Jefferson), 91, 234
novels, 12, 81, 100, 104, 141, 153, 158–60. See also *Algerine Captive, The*
Nullification, 178, 185, 231

"On the Intercourse of the American People with the Indians" (Hall), 214–16

Panther, Abraham, 153–54
Pennsylvania Town and Country-Man's Almanack, 62–66
Poor Richard Improved, 62, 69, 85, 86, 249n29
Poor Will's Almanack, 74, 77, 248n3
print culture, U.S., 6, 12–15, 27; African Americans and, 89–98, 231–40; almanacs and, 6, 7, 12, 55–59, 66–67; captivity narratives and, 6, 7, 15, 139–43, 153–54; federal imagery and, 36–49; federalism and, 6–8, 11–13, 52–54, 87–88, 101–2, 128–29, 153–54, 180–83, 186, 201, 219, 240; local dimensions and, 8, 66–67; magazines and, 6, 7, 12, 14, 99–104, 126–29; Native Americans and, 154–58, 215, 221–30, 239–40; print culture thesis, 8; regional representation and, 180–83, 192, 200; satire and, 6, 7, 12, 14, 54, 100–101; U.S. nationalism and, 6, 8, 11–12, 58–59, 99; women and, 129–30, 133, 135–37, 240. *See also* almanacs; captivity narratives; federal literacy; magazines; novels; western literary culture
Pufendorf, Samuel von, 3, 18, 21

race, 16, 29–30, 143; African Americans and, 89–95, 165–69, 231–39; federalism and, 10, 16, 26–27, 89–98, 143, 165–67, 179, 196, 199, 213, 217–20, 230–31, 234–35, 237, 240; Native Americans and, 154–58, 198, 213–18, 219–30. *See also* African Americans; Cherokee Nation; Native Americans
reader response, 2–3, 7–8, 68–69, 73–74, 76–79, 96–97. *See also* federal literacy
Redeemed Captive Returning to Zion, The, 156
regions, 8, 9; *The Algerine Captive* and, 160, 164–68, 173; almanacs and, 13, 59, 61–67,

71–73, 78, 88, 97; conflicts and rivalries, 16, 28, 35, 178, 182, 187, 192, 220; federalism and, 10, 16, 26–27, 165, 173–75, 176–77, 180–81, 185, 189, 193, 198, 213; mid-Atlantic, 14, 66, 67, 73, 177, 180, 183, 200; New England, 14, 21–22, 68, 73, 114, 161, 164–66, 192, 200, 206–9, 216; stereotypes, 206–7. *See also* South; West
"Remarks on the Importance of Promoting Literary and Social Concert in the Valley of the Mississippi" (D. Drake), 194–95
Rittenhouse, David, 94, 249n29
Rousseau, Jean-Jacques, 18
Rowlandson, Mary. See *Narrative of Mrs. Mary Rowlandson, The*

satire, 6, 7, 62, 99–103, 160; federal literacy and, 12, 101–3, 116, 118–20, 128–29, 219; federal nationalism and, 12–15, 54, 101–3, 107, 118–19, 129; plural dimensions, 101, 102–3. See also *Anarchiad, The*; *Foresters, The*; *M'Fingal*; Murray, Judith Sargent
seal, national, 5, 37–42, 38, 39, 40, 41, 104
seal, state, 34, 43, 44, 46
sectionalism, 11, 23, 178, 181–82, 186, 188
Shay's Rebellion, 115, 125
Simitière, Pierre Eugène du, 37, 38, 41, 100
Sketches of the West (Hall), 205
slavery, 11, 28, 168–69, 220–21, 231–39; abolition and, 90, 92, 94, 96, 167; federal contradictions and, 30, 90, 94–97, 165–68; states and, 11, 16, 166–67, 175, 177; U.S. expansion and, 174, 220. *See also* African Americans; *Algerine Captive, The*; almanacs; Walker, David
Smith, Adam, 4
Soldier's Bride and Other Tales, The (Hall), 205
South, 11, 174, 187, 232; *The Algerine Captive* and, 163, 164–68; almanacs and, 14, 61–66, 73, 96; magazines and, 183–84, 201; regional rivalries and, 28, 176–77, 206. *See also* African Americans; Nullification; regions; slavery
South-Carolina and Georgia Almanack, 62, 64–66
sovereignty: divided sovereignty, 4–5, 17–19, 21–22, 140–42, 145–46, 149–51, 185; Native Americans and, 212–16, 219, 221–30, 239–40; state sovereignty, 34, 43, 115, 167–68; tensions between local and national, 105–7, 149–51
Sovereignty and Goodness of God. See *Narrative of Mrs. Mary Rowlandson, The*

Spanish colonial west, 11, 174, 204; cultural influence on United States, 16, 174, 179, 195–96, 199, 203, 205–6, 210–11; represented in fiction, 204–5, 210–12. *See also* Hall, James

Stamp Act, 106, 142

states' rights, 16, 30, 110, 226, 231, 236

Supreme Court, 212–13, 246n30

Surprising Account of the Captivity and Escape of Philip M'Donald and Alexander M'Leod, A, 157

Surprising Account of the Discovery of a Young Woman Discovered in a Rocky Cave, A (Panther), 153–54

Switzerland, 3, 21

Tales of the Border (Hall), 205

Tariff of 1828, 182, 1885

Thomson, Charles, 38–41, *41*

Tobler, John, 62–69, *63*, 65, 80, 84, 249n20. *See also* almanacs

transnationalism, 9, 12, 82, 204

transportation networks, 11, 20, 165, 189, 195, 259n49

treaties, Native American, 22, 212–14, 219, 227–29, 264–65n120, 266n15

Treaty of Paris, 31, 34, 38

True Narrative of the Sufferings of Mrs. Mary Kinnan, A, 139, 153, 156

Trumbull, John, 14, 101, 114, 115, 118, 120, 124. See also *Anarchiad, The*; *M'Fingal*

Tyler, Royall, 10, 15, 158, 16–68, 173, 220. See also *Algerine Captive, The*

United Colonies of New England, 21–22

United States, grammatical usage, 11, 25–26, 246n30

United States Almanack, 62, 70, 79, 80

Universal Calendar and North American's Almanack, 83, 84

variety, U.S., 2–6, 8, 10–11, 20, 26–27, 37, 42, 135–36, 189; cultural and ethnic, 10, 14–16, 26–27, 139–40, 154–58, 160, 168–70, 172, 174–75, 179, 195–99, 202–13, 217–18, 220; geographic, 1–2, 9, 17, 11, 27–28, 61–62, 159, 174–75, 194–95, 197, 220; intellectual, 131–32; political, 10, 14, 15–16, 17, 25, 27, 52, 62, 65–66, 115–16, 119–20, 121–23, 125, 150–51, 160; professional, 49–50, 164, 174; racial, 26–27, 29–30, 91–92, 94–95, 174, 196, 213–18, 219–40; regional, 27–28, 61–66, 160, 164–69, 176, 183–85, 187, 198, 208; religious, 10, 15, 26, 29, 95, 158, 169–74, 202–3, 224–25. *See also* federalism; federal literacy; race; regions

Virginia Almanack, 62, 69, 72, 73, 249n29

Walker, David, 10, 219–21, 230–40. See also *Appeal to the Coloured Citizens of the World*

Washington, D.C., 91–92

Washington, George, 43, *44*, 56, 74, 76, 193, 246n31; almanac diaries of, 69, 73; "Farewell Address," 142–43; *M'Fingal* and, 121; magazines and, 99, 104–5, 113; Murray and, 130; Washington, D.C., and, 91; Whiskey Rebellion and, 150, 159

Webster, Noah, 25–26, 27, 101, 121

West, 174–218; Anglo-American cultural dimensions, 174, 188, 195–98, 202–3, 204, 209, 216, 218; comparisons with other regions, 176, 180–84, 187, 192–95, 205–9; cultural and ethnic diversity, 195–99, 202–13, 216, 218; distinctive regional characteristics, 176–77, 181, 192–93, 194–96, 201, 203–5; empire and, 176; literary culture (*see* western literary culture); Native Americans and, 174–75, 179, 196, 198–99, 212–18; nativism and, 197–98, 202–3. *See also* French colonial culture; Spanish colonial west; western expansion; western literary culture

western expansion, 15, 25, 173–78, 181, 188, 197

western literary culture, 188–218; Buck-Eye Club, 192–93; Cincinnati, 179, 180, 188–93, 198, 200; East Coast literary culture and, 177, 180–81, 192, 197, 200; federal literacy and, 176–79, 182–83, 185–89, 198–99, 201–2, 210, 215–16, 219; federal nationalism and, 173, 176–83, 185–86, 193–95, 199, 208–19; Flint and, 15, 176–88; institutional dynamics, 178–79, 186–93, 200–202; libraries, 178, 189, 190; literary and social clubs, 178, 189–93; lyceums, 189, 191–93; museums, 189, 190; professional organizations, 178, 186, 188, 189, 190–91; reader engagement and, 178, 181–89, 201–5, 208–10, 215–18; schools, 178, 181, 186, 188–89; Semi-Colon Club and, 192–93. See also Drake, Daniel;

Hall, James; *Illinois Monthly Magazine*; West; *Western Monthly Magazine*; *Western Monthly Review*

Western Monthly Magazine, 177, 179, 200; comparisons with *Western Monthly Review*, 201; East Coast literary culture and, 200; federal literacy and, 201–2, 215–16; federal nationalism and, 177, 178, 199, 201–3, 212–14; Native Americans and, 213–14; *A Plea for the West* and, 202–3; reader engagement and, 178, 201–2, 204, 210–13; representation of conflict, 177, 201–4; role of fiction in, 199, 204–5, 210–13; western cultural diversity and, 199, 203–5, 210–13, 216. *See also* Hall, James; *Illinois Monthly Magazine*; West; western literary culture

—fictional works: "Isabelle and Her Sister Kate and Their Cousin," 204; "James Kirkwood," 204. *See also* Hall, James: works

Western Monthly Review, 179–88, 201; diverse content, 182–85; East Coast literary culture and, 180; federal literacy and, 178, 183, 185–87, 188; federal nationalism and, 178, 180–82, 185–88; Flint and, 15, 176–88; formal structure, 182–83, 188; institutional forms of federalism and, 186–88; reader engagement and, 183, 185; representation of the West, 180–81; representations of conflict, 177, 184–86, 188; sectionalism and, 181–82. *See also* West; western literary culture

Western Souvenir, The (Hall), 200, 209, 217

Whiskey Rebellion, 25, 125, 142, 150, 159

Wilmington Almanack, 85, 86

Wilson, James, 21, 36

Witherspoon, John, 3, 4, 21, 161

women, 10, 29–30; almanacs and, 61; alternative national roles, 130, 143, 151–54, 158; coverture and, 30, 130, 256n89; domestic sphere and, 130, 132–33, 143, 151–53; education and, 131–32, 189; equality and, 15, 130–33, 143, 151; federal exclusion and, 47, 220; federal literacy and, 133–37; federal representation and, 15, 30, 130, 131–32, 135–37, 153, 240; magazines and, 104, 129–30; print culture and, 129–30, 132, 133; republican motherhood, 132; Seneca Falls convention and, 240. *See also* captivity narratives; Murray, Judith Sargent

Wonderful Escape of Dr. Knight and John Slover from Captivity, The, 156

www.ingramcontent.com/pod-product-compliance
Lightning Source LLC
Chambersburg PA
CBHW022100230426
43672CB00008B/1237